Illusion and the Drama

Illusion and the Drama

Critical Theory of the Enlightenment and Romantic Era

Frederick Burwick

The Pennsylvania State University Press
University Park, Pennsylvania

Library of Congress Cataloging-in-Publication Data

Burwick, Frederick.
    Illusion and the drama : critical theory of the enlightenment and romantic era / Frederick Burwick.
        p.   cm.
    Includes bibliographical references and index.
    ISBN 0-271-00732-X (alk. Paper)
    1. European drama—18th century—History and criticism.
2. European drama—19th century—History and criticism. 3. Illusion in literature. 4. Criticism—History. I. Title.
PN1841.B87   1991
809.2'033—dc20   90-45894
                                                                                               CIP

Copyright © 1991 The Pennsylvania State University
All rights reserved
Printed in the United States of America

It is the policy of The Pennsylvania State University Press to use acid-free paper for the first printing of all clothbound books. Publications on uncoated stock satisfy the minimum requirements of American National Standard for Information Sciences—Permanence of Paper for Printed Library Materials, ANSI Z39.48–1984.

Contents

List of Illustrations *vii*

Acknowledgments *ix*

Introduction *1*

1 Perfect Illusion and the Skeptics: Rousseau, Johnson, and Stendhal *19*

2 Illusion and the Players: Diderot, Tieck, and Lamb *41*

3 Illusion and the Audience: Lessing, Mendelssohn, and Schiller *81*

4 Illusion and the Play: A. W. Schlegel *127*

5 Illusion and the Poetic Imagination: Coleridge *191*

6 Illusion and the Stage: Goethe and Hugo *231*

7 Illusion and Metadrama: Coleridge and Tieck *267*

Bibliography *305*

Index *319*

List of Illustrations

(Illustrations follow page 229)

1. Goethe's sketch for *Faust:* "Prolog im Himmel."

2. *Faust* (as performed at the Lyceum), engraved by R. Taylor.

3. Faust and Mephisto (as performed at the Comédie français, Paris), illustrating the *trappe anglais.*

4. Goethe's sketch for *Faust:* "Erscheinung des Erdgeistes."

5. Goethe's sketch for *Faust:* "Studierzimmer. Pudelbeschwörung."

6. Goethe's sketch for *Faust:* "Hexenküche."

7. "Hexenküche," line engraving by Moritz Retzsch (1816).

8. Goethe's sketch for *Faust:* "Auf dem Brocken."

9. Goethe's sketch for *Romeo and Juliet,* Act V.

10. Goethe's sketch for the witches in *Macbeth.*

11. Hugo's sketch for *Les Jumeaux* (1839).

12. *Hernani*, Act II (first performance: Comédie française, 25 February 1830; Michelot as Don Carlos, Firmin as Hernani, Mlle Mars as Dona Sol).

13. The death scene from *Hernani* (Joanny as Don Ruy Gomez), Act V, by Louis Boulanger.

14. "La Bataille d'Hernani," by Granville.

15. Hugo's sketch for *Le Roi s'amuse*, Act II.

16. Hugo's sketch for *Ruy Blas*, Act I.

17. *Ruy Blas*, Act V (first performance: Théâtre de la Renaissance, 8 November 1838; Frédérick Lamaître as Ruy Blas, Atala Beauchêne as Dona Maria, Queen of Spain).

18. Hugo's sketch of "Le Burg à la Croise."

19. Hugo's sketch for *Les Burgraves*, Act I.

Acknowledgments

My inquiry into aesthetic illusion has been encouraged by Murray Krieger, who also read through my introduction, in which I give attention to his ideas on poetic presence and attempt to place them in the context of contemporary criticism. When I began my study of Coleridge's concept of illusion, Reginald Foakes kindly made available the proof-sheets of his edition of Coleridge's *Lectures 1808–1819 On Literature* (1987), which had not yet appeared in the Bollingen *Collected Works*. The notes and commentary to his edition have been invaluable. I am also grateful for his suggestions on my presentation of Schlegel and Coleridge. Bernard Ribémont and Dalton Kraus read parts of the manuscript at various stages and helped to shape the revisions. Richard Fadem and Thomas McFarland gave the entire manuscript their meticulous attention and provided me with wise and useful notes for preparing the final draft.

Support for writing this work was provided by the Research Institute in the Humanities and Social Sciences, Universität Siegen, where the author was in residence as Research Professor in 1987. Further assistance came from the College Institute, UCLA, which funded the project with a Research Grant for 1987.

Parts of chapters 5 and 6 have appeared in a slightly different form in *Word and Image* 4 (1988), and *The Wordsworth Circle* 19: 1 (Winter 1988). The author is grateful to the editors of these journals for permission to use the material here.

For Roswitha Burwick

Introduction

In order to appraise the function of "illusion" in eighteenth-century aesthetics and dramatic criticism, I find it necessary to put aside some of the misconceptions fostered in the name of "history of ideas." As critics of the "new historicism" rightly remind us, literary and philosophical notions inevitably bear the imprint of social, political, and cultural factors. The "history of ideas" approach tends to ignore the peculiarities that mark a given time and place. Seeking organic growth and continuity from age to age, this approach has considered those ideas not perpetuated from one generation to the next as dead ends to be ignored or, if acknowledged at all, as miscreations eliminated in a process of natural selection. Even those ideas which survived suffered the abuse of oversimplification. Moreover, because such an approach emphasizes tracing the propagation of ideas, it slights the differences and nuances among them. Dedicated to the task of charting historical developments, these critics would not have considered themselves participants in a consciously deliberated scheme to uphold a canon and tradition. Nevertheless, they were highly selective in mustering evidence.

One of the consequences of such criticism is that various statements on the nature of illusion, sympathy, and emotional response are lumped together. In fact, even among those writers who grant the importance of illusion in the drama, there is considerable debate over its causes, purposes, and functions. Adherents of opposing philosophical schools might agree that illusion is crucial to aesthetic experience, then disagree on every point that follows. Yet in the "history of ideas" radical disagreements are often forgotten. It is not just that the Romantics are said to be repeating and perpetuating the ideas of the Enlightenment, we are not told how radically Diderot differed from Rousseau or Lessing, much less how Lessing could vehemently disagree with Mendelssohn and Nicolai, though these were friends whose philosophical opinions he highly prized.

Among the several problems involved in the discussion of dramatic illusion, a frequently repeated issue has been whether the experience is voluntary or involuntary. Critics such as Schink or Weisse, for example, maintain that the purpose of bourgeois drama is to offer such an accurate representation of domestic life that the spectators become perfectly convinced during the performance that they are looking upon real events affecting real persons. The emotional response is involuntary and so intense that reason is temporarily overwhelmed.[1] For other critics, such as Marmontel or Mercier, the purpose of the drama is to provide pleasure; we willingly indulge illusion in order to experience most fully the pleasure that dramatic fiction affords.[2] Proponents of the *involuntary* response make no distinction between illusion and delusion. They allow for no conscious awareness of the fictionality of the performance to attend the illusion; indeed, they condemn any intruding awareness as a disruption that destroys illusion. Those who argue the *voluntary* nature of illusion, however, savor the simultaneous modes of response: *aesthetic immediacy* (participating in the illusion) together with *aesthetic distance* (detached attention to the stage performance). A third position, modifying the concept of a complete and overwhelming illusion, was forwarded by such critics as Darwin or Stendhal, who argued that the experience of illusion was never long sustained; they defined the response, similar to a twilight flickering between waking and dreaming, as alternating belief and

---

1. Schink, *Dramaturgische Fragmente*, 458; Weiße, Preface to *Das Fanatismus, oder Jean Calas*, 2–3; see also "Rezension: Trauerspiele von C. F. Weiße," in *Allgemeine deutsche Bibliothek* (1782), 136–37; Schmitt, "Christian Felix Weißes *Jean Calas*, 2–30.

2. Marmontel, *Poétique François* II, 112; Marmontel, "Illusion," in *Encyclopédie* VIII; Mercier, *Du Théâtre*.

disbelief.³ Finally, there were those, such as Du Bos, who granted that pleasure was indeed the object, but insisted that illusion had no part in the response; rather, the spectator remained attentive to the staging and acting, to the aesthetic attributes of the play and the performance.⁴

Marian Hobson, in *The Object of Art* (1982), has written a comprehensive study of the various accounts of illusion in eighteenth-century France. Although she makes no effort to relate developments in French theory to the similar concerns that were emerging in Germany and England, she does provide a well-integrated discussion of illusion in the novel, poetry, painting, music, as well as the drama. She distinguishes very usefully between a *bipolar* and *bimodal* conception of illusion. The former presumes an error in perception: the spectator is deceived, if only for a moment, into mistaking art for reality. The latter allows for "involvement and awareness" to coexist in the aesthetic experience. In the bipolar experience, the spectator either maintains rational control or is victimized by the deception. The bimodal experience works as a kind of self-deception in which the spectator becomes an accomplice in conjuring illusion. Theories of bimodality, according to Marian Hobson's account, were first proliferated among critics of painting.⁵ Discussion of illusion in the drama, throughout most of the eighteenth century, continued to rely on the bipolar model.

The efforts to describe illusion usually involve testimony of stark physical response. Watching Othello in his jealous rage about to murder the innocent Desdemona, the spectator feels his pulse race and sweat bead upon his brow. The skeptics, unconvinced, reply that the spectator does not leap to the stage to prevent the crime.⁶ If the mind remains aloof, why does the body react? Is it possible for the emotions to become so intensely engaged that rational objectivity is forgotten? Is there, after all, an oscillating acceptance and rejection of the illusion? Or is some aspect of consciousness stimulated while other faculties or facilities of mind are in abeyance? Illusion, as some critics define it, takes place through a process of identification or vicarious response that leads to a mediated participation in the dramatic

---

3. Darwin, *The Botanic Garden* II, 87; Stendhal, *Racine et Shakespeare* (1823), in *Oeuvres complètes*, ed. Eudes, XVI, 11–19.

4. Du Bos, "Que le plaisir que nous avons au Théâtre n'est point produit par l'illusion" (Section XLIII), in *Réflexions critiques sur la poésie et sur la peinture*, 451–57.

5. Hobson, *The Object of Art*, 6–12, 47–50, 299–300.

6. Stendhal, *Oeuvres complètes* XVI, 15, refers to a Baltimore soldier who did shoot the actor playing Othello.

action. Lessing, for example, proposed in his *Hamburgische Dramaturgie* that illusion was mediated through sympathy.[7] Coleridge, in his lectures on Shakespeare, described how illusion was engendered through the creative imagination.[8] In spite of the frequently reiterated accusations that Coleridge took his theory of dramatic illusion from A. W. Schlegel, their concerns, as we shall see, were very different. Schlegel emphasizes the playacting strategies in Shakespearean drama. When Shakespeare has a character put on a disguise and feign another role, he has thematized illusion and made the spectator a coconspirator in the plot.[9]

One approach to illusion is to define it as a subjective affect and attempt to explain the response in psychological terms. Another approach is to define it as objective, centering it in the staging and acting. Diderot, for example, gave primary attention to the acting as the source of illusion.[10] Goethe and Hugo were among those who recognized the visual enchantment of stage effects as a means of supporting and enhancing illusion.[11] For Diderot, illusion is still to be concealed through the actor's mastery of his art. The actor's semiotic presence is invisible: the audience sees only the spontaneous action and passion of the character. Goethe was less concerned with concealing the artifice. The optical illusions of the *laterna magica* would still add perceptual intrigue to a scene, whether or not the audience managed to figure out how the effects were wrought. Hugo, for his part, sought to elaborate the interaction between character and setting, recognizing that the very stage props, no less than the actor's movement and gesture and the lines that he would speak, were copresent constituents in the verbal/visual medium of the drama.

Opposing those who consider illusion an essential attribute of the drama, other critics hold that illusion is a condition to be enhanced or disrupted as the playwright sees fit. What these critics emphasize is not the alternating response of the spectator, but the alternating conditions of dramatic representation. In the tradition of the Aristophanic *parabasis*, the actor can be made to appear as if he is stepping in and out of his role.[12] The pretense, of

7. Lessing, *Hamburgische Dramaturgie* (1767–69), in *Werke*, ed. Göpfert, et al., IV, 231–720.
8. Coleridge, *Lectures 1808–1819: On Literature*.
9. Schlegel, *Vorlesungen über dramatische Kunst und Literatur* (1809–11).
10. Diderot, "Entretiens sur le Fils naturel" (1757), in *Oeuvres complètes* VII, 85–168; *De la poésie dramatique* (1758), in *Oeuvres complètes* VII, 299–394.
11. Goethe, *Werke*, division IV, vol. 31, 163–64; Hugo, *Préface de Cromwell*, in *Oeuvres dramatiques et critiques complètes*, 139–53.
12. McLeish, *The Theatre of Aristophanes*, 79–92.

course, involves not a disruption of illusion, but a shift to another dimension of illusion. Like the play-within-a-play, the artifice of stepping out of the play augments the illusion and gives it more complex dimension. The metadrama of the twentieth century (Pirandello, say, or Stoppard) has antecedents in age-old strategies of irony and paradox. In the Enlightenment, the games of trespassing the supposed boundaries of illusion are evident in Marivaux's *Les Sincères* and Gozzi's *Fiabe dell' amore delle tre melarancie*.[13] In the Romantic era, skirmishes with illusion become thematic as well as structural in Tieck's *Der gestiefelte Kater* and Coleridge's *Remorse*.[14]

If illusion is such dubious stuff, a deception sustained by emotion or imagination, perhaps it would be better to dispense with it altogether. As Jonas Barish has observed, playwrights and producers are themselves sometimes a party to the enduring and widespread prejudice against the deceits of theatricality. Barish calls attention to the ways in which dialogue and staging may be deliberately directed toward the destruction not just of illusion, but of the very presumptions of theater. In the later plays of Samuel Beckett, the extravaganzas of Robert Wilson, the assault tactics of Antonin Artaud, and the dramatic sabotage of Peter Handke, the theater turns against itself in sundry acts of self-refutation or self-annihilation.[15] Since the 1920s, the banner of *Anti-Illusion* has been hoisted by several parties. Setting forth his principles of Modernist experimentation at the Cambridge Festival Theatre, Terence Gray called for a total extermination of the "hocus pocus and bamboozli" involved in draping the stage with "the cobwebs of external reality." Gray wanted nothing to distract from the formal symbolism of acting.[16]

Bertolt Brecht, albeit for very different reasons, also wished to free the theater from the false adornments of illusion. He scorned illusionist drama as "a carrousel ride on a wooden pony" that appealed only to childish desires. By engaging the desires, illusion effectively transformed the audience into "an intimidated, believing, 'captivated' crowd."[17] Promulgated by the moral dictates of the ruling class and sustained by the compelling course of whatever story has been adapted to stage, illusion presumes a general acquiescence to fate. As an ideological ploy of the establishment to conceal

---

13. Marivaux, *Théâtre complet*, 1271–1305; Gozzi, *Fiabe Teatrali*, 113–49.
14. Tieck, *Der gestiefelte Kater;* Coleridge, *Remorse*, in *Complete Poetical Works*.
15. Barish, *The Antitheatrical Prejudice*, 450–64.
16. Gray, "This Age in the Theatre," 11; "The Festival Theatre in Cambridge," 585–86.
17. Brecht, *Kleines Organon für das Theater* (1948), in *Gesammelte Werke* XVI, 675; §§28–29.

the real causes of conflict, illusionist drama perpetuates the doctrine of heroic suffering and inevitable destiny always encouraged by the ruling class. Dramatic illusion is no better than a legalized mode of "bourgeois drug dealing."[18] The audience should be suspicious of what the theater declares to be ineluctable.

Work and productivity are the values, Brecht declared, that ought to replace the aesthetics of a futile struggle against fate. Not illusion but *alienation* should be the effect of dramatic representation (*Verfremdungseffekt*). The actor, since his purpose is not to put the public into a trance, should be careful not to fall into a trance himself. Alienation allows both players and audience to deliberate upon the action with full awareness of how events are manipulated. The actor should not conceal but rather reveal that his role is only a role. By suspending the presumption of illusion, the player stands aloof from the character he plays: "out of 'I do this' emerges 'I did this,' and then from 'he did this' follows 'he did this, and nothing else.' " Thus is revealed not causal necessity but precisely the sort of paradox between character and deed that is evident in real life. The approach is political, and the action avowedly engages in class conflict. The pretense that art should be apolitical, Brecht said, is advocated only by those who belong to the dominant party.[19]

Although he thought that aesthetic illusion could be dispelled by emphasizing production, Brecht succeeded only in shifting the ground of illusion. Brecht's *Verfremdungseffekt*, as Theodor Adorno has pointed out, is itself an illusion.[20] In spite of the pretense of rescuing the audience from aesthetic and/or ideological entrapment, Anti-Illusionist drama simply provided another mode of metadramatic play with the essential paradox of art. Art is not a medium that may or may not produce illusion: art is illusion. For Adorno, who adapts the dialectics of Hegel, art not only exploits sensory appearances but also exercises the intellectual discovery of the illusory nature of sensation.

Because perception and cognition build upon the illusory data of the senses, all experience challenges the mind's capacity to cope with illusion. It is a mistake, therefore, to think of illusion as an antonym of reality. As Kant

---

18. Ibid., 661. Brecht's appraisal of the theater as "a branch of bourgeois drug-dealing" follows Karl Marx's condemnation of religion as "the opium of the people" (Introduction, in *Critique of the Hegelian Philosophy of the Right*, 1844).

19. Ibid., 666, 672, 680–87, 698, 700; §§9, 23, 42–55, 72, and 77.

20. Adorno, *Ästhetische Theorie*, 123, 156–58. See also Rath, "Dialektik des Scheins—Materialien zum Scheinbegriff Adornos," 51–61; Huhn, "Adorno's Aesthetics of Illusion," 181–89.

observed, illusion is rather the antonym of delusion.[21] But if illusion is a part of all experience, what makes art and aesthetic experience special or different? Kant answered this question by intellectualizing the response and grounding aesthetic judgment in disinterestedness. While he argues that reason reveals itself in the mind's ability to order sensory data and to develop concepts out of the raw material of sensory perception, he also acknowledges that people enjoy indulging the illusions of the senses.[22] But the experience of art, he insists, cannot occur under the sway of sensual indulgence.

Tragedy, for example, is possible in art only when the causes of danger are removed. Free from threatening immediacy, objects of horror or terror may provide aesthetic pleasure. Similarly, representations of the beautiful in art must never arouse erotic interest. Kant bases his aesthetic on subjective response, but he wants to intellectualize that response and set it apart from sensual excitement and indulgence. He declares, for example, that "nothing sensual is sublime." Our concepts of the beautiful and sublime must originate, however, in the senses: "The beautiful is that which, without concept, generally pleases." Kant's analysis of the beautiful pertains to the "moment" of aesthetic judgment. He admits that, "in the reflections to which this power of judgment addresses its attention," he has "sought to judge according to logical functions (for a relation to the understanding is always contained in judgments of taste)."[23] Kant thus argues that the beautiful pleases "without concept" but is judged beautiful only with and through conceptual understanding. He prescinds the aesthetic experience from the sensual experience.

Although Hegel, too, intellectualizes the aesthetic experience, he attempts to reconcile rational and sensual involvement. What must be prescinded is not the sensual response to the object, but its otherness as object. The artist accomplishes this by transforming the external thing and giving it the imprint of his internal self. By taking from the external world its obstinate otherness, the artist, as free subject, enjoys in the shape of things

---

21. Kant, *Anthropologie in pragmatischer Hinsicht*, §13, in *Werke* VI, 445–46.
22. Ibid., §§12 and 22, in *Werke* VI, 443, 457; §12: "der Hang, sich gerne täuschen zu lassen"; §22: "der Hang, in sich selbst gekehrt zu sein, . . . samt den daher kommenden Täuschungen des inneren Sinnes"; §22: "der Hang, das Spiel der Vorstellungen des inneren Sinnes für Erfahrungserkenntnis anzunehmen."
23. Kant, *Kritik der Urteilskraft* (1790), §§13, 48, 23, 9, 1; in *Werke* V, 302–3, 410–12, 330, 298, 279.

only an external reality of his own identity. As product of the artist's active involvement, the work of art reconciles rational and sensual responses; the sensual in art is intellectualized (*vergeistigt*) while its intellectual content is made to appear sensualized (*versinnlicht*).[24]

In the opening chapters of *Phenomenology of Mind*, Hegel explained that sensory certainty (*sinnliche Gewißheit*) is always illusory. Even through philosophical deliberation of the relation of subject and object, the mind cannot exorcize the phantoms of illusion:

> The healthy understanding is prey to the same thoughts which drive him around in their spinning circles. In the effort thereby to give them truth, the mind—now taking their untruth unto itself, now calling the illusion an appearance of unreliable things, separating the essential of a thing from its necessary and yet inessential propensity, and clinging to that essence as its truth—surrenders itself to the untruth.[25]

Through the dialectic interaction of self and other, which reveals being in-and-for-itself, mind comes to recognize the abstraction of truth and the inevitable presence of illusion.

What art accomplishes is a revelation of illusion as the "truest reality." Dismissing the pejorative deprecation of illusion as subjective and sensual indulgence, Hegel defends illusion in aesthetics as coequivalent to thinking in epistemology and moral premises in ethics. By seeming to give back to nature the very appearance of things, art reenacts the mental grappling with the object of perception in terms of its essence. The accompanying awareness of appearance not only restores the perception of the thing in-and-for-itself, but also allows the artist to complement and enhance the illusion.

> Art takes the appearance and the illusion of this wicked, transitory world forth from the true content of its manifestations and gives

---

24. Hegel, *Vorlesungen über die Ästhetik*, in *Werke* XIII, 44–64.
25. Hegel, "Die Wahrnehmung oder das Ding und die Täuschung," chap. 2 of *Phänomenologie des Geistes*, in *Werke* III, 93–107: "Der gesunde Verstand ist der Raub derselben, die ihn in ihrem wirbelnden Kreise umhertreiben. Indem er ihnen die Wahrheit dadurch geben will, daß er bald die Unwahrheit derselben auf sich nimmt, bald aber auch die Täuschung einen Schein der unzuverlässigen Dinge nennt und das Wesentliche von einem ihnen Notwendigen und doch Unwesentlichsein-sollenden abtrennt und jenes als ihre Wahrheit gegen dieses festhält, erhält er ihnen nicht ihre Wahrheit, sich aber gibt er die Unwahrheit."

them a higher reality conceived by mind. Far removed, therefore, from being mere appearance, to art may be ascribed a higher reality and more truthful existence in contrast with common reality.[26]

Even though the artist draws upon the sensual experience, his work is said to transform sensation into idea. In intellectualizing the aesthetic experience, Hegel, no less than Kant, endeavors to subordinate its sensual origins.

Literary developments from Rousseau through modernism have been caught in the dilemma of a subjective aesthetics embarrassed by its own subjectivism. Approaching art in terms of its power to excite the senses, artists and critics have nevertheless sought to oppose or expose the evocation of illusion and to intellectualize the sensual involvement.[27] The debate over illusion continues to beleaguer and perplex contemporary critics. Although it is my intention to present the critical theories of the Enlightenment and Romantic Era without appeal to more recently elaborated analyses of aesthetic illusion, it is useful and germane to remind ourselves of current arguments concerning illusionism. While it would take another book to survey developments in the twentieth century, it is possible to review briefly those ideas which have been most influential in recent discussion. The ways in which Adorno, Husserl, Gadamer, Gombrich, and Derrida have reacted to the subjectivism of the illusory experience will help introduce the complexity of those issues which were being discussed in the context of very different social, political, and philosophical presumptions some two hundred years earlier.

The definition of illusion as an involuntary emotional response Adorno refers to as *sensualism*. The revolt against sensualism brought about the intellectualizing of aesthetic experience evident in the idealism of Kant and Hegel. The revolt against idealism, promulgated under the ideological protest of the twentieth century, then denounced the pretensions of a privileged intellectual class and advocated an art free of illusory aura. Adorno argues for the "salvation of illusion" ("Rettung des Scheins"), not because he thinks aesthetic illusion is about to be eradicated, but because he sees the

---

26. Hegel, "Einleitung" (introduction) to *Vorlesungen über die Ästhetik*, in *Werke* XIII, 21–23: "Den Schein und die Täuschung dieser schlechten, vergänglichen Welt nimmt die Kunst von jenem wahrhaften Gehalt der Erscheinungen fort und gibt ihnen eine höhere, geistgeborene Wirklichkeit. Weit enfernt also, bloßer Schein zu sein, ist den Erscheinungen der Kunst der gewöhnlichen Wirklichkeit gegenüber die höhere Realität und das wahrhaftigere Dasein zuzuschreiben."
27. Jauß, "Der literarische Prozeß des Modernismus von Rousseau bis Adorno," 252, 262, 265.

presumptions of Anti-Illusionism, as in the drama of Brecht or Beckett, as misdirected.

The *affect* of art is more than the work of art. The old formulation that "the whole is equal to more than the sum of its parts," does not explain the nature of this "more," nor does the psychological account of perception and cognition as a "Gestalt" explain the aesthetic affect.[28] The "more," although mediated by the work of art, appears to be an immediate constituent. If it were a constituent, then, as the Anti-Illusionists have presumed, it might be removed. As a mediated factor, however, it emerges from the very dialectics of art: sense/intellect, subject/object, form/content. The subjective, to be reproduced in art, must be expressed objectively; the interior phantoms of consciousness must take on the form and language of the exterior world. The objective, even strict mimetic representation or documentary record, is altered by the subjective conditions of representing and recording. Art may pretend to emancipate idea from sensation, content from form, but the one exists only in and through the other.

> What is legitimate in the rebellion against illusion as well as what makes the effort illusionary—the hope that aesthetic illusion might lift itself from the quagmire by its own pigtail—are fused together. Evidently the immanent character of appearance in a work, as well as in a latent imitation of reality, cannot be separated from the work nor, therefore, from the illusion. For every ingredient of form and material, mind and matter, which goes into a work of art, emigrates from reality into the work of art where it surrenders its reality: and that is how the ingredient of art becomes its affect.[29]

Art is illusion, but its illusion is always immanent. Its "truths" are necessarily communicated through its artifice. The illusion is always accompanied by the evidence that the illusion is only an illusion. Thus the triumph of illusion

---

28. Adorno, *Ästhetische Theorie*, 122; Köhler, *Gestalt Psychology*, 42–59; *The Selected Papers of Wolfgang Köhler*, 125–67.

29. Adorno, *Ästhetische Theorie*, 158: "Das Legitime an der Rebellion gegen den Schein als Illusion und das Illusionäre an ihr, die Hoffnung, der ästhetische Schein könne am eigenen Zopf sich aus dem Sumpf ziehen, ist aber miteinander verquickt. Offenbar ist der immanente Scheincharakter der Werke von einem Stück wie immer auch latenter Nachahmung des Wirklichen, und darum von Illusion, nicht zu befreien. Denn alles, was die Kunstwerke an Form und Materialien, an Geist und Stoff in sich erhalten, ist aus der Realität in die Kunstwerke emigriert und in ihnen seiner Realität entäußert: so wird es auch zu deren Nachbild."

is never more than a convenient capitulation. By the same token, however, the pretense of annihilating illusion—as in the Aristophanic *parabasis*, Romantic irony, or Anti-Illusionism—only thematizes the inherent dialectics of art.[30]

Although Husserl insisted that he pursued phenomenology as a psychology, Adorno saw him trapped within the confines of systematic epistemology. Husserl follows Kant in determining a structure of imagination within the immanence of consciousness. Like Kant and Hegel, Husserl developed a fully intellectualized concept of illusion. Arguing that we can direct our attention to "pure" consciousness through an act of *transcendental reduction*, he claimed to liberate the eidetic intuition from the empirical process. The imagined object, thus bracketed, is separated from events outside the mind. Its relation to our knowledge and awareness of the external world is neutralized. Developed through play with possibilities, the imagined object offers an alternate reality. Its referentiality ceases to address the real world. It becomes self-referential, addressing only its own *as-if* being. As the product of fantasy is formed, the image is first represented within consciousness as a real perceptual object; its reality is then neutralized. The same process occurs with signs and symbols.[31] The world wrought through this conscious activity functions as a teleologic universe coextensive with empirical reality. Once prescinded from external being, its constituent images—whether grandparents or griffins—have equal verity.

As appraised by Adorno, Husserl's transcendental reduction annuls the ontological difference of being and elaborates an "illusion of concretization."[32] While Adorno opposes Husserl's system of intellectualizing illusion, he, too, argues the self-referentiality of illusion. He is concerned, however, with self-reference occurring within the work, not within the mind. Through the dialectic of defining the illusion and negating its implications, Adorno tells us that we reveal the ideology of illusion and thus come closer to determining truth.

As criticized by Derrida, Husserl's concept of self-referentiality leaves him

---

30. Furst, *Fictions of Romantic Irony*, 239, observes that "the authenticity of the self-contained illusion remains intact in traditional irony, whereas it is incessantly undermined and questioned in romantic irony." The "progressive destruction of illusion," far from being a mere game with the artifices of fiction, is "potentiated into an irony of fictional irony—and of the fictionality of existence."

31. Husserl, *Ideen zu einer reinen Phänomenologie und phänomenologische Philosophie*; *Phantasie, Bildbewußtsein, Erinnerung.*

32. Adorno, *Zur Metacritik der Erkenntnistheorie*; *Ästhetische Theorie*, 155, 158–59, 335, 337, 351; *Negative Dialektik*, 382, 384, 394.

with a solipsistic "theory of presence."[33] In contrast to other theories of illusion as fictions of the imagination with no reality, Husserl posits that illusion has a determinate reality as product of consciousness. Illusion has mental existence. The images are really there in consciousness where they are determined by an as-if teleology independent of external reality. Reference to images or signs is an act of making what has already been formed in the mind present to consciousness. As referents, of course, they cannot be expressed without referring to something other than themselves. Since they are always derived and modified forms of that which constitutes presence, Derrida concludes that Husserl trapped himself in the presence of consciousness.

Some such entrapment seems to occur in each of the various modes of illusion. For example, when we play the optical game with a Necker cube, manipulating its shape by reversing front and back, the illusion may be conscious and voluntary, but we have nevertheless lost our perception of its two-dimensional form as we play with its fictive three-dimensionality. Similarly, illusions of referentiality occur only when we accept signifier as the signified—even though we know better.[34] Illusions of spontaneity take place when we accept as immediate dialogue lines that we know the actors have memorized and rehearsed.[35] Illusions of self-referentiality, whether or not we are persuaded by Husserl's theory, occur when we follow Frodo and Sam Gamgee through Tolkien's Middle Earth.

To be trapped or captivated by illusion, however, need be no worse than to be taken off to prison in a nursery game of "London Bridge is falling down." When Coleridge defined the act of "poetic faith" as "a willing suspension of disbelief for the moment," he recognized that volitional acquiescence kept the mediating referentiality intact even while shifting our attention from signifier to signified.[36] For the same reason, recent accounts of illusion—from Sartre and Merleau-Ponty to Foucault and Iser—have avoided the either/or dichotomy of phenomenological aesthetics by emphasizing mediation and process. Iser, for example, has defined the fictive, not as the opposite of the real, but as that which mediates between the real and the imaginary.[37] In the fictive, the real, evoked only as image or sign, is necessar-

33. Derrida, *La voix et le phénomène*.
34. Issacharoff, "How Play Scripts Refer," 84–94.
35. Schlegel, "Über den dramatischen Dialog" (1796), in *Kritische Schriften und Briefe* I, 110–12.
36. Coleridge, *Biographia Literaria* II, 6.
37. Sartre, *L'Imaginaire;* Merleau-Ponty, *Phénoménologie de la perception* and *L'oiel et l'esprit;* Foucault, *Les mots et les choses;* Iser, "Akte des Fingierens," 121–52.

ily removed from its determinate context and becomes irreal, while the irreal is objectified as image or sign and is made to appear real. Illusion takes place in this middle ground when perception turns from empirical observation and witnesses the processes of mediation.

Murray Krieger escapes the either/or dichotomy by positing a both/and as well as a neither/nor. This strategy also enables him to affirm poetic presence without that presence becoming an entrapment of consciousness, as Derrida said it was for Husserl. In Krieger's tropological analysis, illusion is constructed and deconstructed in the "duplicitous act" of metaphor. Countering the linguistic dichotomy defined by Jakobson as "the metaphoric and metonymic poles" of discourse, Krieger affirms a sense of identity and difference in a use of metaphor that "includes metonymy, comes after it, and thereby transforms itself into irony." Metaphor, as that trope which endeavors "to produce the illusion of verbal identity," closes the gap between signifier and signified and thus conjures a sense of presence. This illusory presence is achieved only as a "momentary trick with a full awareness of the differential nature of language which precedes and coexists with it." Metaphor, then, is not a static figure: its presentation of *idem in alio* exists in a temporal flux. Just as the Necker cube is experienced as a multistable image that we see now one way and now another, metaphor is a multistable trope that engages consciousness in a series of gestalt-shifts: "The sequence seems to move from an immediate, prediscursive, subjective identity (metaphor) to the particularizing differentiation, as of items in a contiguous series (metonymy), to the totalizing of particulars into generalizations (synecdoche), to the self-consciously subversive reflection upon the entire process (irony)."[38] An apparent contradiction is evident: metonymy precedes, Krieger says, and metaphor comes after; but he also states that the sequence moves from metaphor to metonymy.

This chicken-egg dilemma is the same as the one Herder attempted to resolve in his essay on the origin of language. If man is only rational because he has language, how was man before he had language able to invent language? The interdependency of language and thought, for Herder, is progressively concretized and formalized by retentive consciousness (*Besonnenheit*).[39] In order to escape the entrapment of "concretization" (Adorno) and "pres-

---

38. Krieger, *Poetic Presence and Illusion*, xi, xi–xiii, 185; Jakobson and Halle, *Fundamentals of Language* (1956), chap. 5.
39. Herder, *Sprachphilosophische Schriften*, 5–7, 21–25, 28–44.

ence" (Derrida), consciousness must also de-concretize the verbal relationships between thoughts and things. This is what Krieger accomplishes by distinguishing between "consciousness of language" and "consciousness because of language." Presence and illusion involve the chicken-egg dilemma because the pattern of discourse reflects the history of consciousness (ontogeny recapitulates phylogeny).

In emphasizing illusion as momentary, Krieger might seem to resort to the notions of an oscillating or flickering response (Darwin, Stendhal). He tells us, however, that the illusionary identity coexists with the differentiation of terms and concepts. On the other hand, in asserting that illusion is not "a false substitute for 'reality'," but "is itself a real and positive force," he might seem to affirm illusion as the separate reality of consciousness (Husserl). Yet the reality that he attributes to illusion is not absolute and determinate, but only conditional and constitutive. Even while participating in the illusionary context, we deconstitute its illusionary presumptions. The tropical *idem in alio* is also *idem qua alio*. The as-if reality neither replaces nor is confounded with factual reality. Neurologically akin to seeing, reading stimulates a seeing. While reading enables us to behold the presence of metaphor, its visual presence is "seen" as mediated through its verbal sign. The perception, then, requires a double sense. In order to sustain the illusion of identity we must persist in attending to the difference: we read in order to see. We allow the illusion to develop its own self-referentiality, yet we intrude upon the process because self-referentiality always exposes the metaphor as metaphor, revealing its metonymy and irony.[40]

The consequences of the paradigm shift from an involuntary to a voluntary theory of illusion continue to trouble aesthetics. In their efforts to defend the voluntary action, theorists have sought to avoid the deterministic entrapments of language and of mind. Thus many have resorted to mediation and to play. Positing the play-drive as mediating between the rational form-drive and the sensual matter-drive, Schiller sought to free aesthetics from sensual and intellectual bondage. With the mediating freedom of play, the intellectual dimension is not allowed to impose didactic authority ("one should only *play* with the beautiful"); nor is the sensual dimension permitted to lapse into self-indulgence ("one should play *only with the beautiful*"). Through play art achieves its illusion of freedom. It becomes "a happy

---

40. Krieger, *Poetic Presence and Illusion*, 3–27, 139–96; see also Krieger, "Mediation, Language, and Vision in the Reading of Literature."

citizen who calls to me, 'Be free like me.' " Schiller never claims that art is free, only that it communicates "freedom in appearance" (*Freiheit in der Erscheinung*).⁴¹ The media of expression determine and constrain the act of expression. Although art cannot be autonomous, it can and should seem autonomous.

Krieger, it should be noted, does not resort to play in discussing the paradoxical nature of illusion and presence. The way in which poetry shifts from metaphor to metonymy to irony in its self-contradictory propositions, he sees not as a matter of play but as a matter of necessity. The duplicitous *idem in alio* is poetry's way of opposing the self-enclosure that otherwise constrains discourse. This act, too, is no more than a "freedom in appearance," for the consciousness of its own self-enclosure only breaks down, not breaks out of, the construct of discourse.⁴²

Gadamer, by contrast, builds his hermeneutics on an ontology of play in order to free art from subjectivism. Kant's doctrine of a pure and intellectual aesthetic judgment he considers fatal to the aesthetic experience. As we have seen, Kant acknowledges the inclination to illusion but seeks to dispel it through deliberate "disinterestedness." Gadamer restores illusion to the aesthetic experience as *a priori* interest. Play he defines as a purposeless purpose, that is, a game of discovery and confrontation with one's own latent interests. It is purposeless because it has no foreordained obligations; it is purposeful because it excites the vital feelings and brings imagination and understanding into interaction. By reengaging the illusion that Kant had denied to aesthetic judgment, Gadamer's concept of play avoids the ontology of a prescinded consciousness (Kant, Husserl).

In Schiller's aesthetics, play still occurs in the Kantian playground of subjectivism: one plays with one's own sensual and intellectual drives. Gadamer's concept of play involves the game strategy predicated by the work of art; instead of looking *at* the work as an object, one looks *through* it. Like Alice through the looking glass, the player enters into the world of illusion and engages its conditions. The player knows that he is only playing, but he takes the game seriously. The player is not the subject, the game itself is. It is a subject discovered only through playing. Gadamer insists on the primacy of playing as opposed to the consciousness of the player. Play

---

41. Schiller, *Kallias Briefe*, Letter 5, 23 February 1793, and *Ästhetische Erziehung*, Letters 12–15, in *Sämtliche Werke* V, 409–26, 604–19.
42. Krieger, *Poetic Presence and Illusion*, 98–99, 196.

has regulated order and movement: its purposeless purpose is achieved in the performance. It may require great effort, but it is not work, for we do not labor at, but take pleasure in, its creative movement. Its arbitrary rules challenge rather than inhibit performance.[43]

Gombrich's play theory in *Art and Illusion* was published in the same year as Gadamer's in *Wahrheit und Methode*. Gombrich also opposes aesthetic subjectivism and the pretense of disinterestedness. He too develops the distinction between looking at and looking through the work of art, but he also raises the question whether we can watch ourselves in the process. There are two key attributes of Gombrich's account of illusion: (1) We may know that we are having an illusion, but "we cannot, strictly speaking, watch ourselves having an illusion"; (2) illusion rests directly on the artistic recreation of the conditions that influence perception, but it is also affected by deliberate distortion through convention, manner, and style. Gombrich seems to grant us dual perception, so that "we may be intellectually aware of the fact any given experience *must* be an illusion." Like Mendelssohn, who also fretted over the mind's capacity to monitor itself, Gombrich examines the processes by which the art refers to the visible world and determines that we cannot observe the process of reference and the object of reference at the same time. Just as in the optical game with the Necker cube, we lose perception of the means in order to engage the illusion.[44]

In the dramatic criticism of the Enlightenment and the Romantic Era, the effort to sort out the differences between delusion and illusion raised issues of ontology and freedom that twentieth-century theorists continue to address. Since I began by objecting to the reductionism of "history of ideas," I will not now claim genetic continuity in aesthetics. Krieger may confess his Kantian and Coleridgean antecedents, but Kant and Coleridge would have been startled by the existentialist negation and the deconstruction of language evident in his account of metaphor as paradoxical self-affirmation and self-denial. Twentieth-century theorists have been more alert to ideological implications and more preoccupied with the presumptions of discourse and the instability of mediation than any of their predecessors.

To be sure, Rousseau was quite concerned with the ideological impact of the theater. Furthermore, there were political and cultural forces at work in

43. Gadamer, *Wahrheit und Methode*, 41–49, 97–105.
44. Gombrich, *Art and Illusion*; Mendelssohn, "Von der Illusion," in *Gesammelte Schriften*, ed. Mendelssohn, IV-1, 44–45.

the eighteenth-century effort to establish a freedom of choice in aesthetic experience and to raise it from its debased status as emotionalism or sensationalism. Nevertheless, critics did not scrutinize how illusion might replicate an ideological structure and its causality. Kant's diagnosis of the antinomies, amphiboles, and paralogisms of transcendental dialectics was not seen as symptomatic of the general pathology of language. The impasse of discourse, however, is recognized in Schiller's distich: "When the soul *speaks*, the *soul*, alas! speaks no longer," and in Hegel's pun that in language "I can never mean (*meinen*) what is mine (*mein*)."[45]

While definitions developed during the Enlightenment and the Romantic Era do not center illusion in an ontology of language or of political structure, there is an effort to locate illusion in an *ontic* place. I have organized the following chapters according to the assumptions about location. Diderot, as we shall see, elaborates the paradoxicality of illusion but he places it in acting not, as Krieger does, in metaphor. Goethe and Hugo also put illusion on stage, not in the acting but in the stage setting and stage effects. Schlegel locates illusion in the play itself, emphasizing how dramatic action thematizes illusion through strategies of deception and disguise. While the ontological status of play, player, or playhouse depends upon its intersubjective efficacy, the critic can at least sustain a dialectic of self and other. That advantage is rendered *sub rosa* when the ontology is internalized. Fully aware of the subjective entrapment, Coleridge locates illusion in the imagination and endeavors to elaborate the grounds for illusion as a free and self-conscious act.

The closing chapter examines how the theoretical quest for illusion informs the metadramatic play with illusion. I examine the ways in which Coleridge's *Remorse* and Tieck's *Der gestiefelte Kater* ironically undermine intentionality and referentiality, not destroying illusion but rendering it far more complex than the more-or-less constant intention and reference of mimetic drama.

---

45. Schiller, "Sprache," in *Sämtliche Werke* I, 313: "Warum kann der lebendige Geist dem Geist nicht erscheinen? / Spricht die Seele, so spricht ach! schon die *Seele* nicht mehr"; Hegel, *Phänomenologie des Geistes*, in *Werke* III, 86.

1

Perfect Illusion and the Skeptics: Rousseau, Johnson, and Stendhal

The strongest arguments for the power of the aesthetic experience have always come not from its advocates but from its antagonists, from those who consider the arts detrimental and seek to censor their influence. Arguments on moral corruption through aesthetic experience have a venerable history. The classical text is Plato's *Republic* (book X) where the effects of art are called "irrational, useless, and cowardly," exciting "the passionate and fitful temper," rather than pleasing the rational disposition. Plato condemns the poet because he "sets up in each individual soul a vicious constitution by fashioning phantoms far removed from reality."[1] In the eighteenth century that history could be documented from Jeremy Collier's *Short View of the Immorality and Profaneness of the English Stage* (1698) to John Styles's *An Essay on the Character, Immoral, and Antichristian Tendency of the Stage* (1806), with Jean-Jacques Rousseau's *Lettre à d'Alembert sur les spectacles* (1758) as philosophically the most vigorous and rigorous of all indictments of the stage.

Plato, of course, also provides an extensive inquiry into the nature of

---

1. Plato, *Republic*, book X (§§604–5), in *The Collected Dialogues*, 830.

illusion. If the artist's attempt to represent likenesses (*mimesis* or *homoiosis*) derives from the relation of being to idea, expressing the harmony of the soul, then we would have a possibility of true images (*eikon*). If the artist gives his attention merely to being, representing the objects of the senses, then we would have only counterfeit images (*eidolon, phantasma*). As Plato argues in the *Republic*, the latter circumstance dominates the arts because the senses command the body.[2] The difficulties in relating idea to being, or soul to body, also burden the effort to relate meaning to word, or signifier to signified. In the *Cratylus*, Plato ponders the question whether a sign (*semeion* or *semainon*) has meaning without the copresence of a reflection or shadow of an image (*eikon*), whether the meaning of an image, in turn, does not depend upon an ontological idea. Through similarity or likeness, an image could offer no more than a clumsy approximation of the truth. Truth, then, is not to be acquired through oblique similitude but only through perfect duplication. The illusion of artistic representation is necessarily a deception; the perfect illusion, truth, would require not a copy but another original. Socrates, after pondering whether Homer's poetry might be returned to the Republic, is forced to reject it, "for we have come to see that we must not take such poetry seriously as a serious thing that lays hold on truth."[3] Worse than simply lacking truth, the phantom images are set loose as a contagion of deceit.

The conviction that the drama was responsible for "Debauching the Age" prompted Jeremy Collier to pen the attack that gave rise to a virtual storm of defenses and counterattacks.[4] Collier simply assumes rather than describes the illusory appeal. Depictions of lewdness arouse lewd passions and lewd behavior. By "making their *Top Characters Libertines*, and giving them *Success* in their *Debauchery*," playwrights "encourage" spectators to go and do likewise. Lascivious impulses and desires may be held in check by moral principles, but these, Collier believes, are enforced only by the inhibitions of shame and fear. By soliciting admiration for characters who indulge the passions, the drama dispels all vestiges of shame and fear. Its provocations then become spontaneous and inevitable, working upon the audience as

2. Ibid. (§602), 827.
3. Plato, *Cratylus* (§§432, 440), in *The Collected Dialogues*, 466, 474; Derbolav, *Der Dialog "Kratylos" im Rahmen der platonischen Sprach- und Erkenntnisphilosophie* (1953) and "Das Problem des Metasprachlichen in Platons 'Kratylos,' " in *Lebendiger Realismus* (1962).
4. Anthony, *The Jeremy Collier Stage Controversy, 1698–1726;* Barish, *The Antitheatrical Prejudice,* 221–35.

cause upon effect. Because dramatic representation solicits a passive submission of the senses, the spectator has no power to resist the promiscuity of the stage:

> It cherishes those Passions, and rewards those Vices, which 'tis the business of Reason to discountenance. It strikes at the Root of Principle, draws off the Inclination from Virtue, and spoils good Education; 'Tis the most effectual means to baffle the Force of Discipline, to emasculate peoples Spirits, and Debauch their Manners.[5]

The individual is thus bereft of moral defense against the attractive representation of vice upon the stage. The effects are as dire as those Plato described in the *Republic*. Even a man of education and principle is rendered spiritually "emasculate" when exposed to the irresistible temptations of theatrical vice.

If we were to give detailed attention to the moral indictments written by the subsequent generation of critics against the vile influences of the stage, we would find that they gave increasing attention to the illusory spell and its power to vitiate the will. Whether the experience of illusion is voluntary or involuntary becomes the moral crux. John Styles, a century after Collier, argues that drama has a debilitating effect on the will. He appropriates the Platonic distinction to describe two kinds of illusion, one evoked by the true imagery of the church and the other by the counterfeit imagery of the theater. He acknowledges that religion and drama have, in classical as well as in medieval times, shared common interests. While efforts to represent the manifestation and incarnation of divine spirit persist almost unchanged in Christian liturgy, the imagery of the theater has turned to ever more wayward attempts to titillate the sensual response. Since theatrical illusion is produced by stimulating physical excitement, the exacerbated senses leave the spectator in a delirium when the curtain falls. The aftereffects may continue to stir his imagination for days. Condorcet and Godwin, who defend the theater "in their wild and beautiful theories," Styles observes, "possess every thing to make them charming—but truth." The moral arguments of Dr. Johnson and Rousseau are both quoted, but both are put

---

5. Collier, *Short View of the Immorality and Profaneness of the English Stage, Together With the Sense of Antiquity upon this Argument*, i, 2, 4–8, 140–45, 155–56, 179, 287.

aside as humanist rather than Christian. He grants that the stage may aspire to "literary refinement and taste," but even if it seems to coincide with Christian ethics, its means and methods of appeal are always and necessarily physical, sensual, and emotional, but never spiritual. Thus the drama degrades the human condition, not the least when it pretends to exalt and ennoble man in terms of "heroic" passions. Since drama is always an invitation to sensual indulgence, its effects are idleness and dissipation. It "relaxes the nerve of industry" and "transforms the citizen, the tradesman and the mechanic into the man of fashion, the lounger and the libertine."[6]

Rousseau, too, had argued that the effect of the drama was to dissipate the will and turn industry to idleness. In his *Lettre à d'Alembert sur les spectacles*, he denies that dramatic illusion is capable of improving man's moral sensibility. Contrary to Collier, he also denies that theatrical scenes of lewdness excite the spectator to lewd behavior. Illusion, according to Rousseau, engages the sentiments without touching moral interests, personal convictions, or behavior. Its effects are trifling and self-serving, indistinguishable from habitual hypocrisy and other displays of feigned emotion.

> I hear it said that tragedy leads to pity through fear; so it does. But what is pity? A fleeting and vain emotion, which lasts no longer than the illusion which produced it; a remnant of natural sentiment, stifled soon by the passions; a sterile pity, which nourishes itself with a few tears, and which has never produced the slightest act of humanity.... If, according to the remark of Diogenes Laertius, the heart attends more voluntarily to feigned ills than to true ones, if theatrical imitations draw forth more tears than would the presence of the objects imitated, it is less because the emotions are feebler and do not reach the level of pain, as the Abbé du Bos believes, than because they are pure and without mixture of anxiety for ourselves. In giving our tears to these fictions, we have satisfied all rights of humanity without having to give anything more of ourselves.[7]

6. Styles, *An Essay on the Character, Immoral, and Antichristian Tendency of the Stage*, 2–5, 19–23, 27–29, 37, 74–78, 125–32.

7. Rousseau, *Lettre à d'Alembert sur les spectacles*, in *Oeuvres* VIII, 34–36: "J'entends dire que la tragédie mène à la pitié par la terreur; soit. Mais quelle est cette pitié? Une émotion passagére et

The rules of the drama contribute little to creating illusion, for illusion is simply the game an audience plays to amuse itself. *Mimesis* is a futile pretension:

> Behold a well planned imitation, which proposes for its object that which does not exist at all, and leaves, between defect and excess, that which is like a useless thing! But of what importance is the truth of imitation, provided that the illusion is there? The only purpose is to excite the curiosity of the public.[8]

Although he argues that illusion works through the emotions, he does not conclude that the spectator is then persuaded to adopt or imitate the spurious values of the drama. How much worse would be the corruptive influence, if we always exercised the same tolerance of crimes as Corneille and Racine expect from us:

> It is not even true that murder and parricide are always repugnant in the theater. Favored by a few easy suppositions, they are rendered permissible, or pardonable. It is hard not to excuse Phaedra, who is incestuous and spills innocent blood: Syphax poisoning his wife, the young Horatius stabbing his sister, Agamemnon sacrificing his daughter, Orestes cutting his mother's throat, do not fail to be interesting characters.[9]

---

vaine, qui ne dure pas plus que l'illusion qui l'a produit; un reste de sentiment naturel, étouffé bientôt par les passions, une pitié stérile, qui se repaît de quelques larmes, et n'a jamais produit le moindre acte d'humanité.... Si, selon la remarque de Diogène-Laërce, le coeur s'attendrit plus volontiers à des maux feints qu'à des maux véritables; si les imitations du théâtre nous arrachent quelquefois plus de pleurs que ne feroit la présence même des objets imités, c'est moins, comme le pense l'abbé du Bos, parceque les émotions sont plus foibles et ne vont pas jusqu'à la douleur, que parcequ'elles sont pures et sans mélange d'inquiétude pour nous-mêmes. En donnant des pleurs à ces fictions, nous avons satisfait à tous les droits de l'humanité, sans avoir plus rien à mettre du nôtre."

8. Ibid., 39: "Ne voila-t-il pas une imitation bien entendue, qui se propose pour objet ce qui n'est point, et laisse, entre le défaut et l'excès ce qui est, comme une chose inutile! Mais qu'importe la vérité de l'imitation, pourvu que l'illusion y soit? Il ne s'agit que de piquer la curiosité du peuple."

9. Ibid., 47–48: "Il n'est pas même vrai que le meurtre et le parricide y soient toujours odieux. A la faveur de je ne sais quelles commodes suppositions, on les rend permis, ou pardonnables. On a peine à ne pas excuser Phèdre incestueuse et versant le sang innocent: Syphax empoisonnant sa femme, le jeune Horace poignardant sa soeur, Agamemnon immolant sa fille, Oreste égorgeant sa mère, ne laissent pas d'être des personnages intéressants."

In his exposition of Molière's comedies, Rousseau shows us how virtue is ridiculed and vice applauded.[10] Still his argument is not that the topsy-turvy morality of the drama might pervert and corrupt the audience. He is not willing to grant such suasive power to illusion. As he defines it, illusion is no more than an indulgence of imagination for amusement's sake. The highest ideals of the theater cannot improve society, nor can its crudest displays be blamed for corrupting the people. Yet the theater does corrupt.

Immorality is propagated only indirectly by the theater. When we witness, play after play, how the conditions of morality are suspended or altered, all that happens is that we relax our expectations of moral justice and anticipate the excitement of the passions. Rousseau observes that contemporary drama is unduly preoccupied with love, a most "contagious passion." After the play has aroused sexual feelings in the spectator, it little matters whether morality is then preserved on stage.

> Is it not absurd to pretend that, after the event, the movements of the heart can be governed by the precepts of reason, and that the results must be awaited to know with what impression one ought to receive the situations which lead to them? The harm for which the theater is reproached is not precisely that of inspiring criminal passions but of disposing the soul to feelings which are too tender and which are later satisfied at the expense of virtue.[11]

The emotional enchantment of Voltaire's *Zaïre*, whatever moral lesson might be drawn from Orosmane's jealousy and his suicide after murdering his mistress, leaves the audience thoroughly entranced by the power of love. "However love is depicted for us, it seduces or it is not love." We delight in the "delicious sentiment" and ignore the moral tribulations. We are encouraged to indulge rather than "to distrust the illusions of love." By making "a lover estimable or detestable according to whether well or ill received in his loves," love itself becomes a virtue.[12]

---

10. Ibid., 50–66.
11. Ibid., 75: "N'est-il pas plaisant qu'on prétende ainsi régler après coup les mouvements du coeur sur les préceptes de la raison, et qu'il faille attendre les évènements pour savoir quelle impression l'on doit recevoir des situations qui les amènent? Le mal qu'on reproche au théâtre n'est pas précisément d'inspirer des passions criminelles, mais de disposer l'ame à des sentiments trop tendres, qu'on satisfait ensuite aux dépens de la vertu."
12. Ibid., 81: "Qu'on nous peigne l'amour comme on voudra: il séduit, ou ce n'est pas lui"; VIII, 82: "On croit faire merveilles de rendre un amant estimable ou haïssable, selon qu'il est bien ou mal

Still, Rousseau's point is not that these voluptuous illusions immediately or directly corrupt an audience.[13] The process is indirect and gradual, for in entertaining the emotions the theater takes us away from practical and useful activities.

> In favoring all our penchants, it gives a new ascendancy to those which dominate us. The continual emotion which is felt in the theater excites us, enervates us, enfeebles us, renders us much less able to resist our passions; and the sterile interest taken in virtue serves only to satisfy our self-esteem without constraining us to practice it.[14]

The theater corrupts by institutionalizing amusement, by giving social priority to gathering for no other purpose than self-indulgence.[15] As we can observe in his *De l'imitation théâtrale*, the essay he wrote in preparing his reply to d'Alembert's proposal to bring the theater to Geneva, Rousseau made a close study of book X of Plato's *Republic*. There he adheres more closely to Plato's argument that the imitation itself is the cause for immorality.[16] D'Alembert asserted that the theater would liberate the people from the repression of a Socinian clergy and bring them the enlightenment of art.[17] Rousseau chose to answer d'Alembert's argument for social improvement on social grounds. Thus he emphasizes that the corruptive forces are social and economic: the pleasure principle replaces the work ethic. Rousseau is concerned only with protecting the values of Geneva against the decadence of Paris. Where people are virtuous, the theater can only corrupt and pervert. The French, however, do well to support the theater.

---

accueilli dans ses amours; de faire toujours approuver au public les sentiments de sa maîtresse, et de donner à la tendresse tout l'intérêt de la vertu: au lieu qu'il faudroit apprendre aux jeunes gens à se défier des illusions de l'amour."

13. Ibid., 83: "Encore une fois, je n'entreprends point de juger si c'est bien ou mal fait de fonder sur l'amour le principal intérêt du théâtre; mais je dis que, si ses peintures sont quelquefois dangereuses, elles le soront toujours quoi qu'on fasse pour les déguiser."

14. Ibid., 84: "En favorisant tous nos penchants, il donne un nouvel ascendant à ceux qui nous dominent; les continuelles émotions qu'on y ressent nous énervent, nous affoiblissent, nous rendent plus incapables de résister à nos passions; et le stérile intérêt qu'on prend à la vertu ne sert qu'à contenter notre amour-propre sans nous contraindre à la pratiquer."

15. Ibid., 85–96.
16. Rousseau, *De l'imitation théâtrale*, in *Oeuvres* VIII, 219–45.
17. d'Alembert, "Genève" (1757), in *Encyclopédie* VII, 578.

Where people are already wicked, plays may distract them from further wickedness.[18]

To claim that drama has the power to overwhelm the reason and delude the senses implies that the aesthetic experience is a rape rather than a seduction. Coleridge was later to object to the definition of the mind as "a lazy Looker-on," a mere *camera obscura* or *tabula rasa*, passively receiving and recording external data through the senses, and he was to insist upon desynonymizing *illusion* and *delusion* to distinguish the conscious engagement of the aesthetic experience from the passive acquiescence to deception.[19] But for many critics of the Enlightenment, the only explanation of how drama could work so powerfully upon our feelings was that the reason was either overwhelmed or, at least momentarily, convinced that the scene on the stage was real.

From this assumption, it would follow that the most effective drama would be that which engenders a perfect illusion. The scene presented on the stage must be rendered indistinguishable from real life. Jean-Baptiste Du Bos, who based his critical theory on the pleasure of the aesthetic response, saw the difficulties of this assumption and deliberately denied the importance of illusion in the drama.[20] Charles Batteux was another skeptic who rejected "perfect illusion." He argued, nevertheless, that playwright and players should strive for perfection, not in the vain attempt to secure illusion but simply to enhance the spectator's pleasure.[21] But many later critics were convinced that the success of the drama ought to be measured in terms of its evocation of a perfect illusion.

For Johann Friedrich Schink, a partial dallying with an illusory experience was a useless enterprise for the drama. Illusion, he declares in his *Dramaturgische Fragmente* (1781–82), must work a total and involuntary spell. Nevertheless, "perfect illusion" meant for Schink the opposite of what it meant for Plato. As noted above, Plato's concept of "perfect illusion,"

---

18. Rousseau, *Lettre à d'Alembert* VIII, 85–88, 96: "Quand le peuple est corrompu, les spectacles lui sont bons, et mauvais quand il est bon lui-même"; Barish, *The Antitheatrical Prejudice*, 256–94, argues that Rousseau substitutes effect for cause in presenting the theater as central trope for the charades and masquerades, pretensions and hypocrisies, that infect society; the theater conveniently symbolized for Rousseau the deceit and disguise of social mannerism.

19. Coleridge to Thomas Poole, 23 March 1801, *Collected Letters of Samuel Taylor Coleridge* II, 709; *Lectures 1808–1819: On Literature* I, 35, in *The Collected Works of Samuel Taylor Coleridge* 5.

20. Du Bos, *Réflexions critiques sur la poésie et la peinture*, section XLIII. "Que le plaisir que nous avons au Théâtre n'est point produit par l'illusion," 451–52.

21. Batteux, *Les Beux Arts réduits à un même principe* III, 318–29; VI, 191–92.

required a "true image" to replicate the inherent relation of being to idea, body to spiritual essence, whereas only a counterfeit image could be achieved by imitating the objects of the senses. Schink's "perfection" is Plato's "counterfeit." The truth, for Schink, is not in the object, as object, but in the sensations and feelings that it arouses: "What does not affect the human heart is not true." "Perfect illusion" is irresistible. Once the sensations and feelings are implicated, the spectator no longer perceives merely the appearance but participates fully in the illusion: "Through illusion the spectator believes himself transplanted from the theater out into the real world." He experiences the drama not as an imitation, but as the matter itself, without conscious awareness of player or stage. Drama based on appearance and probability (*Schein* and *Wahrscheinlichkeit*) can only disappoint, "because mere appearances can never replace reality nor maintain vitality." Illusion, on the other hand, "heightens our interest to such a degree that we forget the playwright and the player, and live before the stage as in the real world"; illusion is "the animating force, . . . which alone transforms dramatic literature into truth." Schink's "perfect illusion" can tolerate no metadramatic or self-reflexive irony on the stage, for any disruption of illusion (*Illusionszerstörung*) destroys the entire effect of the play and "rips one with force out of the events and out of the human life."[22]

Dr. Samuel Johnson is often cited as the pragmatic critic who rejected the concept of illusion: "The truth is, that the spectators are always in their senses, and know, from first act to last, that the stage is only a stage, and that the players are only players."[23] Before we conclude, however, that Johnson was an utter skeptic who deined the efficacy of illusion, we would do well to recollect how frequently he warned against the indulgence of illusion. In *Rambler* No. 4, for example, he commends fiction for its power to influence the mind by engaging the imagination. Because of this power, the author fulfills a moral responsibility in avoiding the "wild strain of imagination" and showing, instead, "life in its true state, diversified only by accidents that daily happen in the world, and influenced by passions and qualities which

---

22. Schink, *Dramaturgische Fragmente*, 699, 65, 420, 534, 758; p. 15: "Was nicht auf menschliches Herz wirkt, ist nicht wahr"; p. 650: "Der getäuschte Zuschauer [glaubt] sich aus dem Theater in die wirkliche Welt ersetzt"; 1039: "weil blosser Schein die Wirklichkeit nie ersetzt, . . . und lebendig erhält"; p. 458: "[Illusion erhöht] unser Interesse zu einem Grade, daß wir Dichter und Schauspieler darüber vergessen, und vor der Bühne, wie in der wirklichen Welt leben"; "[Illusion ist] die belebende Kraft, . . . die allein die dramatische Dichtung zur Wahrheit erhebt"; p. 441: "einen mit aller Gewalt aus Begebenheit und Menschenleben herausrücken."
23. Johnson, "Preface to Shakespeare," *The Works of Samuel Johnson* XII, 9.

are really to be found in conversing with mankind." Johnson thus endorses the principles that underlie the "mirror of life" realism in the novel and in the domestic drama of the eighteenth-century stage. Observing that fiction is "written chiefly to the young," Johnson asserts that judicious constraint is all the more necessary, for the imagination is easily excited among young readers:

> They [works of fiction] are the entertainment of minds unfurnished with ideas, and therefore easily susceptible of impressions; not fixed by principles, and therefore easily following the current of fancy; not informed by experience, and consequently open to every false suggestion and partial account.

If Johnson did not assume that images could work with compelling vivacity in a youthful mind, he would not insist "that nothing indecent should be suffered to approach their eyes or ears." As an imitation of reality, fiction must exercise care "in representing life, which is so often discolored by passion or deformed by wickedness." An author must omit the noisome and squalid details and not allow "the world to be promiscuously described."[24]

Nor is this susceptibility to the influences of fancy a frailty confined to youth. A major tenet of Johnson's moral philosophy is that the reason must be alert to the impositions of the imagination. Although he granted in *Rambler* No. 4 that the "current of fancy" flowing from fiction could be positive and educative, in his *Dictionary* he defined illusion only in negative terms: "mockery; false show; counterfeit appearance; errour." *Rambler* No. 5 presumes that "every man is sufficiently discontented with some circumstance of his present state, to suffer his imagination to range more or less in quest of future happiness." *Rambler* No. 203 makes the similar argument that because "the time present is seldom able to fill desire or imagination, . . . we are forced to supply its deficiency by recollection or anticipation." *Idler* No. 58 tells us that "the most active imagination will be sometimes torpid" and will thus seek out stimulations to excite pleasure—only to have the expectations blighted by disappointments that reveal "the fallacies of imagination." The opening lines of *Rasselas*—"Ye who listen with credulity to the whispers of fancy, and pursue with eagerness the phantoms of

---

24. Johnson, *Works* I, 19–26.

hope"—make clear that this, too, is a cautionary tale concerned with the dangers of the imagination.[25]

Such often-reiterated caveats should remind us that Johnson belongs to the tradition of critics who recognize a moral danger in the power of the imagination. Even though a spectator knows "that the stage is only a stage, and that the players are only players," the drama may still work upon his credulity. The senses and emotions may be so affected that the reason itself is misdirected. When in *Rambler* No. 125 he reflects upon the problem of defining the boundaries between comedy and tragedy, he grants that the mercurial nature of the literary imagination, "a licentious and vagrant faculty, unsusceptible of limitations, and impatient of restraint," resists the efforts of critical definition. "If the two kinds of dramatick poetry had been defined only by their effects upon the mind," he argues, it might have been possible to avoid "absurdities" in the drama. His concern with the "effects upon the mind," however, leads not to defending the imagination, but to upholding propriety. The rational mind opposes a mixture of serious and farcical elements and requires a prevailing uniformity of effects. By removing all comic elements from tragedy, contemporary playwrights may not often "move terrour or pity" nor attain "that dominion over the passions which was the boast of their predecessors," but neither are they apt to disrupt a tragic scene by provoking laughter.[26] The illusion resides not in the perception of the stage as reality, but rather in the affective response.[27] What thrills him in the theater, the spectator may continue to rehearse in his mind and even act out in his own life. Like Rousseau, Johnson had a low opinion of players, the stage, and habitual playgoers. In *Idler* No. 47, a homely version of the letter to d'Alembert, "Deborah Ginger" writes a letter to the editor, describing how her husband's mind has been corrupted by attending plays.[28]

Johnson's "physical limitations of sight and hearing," as J. E. Brown suggests in *The Critical Opinions of Samuel Johnson*, might explain the contrast between his skeptical attitude toward stage illusion and his strong sense

25. Johnson, *A Dictionary of the English Language; Works* I, 27; IV, 182; V, 282–83; VII, 7.
26. Johnson, *Works* III, 80–86.
27. Foakes, "Form to His Conceit: Shakespeare and the Uses of Stage Illusion," 107, points out that this was precisely the argument forwarded by William Kenrick in his attempt to "correct" the seeming contradiction in Johnson's dismissal of illusion. In the commentary published in the *Monthly Review* (October and November, 1795), Kenrick "tried to distinguish between delusion affecting our belief, and delusion affecting our emotions, and claimed that 'the deception goes no farther than the passions, it affects our sensibility, but not our understanding.'"
28. Johnson, *Works* V, 239–43.

of the illusion experienced in reading: "A person gifted with Johnson's extraordinary imagination, but with sight and hearing impaired, might well say 'A play read, affects the mind like a play acted,' and underestimate the amount of illusion possible on the stage, to the average spectator."[29] In his "Preface to Shakespeare" (1765), Johnson interprets the experience of illusion by relating performance to reading: "A dramatick exhibition is a book recited with concomitants that encrease or diminish its effect." Not "stage illusion" but aesthetic illusion, such as wrought by reading the book, furnishes Johnson his model for explaining how the mind reacts, knowing "that the action is not supposed to be real," yet granting credibility to the feelings involved. After having asserted that no "representation is mistaken for reality," that no "dramatick fable in its materiality was ever credible, or, for a single moment, was ever credited," Johnson goes on to argue that credibility derives from the contemplation of the emotional effects:

> It will be asked, how the drama moves, if it is not credited. It is credited, with all the credit due to a drama. It is credited, whenever it moves, as a just picture of a real original; as representing to the auditor what he would himself feel, if he were to do or suffer what is there feigned to be suffered or done. The reflection that strikes the heart is not, that the evils before us are real evils, but that they are evils to which we ourselves may be exposed.... The delight of tragedy proceeds from our consciousness of fiction; if we thought murders and treasons real, they would please no more. Imitations produce pain or pleasure, not because they are mistaken for realities, but because they bring realities to mind.[30]

As in reading a book, Johnson tells us, we retain "our consciousness of fiction." This is why the unities of time and place need not be deemed absolute mandates. Since we cannot suppose "that when the play opens, the spectator really imagines himself at *Alexandria*," we must grant that the illusions of time and place are elements that the imagination may "willingly permit" to be shifted and altered. Indeed, the very "delight" in the experience occurs through a willing acceptance, which allows, in turn, a self-conscious contemplation and reflection upon our own response.

29. Brown, *The Critical Opinions of Samuel Johnson*, 73.
30. Johnson, *Works* XII, 8–11.

In ignoring the presumption of an objective stage illusion and turning instead to the personal response, Johnson avoids that Platonic criterion which requires a representation to be a perfect duplication in order to be "true." In this respect, his explanation is akin to other subjective accounts of illusion. While he saw the possibility of the mind succumbing to the imagination, Johnson nevertheless insisted upon the copresence of reason. Thus he would not extend the subjective ground, as did Henry Home (Lord Kames) by attributing to aesthetic illusion the essentially irrational province of the dream. The dream, as analogical explanation of the aesthetic experience, allows the images of fancy to prevail while reason slumbers. For Johnson, that would mean surrendering the battle without a fight.

Perhaps as a truce, rather than as a capitulation, Lord Kames suggested that the rational faculties might be considered suspended as in a "waking dream." By putting reason in a temporary abeyance and turning consciousness over to the imagination, Kames also endeavors to affirm the notion of a "perfect illusion":

> When a play begins, we have no difficulty to adjust our imagination to the scene of action, however distant it be in time or place; because we know that the play is a representation only. The case is very different after we are engaged: it is the perfection of representation to hide itself, to impose upon the spectator, and to produce in him an impression of reality, as if he were a spectator of a real event; but any interruption annihilates that impression, by rousing him out of his waking dream, and unhappily restoring him to his senses.

Where Johnson saw reason as the arbiter of moral judgment, Kames considered sympathy, the "cement of society," as the moral ground for the arts as well as for all human endeavor. Following Shaftesbury and Hutcheson, Kames had no moral qualms about the sympathetic instincts prevailing over reason in the dreamlike state of aesthetic experience.[31] Like Schink, Kames

---

31. Home, *Elements of Criticism* II, 418; Foakes, in his Introduction to Coleridge's *Lectures 1808–1819: On Literature* I, lvi–lvii, cites this passage as relevant antecedent to Coleridge's account of dramatic illusion as "waking dream"; Foakes also refers to *Elements of Criticism* I, 91 and II, 414–16. On sympathy, see *Elements of Criticism* I, 6–9, 446–47; II, 500; Shaftsbury, *Characteristics of Men, Manners, Opinions, and Times;* Hutcheson, *An Essay on the Nature and Conduct of the Passions and Affections with Illustrations on the Moral Sense*.

thinks it necessary to protect this "perfection of representation" from any distracting elements.

Erasmus Darwin, too, felt that dramatic illusion was a fragile experience that the playwright and the players must protect from disruptions. The dream analogy for Darwin and Kames thus has the added implication that drama must not risk extreme emotional sensations lest the spectator be aroused from the illusion: "If any distressful circumstances occur too forcible for our sensibility, we can voluntarily exert ourselves, and recollect, that the scenery is not real." While Kames does not tell us that the "waking dream" suppresses the will, Darwin explicitly asserts that it is only when we emerge from the illusory state that we can once again "voluntarily exert ourselves." The waking reverie so charms the will that we become "unwilling to relinquish the pleasure." The experience, therefore, is addictive:

> We are at the same time unwilling to relinquish the pleasure, which we receive from the other interesting circumstance of the drama; and on that account quickly permit ourselves to relapse into the delusion; and thus alternately believe and disbelieve, almost every moment, the existence of the object represented before us.

In contrast to Kames, Darwin does not think a "perfect illusion" necessary to the experience or even possible to sustain. He describes, rather, a twilight awareness in which we "alternately believe and disbelieve," and a seduction of the will much like the enchantment he attributes to the opium poppy, conjuring "the thin forms of Fancy and of Dreams," in his "The Loves of the Plants."[32]

The reports on the nature of dramatic illusion are filled with contradictions. What is the source of illusion: the play, the players, the staging, or the self-indulgent reverie of the spectator? If illusion is conjured by the performance on the stage, then the drama might well work an involuntary spell. If illusion depends on the subjective participation of the spectator, then presumably its engagement would require a voluntary acquiescence. The critics disagree. We may listen to Diderot:

---

32. Darwin, *The Botanic Garden* II, 87; see also canto II, lines 267–90.

> Illusion is not voluntary. The poet who says, I wish to create an illusion, is like the man who says, I have a certain experience of life to which I shall pay no attention.[33]

Or to Marmontel:

> Illusion in the theater is voluntary: one knows while attending that one is to be deceived, and far from defending oneself, one should take pleasure in being there, provided that one knows that he is with art.[34]

Since art cannot duplicate reality, Marmontel reasons, then the causes of illusion must lie somewhere other than in the efforts at probability and the semblance of truth. Were illusion perfect, tragedy would only produce pain, and even comedy would be perceived as insipid confusion. The pleasure in dramatic illusion depends not on our mistaking it for reality, but on our half-conscious awareness that it is the work of genius. Thus it is willingly indulged.[35]

The circumstances that provoked Stendhal to pen his pamphlet, *Racine et Shakespeare* (1823), were much the same as those which, four years later, prompted Hugo to write his polemical preface to *Cromwell* (1827). In chapter 6, I shall discuss how Hugo entered the fray between the Classic and the Romantic with his defense of Romanticism as the grotesque. Although Hugo's preface to *Cromwell* became the manifesto of Romanticism in France, Stendhal's dialogue between the Academician and the Romantic had already set forth the major issues. To be sure, Schlegel and Coleridge were much earlier in proposing Shakespeare as the model for Romantic drama. In France, however, the reception of Shakespeare was a difficult matter. In 1822, when a company of English actors in Paris attempted to perform *Othello*, they were hooted by a hostile audience.[36] An English Shake-

---

33. Diderot, *De la poésie dramatique* (1758), in *Oeuvres complètes* VII, 330: "L'illusion n'est pas volontaire. Celui qui dirait: Je veux me faire illusion, ressemblerait à celui qui dirait: J'ai une expérience des choses de la vie, à laquelle je ne ferai aucune attention."
34. Marmontel, *Poétique François* II, 112: "L'illusion du théâtre est volontaire: on sait en y allant qu'on sera trompé, et loin de s'en défendre, on se plaît à l'être, pourvû qu'on le soit avec art."
35. Marmontel, "Illusion," in *Encyclopédie* VIII; for another version of illusion as voluntary self-indulgence, see Mercier, *Du théâtre, ou nouvel essai sur l'art dramatique.*
36. Fayolle, "Criticism and Theory," in *The French Romantics* II, 260.

speare on the French stage too blatantly represented the intrusion of political and aesthetic values at odds with tradition. France, after Wellington's defeat of Napoleon and the restoration under Louis XVIII, was chary of intrusions on tradition.

Stendhal addresses the conflict of Romantic and Classic as essentially ideological, an opposition between the values of the Modern Age and the *ancien régime:*

> *Romanticism* is the art of presenting nations with the literary works which, in the present state of their customs and their beliefs, are capable of giving them the greatest possible pleasure.
> *Classicism*, on the contrary, offers them the literature which gave the greatest possible pleasure to their great-grandfathers.[37]

He nevertheless endeavors to separate the aesthetic issues from the political ones. The debate over the respective merits of Racine and Shakespeare concerns the power of the drama to conjure a "perfect illusion." The Academician assumes that he can win his case for Racine simply on the grounds of an adherence to the three unities. An audience in England or Germany, he declares, cannot really imagine that whole months pass while they are in the theater watching *Macbeth*. Nor could a French audience, replies the Romantic, believe that twenty-four hours pass during a performance of *Iphigénie en Aulide*.[38] Clearly, illusion requires something more than merely constraining lapses in time or shifts in place. What, the Academician and the Romantic must ask, constitutes *illusion?* Does the word mean the same to each of them?

The first point to be established is whether we are capable of analyzing how our senses react to the events on stage. The Romantic attempts to placate the Academician, who insists that he experiences perfect illusion in beholding the plays of Racine.

> Let us not get angry. Condescend to observe with attention that which passes in your head. Attempt to lift for one moment the veil thrown by habit over the actions which take place so fast that you

---

37. Stendhal, *Racine et Shakespeare* (1823), in *Oeuvres complètes* (1927–37), XIII, 64: "*Romanticisme.* L'art de présenter aux peuples les oeuvres littéraires qui, dans le'état actuel de leurs habitudes et de leurs croyances, sont susceptibles de leur donner le plus plaisir possible."
38. Ibid., 12–14.

have already lost the power to follow them with your eyes and to see them *happening*. Let's hear about that word *illusion*. When one says that the imagination of the spectator shapes itself, that he passes through the necessary time for the events which are represented in the scene, one does not hear that the illusion of the spectator would go to so far as to believe that all the time has really passed.[39]

The Academician is surprised that the Romantic insists that theatrical illusion experienced in *Macbeth* is the same as in *Iphigénie en Aulide*. To establish a common ground for interpreting the drama, the Romantic offers an academic definition of illusion, quoting from François Guizot, leader of the *doctrinaires:*

> To have illusions, to be *in illusion*, means to be deceived, according to the Dictionary of the Academy. One *illusion*, says Monsieur Guizot, is the effect of one thing or one idea, which deceives us by a misleading appearance. Illusion refers then to the action of a person who believes the thing that is not, as in dreams for example. Theatrical illusion would then be the action of a person who believes truly those things to exist which pass only on the stage.[40]

Darwin, we recall, compared illusion to the dream and added that it is an experience that we "alternately believe and disbelieve." Stendhal also declares that the dreamlike state is engaged only in alternating moments.[41] An awareness of reality keeps us from being utterly duped by illusion.

The Romantic tells the story of an American soldier on sentry duty at a

---

39. Ibid., 14: "Ne nous fâchons pas, et daignez observer avec attention ce qui se passe dans votre tête. Essayez d'écarter pour un moment le voile jeté par l'habitude sur des actions qui ont lieu si vite, que vous en avez presque perdu le pouvoir de les suivre de l'oeil et de les voir *se passer*. Entendons-nous sur ce mot *illusion*. Quand on dit que l'imagination du spectateur se figure qu'il se passe le temps nécessaire pour les événements que l'on représente sur la scène, on n'entend pas que l'illusion du spectateur aille au point de croire tout ce temps réellement écoulé."

40. Ibid., 15: "Avoir des illusions, être dans l'*illusion*, signifie se tromper, à ce que dit le dictionnaire de l'Académie. Une *illusion*, dit M. Guizot, est l'effet d'une chose ou d'une idée qui nous déçoit par une apparence trompeuse. Illusion signifie donc l'action d'un homme qui croit la chose qui n'est pas, comme dans les rêves, par exemple. L'illusion théâtrale, ce sera l'action d'un homme qui croit véritablement existantes les choses qui se passent sur la scène."

41. Brinker, "Aesthetic Illusion," 191–96, forwards essentially the same argument; although he faults eighteenth-century theories for equating illusion with emotion, he seems to have overlooked the historical antecedents to his own analysis.

Baltimore theater during a performance of *Othello*. Upon beholding the black man about to murder the white woman, the outraged soldier fired a gun shot that shattered the actor's arm. This, declares the Romantic, is the consequence of perfect illusion. An ordinary spectator, however, quickly extricates himself from the depths of the spell. When he applauds in transport the "complete illusion" of Talma's Manlius, it is the actor not the Roman whom he applauds.

> It is impossible for you not to admit that the illusion which one goes looking for in the theater is not a perfect illusion. The perfect illusion is that one of the soldier on guard at the theater in Baltimore. It is impossible for you not to admit that the spectators know well that they are in the theater and that they witness the representation of a work of art and not a true fact.[42]

Since a perfect illusion, if sustained, would reduce the spectator to the same sort of madness that gripped the Baltimore soldier, then the desired effect in the drama must be either scattered moments of perfect illusion or an imperfect illusion, in which our response to the drama is less intense and immediate. The Academician is led to admit that Racine's use of rhetorical declamations frequently disrupts the experience of illusion. Admiration for the acting or the poetic language cannot coexist with perfect illusion, nor can the awareness of our own emotional response to the dramatic experience. The drama solicits long moments of imperfect illusion broken by short moments of perfect illusion. These moments of perfect illusion, argues the Romantic, are less frequent in Racine than in Shakespeare. Racine emphasizes the formal attributes of time, place, and action, but his lengthy speeches interrupt rather than enhance illusion. Shakespeare, however, gathers emotional force and, in spite of his want of regular form, the moments of perfect illusion occur with greater frequency.

In the next chapter, we shall again encounter the presumption of "perfect illusion." Diderot, in *Les Bijoux indiscrets* (1748), imagines a stranger, totally unacquainted with the theater, placed in a private box and told that when the

---

42. Stendhal, *Racine et Shakespeare*, 15–16: "Il est impossible que vous ne conveniez pas que l'illusion que l'on va chercher au théâtre n'est pas une illusion parfaite. L'illusion *parfaite* étaite celle du soldat en faction au théâtre de Baltimore. Il est impossible que vous ne conveniez pas que les spectateurs savent bien qu'ils sont au théâtre, et qu'ils assistent à la représentation d'un ouvrage de l'art, et ne pas à un fait vrai."

curtain rises he will be able to see into the chambers of court and witness the intrigues that take place there. "Do you believe," Diderot asks, "that the illusion of this man will endure an instant?"[43] No more than Stendhal does Diderot accept the notion of "perfect illusion." In chapter 5 we shall come to a different sort of test for "perfect illusion" proposed by Coleridge: a tragedy would represent a current national catastrophe involving, for example, the execution of the king. If we then ask "to which spectacle the person would repair," could even a "perfect illusion" of the execution on stage possibly compete with the actual event?[44] "Perfect illusion," as most of its advocates argue, incapacitates the will. In chapter 2, we shall explore further Diderot's notion of involuntary illusion. At the close of chapter 3, we shall return to the dream analogy in the works of Sulzer and Herder, who, like Kames and Darwin, posit a dreamlike state of mental participation. And in chapter 5, we shall explain why the act of the will was essential to Coleridge's account of the "willing suspension of disbelief."[45] Even among those critics who dismiss "perfect illusion," the concept, as we shall see, is reinvoked in order to demonstrate the operation of the will in mentally shaping the shadows of the imagination. The argument, at least as negative instance, persists.

Kendall Walton, in his recent studies of aesthetic illusion, has resurrected "the classic story of Henry, a backwoods villager watching a theatrical performance, who leaps to the stage to save the heroine." Walton adds several new permutations on the relationship between spectator and performance. If Henry disrupts the action, he has effectively "saved" the heroine. Nor need he be duped by a "perfect illusion." Walton suggests that he may simply feel "so strongly that a beautiful damsel ought to be spared, even in fiction, that he intervenes in her behalf." Illusion, for Walton, depends on an interaction with fictional circumstances. The fictionality is crucial. He poses two questions: "Is it *true* that Henry saves the heroine?" and "Is it *fictional* that he saves her?" The answer to both must be no. It cannot be *true*, because the heroine does not exist and the actress was in no real danger. It cannot be *fictional*, because the fate of the fictional heroine of the drama is unaltered by Henry's disruption of the performance. What might be claimed is that

---

43. Diderot, *Oeuvres complètes* IV, 286–87: "Croyez-vous que, malgré tout le sérieux que j'affecterais, l'illusion de cet homme durât un instant?"
44. Coleridge and Wordsworth, marginalia at 319–20 of Knight, *Analytical Inquiry into the Principles of Taste*. Marginalia transcribed with commentary by Shearer and Lindsay.
45. Coleridge, *Biographia Literaria* II, 6.

Henry assumed authorship and "rewrote" the fiction. Here Walton is indebted to the Romantic concept of the imaginative involvement of the reader or auditor as a reflection or reenactment of the creative process of the author. In correcting Coleridge's "willing suspension of disbelief" to an active, or interactive, play with fiction, Walton changes "suspending disbelief" to "pretending belief." There is no barrier of disbelief that needs to be overcome, he argues, for human beings are eager to "make up stories and tell them to each other."[46] Walton, of course, has taken Coleridge's argument out of context. There is, indeed, a resistance that must be overcome before we pretend.

The mind must constantly monitor the fallibilities and limitations of the senses. The well-practiced facility of compensating for optical illusions, as Bishop Berkeley has argued, becomes so habitual that we assume an undue confidence in our perception.[47] We distrust illusions that we cannot correct. Edmund Burke built his theory of the sublime upon those sensory encounters with vastness and duration that baffle comprehension.[48] Illusion may involve play with fictional possibilities, as theories that presume a voluntary and self-indulgent response have argued. Yet this argument need not be seen as excluding that position which assumes an involuntary response. Several critics describe a maturation of the aesthetic experience in which we progress from delusion to illusion as we learn to monitor and control our senses.

It is the very nature of art to challenge perception. As Lessing observes in the preface to his *Laokoon* (1766), painting and poetry "put before us absent things as present, with the appearance of reality; both cause illusion, and the illusion of both pleases."[49] The source of the pleasure, a matter which we shall investigate further in chapter 3, lies for Lessing in the sympathetic response, which is felt not in terms of the perfection of the illusion but in

---

46. Walton, "Appreciating Fiction: Suspending Disbelief or Pretending Belief?" See also Walton, "Points of View in Narrative and Depictive Representation"; "How Remote are Fictional Worlds from the Real World?"; "Fearing Fictions"; and *Mimesis as Make-Believe. On the Foundations of the Representational Arts.*

47. Berkeley, *An Essay towards a New Theory of Vision* (1709), *The Theory of Vision, or Visual Language* (1733), in *Works* I, 27–112, 371–400.

48. Burke, *A Philosophical Enquiry into the Origin of our Ideas on the Sublime and Beautiful*, in *The Speeches and Writings of Edmund Burke* I, 138–55.

49. Lessing, "Laokoon oder über die Grenzen der Malerei und Poesie," in *Werke*, ed. Göpfert, et al., VI, 9: "[Malerei und Poesie] stellen uns abwesende Dinge als Gegenwärtig, den Schein als Wirklichkeit vor; beide täuschen, und beider Täuschung gefällt."

interaction with its limitations. Goethe delighted in the complicity of deception and revelation in aesthetic illusion; arriving at the Palladio in his *Italian Journey* (1786–88), he described how a divine artistic force "from truth and falsehood built a third, whose hidden being enchants us."[50] The enchantment, however, remains a provocation and paradox: the counterfeit image seems to contain an image of perfection.

50. Goethe, *Italienische Reise*, 53: "aus Wahrheit und Lüge ein Drittes bildet, dessen erborgtes Dasein uns bezaubert."

2

Illusion and the Players: Diderot, Tieck, and Lamb

When Coleridge, in 1808, objected to French critics who had confused "stage illusion" with "actual delusion,"[1] he was referring to the argument for dramatic verisimilitude that extends from D'Aubignac, La Mesnardière, and Corneille through Voltaire and Beaumarchais.[2] Had he known the dramatic theory of Diderot, he would have had to modify his sweeping condemnation, for Diderot, at odds with other French critics, insisted upon a simultaneous immediacy and distance in the aesthetic experience. The theory that Diderot forwarded in his review, "Observations sur une brochure intitulée *Garrick, ou les acteurs anglais*" (1770),[3] he subsequently elaborated into the dialogue, *Le*

---

1. Coleridge, *Lectures 1808–1819: On Literature* 2 vols., I, 135.
2. Hédelin d'Aubignac, *Pratique du théâtre;* La Mesnardière, *La Poétique;* Corneille, *IIIe Discours* and preface to *Don Sanche*, in *Théâtre complet;* Voltaire, *Un Discours sur la tragédie*, preface to *Le Brutus;* Beaumarchais, preface to *Eugénie*, in *Oeuvres complétes;* see T. J. Reis, "Spectacle and the Language of Illusion," in *Toward Dramatic Illusion: Theatrical Technique and Meaning from Hardy to Horace*, 138–55; Villiers, "Illusion dramatique et dramaturgie classique."
3. Circulated in the manuscript *Correspondance littéraire*, Diderot's review addressed the French translation of Hill's *The Actor*. For a study of Diderot's transformation of the review into the dialogue *Paradoxe sur le comédien*, see Sherman, *Diderot and the Art of the Dialogue*, 63–78.

Paradoxe sur le comédien. Although written and revised between 1773 and 1778, Diderot's *Paradoxe* was not published until 1831. Known only to the few who had access to manuscript copies, Diderot's dialogue had limited influence on the subsequent generation of critics. While Johann Georg Hamann and Moses Mendelssohn saw such copies,[4] Ludwig Tieck and Charles Lamb most probably did not, yet they perceived the same problems and raised very similar questions.

There is a temptation to read Diderot's account of the drama in reverse, to begin, that is, with *Le Paradox sur le comédien* (1773) and work backwards, through the *Salon de 1767*, to his *Discours sur la poésie dramatique* (1758) and his *Entretiens sur le Fils naturel* (1757), concluding with the dialogue on dramatic illusion in *Les Bijoux indiscrets* (1748).[5] Because the later work explicitly addresses a paradoxicality that is only implicit in the earlier discussions, the elaborations of paradox in *Paradoxe* are useful in interpreting the earlier works. Admittedly, they are not adequate tools for analysis, yet they do help us understand the problems Diderot was grappling with in the *Discours* and *Entretiens*. Reversing chronology, of course, is apt to falsify the gradual maturation of a writer's thought—especially risky in Diderot's case, for certain key phrases are repeated in his writings but acquire significantly different meanings. Nevertheless, I have succumbed to the temptation. I shall begin by discussing the *Paradoxe* and then turn to the earlier works. I hope to guard against misinterpretation with specific reminders of crucial stages in the development of Diderot's aesthetics.

The first point to be observed about Diderot is that he shows himself throughout his works as a lover of paradox.[6] Whether we read *Le Neveu de Rameau* (1762), or *Le Rêve de d'Alembert* (1769), or *Jacques le fataliste* (1775), we find Diderot so dexterous in juggling dialogical oppositions that his

---

4. First published in *Mémoires, correspondance et ouvrages inédits de Diderot* IV, 1–101; see Wilson, *Diderot* 624, 856n. Mortier, *Diderot in Deutschland, 1750–1850*, 288–91, is meticulous in documenting Diderot's influence in Germany, but he has missed Mendelssohn's response to Diderot's *Paradoxe sur le comédien*.

5. Diderot, *Entretiens sur le Fils naturel* (1757) and *Discours sur la poésie dramatique* (1758), in *Oeuvres complètes* (= *OC*) VII, 85–168, 299–394. For the *Salon de 1765*, I cite the critical edition of Bukdahl and Lorenceau; for the *Salon de 1767*, I cite Diderot, *Salons*, ed. Seznec and Adhémar, III. *Paradoxe sue le comédien* (1773) and additional texts will be cited from *Oeuvres esthétiques* (= *OE*), ed. Vernière. Reference to these editions will be given parenthetically in the text.

6. The opposite opinion has been forwarded by Belaval, *L'Esthétique sans Paradoxe de Diderot*; see, however, the review by Dieckmann, "Yvon Belaval"; Villiers, "A propos du *Paradoxe* de Diderot"; Hobson, "Le 'Paradoxe sur le comédien' est un paradoxe"; and Hobson, *The Object of Art. The Theory of Illusion in Eighteenth-Century France.*

exposition of alternatives seldom closes upon a fixed and definite resolution.[7] The efforts at determining "truth" remain indeterminate, conclusions inconclusive, and paradoxes appear instead of resolutions. Diderot knew a variety of verbal and logical strategies for producing different sorts of paradox. Many "truths," as De Quincey was later to observe, deserve paradoxical exposition for they are not "truths" at all, but ambivalent or factional matters of *pro* and *con* that may be viewed from opposite sides; paradox may thus reveal the error of popular opinion and challenge the orthodox by exclaiming: "Here, reader, are some extraordinary truths, looking so very like falsehoods that you would never take them for anything else if you were not invited to give them special examination."[8] While the *paradictum* contradicts the *orthodictum*, it rises above mere *contradictum*. In such an instance, what is false or true is then to be demonstrated.

Some paradoxes, however, defy resolution. For example, I swear that I always tell the truth, and my friend promptly says of me, "This man always lies." At this point, we have no paradox, only a contradiction. When I affirm that my friend's assertion is correct, the contradiction has been turned into a paradox, for if I always speak the truth, then his statement that I always lie must be true for I have affirmed it. But if it is true, then my own statement is a lie, and so, too, my affirmation of his statement.[9] Whereupon we see that the statements, like an image caught up between two opposing mirrors, reverse one another in an endless series of counter-reflections. The possibility of resolution is baffled. Diderot, when he investigates the nature and experience of illusion, redresses several contradictions to orthodoxy, but he also exploits some inherent and some only seeming contradictions. Our task in reading his excursions on illusion

---

7. Furst, *Fictions of Romantic Irony*, 159–87; see also Jauß, "Der dialogische und der dialektische *Neveu de Rameau* oder: Wie Diderot Sokrates und Hegel Diderot rezipierte"; Jauß, "Diderots Paradox über das Schauspiel (Entretiens sur le Fils Naturel)"; Jauß, "Nachahmungsprinzip und Wirklichkeitsbegriff in der Theorie des Romans von Diderot bis Stendhal"; and Bremner, *Order and Change. The Pattern of Diderot's Thought.*

8. De Quincey, "Rhetoric" (1828) and "Secret Societies" (1847), in *The Collected Writings of Thomas De Quincey* X, 90–91, and VII, 205–6; *paradox* defined in contrast to *fallacy:* I, 199 and IX, 137. A similar definition of paradox is forwarded by Dieckmann in his review of Belaval: "Very few of Diderot's critics seem to be willing to read the *Paradoxe* and take it for what it is, or what, at least at the outset, it meant to be: a well-known classical genre, in which the author treats a statement which is contrary to general or received opinion and in appearance absurd, but in reality partly well founded," 65.

9. Martin, *The Paradox of the Liar;* Poundstone, *Labyrinths of Reason. Paradox, Puzzles, and the Frailty of Knowledge*, 18.

requires that we sort our way between resolvable and irresolvable, real and apparent paradoxes.

In the next chapter, we shall look into the question of audience response. During the eighteenth century, dramatic illusion was generally defined as the heightening of emotional response to the point that the reason is overwhelmed. The spectator is then affected by the dramatic imitation as if it were reality. Illusion in these circumstances is often attributed directly to the success of the actor. The actor, so it seems, ceases to be himself and becomes the character he plays. In examining how this apparent transfer is wrought, critics argued the same distinction between reason and emotion in acting that they used to address the problem of audience response. But here the argument took a different turn. The idea of artistic control conflicted with the notion of "feeling" the part.

Diderot takes up this problem in *Le Paradoxe sur le comédien*. If an actor is actually in the throes of emotion, he loses all command of his skills in mime, gesture, elocution. Thus to create the illusion of powerful emotions affecting a character, he must play the role with studied deliberation. *Nulle sensibilité* and *sang-froid* constraint enable the actor to concentrate all his artistic training and skill to performing the very extremes of passion. Diderot refers to the acting of David Garrick and Claire-Joseph Clairon as examples of this paradoxical doctrine of the illusion of overwhelming emotion achieved through total emotional constraint.[10] Should an actor actually surrender himself to the sway of feelings, the performance will be awkward and uneven. The paradox thus has a positive and negative aspect: if the spectator ceases to behold the actor and sees only the character caught up in emotional agitation, then it is certain that the actor has repressed emotion to achieve the effect; contrarily, if the spectator is aware of the actor and an inconsistent representation, the fault may well lie in the actor's allowing himself to be affected by the emotional conditions of the role. The emotional response is excited in the audience when it is only mediated, not felt, by the actor.

These are the attributes of Diderot's paradox that have received most attention in the theory of acting from Beatrix Dussane and Jacques Copeau

---

10. Garrick, *Private Correspondence;* in his letter to Jean-Baptiste-Antoine Suard, 7 March 1776, Garrick promises a commentary on Diderot's *Paradoxe sur le comédien*. Clairon, *Mémoires d'Hippolyte Clairon;* on La Clairon's acting, see Lancaster, *French Tragedy in the Time of Louis XV and Voltaire, 1715–1774.*

down through Konstantin Stanislavski and William Archer.[11] Seen merely in the terms described, it may seem that Diderot expects the actor to be cold and dispassionate. The opposite is true; it is not *insensibilité* but extreme *sensibilité* that belongs to the psychological nature of the actor. Here we are at one of those cruxes where we need to pay attention to chronology. In the *Entretiens sur le Fils naturel* (1757), Diderot had declared that actors, like all artists, must possess an exquisite sensibility:

> The poets, the actors, the musicians, the painters, the singers of the first order, the great dancers, the tender lovers, the truly devout, all this enthusiastic and passionate troop feel vividly but think very little.[12]

It must be recognized, too, that Diderot saw himself not only as a poet, but also as a philosopher. Unfortunately, artistic sensibility tends to interfere with rational deliberation. This was the paradox of his own life, which he struggled to resolve. Clearly, he had not resolved it at the time of *Entretiens sur le Fils naturel*. Over a decade later, in *Le Rêve de d'Alembert* (1769), he had come to a possible resolution: The man of extreme sensibility, who is not dissipated by his sensual responsiveness but learns to master his own physical drives, has the makings of "a great artist, especially a great actor, a great philosopher, a great poet, a great musician, a great physician" (*OC* II, 171). In *Le Paradoxe sur le comédien*, the actor who represses his emotions in playing a role actually possesses acute sensitivity to the emotions involved: he demonstrates their effects without allowing himself to be ruled by their causes. A second level of the paradox of acting, therefore, is that the actor knows through personal experience the very power of emotions that he must then show only *as if* he were experiencing them while playing the role.

There is a third level of paradoxicality in *Le Paradoxe sur le comédien*. This is the paradox of art and reality that Diderot had worked out a few years before in his *Salon de 1767*. The actor, like the artist, imitates reality. While other theories of illusion, as we shall have ample occasion to observe, pre-

---

11. Diderot, *The Paradox of Acting*, xii. See also Diderot, *Paradoxe sur le comédien, avec recueilles et présentées sur l'art du comédien*, 79–137.

12. *OC* VII, 108: "Les poètes les acteurs, les musiciens, les peintres, les chanteurs de premier ordre, les grands danseurs, les amants tendres, les vrais dévots, toute cette troupe enthousiaste et passionnée sent vivement, et réfléchit peu."

sume the fidelity of imitation as the source of illusion, Diderot long wrestled with the idea of difference, the ideal that transformed the imitation of the real. In chapters 3 and 5 we shall refer to the concept of aesthetic "difference" as forwarded by Johann Jacob Bodmer in his correspondence with Pietro di Calepio (1736) and by Samuel Taylor Coleridge in his Shakespeare lectures (1808–19). But there is a difference in Diderot's "difference"; it is the difference between the real and the ideal. In his encyclopedia article, *Beau* (1752), he had endeavored to define the beautiful as real; in spite of his empirical approach, he could affirm only a semiotic "reality" of the *beau réel*. In his *Salon de 1767*, however, he proposed that the most effective illusion was created through the *modèle idéal*.

Thus it might seem that in positing a *modèle idéal* Diderot abandoned his early empiricism and adopted a Platonic idealism. This is not the case. Diderot's ideal model of beauty is firmly anchored in real experience: it is not received through rhapsodic inspiration; it is developed inductively through observation and study. The perfect replica of reality is impossible, perhaps not even desirable, in art. The artist may copy nature, but his copy is inevitably different. The more meticulously the artist has copied, the more disappointing the results. The difference is worse, not better. To make the difference better, the artist needs an ideal model. Whence does he derive his ideal model? From the study of nature, but also from the study of the ancients. From the complete indulgence of his feelings, but also the exercise of complete self-control. How does this lead to an ideal model? From his study and experience, inductively and intuitively, the artist derives a summation of the essential and characteristic. No longer distracted by the extraneous detail of a mere copy, he conceives an ideal model that will allow him to give shape and form to his subject. He now copies with a difference informed by his ideal model (*Salon de 1767*, 59–64).

It may be objected, here, that I am reaching too far afield in drawing from the *Salon* to interpret the *Paradoxe*—the one, after all, has to do with painting, the other with acting. But both are concerned with how the artist creates illusion: the painter with his paints, brush, and canvas, the actor with his body and voice. More importantly, Diderot himself made the connection. Testimony for his concept of *modèle idéal* he took from the Garrick's advice on acting: "There is an imaginary being whom you must take for a model" (*Salon de 1767*, 63). Without this ideal model, the actor, or any other artist, will never rise above mediocrity. Having defined it in the *Salon de*

1767, Diderot continues to refer to the *modèle idéal* in his *Paradoxe*.[13] In order to give his performance the appearance of reality, the actor must discover and enact the very *modèle idéal* conceived by the poet. The illusion of reality is created not by copying the real, but by "realizing" the ideal model.

A fourth level of paradoxicality in *Le Paradoxe sur le comédien* is the resolution described in the concluding dream. In this dream "l'homme paradoxal" argues, in a dialogical monologue, that to imitate nature, the artist must not "imitate" nature. Just as the actor maintains a cool control over his art when exhibiting the passions, it is his art, not mere copying or imitating, that enables him to express the *modèle idéal* (*OE* 375–77). Diderot's "l'homme paradoxal" does more than recapitulate the previous argument. His function is to demonstrate the art/reality paradox. The demonstration, as we might well expect, is itself paradoxical: "l'homme paradoxal" appears in a dream, usurps the roles of the two interlocutors, and continues their dialogue by himself in two voices. Are we to believe the dream figure rather than the interlocutors to whom he appears? Which of his two voices is the more trustworthy? Such questions cannot be answered; nevertheless, the demonstration of mimetic paradox is clear. The differences between art and reality are resolved, after all, only in aesthetic illusion. Within the illusion of the dream, Diderot's "l'homme paradoxal" insists upon the disparities of "l'homme de la nature, l'homme du poète, l'homme de l'acteur" resolved in the union of the three models as the one ideal model perceived by the theater audience. The resolution is an illusion; the paradox persists.

While *Le Paradoxe sur le comédien* provides us with Diderot's mature deliberation on the paradoxical nature of acting, his earlier essays deserve attention not because they expose unripened stages of his thought, rather because they address other attributes of theatrical illusion. *Discours sur la poésie dramatique*, written to accompany his play *Le Père de famille* (1758), provides a rationale for the genre of domestic drama, "la comédie sérieuse." In arguing that illusion is the end or purpose of drama, Diderot addresses the paradox of intellectual awareness. Coleridge, as we shall see in chapter 5, develops the notion of an intellectual awareness of illusion simultaneous with the imaginative participation in illusion. Had Diderot formulated such

---

13. Wilson, *Diderot*, 625, notes that Diderot refers to the *modèle idéal* twelve times in the *Paradoxe sur le comédien*.

a theory of illusion fifty years earlier? If we consider only the issue of simultaneity, the answer would seem to be yes. But Coleridge emphasized the act of will in achieving "that willing suspension of disbelief for the moment which constitutes poetic faith."[14] For Diderot, the psychological response was involuntary and emotional; for Coleridge, illusion required the will and the imagination. Diderot defined the response to the drama as a behavioral response triggered by circumstances similar to those which may be observed in other social contexts. The conditions that arouse our anger, fear, laughter, contempt in real life will arouse the same emotions when represented in the drama. In contrast to his later insistence that the actor must exercise complete control over his emotions, Diderot here declares that the nature of emotional stimulus-response is a matter of sensibility, not of willful choice. Illusion overwhelms the spectator, whether or not he desires the effect or believes the conditions.

The involuntary nature of illusion conceals another of Diderot's paradoxes: When he says that we cannot will to make it happen, he refers not just to the spectator but to the actor and the playwright as well. Thus the playwright must accept that illusion is the purpose of his art, but he cannot choose to create an illusion: "Illusion is not voluntary. The poet who says, I wish to create for myself an illusion, is like the man who says, I have a certain experience of life to which I shall pay no attention" (*OC* VII, 330). In providing his play with an "experience," the playwright assembles circumstances and situations according to inexorable laws of cause and effect. Illusion is involuntary; it also goes hand-in-hand with causal necessity. The playwright may achieve his purpose indirectly by revealing a compelling causality at work in his dramatic action: "It is the poet who creates, who produces from nothing, with this difference, that in nature we see only a vast succession of effects, the causes of which are unknown to us, whereas the dramatic movement of a play is never obscure; and that, if the poet hides a sufficient number of his mechanisms to stimulate us, he always allows us to glimpse enough of them to satisfy our curiosity" (*OC* VII, 328).[15] His model

---

14. Coleridge, *Biographia Literaria* II, 5–6.
15. *OC* VII, 330: "L'illusion n'est pas volontaire. Celui qui dirait: Je veux me faire illusion, ressemblerait à celui qui dirait: J'ai une expérience des choses de la vie, à laquelle je ne ferai aucune attention." VII, 328: "C'est lui [le pòete] qui crée, qui tire du néant; avec cette différence, que nous n'entrevoyons dans la nature qu'un enchaînement d'effets dont les causes nous sont inconnues; au lieu que la marche du drame n'est jamais obscure; et que, si le poète nous cache assez de ses ressorts pour nous piquer, il nous en laisse toujours apercevoir assez pour nous satisfaire."

is history, but history is then contrived so that its hidden causal springs may be exposed to scrutiny.

Even if the poet gives us extraordinary events, he must make them appear historical. "Where is the boundary at which the absurdity ends and credibility begins? How can the poet sense how far he dare venture?" Diderot raises these questions only after he has already provided the answer. The boundary line, the limit of credibility, is defined by the poet's capacity to represent a convincing causality determining the action. The marvelous, rare but possible, remains within the playwright's province. What he must reject is the miraculous and the romantic—the former because it transcends natural causality; the latter because it presents the marvelous by coincidence and chance rather than by causal necessity.

> But, while the relation of events often escapes our notice in nature, and while, owing to our want of an overall view of things, we only perceive a fatal association of circumstances, the poet insists that throughout the entire texture of his work there be a visible and palpable connection, and in this respect his work is less true, but has more verisimilitude, than that of the historian.[16]

Recognizable, here, are the rudiments of one of those paradoxes later asserted in *Le Paradoxe sur le comédien*: the poet's historical model, like the *modèle idéal*, enables him to represent events with "more verisimilitude" than the natural events themselves. Even the incredible becomes credible. The poet cannot govern the laws of causality, but he can show us a sequence of events that seems to be causally determined. Where the dramatic situation baffles his effort to create the appearance of causal relations, he must nevertheless convince us that the relations are possible, that there may indeed be hidden causes. Dramatic action, the marvelous no less than the commonplace, must seem to unfold according to an inevitable and inexorable progression.

Illusion cannot be created, but it can be conjured. Dramatic illusion

---

16. Ibid., 329: "Mais où est le terme où l'absurdité des événements cesse, et où la vraisemblance commence? Comment le poète sentira-t-il ce qu'il peut oser?"—"Mais, au lieu que la liaison des événements nous échappe souvent dans la nature, et que, faute de connaître l'ensemble des choses, nous ne voyons qu'une concomitance fatale dans les faits, le poète veut, lui, qu'il règne dans toute la texture de son ouvrage une liaison apparente et sensible; en sorte qu'il est moins vrai et plus vraisemblable que l'historien."

depends on circumstances, and it is the causal probability of circumstances that makes "illusion more or less difficult." Illusion he compares to a geometric equation: "On one side of the equation there is illusion, an invariable quantity, equal to a sum of terms—some positive, others negative—whose number and possibility of combination can be varied in endless ways, but the total value of which is always the same." Opposite to illusion, on the other side of the equation, are the terms of the play. The playwright, in developing the dramatic circumstances, may juggle the positive and negative terms: "the positive terms represent ordinary circumstances and situations; the negatives, the extraordinary; one sort is compensated for by the others" (*OC* VII, 330). Diderot's simile of the geometrical equation recapitulates his insistence that the playwright cannot say "I wish to create an illusion." Illusion is on the other side of the equation, apart from the play and the playwright. The separation is to the advantage of the playwright, who need not bother with the individual peculiarities of his spectators.

> When I say that an illusion is an invariable quantity, I mean to a man who judges of various productions, and not to various men. There are probably no two human beings in the world possessing the same measure of certainty, and yet the poet is condemned to make illusions for every one! The poet takes advantage of the reason and the experience of an educated man, just as a governess takes advantage of the stupidity of a child. (*OC* VII, 331)[17]

Although Diderot's discussion of illusion cannot ignore the audience, he does avoid the psychological complexities of aesthetic response. His attitude toward the audience is only a notch above Phineas T. Barnum's credo that "a sucker is born every minute." Taking advantage of an educated man is essentially the same as taking advantage of a child's stupidity. We spectators,

---

17. Ibid., 330: "On sait ce qu'ils appellent une équation. L'illusion est seule d'un côté. C'est une quantité constante, qui est égale à une somme de termes, les uns positifs, les autres négatifs, dont le nombre et la combinaison peuvent varier sans fin, mais dont la valeur totale est toujours la même.... Les termes positifs représentent les circonstances communes, et les négatifs les circonstances extraordinaires. Il faut qu'elles se rachètent les unes par les autres." VII, 331: "Quand je dis que l'illusion est une quantité constante, c'est dans un homme qui juge des différentes productions, et non dans des hommes différents. Il n'y a peut-être pas, sur toute la surface de la terre, deux individus qui aient la même mesure de la certitude, et cependant le poète est condamné à faire illusion également à tous! Le poète' se joue de la raison et de l'expérience de l'homme instruit, comme une gouvernante se joue de l'imbécillité d'un enfant."

Diderot assures us, "are merely witnesses of events which ignore us" (*OC* VII, 340).

In *Le Paradoxe sur le comédien*, he emphasizes the role of the actor in conjuring illusion, but he carefully disassociates the actor from directly experiencing the illusion. The division of terms remains constant in Diderot's dramatic theory. In section X of the *Discours*, "Du Plan," Diderot addresses illusion as conjured by the playwright's manipulation of circumstance. He begins section XI, "De l'intérêt," by granting the importance of arousing interest, but asking in whom the interest is to be aroused. Since most of us would assume that interest should be aroused "in the minds of the audience," we may be wary of another paradoxical ploy when Diderot dismisses the audience and has his interlocutor voice an astonished question: " 'Then must one keep the characters in mind and interest them?' " (*OC* VII, 340). Precisely. Diderot's focus is on the players not on the spectators; his concern is with causes of illusion not with its effects.

"One discovers in my ideas," Diderot says in mock dismay, "as many paradoxes as one wants" (*OC* VII, 341). The paradox involved here is quite simple: if the playwright and the actors keep the characters interested in the action, the interest of the audience will naturally follow. To keep the characters interested, however, there must be anticipation rather than surprise. By developing the interest of the characters in the course of events, the playwright also has occasion to reveal the causal relations. All the attention must be given to the events on stage.

> Both author and actor must forget the spectator. All interest should be centered in the characters. One would not often read in poetics: If you do this or that, you will produce this or that effect on the spectator. One might read, on the contrary: If you do this or that, this is what will happen to your characters. (*OC* VII, 344)[18]

The "fourth wall" of the stage, the invisible wall which conceals the audience from the players but not the players from the audience, also contributes to paradox. So long as the wall is intact, so too is the dramatic

---

18. Ibid., 341: "On trouvera, dans mes idées, tant de paradoxes qu'on voudra." VII, 344: "Il fallait cependant que l'auteur et l'acteur oubliassent le spectateur, et que tout l'intérêt fût relatif aux personnages, on ne lirait pas si souvent dans les poétiques: Si vous faites ceci ou cela, vous affecterez ainsi ou autrement votre spectateur. On y lirait au contraire: Si vous faites ceci ou cela, voici ce qui en résultera parmi vos personnages."

illusion, for illusion depends upon utterly ignoring the spectators. The playwright is responsible for constructing the wall, the actor keeps it in place. "If, instead of taking part with his characters and allowing the audience to take care of themselves, the poet steps down from the stage into the parterre, he will harm his plot." The playwright who becomes more concerned with dazzling the audience sacrifices development of plot and character for a few theatrical effects. Moreover, if the playwright caters to the audience, so will the actor.

> And the actor, what will become of him, if you are occupied with the spectator? Do you believe he will not sense that what you have put in this passage or in that one has not been imagined for him? You thought about the audience; he addresses them. You wanted their applause; so will he. And then what will become of your illusion?[19]

When Diderot pontifically reasserts his claim that actor and playwright should keep the fourth wall inviolable and "think no more of the audience than if it had never existed," his interlocutor interrupts with a reminder of that stunning moment at the end of Act IV in Molière's *The Miser* (1668), when Harpagon, who has lost his chest, asks the audience "Messieurs, is not the thief among you?" While genius may break down walls and trespass boundaries, Diderot will not allow the exception of genius to disprove the rule of commonsense. Most clever playwrights find that they cannot speak to their audience without stopping the action. For Diderot, the fourth wall is more than simply a part of the illusion, it supports the very structure of illusion.

Because he keeps the fourth wall securely in place, the wonderful metadramatic apparatus that Diderot constructed for *Le Fils naturel* does not occur metadramatically; he does not allow the play with illusion to intrude upon the play itself. Diderot saves his playful paradoxes for his dialogues. The drama is serious business. Indeed, his new genre is the *genre sérieux*. He places it between comedy and tragedy, models it on the domestic drama of Lillo's *London Merchant*, and requires that it be moral and true. Just as *Discours sur la poésie dramatique* was written as a rationale to accompany *Le Père de famille* (1758), the *Entretiens* offer a justification of *Le Fils naturel*

---

19. Ibid., 345: "Et l'acteur, que deviendra-t-il, si vous êtes occupé du spectateur? Croyez-vous qu'il ne sentira pas que ce que vous avez placé dans cet endroit et dans celui-ci n'a pas été imaginé pour lui? Vous avez pensé au spectateur, il s'y adressera. Vous avez voulu qu'on vous applaudît, il voudra qu'on l'applaudisse; et je ne sais plus ce que l'illusion deviendra."

(1757). In the *Entretiens,* he tells us that the story of the natural son is based upon actual incidents relating to the return of the father and the ensuing double marriage, and that the play itself was written by the son for family performance commemorating the anniversary of the event. The boundaries between fiction and reality are suspended as Diderot engages in dialogue with Dorval, a character in the play but also its supposed author.

The *Entretiens* are introduced with an account of the dissatisfaction with *Le Fils naturel:* Lysimond, Dorval's father, charges that the play is unconvincing. Despite the truth of its subject, the performance is artificial (*OC* VII, 85–86). The first of the three conversations begins with the fictional character called upon to explain illusion: "J'en ai remarqué plusieurs qui ont un caractère de fiction qui n'en impose qu'au théâtre, où l'on dirait qu'il y a une illusion et des applaudissements de convention" (*OC* VII, 87). This is a two-way paradox, a double bind. Ostensibly "le vraisemblable" of convention theater is not enough: what is required is "le vrai" itself. The "true" play, however, is by no means true, nor even reasonably probable. The plot is borrowed from Carlo Goldoni's *Il Vero Amico* (1750), and the causal relations, by Diderot's definition in the *Discours,* are romantic. But Diderot has nothing to worry about, for he has turned his authorship over to Dorval with whom he now converses as the sympathetic interlocutor "Moi."

Dorval's task in the *Entretiens* is to defend the play that he wrote in terms of the kind of play that he wanted to write as well as the kind of play that he did not. Dorval points out much that was wrong with conventional theater: wealthy patrons held seats upon the stage; the rhetorical declamation of the actors was stiff and unnatural; no attention was given to authentic costuming; stock settings were used; stage dynamics were neglected; the subject matter had little in common with the experience of the audience. *Le Fils naturel* was intended to bring about reform. Conventional theater was pursuing a corrupt doctrine of "vraisemblance" and "bienséance." Dorval wants to replace the artificial with the real. Why then, we might well ask, did Diderot take such an improbable romance as the plot for his new *genre sérieux?*

Dorval, an illegitimate son, is visiting his friend Clairville. Dorval and Rosalie, Clairville's fiancée, are attracted to each other, while Constance, Clairville's sister, thinks Dorval is in love with her. Act I: Dorval has decided he should leave before the situation gets worse; Clairville, who has no suspicion, asks his friend to stay and to speak with his fiancée, whose affections have grown inexplicably cold. Act II: Dorval pens a letter to Rosalie, but before he can finish it he is called to save Clairville from an assault by thieves. Constance finds the letter and thinks it is addressed to her. Act III: Clairville learns from Constance of Dorval's love for her and, in gratitude to his friend for saving his life, generously announces the marriage. Dorval is disconcerted; Rosalie faints. A servant announces that Rosalie's father is about to return—bereft of the riches he had garnered in the Indies. Dorval secretly commissions his banker to transfer a share of his wealth to Rosalie. Act IV: Constance dismisses Dorval's claim that he is not good enough for her; his birth may be ignoble, but his character is virtuous. His children, she promises him, will be noble and proud. Act V: Dorval persuades Rosalie that she must marry Clairville and he must accept Constance. Rosalie's father arrives and he turns out to be Dorval's missing father as well. The strange attraction Rosalie and Dorval felt for one another was the love of brother and sister. The curtain falls with the joyful reunion and the prospects of a double wedding.

One has to keep in mind that this play, which honors nobility of character over nobility of birth, which makes the individual rather than the church the arbiter of morality and virtue, could scarcely be endorsed by the *ancien régime*. The reform of the theater had significant political implications. Diderot sets his play not in an aristocratic court, but in a middle-class home—not in the remote past or in some distant place, but right now, just outside of Paris. The scene between Dorval and the servant stresses mutual respect, a relationship based on character rather than condition to which Dorval proudly refers in the *Entretiens*. Dorval recommends a full-scale reform of the theater:

> Domestic and bourgeois tragedy must be created. The *genre sérieux* must be perfected. The conditions of men must be substituted for their characters, perhaps in all genres. Mime must be closely associated with dramatic action. The stage must be altered; and *tableaux* must be substituted for *coups de théâtre*, a new source of invention for the poet and of study for the actor. For what use is it if the poet imagines *tableaux* and the actor remains faithful to his symmetrical positioning and stilted acting style? Real tragedy must be introduced into the lyrical theater. Finally the dance must be converted to a real poetic form, to be written down, and distinguished from any other imitative art.[20]

20. Ibid., 161: "La tragédie domestique et bourgeoise à créer. Le genre sérieux à perfectionner. Les conditions de l'homme à substituer aux caractères, peut-être dans tous les genres. La panto-

The introduction of *tableaux* and mime are intended to replace the symmetrical placing of the actors on stage and the declamatory manner of delivery. The *tableaux* are not intended to be static *tableaux vivant* in which the actors pose without moving as if in a painting; they are to move with more lively animation than was usual in the Comédie française, but they are to manage setting and grouping as in an artful domestic scene (Diderot has the paintings of Greuze in mind). The actors are urged to study mime so that they learn to use body, gesture, facial expression instead of relying merely on vocal delivery. An actor should be acting even when not speaking.

The reality and truth Dorval wants in the drama are made to stand in stark contrast to the *vraisemblable* and *bienséance* of conventional theater. But the dialogue also reveals that this reality and truth has little in common with the real world. The purpose of the drama is "to inspire man to a love of virtue and a horror of vice" (*OC* VII, 149). To make dramatic illusion strong and convincing, the attributes of the real world must be faithfully imitated, but the circumstances must be changed. The drama does not show the world as it is, but as it should be. The women in the audience will laugh, says "Moi," at Constance's frank declaration of love. "What women, if you please!" objects Dorval; perhaps "the women of the past," but not enlightened women. The illusion of the drama is not just for the moment, it aspires to change our perception of reality.

As early as his encyclopedia article *Beau* (1752), Diderot began deliberating the Platonic problem of ideal vs. real. Everyone experiences the beautiful and attempts to reason about it, Diderot begins his encyclopedia article, but not even the experts have succeeded in explaining its origin and essence or in defining its meaning. Is the beautiful absolute or relative? Is the beautiful an essential, eternal, immutable idea? Are the rules and models by which it can be expressed art? Or is the beautiful a matter of mode and fashion? (*OE* 391). The question of absolute vs. relative is further complicated by an inquiry into individual taste vs. universal appreciation, subjective perception vs. objective manifestation (*OE* 392). According to Du Bos, the beautiful resisted rational definition precisely because it was an irrational experience. Not reason but emotion, feeling, instinct receive those pleasur-

---

mime à lier étroitement avec l'action dramatique. La scène à changer, et les tableaux à substituer aux coups de théâtre, source nouvelle d'invention pour le poète, et d'étude pour le comédien. Car, que sert au poète d'imaginer de tableaux, si le comédien demeure attaché à sa disposition symétrique et à son action compassée? La tragédie réelle à introduire sur le théâtre lyrique. Enfin la danse à réduire sous la forme d'un véritable poème à écrire et à séparer de tout autre art d'imitation."

able stimuli which we call beautiful. Thus the beautiful can only be defined in terms of its psychological and sensual effects.[21] Diderot's major effort in this article is to put aside the sensualist/hedonist argument and to resolve the disparity of the *beau absolu* and *beau relatif* by establishing an empirical ground for the *beau réel*.

Diderot found his empirical ground in Shaftesbury and Hutcheson (the same sources, as we shall see in chapter 3, from which Lessing drew his aesthetics of sympathy).[22] Diderot affirmed that the beautiful may be fully realized in the object; therefore, the beautiful is real, essential, true. The beautiful that we perceive in art and nature actually exists in the entity as we perceive it. The test of empirical validity is in the experience. Although Diderot is following Shaftesbury in this argument, he found Shaftesbury's aesthetics insufficiently empirical. When Shaftesbury documents the experience of the beautiful, he attributes the affect to a "higher Majesty or Grandeur." Diderot resists this appeal to an ideal outside of empirical experience. He addresses the reality of the beautiful as fully accessible through perception (*OE* 33). Diderot found that Hutcheson also deviated from his own empirical principles. Hutcheson defined the beautiful as a "pleasant Idea" and a "delightful Perception of the Whole," then he, too, moved beyond the strictly empirical by claiming that "our Power of perceiving these Ideas" resides in "an *Internal Sense.*" As Diderot saw it, the empirical method had fallen into the trap of rationalism. Because the feelings were separated from the reason, there was no way to *know* the beautiful through the senses. Hutcheson's resolution through a rationally determined "*Internal Sense,*" no less than Du Bos's appeal to a "*sixième sens,*"[23] departed from the strictly empirical definition that Diderot wished to forward.

Instead of the rationalist division between reason and feeling, Diderot posited the Lockean cause-effect confluence of sensation and reflection. Not even Locke, however, could provide Diderot with the support he needed in affirming the *beau réel*. In terms of perception, he could come no closer to that reality than Locke's "secondary qualities." Primary qualities ("solidity, extension, figure, motion or rest, and number") reside in the object. Secondary qualities ("colours, sounds, tastes, &c.") "are nothing in the objects themselves, but powers to produce various sensations in us by

---

21. Du Bos, *Réflexions critiques sur la poésie et sur la peinture* II, 340–48, 516.
22. Cooper, *Characteristics of Men, Manners, Opinions, and Times* (1711); Hutcheson, *Inquiry into the Origin of our Ideas of Beauty and Virtue* (1725); see below, chapter 3, note 11.
23. Du Bos, *Réflexions* II, 341–42.

their primary qualities." Secondary qualities (color, for example) derive from primary qualities that are otherwise "insensible." Even if Locke had admitted the "beautiful" among the secondary qualities, their subjectivity would not have helped Diderot establish the objectivity of the *beau réel*. Diderot, however, did not trap himself in the argument that the beautiful was known simply through sensory data. He turned, instead, to Locke's argument on signs as mediators between perception and conception.[24] The beautiful, in Diderot's definition of 1752,[25] is a quality represented as a sign, directly experienced but understood and appreciated only in reflection (*OE* 416–17). Persistently "becoming" what it only represents, the sign is the root element of illusion.

In the discussion of the drama in *Les Bijoux indiscrets* (1748), Diderot has Mirzoza, the Sultan's favorite, repudiate the pretensions of dramatic illusion. A stranger, who is supposed to be familiar with the manners and intrigues of court but who has never visited a theater, is told of a courtly scandal (apparently sketched from Racine's *Phèdre*) which he is to witness from a secret room where he may look into the palace. With all precaution to preserve the ruse, the stranger is taken to a private box in the theater and informed that when the curtains are drawn he will be able to see what is taking place in the royal hall. Mirzoza then poses the question:

> Do you think, in spite of all the seriousness which I have pretended, the illusion of this man will last an instant?[26]

Although Lessing translated this episode from *Les Bijoux indiscrets* into his exposition of illusion in the *Hamburgische Dramaturgie*, he did not come to

---

24. Locke, *An Essay on Human Understanding*, book II, chap. 8, §23; book III, chap. 2.
25. Dieckman, *Cinq Leçons sur Diderot*, 102, claims that the pseudo-empirical argument on the *beau réel* should not be seriously considered as a point of departure for the subsequent aesthetics of his *Salons;* the opposite position is argued by Deuchler, "Diderots Traktat über das Schöne," and by Chouillet, "La formation des idées esthétiques de Diderot."
26. *OC* IV, 286–87: "Je suppose ... un nouveau débarqué d'Angote, qui n'ait jamais entendu parler de spectacles, mais qui ne manque ni de sens ni d'usage; qui connaisse un peu la cour des princes, les manéges des courtisans, les jalousies des ministres et les tracasseries des femmes, et à qui je dise en confidence: 'Mon ami, il se fait dans le sérail des mouvements terribles. Le prince, mécontent de son fils en qui il soupçonne de la passion pour la Manimonbanda, est homme à tirer de tous les deux la vengeance la plus cruelle; cette aventure aura, selon toutes les apparances, des suites fâcheuses. Si vous voulez, je vous rendrai témoin de tout ce qui ce passera.' Il accepte ma proposition, et je le mène dans une loge grillée, d'où il voit le théâtre qu'il prend pour le palais du sultan. Croyez-vous que, malgré tout le sérieux que j'affecterais, l'illusion de cet homme durâit un instant?"

terms with its paradoxical implications. Hans Robert Jauß, however, drew from Mirzoza's arch question an apt introduction to his essay on Diderot's paradox of the drama.[27]

Mirzoza insists that the many blatant artifices of theatrical performance render the illusion impossible. The extravagances of gesture and delivery, the peculiarities of poetic language, the inappropriate fashion of costume and setting, are among the attributes that belie the pretenses of *imitatio naturae*. Although traditional theater does not provide the "illusion of reality," Diderot confirms the possibility of illusion. In Jauß's analysis, which turns attention to Dorval's program for the *genre sérieux* in the *Entretiens sur le Fils naturel*, Diderot did not merely propose a reform of subject matter and style to fulfill more convincingly the expectations of *imitatio naturae*. For Diderot, Jauß argues, the successful imitation of nature achieves its most perfect illusion when it allows within the truth of imitated reality a simultaneous revelation and recognition of the secret harmony of the "système de la nature."[28]

In answering her own question, Mirzoza is restricting the meaning of illusion to a confusion with reality, or at least that version of reality enacted in the royal court. But Sélim and Ricaric, Mirzoza's partners in this dialogue, had already set forth other conditions for illusion—the efficacy of which apparently does not depend on faithful imitation of nature. Mirzoza's question, in the context of chapter 38, "Entretien sur les lettres," involves a more basic problem: If *imitatio naturae* is not the source of illusion, what is? If drama does not imitate nature, what does it imitate? When Diderot brings this chapter to a close, the paradox of illusion is left in a state of self-contradiction. The theater conjures illusion, but its very methods of conjuration expose and dispel the illusion. Almost twenty years were to pass before Diderot, in positing the *modèle idéal*, was prepared to argue that, while art may refer to the real conditions of life, the efficacy of illusion was to be attained only by rising above strict imitation. Neither the sublime moonlit seashore of Vernet nor the provocative still life of Chardin prompt us to confuse the representation with reality, but both engage the spectator in an illusion that is a dreamlike revelation of the ideal essence of the real.[29]

27. Jauß, "Diderots Paradox über das Schauspiel," 380–81.
28. Ibid., 401.
29. Diderot, *Salon de 1765; Salon de 1767*, in *Salons* III; Fried, *Absorption and Theatricality. Painting and Beholder in the Age of Diderot;* Carr, "Diderot and the Paradox of the Spectator," and "Painting and the Paradox of the Spectator in Diderot's Art."

Although Diderot ranked *Réflexions sur la poésie et sur la peinture* among the major works of critical theory (*OC* III, 486), he opposed Du Bos's sensualist argument, emphasizing instead the intellectual and empirical grounds for aesthetic experience. Where Du Bos had defined the beautiful in terms of its psychological and sensual affects, Diderot's major effort, following his article on *Le Beau*, was to escape the hedonism of Du Bos's pleasure principle. Du Bos's appeal to a *"sixième sens"* was at odds with the empirical definition that Diderot wished to forward. Du Bos supposed that aesthetic pleasure derives from a sixth sense capable of moderating the stimulation of the other five senses. Two key elements in his *Réflexions* are (1) his affirmation of an affective excitement and inspiration through the suasive power of art (following Longinus and Quintilian) and (2) his interpretation of *ut pictura poesis* (Horace) as the essential identity of the sensory response to word and image. Having based his aesthetic on the pleasure of sensory stimulation, Du Bos had to avoid the implication of painful emotions agitated through dramatic illusion. Thus he declared that the pleasure which we have in the theater is not a product of illusion.[30] Du Bos recognized, of course, that illusion is an essential attribute of aesthetic experience; he simply wanted to liberate sensual pleasure from the spell of illusion. Illusion stimulates the senses, but the pleasure derives from the capacity of the sixth sense in monitoring the activity of the other senses. If Du Bos had transferred this monitoring capacity from the senses to the reason or imagination, he would have resolved a major dilemma in eighteenth-century aesthetics. Du Bos, however, has acknowledged only the response of the *sensus communis*.[31] His sixth sense is sensory intuition; its function is to sense the other senses.

Because he understood art as an appeal to sensation, Du Bos naturally assumed that aesthetic experience was mediated through sensual and emo-

---

30. Du Bos, *Réflexions*, 451–57: "Que le plaisir que nous avons au Théâtre n'est point produit par l'illusion" (Section XLIII); Du Bos observed the paradox of Boileau and Chapelain: "Un charme secret nous attache donc sur les imitations que les Peintres et les Poëtes en sçavent faire, dans le temps même que la nature témoigne par un frémissement intérieur qu'elle se soulève contre son propre plaisir" (I, 2); he affirmed sensory excitement through illusion: "Ces fantômes de passions que la Poësie et la Peinture sçavent exciter en nous émouvant par les imitations qu'elles nous présentent satisfont au besoin ou nous sommes d'être occupés" (I, 27); but he located aesthetic pleasure neither in illusion nor in excitement, but in the sixth sense: "C'est ce sixiéme sens qui est en nous, sans que nous voyions ses organes" (II, 341–42); see Hogsett, "Jean Baptiste DuBos on Art as Illusion," 161.

31. For an account of the *sensus communis* in the history of perception theory, see Schipperges, *Welt des Auges. Zur Theorie des Sehens und Kunst des Schauens*.

tional processes. It followed, then, that only the actor who is moved by the emotional situation of the character he plays can communicate that emotional affect to the audience. Diderot opposed affective acting in his *Paradox* and insisted upon the artist's rational control in creating illusion. In his "Reply to a couple of Questions on Dramatic Art" (1774),[32] Mendelssohn turned to Diderot's argument. Mendelssohn had previously debated with Lessing on the nature of dramatic illusion (this debate—*Correspondence concerning Tragedy, 1756–1757*—will be discussed in chapter 3). While he granted that the senses were stimulated through rhetoric and gesture, Mendelssohn did not place illusion in the acting. Illusion occurs, he agreed with Du Bos, through the excitement of the senses; only when the excitement subsides may the aesthetic experience be appraised and evaluated by the reason. Later, in his *Rhapsodie* (1771), Mendelssohn granted the persistence, even in the midst of illusion, of "a secret consciousness that we have an imitation, and not the truth, before our eyes." But he insists that rational judgment cannot intrude without disrupting the illusion. Aesthetic experience is thus separated from aesthetic judgment. Experience reanimated through judgment, according to the argument that he adapts from Diderot's *Paradox*, enables the actor to produce illusion.

Mendelssohn's first question is given in two forms: "Can one become a good actor through rules, without inner feeling?" (The answer is no.) "And was that actress right in claiming that her understudy, who confessed that she had never loved, was unsuited to play the role of a woman in love?" (The answer is yes.) The rules can only address external appearances. Through training and practice the player learns to control facial expression, bodily movement, modulation of voice. But the feelings that are to accompany and inform the gestures must be drawn from experience. Mendelssohn likens the process to reading a text silently as if we were actually speaking it. We can properly move our lips and tongue only if we think of the sounds. So, too, the player must draw upon the feelings to inform the physical actions. When he declares that "inner feeling" is therefore necessary, Mendelssohn would seem to follow Du Bos rather than Diderot. He breaks from Du Bos, however, with this amendment: the player must not experience this "inner feeling" in his own person, but only in the person of the character he portrays.

---

32. Mendelssohn, "Beantwortung einiger Fragen in der Schauspielkunst" (1774), in *Gesammelte Schriften*, ed. Elbogen, et al., III-1, 311–12.

How the player is to become this dual being, self and character, is deliberated in response to his second question: "What does illusion do for the enthusiasm of an actor?" In order to express the emotions of a character, the player must feel them. He should accomplish this, however, not immediately but through "intuitive illusion" (*anschauende Illusion*). In silently mouthing the words of a text, we keep from voicing the sounds we shape. So too in expressing the emotions; the player feels them only through his illusory being. The success of the actor in expressing this illusory being depends on how well he can intuit the affects. Once he has rationally determined the dramatic situation and intuitively entered into the character, he must allow his emotional capacities to participate fully in the illusion. Two difficulties may beset the actor in sustaining this illusory being: he must be on guard that his rational faculties do not contradict the illusion; and he must not act, or react, in his own person, rather than in the person of his character.[33] Mendelssohn has altered the paradox by containing both of its elements—expression of feeling and rational control—within the illusion of the player. Furthermore, he requires the player to maintain precisely that dual perception which he says is available to the spectator only sequentially (first the aesthetic experience of illusion, afterward the evaluation and judgment).

Ludwig Tieck also developed different accounts of illusion during his long career. His comic play *Puss-in-Boots* (*Der gestiefelte Kater*, 1797) will be discussed in the concluding chapter, "Illusion and Metadrama," for it experiments more radically with the ironies of illusion than any other drama prior to the baffling contests of illusion and counterillusion in twentieth-century drama from Luigi Pirandello to Tom Stoppard. Tieck's ideas on dramatic illusion are derived, in large part, from his study of Shakespeare. Early in 1797, August Wilhelm Schlegel reviewed Tieck's translation of *The Tempest* as well as his plays *Puss-in-Boots* and *Bluebeard;* the two did not meet, however, until May of 1798.[34] Both wrote numerous critical commentaries

---

33. Ibid., 312: "Er muß sich nur hüten, mit seinen obern Seelenkräften dieser Illusion zu widersprechen"; "Wenn der Akteur zornig ist, so agirt er seine eigene Person, und nicht die des Helden, den er vorstellen soll: denn die Ursachen seines Zornes halten ihn ab, in alle die Begriffe einzugehen, die zu seiner intuitiven Begeisterung nöthig sind."

34. Schlegel, Rezension "Ritter Blaubart und der gestiefelte Kater," in *Kritische Schriften*, ed. Reimer, I, 311–21. For the meeting between A. W. Schlegel and Tieck, see Köpke, *Ludwig Tieck. Erinnerungen aus dem Leben des Dichters nach dessen mündlichen und schriftlichen Mitteilungen* I, 232; *Friedrich Schlegels Briefe an seinen Bruder August Wilhelm*, ed. Walzel, 384 and 390; the letters of 13 and 28 April 1798 state Tieck's intention to visit August Wilhelm in May.

on Shakespeare and the drama; in consequence of their shared interest, they agreed to collaborate in translating the plays.[35]

Before he met Schlegel, Tieck had already developed, in both theory and practice, his ideas on dramatic illusion. In Schlegel's theory of illusion, chapter 4, we will recognize several ideas that Schlegel borrowed from Tieck. Tieck's attention to audience participation (*Teilnahme*) becomes a mainstay in Schlegel's *Lectures on Dramatic Art and Literature* (*Vorlesungen über dramatische Kunst und Literatur*, read in 1808; published 1809–11).[36] Tieck, in analyzing "Shakespeare's Use of the Marvelous" ("Shakespeare's Behandlung des Wunderbaren," 1793), already argues the aesthetics of illusion in terms of audience participation.[37]

Were there no more to Tieck's theory than a concern with audience participation in illusion or the metadramatic exploitation of illusion, our attention to his ideas might well have waited until these topics are addressed in chapters 3 and 4. But Tieck stands apart from other German critics— with the exception of Mendelssohn—in describing illusion as manipulated by the actor. Like Diderot, Tieck observes the illusory *dédoublement* in the semiotics of acting. His comments on the actor as illusionist are scattered throughout his earlier theater reviews, and he explains the paradox of studied "passion" in his volume of *Remarks, Impressions, and Crotchets concerning German Theater* (1825).[38]

The problematic element in his early essay on "Shakespeare's Use of the Marvelous" is not his notion of participation as a kind of trance, but his persistent attention to factors that might disrupt the trance. To destroy illusion, of course, has been claimed as the purpose of *romantic irony*. As one of the current handbooks of literary terms defines it, romantic irony is "a mode of dramatic or narrative writing in which the author builds up artistic illusion, only to break it down by revealing that the author, as artist, is the arbitrary creator and manipulator of the characters and their actions."[39] This definition, identified with Friedrich Schlegel, is at best a radical over-

---

35. Tieck translated *The Tempest* and *Love's Labour's Lost;* these translations, however, were not included in the *Dramatische Werke* of Shakespeare, which includes the translations of A. W. Schlegel and Dorothea Tieck.
36. Schlegel, *Vorlesungen über dramatische Kunst und Literatur.*
37. Tieck, "Shakespeare's Behandlung des Wunderbaren" (1793), in *Kritische Schriften* (= *KS*) I, 37–74. Reference to this edition will be given parenthetically in the text.
38. Tieck, "Soll der Schauspieler während der Darstellung empfinden? soll er kalt bleiben?" *Bemerkungen, Einfälle und Grillen über das deutsche Theater* (1825), in *KS* IV, 79–82.
39. Abrams, *A Glossary of Literary Terms*, 94.

simplification of Schlegel's concept of irony as a "form of paradox," a "permanent parekbasis" and a "transcendental buffoonery," rendering the reader or audience unable to distinguish instinct from intent, naivete from affectation, seriousness from jest.[40]

The simple formula—that after building up illusion the author then breaks it down and exposes his own artistic ploy—may well have been endorsed by Tieck early in his career. But he soon came to the more complex concept forwarded by Friedrich Schlegel, in which the "building up" and "breaking down" are not discreet but simultaneous and pervasive, resulting not in a clearly exposed sense of artistic control but rather in irresolvable paradox. When Tieck wrote on "Shakespeare's Use of the Marvelous," he seemed to think that the "destruction of illusion" (*Illusionszerstörung*) was an aesthetic vice to be avoided. In his own experiments with fiabesque drama, he discovered advantages in the satirical tactics of undermining illusion. It gradually became evident to him that there was greater tenacity in aesthetic illusion than he had supposed. As he demonstrates in *Puss-in-Boots*, the constant disruption of illusion actually heightens illusion. Tieck's *Illusionszerstörung* becomes, then, the means of attaining "permanent parekbasis."

In "Shakespeare's Use of the Marvelous," Tieck assumes that "the illusion of the spectator" is the purpose of the drama, and, in typical eighteenth-century terms, he argues that illusion is possible only when the artist is capable of "putting the judgmental understanding to sleep." Those critics who are preoccupied with antecedents to Coleridge's analogy of illusion and dream and his definition of "poetic faith" as a "willing suspension of disbelief"[41] may add to the list Tieck's account of illusion,

> that the poet does not rely on our good humor; rather, even against our will, he so heightens the fantasy that we forget all rules of aesthetics, with all the principles of our more enlightened century, and give our selves up to the beautiful madness of the poet; that the soul, after this intoxication, willingly surrenders itself anew to the

---

40. F. Schlegel, *Lyceum*–Fragmente §§42, 48, 108; *Athenäum*–Fragmente §§51, 116, 121, 238, 305, 418; and *Philosophische Fragmente* (1797), §668, in *Kritische Ausgabe* II, 152, 153, 160, 172–73, 182–85, 204, 217, 244–45; XVIII, 85. See my chapter on Friedrich Schlegel in *The Haunted Eye: Perception and the Grotesque in English and German Romanticism*, 72–92.

41. Coleridge, *Biographia Literaria* II, 6.

enchantment, and the playing fantasy is not awakened from its dreams by any sudden and offensive surprise.[42]

In spite of Tieck's assumption that this engagement of illusion defies the rules of Enlightenment aesthetics, his formulation is quite in accord with the arguments of Gottsched, Bodmer, or Mendelssohn. The "rules" are produced by reason, while illusion, as understood by these eighteenth-century critics, occurs only when the reason has been overcome by the feelings.[43] What Tieck means, of course, is that Shakespeare has defied the "rules" and succeeds in creating illusion even against those criteria of *mimesis* presumed necessary to the drama. Although Tieck still endorses the opposition between reason and emotion that had been crucial to Enlightenment aesthetics, he expands the psychological territory of illusion. For him illusion is more than reason overwhelmed by intense emotion; the dreamlike consciousness is sustained by the play of imagination or fantasy. This explains the apparent contradiction in his declaring that illusion is both involuntary and voluntary. It may be wrought "even against our will," but we "willingly surrender" once we have experienced the aesthetic intoxication.

Tieck's essay attempts to explain the different strategies Shakespeare uses in conjuring illusion with the supernatural beings in his comedies (*The Tempest, Midsummer Night's Dream*) and in his tragedies (*Hamlet, Macbeth*). Tieck's problem is that he cannot untangle the contradictions and show us how they are only apparent contradictions after all. As a result, he wants to have the dramatic situation two ways: The spectator's response must be involuntary but also voluntary; the plot must be causally consistent but also full of inconsistent surprises. Inconsistency, he argues, will disrupt the illusion, but he goes on to observe how Shakespeare enhances illusion through inconsistencies. On the one hand, he insists that absurd and insipid elements must be eliminated; on the other, he acknowledges that

---

42. *KS* I, 37–38: "Daß der Dichter nicht unsere Gutmüthigkeit in Anspruch nimmt, sondern die Phantasie, selbst wider unsern Willen, so spannt, daß wir die Regeln der Aesthetik, mit allen Begriffen unsers aufgeklärteren Jahrhunderts vergessen, und uns ganz dem schönen Wahnsinn des Dichters überlassen; daß sich die Seele, nach dem Rausch, willig der Bezauberung von neuem hingibt und die spielende Phantasie durch keine plötzliche und widrige Ueberraschung aus ihren Träumen geweckt wird."

43. Gottsched, *Versuch einer Critischen Dichtkunst vor die Deutschen*, 492–93, 614–15; Bodmer, *Critische Abhandlung von dem Wunderbaren in der Poesie*, 14–18, 150, 166–67; Mendelssohn, "Von der Herrschaft über die Neigungen" (1757), in *Gesammelte Schriften*, ed. G. B. Mendelssohn, IV, part 1, 38–45.

they contribute effectively to the portrayal of such characters as Bottom and Caliban.

His first point is that the "marvelous world" must be complete—that is, it must be self-consistent and coherent. The task in narrative is easier, for the reader is initiated into the fantastic "through the eyes of the poet." In the drama, the "marvelous world" is supposed to be viewed directly by the spectator. While an imitation of real life involves conditions already known, the spectator must be shown a new set of conditions, those which govern the marvelous and supernatural. The poet may take advantage of the spectator's "propensity for illusion" (*Hang zur Illusion*),[44] but he can hold it only by providing a logical continuity to his dramatization of the fantastic. The slightest trespass will alert the reason and destroy the illusion. Tieck argues that this logical continuity is similar to that which governs the combinations and associations in dreams (*KS* I, 41–43).

Allegory, in contrast to both narrative fiction and the drama, is addressed to the understanding and does not exercise "illusory power" (*täuschende Kraft*). Thus it is a mistake for the storyteller or the playwright to engage the moral and philosophical manner of allegorical representation. Intellectual discrimination is engaged and the play of fantasy ceases: "In precisely that instant, the understanding speaks its damning judgment over the whole remaining composition." As an example of the poet violating the whole through an inconsistent poetic exposition, Tieck cites the allegorical dream at the conclusion of Goethe's *Egmont*. Goethe, whose attention to illusion will be studied in chapter 6, argued that a total appeal to the fantasy was at odds with the purpose of the drama and that the audience must grapple both mentally and emotionally with the drama.[45] Egmont's dream, for Goethe, was not inconsistent but apt and essential. To be sure, Tieck himself has difficulties in applying his formula for "a whole marvelous world" and the necessity of "uninterrupted illusion." While he considers the dramatic illusion of *Egmont* disrupted by the allegorical dream, he sees the allegorical masques in Shakespeare's *Tempest* fully absorbed into the illusory action of the drama. They retain, Tieck insists, only a "shade" of their allegorical character and thus do not disturb.

Even though he repeats his aesthetic principle that illusion must not be

---

44. Tieck's claim that we possess a natural "Hang zur Illusion" is elaborated by Kant: "Die Natur hat den Hang, sich gerne täuschen zu lassen, dem Menschen weislich eingepflanzt," *Anthropologie in pragmatischer Hinsicht* (1798, 1800) §12; in *Werke* VI, 443.
45. Goethe "Weimarisches Hoftheater," in *Werke*, div. 2, vol. 40, 79.

broken, he continues to confront in the plays evidence that Shakespeare flirted with those very factors which threaten illusion. What gradually emerges in his examination of the marvelous in Shakespeare, in spite of Tieck's governing thesis, is that illusion thrives on disruptive antagonism. Even in dreams a certain disruptive antagonism has the effect of enhancing the power of illusion:

> In the midst of a dream, the soul itself is very often prompted not to believe the phantoms, to tear itself free from the illusion and explain all as the deceptive figures of dreams. In such moments, when the mind is in conflict with itself, the slumberer is always close to waking, for the fantasies lose their illusory reality, the judgment sets itself apart, and the entire spell is on the verge of disappearing. If one persists in dreaming, however, the non-disruption of illusion always results from the infinite abundance of new magical figures which the fantasy brings forth inexhaustibly.[46]

Even in dreams, Tieck acknowledges, illusion is conditional; even in authoring dreams, the dreamer somehow violates his own illusions. One faculty of mind rebels against the other, and judgment is prepared to intrude. At this juncture something peculiar happens, which Tieck can only describe rather than explain. The "non-disruption of illusion" becomes both cause and effect of a renewed imaginative vigor. Because the impending disruption has been forestalled, it turns into a positive attribute that reinforces the illusory experience. Somehow the challenge, imposed by reason and judgment, serves as test or proof. Thus tempered, illusion acquires greater resiliency and strength.

Again, Tieck has described a response in two stages, resistance and acquiescence. In setting forth the involuntary and voluntary conditions, he stated that illusion could be conjured "even against our will"; yet we would "willingly surrender" once we were initiated into the experience. He then

---

46. *KS* I, 44: "Mitten im Traume ist die Seele sehr oft im Begriff, den Phantomen selbst nicht zu glauben, sich von der Täuschung loszureißen und alles nur für betrügerische Traumgestalten zu erklären. In solchen Augenblicken, wo der Geist gleichsam mit sich selber zankt, ist der Schlafende immer dem Erwachen nahe; denn die Phantasien verlieren an ihrer täuschenden Wirklichkeit, die Urtheilskraft sondert sich ab und der ganze Zauber ist im Begriff zu verschwinden. Träumt man aber weiter, so entsteht die Nichtunterbrechung der Illusion jedesmal von der unendlichen Mengen neuer magischen Gestalten, die die Phantasie unerschöpflich hervorbringt."

tells us that even in dreams the mind, monitoring its own fantasies, will bring judgment against the deceptions unless the dream replenishes the illusion with greater fecundity of images. Once the dreamer has entered into this second stage, the monitoring mind and impending judgment are rendered impotent:

> We lose in an unceasing confusion the instruments with which we are accustomed to measure the truth; because nothing real attracts our attention, we lose in the uninterrupted activity of our fantasy, all recollection of reality.[47]

Illusion is defined in terms of negatives: through "non-disruption" we forget reality; surrendering to "unceasing confusion" and "uninterrupted" fantasy, we lose ourselves in another world.

The highest form of illusion occurs, Tieck claims, when we become so thoroughly naturalized as inhabitants of the alternate world that we negate all connections to the real world (*KS* I, 44–45). If this is true, however, how can he praise Shakespeare for reaffirming the connections to the real world in the very midst of the marvelous world of Prospero's island? The intrigue of court and the love of Miranda and Ferdinand require persistent attention to that world which was supposed to have been forgotten. As Tieck explains it, the real world does not disrupt, rather it merges with the marvelous world. Miranda neither recognizes nor recollects; she sees in Ferdinand only the creature of a "brave new world." The audience, however, witnesses something known and familiar in Miranda's response. "Through her character," Tieck says, "Shakespeare has exquisitely combined the marvelous with the real world; the latter must win for itself the spectator's feelings, lest the former never allow him to return from his astonishment and the consequent illusion" (*KS* I, 46–47).

Tieck insists that illusion depends upon the total displacement of reality, but he then stipulates that real conditions must be copresent to prevent illusion from lapsing into a permanent delusion. Prospero's magical power may be incomprehensible, but Shakespeare gives it dramatic probability by initiating his audience into its workings. The spectator is witness to the spell

---

47. Ibid.: "Wir verlieren in einer unaufhörlichen Verwirrung den Maßstab, nach dem wir sonst die Wahrheit zu messen pflegen; eben, weil nichts Wirkliches unsere Aufmerksamkeit auf sich heftet, verlieren wir, in der ununterbrochenen Beschäftigung unserer Phantasie, die Erinnerung an die Wirklichkeit."

that Prospero casts upon Miranda and to his magical control over Ariel and Caliban. Because the spectator has seen the preparations for each magical event, he is not surprised by the consequences (*KS* I, 47–48). Even while the supernatural causality is at work, however, dramatic action is also developed through the natural causality of human passions: the love of Ferdinand and Miranda, the villainy of Sebastian and Antonio, the comic insurrection of Stephano and Trinculo.

The human sympathies, in other words, must be governed by a natural causality, even though some of the circumstances are magical or supernatural. The attention must be completely seduced by the marvelous enchantment, for if the spectator is distracted by reality, "the phantoms of the poet will be destroyed" (*KS* I, 48). Although the "marvelous world" is not "total," Tieck declares that partial illusion is impossible (*KS* I, 50). The real must coexist with the marvelous, yet it must do so invisibly and unobtrusively. Should the combination become evident, no illusion at all is possible. The results are insipid. He cites Marmontel's *Zémire et Azor* as an example of the insipid conflict. Once again, however, Tieck contradicts himself. He has already asserted that a proliferation of images will obviate *Illusionszerstörung* and reinforce the illusion. He therefore stipulates that in addition to self-consistent totality, the marvelous world should also have variety. Mere abundance will not excite the fantasy; there must be novelty and surprise (not *Menge*, but *Mannigfaltigkeit*). Variety, of course, requires the poet to generate new forms, to depart from established patterns.

With this second principle, Tieck worries about two more threats to illusion, discontinuity and emotional extremes. Shakespeare's mastery, Tieck asserts, is evident in his careful observance of the boundary between tragic and comic. In the shipwreck scene, in Alonso's grief for his presumably drowned son, in the plots to murder and usurp, Shakespeare stalks the boundary without trespassing. He ameliorates the emotional response. Should the spectator experience too intensely the tragic suffering, he will reject the illusion. The tragic implications are present, but Shakespeare does not allow them to dominate the action. Variation of character and action is attended by a moderation of effects. The contrasts of love and hate, tragic and comic, provide the necessary variety in plot as well as character. The love of Ferdinand and Miranda is set off against the assassination of Alonso planned by Sebastian and Antonio, which, in turn, is parodied in Caliban's scheme with Stephano and Trinculo to kill Prospero (*KS* I, 51–55). The scenes, however, are so modulated that neither heightened emotions nor astonishment at the changes disrupt the illusion.

Tieck's first principle for the use of the marvelous stipulates a self-consistent totality; his second principle invites inconsistency and unpredictability; his third principle calls for ironic combinations and comic confusion. Confusion is necessary, he says, to keep the magical phantoms from acquiring "corporeal consistence." If Ariel and Caliban seem too human they lose their supernatural identity. Magical figures must be improbable to be probable. The marvelous requires confusion. Following this line of reasoning, Tieck controverts what he had earlier asserted about self-consistency and the associative logic of dreams. Inconsistent and contradictory events, as he deals with them in this context, no longer destroy illusion; rather, they enhance illusion by adding paradoxical dimensions to the aesthetic experience. To be sure, he had earlier defended the ridiculous and repulsive Caliban as appropriate contrast to Ariel (*KS* I, 48), but contrasting effects were not to lapse into the insipid and absurd (*KS* I, 50). Having thus rejected the insipid, he now comes to its defense: The spectator's fantasy "delights in the burlesque and insipid" ("ergötzt sich an dem Burlesken und Abgeschmackten," *KS* I, 56).

Only with an emotional affect that had been softened and constrained would Tieck allow tragic events to take place in comedy; nevertheless, he fully approves the union of the frightful and the ludicrous. The fantasy is accustomed to observing a given object as attractive or repulsive, comic or terrifying. What first prompts our laughter may in the next moment cause us to shudder in horror. The grotesque turnabout results from that mobility of the imagination which enables us to perceive an object as seductive but dangerous, or ridiculous but horrible. The ghosts and witches in folktales typically elicit such dual response. In dreams, too, ghastly circumstances are often modified by comic elements. When the two are combined, the experience is rendered more believable, for the comic draws the horrific back into the ordinary.

Because a sense of the paradoxical or contradictory accompanies the combination, the power to discriminate and judge is confused: "The soul is transposed into a kind of giddy state, in which it is ultimately compelled to acquiesce to illusion because it has lost hold on all signs of truth or error."[48]

---

48. Ibid., 57: "Die Seele wird in eine Art von Schwindel versetzt, in welchem sie sich am Ende gezwungen der Täuschung überläßt, da sie all Kennzeichen der Wahrheit oder des Irrthums verloren hat."

At this point, Tieck describes precisely that sort of irresolvable structure which Todorov forwarded in his definition of the fantastic as the genre of uncertainty. In documenting the fantastic as that genre which prevents the reader from determining whether the narrative events are to be interpreted as real or imaginary, Todorov refers again and again to Jacques Cazotte's *Le Diable Amoureux* (1772).[49] Tieck, too, quotes from the conclusion of Cazotte's tale to support his argument that paradoxical combinations have the effect, by undermining rational resolution, of "forcing" illusory response.[50]

In spite of his appeal to a self-consistent "world," Tieck, unlike Todorov, is not concerned with structurally sustained irresolution. As is evident in his application of this principle to *Midsummer Night's Dream*, it suffices for Tieck if the efforts of rational resolution are momentarily distracted. The comic and terrible must merely preoccupy our attention, so that we are prevented from scrutinizing too closely the presumptions upon the imagination. As does Todorov, Tieck, too, excludes those texts that give us only imaginary events without implicating their "reality." If the events are purely romantic and strange (*romantisch, abenteuerlich*) they involve no illusion: "The marvelous would cause no illusion precisely because it is too marvelous" (*KS* I, 58). Todorov's fantastic is delicately perched at the apex of a triangle whose sides descend into the marvelous (unnatural events actually occur) or into the uncanny (unnatural events are revealed to be imaginary). Tieck's model for illusion is essentially the same, but he does not insist on logical or structural coherence.

Even if a coherent and irresolvable combination of natural and unnatural elements is not necessary, Tieck forwards no other determinate criteria. As a result, he contradicts himself. He tells us that the intrusion of surprising or shocking elements will disrupt the illusion (*KS* I, 48), but that they also may add variety and enhance illusion (*KS* I, 50–51). A dialectic is apparently necessary, but he cannot define this principle to discriminate success from failure. In *Midsummer Night's Dream* and *The Tempest*, he finds that the

49. Todorov, *The Fantastic*, 24–25, 27, 31, 45, 52, 82, 85, 101, 127–28, 129, 130–31, 166.
50. *KS* I, 57; Jacques Cazotte, *Le Diable Amoureux:* (the old priest to Alvaro) "Après vous avoir ébloui autant que vous avez voulu l'être, contraint à se montrer à vous dans toute sa difformité, il obéit en esclave qui prémédite la révolte; il ne veut vous laisser aucune idée raisonnable et distincte, mêlant le grotesque au terrible; le puérile de ses escargots lumineux, à la découverte effrayante de son horrible tête; enfin le mensonge à la vérité; le repos à la veille; de manière que votre esprit confus ne distingue rien, et que vous puissiez croire, que la vision qui vous a frappé, était moins l'effet de sa malice, qu'un rêve occasioné par les vapeurs de votre cerveau."

appearance of the commonplace amidst the supernatural actually heightens illusion (*KS* I, 58–59).

But the same combination, Tieck says, does not work for Carlo Gozzi. Gozzi, too, brings together the natural and supernatural, the commonplace and the extraordinary, but he achieves no synthesis. Later, in his *Puss-in-Boots* (1797), Tieck will develop a complex structure of metadramatic irony out of the antagonism of magical and mundane which he had found in Gozzi's fiabesque drama (see chapter 7). In his essay on "Shakespeare's Use of the Marvelous," he acknowledges how Gozzi's use of the *fiabe* provides "a windup toy for the eyes of the spectator, who is often enough surprised by the transformations"; nevertheless, he accuses Gozzi of lacking dramatic development. Content merely to entertain and amuse, Gozzi uses the combination only for "bizarre and grotesque" effects. Thus he lapses into farce. Not drama, but "dramatic abortions" ("dramatische Mißgeburten," *KS* I, 60) are the result.

In tragedy, Tieck observes, the supernatural must remain distant and unexplained, influencing the action only indirectly by working upon the characters in the natural world. Used only in brief interludes, the supernatural scenes give us a glimpse into a character's anxieties and fears. So long as the marvelous appears on stage but for a momentary revelation of horror, as if exposed by a sudden flash of lightning (*KS* I, 63), then it may succeed in startling or even frightening us. Such scenes cannot be long sustained, however, or brought directly into the tragic action. The reason would rebel against the emotional affect and the illusion would be destroyed. The illusion is only possible so long as the fear that we feel prevents the judgmental understanding from intervening.[51]

In tragedy, then, the marvelous need not seem probable. Its affects are emotional and irrational. The marvelous in comedy is directly involved in the action; in *Midsummer Night's Dream* and *The Tempest* the magic is fully acknowledged. The marvelous in tragedy is a brief and indirect intrusion; in *Hamlet* and *Macbeth* the supernatural remains inexplicable—we suspect more than we perceive (*KS* I, 64–65). Nevertheless, the audience must be prepared for the intrusion. The playwright must give us some anticipation of

---

51. Ibid., 63: "Das Wunderbare tritt hier in den Hintergrund zurück; wie ein Blitzstrahl bricht es dann plötzlich hervor, und eben darum ist hier die Kunst des Dichters, es wahrscheinlich zu machen, nicht notwendig; wenn er es nur dahin bringt, daß es nur eintritt, uns zu erschrecken und zu erschüttern, so wird schon dadurch unsere Illusion völlig gewonnen, denn der Schreck, den wir empfinden, läßt den richtenden Verstand nicht zur Sprache kommen."

superstitious beliefs before his character confronts the manifestation of his own fear. This preparation is necessary to the illusion, but even with heightened anticipation, the apparition cannot remain long without losing its illusory power (*KS* I, 69–70). Since tragedy builds on the causal conditions of human action, the playwright must always allow for a natural explanation of the marvelous. When the ghosts appear to Richard III on Bosworth Field or when the ghost of Banquo takes his place at Macbeth's table, the spectator must realize that he is seeing the supernatural through the eyes of the character (*KS* I, 70–74). The illusion is sustained only as a dramatization of delusion, the irrational that has momentarily intruded upon the mind of the character.

Although Tieck generally ignores staging and acting in his 1793 essay, he does grant that "a completely mechanical artifice" may reinforce illusion. Shakespeare relies on music to provide such artificial support. The imaginative flight of lyric song, Tieck argues, may prepare the audience for certain departures from natural events. Music and song overcome our resistance to the improbable and allow us to tolerate the magical fairy tales of operetta (*KS* I, 61). In his subsequent criticism of the drama, Tieck departs from the eighteenth-century model of emotion vs. reason in accounting for illusion. He comes to distinguish "crude illusion" from the "true and valid" aesthetic illusion. The former depends on "slice of life" verisimilitude, while the latter engages the imagination. Tieck's contrast is essentially the same as the one Coleridge forwards in his Shakespearean lectures when he distinguishes between "copy" and "imitation" (see chapter 5). Domestic drama may draw directly from nature, Tieck observes, but it wants artistic refinement; raw emotions may be accurately portrayed, but the appeal is sentimental not imaginative.[52]

Tieck also begins to give more attention to acting. His essays on the backgrounds of English and German theater address changing fashions of acting and staging. And when his own plays are to be produced, Tieck engages in a vigorous correspondence with director and players.[53] In recognizing drama as performing art, he sees that the mediation of the players is crucial: The interpretive skills of the player determine and direct how the

---

52. Tieck, Preface to *Dramaturgische Blätter*, in *KS* III, xii.
53. Tieck, "Das alt-englische Theater," preface to *Alt-Englisches Theater* (1811, 1823, 1828), and *Vorschule zu Shakespeare*, in *KS* I, 215–322; "Die Anfänge des deutschen Theaters," preface to *Deutsches Theater* (1817), in *KS* I, 325–88; for his correspondence concerning the performance of *Der gestiefelte Kater* and *Blaubart*, see *Ludwig Tieck, Dichter über ihre Dichtung* I, 112–18, 144–48.

audience anticipates, experiences, and judges illusion. His appraisal of acting emphasizes the very paradox that Diderot had observed. Tieck poses the question: "Should the actor respond feelingly during the performance, should he remain cold?" (1825). Neither here nor elsewhere does he refer to Diderot's *Paradoxe sur le comédien* or Mendelssohn's "Reply to a couple of Questions on Dramatic Art." While it may be observed that his way of formulating the problem is closer to Mendelssohn, Tieck follows Diderot in referring to the acting technique of Claire-Joseph Clairon.[54] To be sure, as Tieck himself grants, it is an old question often raised.

Whether the actor should be impassioned or aloof, as Tieck sees it, is only a variation on the question about nature and art. Why must an actor rely on the art of acting? Why may he not assume the same expressive freedom as the poet and give free play to his natural instincts, his enthusiasm, inspiration, and feeling? So asks Tieck's fictive youthful actor, and an old professional defends the art as providing formal order. Inspiration is fleeting, feelings are uncertain and changing. Since an actor may easily lose his passionate mood in the midst of a scene, what becomes of the character he is playing? There is another problem of relying on individual feeling: it is not only inconstant, it is also raw and uninformed. Untempered by art and reflection, natural spontaneity is erratic and cannot sustain dramatic illusion. The emotional exhibitionism interferes with the spectator's attention to dramatic action. Only through the deliberate control of art can the actor portray intense emotion in a manner consistent with the drama.

In setting forth his paradox, in which an illusion of overwhelming emotion is achieved through total emotional constraint, Diderot cited the examples of Mlle Clairon and David Garrick. Tieck quotes from La Clairon, but substitutes Schröder for Garrick—giving to Schröder, however, the same anecdote that Diderot had attributed to Garrick, that the actor was so completely in control of his performance that even in the midst of Lear's rage he could whisper jests to other players. Like Diderot, he also retells the debate between Clairon and Dusmenil. Dusmenil's argument was that art should give way to enthusiasm, "so that we are no longer aware of the intention, and are inspired by that illusion, which is alone the only true

---

54. Tieck, "Soll der Schauspieler während der Darstellung empfinden? soll er kalt bleiben?" *Bemerkungen, Einfälle und Grillen über das deutsche Theater* (1825), in *KS* IV, 80, translates from the *Mémoires d'Hippolyte Clairon* (Paris, 1798); cf. Diderot, *OC*, VIII, 366–67, 373, 377, 393, 403–4.

one."⁵⁵ By reaffirming that artistic control and constraint enables the actor to concentrate all his training and skill to performing the very extremes of passion, Tieck arrives at the paradox of natural spontaneity as an illusion achieved through deliberation. Unlike Diderot, Tieck insists that this is only an "apparent paradox." It is perceived as paradox to those who have experienced only the natural spontaneity and do not understand artistic control. In the creative process, they cease to be antagonistic elements. To the artist, enthusiasm and deliberation are synthesized in art: "The highest inspiration, the true enthusiasm are at the same time the true deliberation and creative clarity."

Similar to Wordsworth's account of poetry as "the spontaneous overflow of powerful feelings" which then "takes its origin from emotion recollected in tranquillity,"⁵⁶ Tieck argues that a poet comprehends intense feeling through a divine peace ("göttliche Ruhe"). If the poet allows himself and his art to be consumed by intense and moving passion, he should not wonder that the results are awkward and amateurish. The passion must be fully appropriated and reengendered within creative deliberation. Similar to Coleridge's definition of poetry as a "reconciliation of opposite and discordant qualities"⁵⁷ is Tieck's declaration that all art, that of the poet as well as that of the actor, is achieved through synthesis of nature and art, passion and deliberation, feeling and observation (*KS* IV, 81).

Charles Lamb, in his essay "Stage Illusion," gives to the actor or actress the entire credit for a successful conjuration.⁵⁸ Illusion, for Lamb, depends upon our recognition and acceptance of a character as a fellow human being. This does not mean that, in order to observe the illusion, we must forget that we are in the theater; it means rather, that we recognize in the actions upon the stage the very kind of role playing that we engage in with our fellow creatures. Stage illusion, then, is a formalization, a dramatization, of our most compulsive social activity. Lamb begins his essay by accepting illusion as a criteria for judging the excellence of a dramatic performance, but he takes issue with the presumption that illusion approaches perfection "when the actor appears wholly unconscious of the presence of spectators."

The actor was supposed to consider the proscenium arch as a "fourth

---

55. *KS* IV, 80: "damit wir die Absicht nicht mehr gewahr, und von jener Täuschung begeister werden, die allein nur die ächte ist." Diderot, *OC,* VIII, 364, 366–67, 381–82, 396.
56. Wordsworth and Coleridge, *Lyrical Ballads,* ed. Brett and Jones, 260.
57. Coleridge, *Biographia Literaria* II, 16–17.
58. Lamb, "Stage Illusion," in *Works* III, 29–34.

wall," yet the most successful actors of the period played for "points" (applause accorded a virtuoso display). Even Diderot, who insisted that "it was necessary for author and actor to forget the spectator" (*OC* VII, 344: "Il fallait cependant que l'auteur et l'acteur oubliassent le spectateur"), granted that genius had the privilege of trespassing the boundaries of common sense. Like Diderot and Tieck, Lamb directs his attention to the acting. Even though he disagrees with Diderot's strictures against "playing to the house," Lamb endorses the emphasis placed on the acting as source of illusion. Lamb's argument on the nature of illusion shares nothing with Coleridge's concern with imagination. The spectator does not necessarily engage in illusion; rather, he is merely a witness to the degree it is achieved by the actors. In disagreeing with this definition, Lamb does not wish to reclaim illusion as the experience of the spectator. He is quite pleased to leave illusion to the actors. What he wishes to correct is the notion that the actor must seem oblivious to the audience in order to produce effective illusion. He grants, of course, the relationship between stage illusion and the power of the performance "to affect the feelings." Similar to Diderot, he sees this power enhanced by the "dédoublement" of actor and character.

Tragedy, because it aims at eliciting pathos, would seem to require an actor to devote "undivided attention to his stage business." Nevertheless, "our cleverest tragedians" repeatedly turn from stage action to audience; "while these references to an audience, in the shape of rant or sentiment, are not too frequent or palpable, a sufficient quantity of illusion for the purposes of dramatic interest may be said to be produced in spite of them." Stage illusion, in other words, may persist even though the actor steps through the invisible "fourth wall" of the stage. This trespass is possible in tragedy and, Lamb argues, necessary in some comedy.

Lamb argues that when the playwright creates a comic character whose actions and manners are too extravagant or morally repugnant, the actor is required to initiate "a tacit understanding with the audience." Neither stepping out of his role, nor directly appealing to the audience, the actor must make the audience "unconsciously to themselves, a party in the scene." This secret shared between audience and player requires "the highest skill" and is achieved only by "the great artists." To clarify what is involved in this conspiracy with the audience, Lamb offers several examples of comic play with illusion.

The first is the coward as comic character. Because "a coward *done to the life* upon the stage would produce anything but mirth," the actor must make the *acting* open or transparent. To his skill in letting the audience see into his role playing, Lamb reports, Bannister owed his success in making his cowards lovable and laughable.

> How was this effected but by the exquisite art of the actor in a perpetual subinsinuation to us, the spectators, even in the extremity of the shaking fit, that he was not half such a coward as we took him for? We saw the common symptoms of the malady upon him; the quivering lip, the cowering knees, the teeth chattering; and could have sworn "that man was frightened." But we forgot all the while—or kept it almost a secret to ourselves—that he never once lost his self-possession; that he let it out, by a thousand droll looks and gestures—meant at *us*, and not at all supposed to be visible to his fellows in the scene, that his confidence in his own resources had never once deserted him.

Lamb proceeds to name other comic types—the miser, the irritable old man—which would be disagreeable or repugnant if not played in such a manner as to reveal "an inner conviction that they are *being acted* before us; that a likeness only is going on, not the thing itself." What is wanted, then, is a consciousness of the counterfeit, "just enough of a likeness to recognize, without pressing upon us the uneasy sense of a reality."

As negative example, Lamb cites the performances of Emery, who does well in characters of a tragic cast, but fails in comedy because he is too insistently natural. Lamb calls attention to the seeming paradox. The actor who plays "*to the life*" misses the antic otherness of a comic character. Comedy is not strictly mimetic: it distorts and exaggerates. Unlike serious scenes, comic scenes play with credibility.

> The degrees of credibility demanded of the two things may be illustrated by the different sort of truth which we expect when a man tells us a mournful or a merry story. If we suspect the former of a falsehood, we reject it altogether. Our tears refuse to flow at a suspected imposition. But the teller of a mirthful tale has latitude allowed him. We are content with less than absolute truth. 'Tis the same with dramatic illusion. We confess we love in comedy to see an audience naturalised behind the scenes—taken into the interest of the drama, welcomed as bystanders, however.

Stage illusion in comedy, then, depends on a deliberate revelation of role playing. Lamb uses a varied vocabulary in defining this sort of acting. Coleridge, in his 1808 lecture on dramatic illusion, referred to the spectator's "half belief," a term which Lamb repeats, but he directs attention towards the actor, rather than the spectator, in speaking of a role being "half put on," of "subinsinuation," of "compromise," of a "judicious understanding, not too openly announced." He uses a similar vocabulary and essentially the same argument in his account of Bannister in "On some of the Old Actors." Bannister is praised for his vocal mastery of the "aside" and the ironic "give-away":

> Jack had two voices, both plausible, hypocritical, and insinuating; but his secondary or supplemental voice still more decisively histrionic than his common one. It was reserved for the spectator; and the *dramatis personae* were supposed to know nothing at all about it. The *lies* of Young Wilding, and the *sentiments* in Joseph Surface, were thus marked out in a sort of italics to the audience.

Lamb by no means claims that such deliberate byplay with a role is appropriate to any character. He does consider the tactics of "half-belief" peculiarly necessary to the "highly artificial comedy of Congreve or of Sheridan." And a technique quite like it is also required in those frequent roles of disguise in Shakespeare's comedies. He cites, for example, Mrs. Jordan's success as Viola in *Twelfth Night*. Not that the audience must see Mrs. Jordan peeping through her characterization of Viola, but that Viola must peep through her disguise as page. Lamb notes especially Viola's "disguised story of her love for Orsino." Viola must be fully visible to the audience, yet the audience must also accept the illusion that Orsino beholds only Cesario. Furthermore, her delivery must be naturally harmonic; the rhetoric and poetry of Shakespeare must fully dissolve in the seeming spontaneity and organic growth of the passion.

While a certain play with illusion is also required in Iago's feigned friendship and sincerity, an actor makes a grave mistake when he renders the villainy transparent. Bensley properly mastered the role when he played Iago without giving the audience a privileged display of his evil cunning and cleverness:

> No spectator, from his action could divine more of his artifice than Othello was supposed to do. His confessions in soliloquy alone put

you in possession of the mystery. There were no by-intimations to make the audience fancy their own discernment so much greater than that of the Moor—who commonly stands like a great helpless mark, set up for mine Ancient, and a quantity of barren spectators, to shoot their bolts at. The Iago of Bensley did not got to work so grossly. There was a triumphant tone about the character, natural to a general consciousness of power; but none of that petty vanity which chuckles and cannot contain itself upon any little successful stroke of its knavery—as is common with small villains, and green probationers in mischief. It did not clap or crow before its time. It was not a man setting his wits at a child, and winking all the while at other children, who are mightily pleased at being let into the secret; but a consummate villain entrapping a noble nature into toils, against which no discernment was available, where the manner was as fathomless as the purpose seemed dark, and without motive.

The actor's "subinsinuations" and "by-intimations" provide for an open form of stage illusion; the closed form does not allow audience to be "let into the secret." In distinguishing between open and closed forms of stage illusion, Lamb also establishes criteria of dramatic propriety for their respective use. Because the satirical exaggerations of the Comedy of Manners produce fictive caricatures rather than mimetic characters, the performance calls for an open illusion.

The essay "On the Artificial Comedy of the Last Century" elaborates further the differences between open and closed stage illusion.[59] The comedy of his own times requires the closed form. Lamb traces the changes from Comedy of Manners, to Sentimental Comedy, to the contemporary comedy of bourgeois morality and melodrama, "the exclusive and all-devouring drama of common life; where the moral point is everything." The Comedy of Manners gave us "fictitious half-believed personages." Modern comedy insists upon real life: "[W]e recognize ourselves . . . the same as in life—with an interest in what is going on so hearty and substantial, that we cannot afford our moral judgment, in its deepest and most vital results, to compromise or slumber for a moment."

59. Lamb, "On the Artificial Comedy of the last Century," in *Works* IV, 275–87; see also "On Some of the Old Actors" and "On the Acting of Munden," in *Works* IV, 257–74 and 288–91. Wayne McKenna, *Charles Lamb and the Theatre*, 37–54.

Having acquired this militant moral attention, the modern audience is no longer capable of enjoying the rakes, libertines, profligates, and strumpets of Congreve, Wycherley, or Farquhar: "The business of their dramatic characters will not stand the moral test." Because of its insistent social realism, present-day comedy is a "tyrant... pernicious to our pleasures." It has taken from us the "middle emotions," the "half belief," and the "imaginary freedom" of the open form. Instead of playing with fictions, we expect a mirror of reality. The pleasure of aesthetic "indifference" has been overwhelmed by "a perpetual moral questioning": "We dare not dally with images, or names, of wrong. We bark like foolish dogs at shadows. We dread infection from the scenic representation of disorder, and fear a painted pustule." And again: "We cling to the painful necessities of shame and blame. We would indict our very dreams."

His case for "artificial comedy," Lamb acknowledges, depends upon the very unlikely condition that a contemporary audience would suspend moral judgment and give attention to the essentially nonmimetic "pageant." He discusses Palmer's rendition of Joseph Surface in terms very similar to his account of Bannister's performance. In total contrast to Bensley's Iago, Palmer's Surface emphasized "the downright *acted* villainy of the part, so different from the pressure of conscious actual wickedness." Bannister, according to Lamb, had "two voices." Palmer was "twice an actor"—that is, "he was playing to you all the while he was playing upon Sir Peter and his lady." Of his attention to the audience, "his fictitious co-flutterers on the stage perceived nothing at all."

3

Illusion and the Audience: Lessing, Mendelssohn, and Schiller

Because they seem at odds with the prevailing emphasis on reason, Sentimental Tragedy and the Cult of Sensibility might be judged mere anomalies, marginal countercurrents in the Age of Enlightenment. They were, in fact, central. In the theater, no plays were more popular than those which effectively "mirrored" familiar domestic trials and tragedy.[1] In philosophy, the very emphasis on reason prompted a number of thinkers to seek a rational defense of sensation and emotion in order to restore the integrity of aesthetic experience. With the two volumes of Baumgarten's *Aesthetica* (1750, 1758), the *feeling* (*aisthesis*) of art gained legitimacy as a specific subject of metaphysi-

---

1. Guthke, "Das bürgerliche Drama des 18. und frühen 19. Jahrhunderts," in *Handbuch des deutschen Dramas*, 79, attributes the popular appeal of the domestic tragedy to the playwright's skill in satisfying moral expectations and in sustaining illusion: "Wenn er dem Zuschauer ununterbrochen und ungetrübte Wirklichkeitsillusion vermittelt, also eine Vorspiegelung des gegenwärtigen 'gemeinen Lebens,' wie das Publikum es aus der täglichen Erfahrung kennt." Wierlacher, *Das Bürgerliche Drama. Seine theoretische Begründung im 18. Jahrhundert*, 111–16, devotes a chapter to explaining "Das Postulat der Illusion." See also Koopmann, *Drama der Aufklärung. Kommentar zu einer Epoche;* Nivelle, *Kunst- und Dichtungstheorien zwischen Aufklärung und Klassik;* Pikulik, "*Bürgerliches Trauerspiel" und Empfindsamkeit.*

cal inquiry.² Not unlike such Puritans as Jeremy Collier, who denounced the theater for abusing the spirit and exciting the emotions,³ the rationalists, following Descartes, also denigrated the senses and the feelings as the source of ignorance and confusion.⁴ We traced these developments in France and England. In Germany, Meier and Wolff deserve major credit for their efforts to secure for art a respectable, albeit subordinate, place within the rationalist scheme of perceiving and knowing.⁵ But could one claim for art a power to reveal the good, the true, the beautiful in such a way as might render it, not subordinate, but equal, perhaps even superior to rational deliberation?

By the mid-eighteenth century, several arguments had been forwarded in the effort to redeem aesthetic experience from its debased position as mere sensual, irrational perception. Du Bos had argued that aesthetic pleasure derives from a sixth sense capable of mediating and judging the stimulation of the other five senses.⁶ While the stimulation of the senses could produce a voluptuous response, our very indulgence of that pleasure was a recreation of self, a consciousness of our own sensual capacities. Wolff combined the pleasure principle of Du Bos with the psychology of Leibniz to demonstrate how sensual perception could lead to self-awareness.⁷ Following Leibniz, another defense of aesthetic experience had been found in the capacity of art to excite and increase the perceptual activity of the "monads." If the activity of the "monads" is essential to rational conception as well as sensual perception, then the stimulation provided by art is not confined to the baser affects.⁸ The empiricists also provided an answer to the Cartesian denigration of the senses. Rather than as a source of confusion and error, sensory data served the empiricists as the building blocks of knowledge.⁹ Bodmer maintained a dualism, not the paradoxical simultaneity later introduced by Diderot, but a sequential interchange of emotional and rational response. He granted that the emotions were aroused by artistic imitation as illusion,

---

2. Baumgarten, *Aesthetica.*
3. Collier, *A Short View of the Immorality and Profaneness of the English Stage.*
4. Descartes, *Meditationes de prima philosophia* and *Discours de la méthode.*
5. Meier, *Abbildung eines Kunstrichters* and *Anfangsgründe aller schönen Künste und Wissenschaften;* Christian Wolff, *Psychologia empirica.*
6. Du Bos, *Réflexions critiques sur la poésie et sur la peinture.* "C'est ce sixiéme sens qui est en nous, sans que nous voyions ses organes" II, 341–42.
7. Wolff, *Psychologia empirica,* §511.
8. Leibniz, *Meditationes de cognitione, veritate et ideis* (1684) and *Monadologie* (1714), in *Kleine Schriften zur Metaphysik.*
9. Locke, *Essay on Human Understanding.*

yet he insisted that the reason was then challenged by the imitation as imitation. As a result, the spectator shifts back and forth: now succumbing to the effects, now scrutinizing the causes.[10] The doctrine of sympathy, especially as it had been forwarded in England by Shaftesbury and Hutcheson, was influential among German philosophers in establishing an innate and intuitive ground for moral action.[11] Natural theology offered an additional defense of aesthetic experience: because the design of God in the physical world is evident through the senses, sensory perception gives man immediate and direct access to divine revelation. Moreover, it is only human reason that has to struggle to link ideas consecutively in discursive thought. In the divine consciousness all ideas are intuitive and spontaneous. Since art, too, is intuitive and spontaneous, aesthetic experience must be similar to the revelation of divine wisdom.[12] Here is a version of the neoplatonic argument that would later reemerge in Coleridge's definition of the "primary imagination" as the "repetition in the finite mind of the eternal act of creation in the infinite I AM."[13]

In their *Correspondence concerning Tragedy* (*Briefwechsel über das Trauerspiel*, 1755–57), Nicolai, Mendelssohn, and Lessing attempted to define the province of tragedy in relation to reason and emotion.[14] The correspondence was prompted by Nicolai's *Discourse on Tragedy* (*Abhandlung vom Trauerspiele*), which had been written to guide fledgling playwrights who would be submitting their plays in the competition for the prize announced in the *Bibliothek*.[15] Nicolai's *Discourse* attempted to ward off heavy-handed moralizing by setting forth an affective account of tragedy. While he affirmed that the purpose of tragedy was to arouse the passions, he also prescinded that

10. Bodmer, *Brief-Wechsel von der Natur des poetischen Geschmackes;* Bodmer and Breitinger, *Von dem Einfluß und Gebrauche der Einbildungs-Krafft zur Ausbesserung des Geschmackes.*
11. Cooper, *Characteristics of Men, Manners, Opinions, and Times;* Hutcheson, *A System of Moral Philosophy;* Hutcheson, *Sittenlehre der Vernunft.*
12. Wolff, *Theologia naturalis* (1736), section 1, §207; *Psychologia empirica,* §§286–89. Cramer, *Von dem Wesen der biblischen Poesie. Poetische Übersetzungen der Psalmen.*
13. Coleridge, *Biographia Literaria* I, 304.
14. Lessing, Mendelssohn, Nicolai, *Briefwechsel über das Trauerspiel,* in Lessing, *Werke,* ed. Göpfert, et al., IV, 153–227; I have also relied on the commentary in *Briefwechsel uber das Trauerspiel,* ed. Schulte-Sasse, 168–237; Heidsieck, "Der Disput zwischen Lessing und Mendelssohn über das Trauerspiel"; "Lessing as Aesthetic Thinker. An Esssay on the Systematic Structure of Lessing's Aesthetics."
15. *Bibliothek der schönen Wissenschaften und der freyen Künste.* The prize competition was announced in a prospectus for the planned *Bibliothek* in Spring, 1756; Nicolai's *Abhandlung vom Trauerspiel* appeared the following year in the first number, *Bibliothek,* vol. 1, no. 1 (Leipzig: J. G. Dyck, 1757), 17–68.

purpose from the concept of *catharsis* as a purgative and moral purification. Lessing responded that Nicolai had imposed a false separation between emotional and moral affects, for the sympathy aroused through the drama was in itself morally good.

Observing that certain passions stirred by the drama, specifically that of "admiration" (*Bewunderung*), could prompt a rational decision to emulate,[16] Mendelssohn's position may seem to provide a compromise between Nicolai and Lessing. In fact, Mendelssohn was in perfect accord with Nicolai and utterly at odds with Lessing. Nicolai, with Mendelssohn, had no difficulty in acknowledging that moral improvement was possible through the subsequent engagement of the reason; the primary response, however, was emotional and therefore necessarily amoral.[17] This is the crux, for Lessing maintained that the moral affect of tragedy was not an after-response of reason, but resided in the immediate emotional engagement of sympathy. The purpose of tragedy, in his definition, was not just to excite the passions, but to exercise and amplify our capacity to feel sympathy, for "the most sympathetic person is the best person." Following Hutcheson, Lessing assumed an innate moral capacity that was not dependent on higher reason. Thus he asserted that sympathy could effect moral improvement in "the man of understanding as well as the ignorant."[18]

All three correspondents attempt to explain and justify the emotional appeal of art in rationalist terms. Mendelssohn candidly confesses his debt to the Leibniz–Wolff school, and all three friends employ the vocabulary of rationalism.[19] In spite of certain shared premises and purposes, the correspondence becomes entangled in disagreement with the very first response from Lessing. Is emotional excitation or sympathy the proper end of the drama? Lessing vehemently asserted the latter, while Nicolai and Mendelssohn upheld the former. If only he and Nicolai could clearly set forth the

---

16. Mendelssohn to Lessing, 23 November 1756, in Lessing, *Werke* IV, 168.
17. Mendelssohn and Nicolai to Lessing, January 1757, in Lessing, *Werke* IV, 198. This is the point of Nicolai's objection to Mendelssohn's assertion: "Wenn Herr Nicolai behauptet,* die Poesie könne sur Besserung der Sitten nichts beitragen, so hat er offenbar Unrecht." Nicolai inserted the asterisk and added the comment: "Wenn—aber merken Sie es sich, mein lieber Lessing, daß ich dieses nicht behauptet." With Mendelssohn he affirms moral improvement, not as a direct effect of tragedy upon an audience, but as a *possible* subsequent effect when reason and judgment evaluate the represented action.
18. Lessing to Nicolai, November 1756; Lessing to Mendelssohn, 28 November and 18 December 1756, in Lessing, *Werke* IV, 163, 175, and 189–90.
19. Mendelssohn to Lessing, 23 November 1756, in Lessing, *Werke* IV, 169–70.

nature of illusion, Mendelssohn was sure,[20] Lessing would see the error of his belief that through sympathy the drama could be immediately and directly moral.

The purpose of all poetry, Nicolai affirms with Du Bos, is to provide pleasure. In tragedy, the poet achieves this end through the excitement of pity and fear; the greater the emotional excitement, the better the play. Even the negative emotions—anger, pain, sorrow, terror—produce pleasure because the spectator feels all of the turmoil and movement of mood without suffering direct physical consequences. Because the excitement is a source of pleasure, scenes of anguish do not disrupt the illusion. The spectator endures the illusory duress in order to feel actual emotion ("die Rührung, welche wirklich geschieht").[21]

Nicolai does not discuss illusion as such, but he is concerned with the importance of sustaining an emotional hold on the audience. Thus he defends a certain adherence to the unities of time and place. His argument is based exclusively on psychological effect and makes no appeal to the structural propriety of the classical genre. He requires that the action unfold according to "apparent time" (*scheinbare Zeit*) because the unnatural extension of time confuses and repulses the audience. Similarly, frequent shifts from place to place are awkward in the drama not because they violate rules but because they disrupt the incremental development of emotional intensity. The major problem with scene changes is that the spectator is forcibly reminded "that the theatrical palaces and gardens are nothing but painted canvas." The disruption is worst at the moment in which the scene change occurs, for the spectator is prompt to accept the artifice. Nevertheless, such reminders of theatricality should be kept to a minimum.[22]

20. Mendelssohn to Lessing, 23 November 1756, December 1756, and January 1757, in Lessing, *Werke* IV, 169, 181, 194–95.
21. Nicolai, "Abhandlung vom Trauerspiele" (1757), in Lessing et al., *Briefwechsel über das Trauerspiel*, 13: "Die Ausbrüche der heftigen Leidenschaften sind so schrecklich, daß wir uns nicht einen Augenblick bedenken können sie zu unterbrechen; es ist also die Stärke der Bewegung die er liebt, auch der schmerzliche Empfindungen unerachtet, die wider das Angenehme der Leidenschaft streiten, in kurzem obsieget, und die heftigsten Folgen hinterlassen. Eine Leidenschaft also die diese Folgen nicht hinterläßt, in welcher der Schmerz über das Vergnügen gerühret zu werden nicht obsieget, muß gänzlich angenehm seyn. . . . unser Geist wird gerühret, er empfindet auch Schmerz, aber ein Schmerz, der nicht wirklich sondern nur nachgeahmt ist, ist eben deßwegen nicht vermögend die Rührung, welche wirklich geschieht, zu überwältigen; das Unangenehme der Leidenschaft verschwindet also, und es bleibet uns nichts übrig als das Vergnügen gerühret zu werden, als das süße Zittern, das von der Bewegung der Leidenschaft hervorgebracht wird."
22. Ibid.: on "scheinbare Zeit," 22–23; on unity of place, 24.

Lessing first responds to Nicolai's complete essay on 2 April 1757. Six months earlier, however, Nicolai had summarized his thesis that the tragic *mimesis* was sensual in nature and that the purpose of tragedy was to excite the passions.[23] It was that letter of 31 August 1756 which prompted Lessing's objections and initiated the debate that continued until 14 May 1757, when Nicolai tried to draw up a ledger of their agreement and disagreement. Nicolai's ledger reveals, more strikingly than the individual letters, how much the disagreement had derived from the inability of Nicolai and Mendelssohn to acknowledge their difference with Lessing's fundamental philosophical position.[24] To be sure, they tried repeatedly to come to agreement on the meaning and function of "pity" and "admiration" (*Mitleid, Bewunderung*). The persistent counter-objections are symptomatic of the conceptual difference in their understanding of the affective nature of illusion.

At the very outset of the debate, Mendelssohn saw that it was necessary to establish the mediation of illusion. Within the experience of illusion, "terror" and "tears" were transformed into modes of pleasure that had nothing to do with Lessing's "sympathy." Thus in his letter of 23 November 1756 he countered Lessing's objections to Nicolai:

> It always seems to me as if any illusion of terror, even unassisted by sympathy, must be pleasurable. An example of this would be the painting of the snake mentioned by Aristotle, or, more appropriately, your own example of the appearance of a ghost upon the stage. The manner and means by which you seek to reduce this terror into a sympathy is all too highly contrived for it to be natural. We will want to discuss this matter more extensively, once we have organized our thoughts concerning the effects of theatrical illusion and concerning the conflict of illusion with the *cognitio clara*.[25]

---

23. Nicolai to Lessing, 31 August 1756, in Lessing, *Werke* IV, 155–59.
24. Nicolai to Lessing, 14 May 1757, in Lessing, *Werke* IV, 214–23.
25. Mendelssohn to Lessing, 23 November 1756, in Lessing, *Werke* IV, 169: "Es scheint mir immer, als wenn eine jede Illusion vom Schrecken, auch ohne Beyhülfe des Mitleidens, angenehm seyn müsse. Ein Beyspiel davon sey die vom Aristotles angeführte gemahlte Schlange, oder vielmehr die von Ihnen selbst angeführte Erscheinung eines Geistes auf der Schaubühne. Die Art und Weise, wie Sie dieses Schrecken auf ein Mitleiden reduciren wollen, ist allzu spitzfindig, als daß sie natürlich seyn könnte. Ueber alles dieses wollen wir uns weitläufiger heraus lassen, wenn wir erst unsere Gedanken von der Wirkung der theatralischen Illusion, und von dem Streite derselben mit der deutlichen Erkenntniß, in Ordnung gebracht haben."

Illusion as the arena of aesthetic experience was essential to Mendelssohn's argument, for he had to explain how and why the otherwise alert capacity of reason was not operative.

Mendelssohn's next letter to Lessing, dated early December, continues to object to Lessing's emphasis on sympathy. For Mendelssohn the act of "admiring" prompts the rational choice to emulate. Lessing, he objects, has reduced "admiring" to a dumfounded "marveling" (that is, Lessing has confounded *Bewunderung* with *Verwunderung*). Mendelssohn goes on to distinguish the higher and lower orders of knowing. In contrast to the rational mode of symbolic knowing, aesthetic experience involves only the sensual mode of intuitive knowing. Taste (*Geschmack*), therefore, may oppose reason and exercise an even greater influence over the will. Similar to the rhetorician in appealing to the passions (what Aristotle called the pathetic *pistis*), the playwright works upon this power over the will. In the theater, the rational mode is in abeyance:

> If the poet, *through the perfectly sensual appeal of his language,* can convince our intuitive understanding of the nobility or ignobility of his characters, then he has our applause. We enjoy obscuring the clear connections of reason, which would otherwise oppose our illusion, so that we might, by the means of illusion, transpose ourselves into another climate, other conditions, amidst other people, in order to feel with full emphasis the strength of the imitation.[26]

Mendelssohn's notion that "we enjoy obscuring the clear connections of reason," may have some remote kinship with Coleridge's "willing suspension of disbelief"; nevertheless, Mendelssohn can offer no concept approaching Coleridge's affirmation of intuitive reason operating through the imagination. For him, intuitive knowing is purely sensual; the reason is operative only *after* the aesthetic illusion subsides. Again promising to prepare with Nicolai a statement concerning theatrical illusion, he explains why the aesthetic experience cannot be immediately moral. Although "admira-

---

26. Mendelssohn to Lessing, early December 1756, in Lessing, *Werke* IV, 181: "Wenn der Dichter, *durch seine vollkommen sinnliche Rede,* unsre intuitive Erkenntniß von der Würde und Unwürde seiner Charaktere überzeugen kann, so hat er unsern Beyfall. Wir verdunkeln gern die deutlichen Vernunftschlüsse, die sich unsrer Illusion widersetzen; so wie wir uns vermittelst der Illusion in ein ander Klima, in andre Umstände, und unter andre Menschen versetzen, um die Stärke der Nachahmung recht nachdrücklich zu fühlen."

tion" may prompt the spectator to emulate the heroic virtue he witnesses on the stage, he can only so determine through reason. This "momentary wish" to emulate virtue does not disrupt the playwright's thrall over "the lower faculties of our soul" ("unsere untere Seelenkräfte"). Because it is only when the illusion is over that reason again assumes control, Mendelssohn must concur with Nicolai in removing the moral affect from the immediate ends of the drama. Reason and emotion, according to Mendelssohn's formula do not operate simultaneously, only consecutively. A direct influence is likely to occur only in a person who has no stock of clear rational knowledge and is thus compelled by the illusion. But this influence overrides all moral choice. Mendelssohn refers to an Englishman who claimed the influence of *Cato* as excuse for committing murder: "What Cato does and Addison approves cannot be wrong."

In his answer to Mendelssohn (18 December 1756), Lessing claims that illusion is no matter of special concern for the playwright. Lessing will later change his mind and discriminate generic differences in the nature of illusion and in the ways in which it may be propagated. For example, in his *Letters on Contemporary Literature* (*Briefe, die neueste Literatur betreffend*, 1759–65), no. 51 (16 August 1759), he distinguishes between the language of poetry and the language of drama. The noble and sublime expression of poetry is ill suited to the stage, for the illusion depends upon the apparent spontaneity of dialogue.

> In the drama especially, every character must have his own manner of thinking as well as his own manner of speaking. The noblest words are precisely for this reason, because they are the noblest, almost never the words which first occur to us in haste or in duress. They betray a previous deliberation, change heroes into declamators, and thereby disrupt the illusion.[27]

While the illusion in epic poetry may be heightened by exalted language, in tragedy the dramatic poet can sustain illusion only by using the most com-

---

27. *Briefe, die neueste Literatur betreffend* (1759–65), in Lessing, *Werke* V, 184: "In dem *Drama* besonders, wo jede Person, so wie ihre eigene Denkungsart, also auch ihre eigne Art zu sprechen haben muß. Die edelsten Worte sind eben deswegen, weil sie den edelsten sind, fast niemals zugleich diejenigen, die uns in der Geschwindigkeit, und besonders im Affekte, zu erst beifallen. Sie verraten die vorhergegangene Überlegung, verwandeln die Helden in Declamatores, und stören dadurch die Illusion."

monplace words to express his character's thoughts. In the *Correspondence concerning Tragedy*, however, Lessing asserts that illusion in the drama is the same as illusion in any other form of literature. Because the effects of illusion may be derived equally from reading, they obviously do not depend exclusively on theatrical performance. Even after Mendelssohn has sent his full deliberation on the nature of illusion, Lessing refuses to grant that, in order to explain "the pleasure in imitations of imperfection," it is necessary to presume "the pleasure in illusion."[28]

While Lessing apparently could not comprehend Mendelssohn's insistence on the mediation of aesthetic experience through illusion, Mendelssohn, for his part, could only conceive of "sympathy" as one among many passions represented upon the stage and capable of exciting response in the spectator ("ein nachgeahmtes Mitleiden"), or as that kind compassion which could shrivel to the meager condescension of "feeling sorry for" (*bemitleiden*).[29] Lessing, of course, meant by "sympathy" the emotional capacity of experiencing any passion felt by another. Lessing carefully repeats Mendelssohn's distinction between the clear knowledge of reason and the obscure knowledge of the senses; he then claims, however, that moral action is not, as Mendelssohn will have it, determined by reason, but rather by the intuitive act of sympathy. Reason and volition cannot produce sympathy, but the tragic poet can call it forth. Sympathy is the one emotional response necessary to the aesthetic experience of the drama.[30] Just as "illusion" is the mediating factor in Mendelssohn's theory, "sympathy" provides for Lessing the necessary mediation between spectator and dramatic performance. The failure to understand these basic differences is evident in Mendelssohn's lengthy letter (January 1757) with the accompanying essay "On the Control of the Desires" ("Von der Herrschaft über die Neigungen").

"You should not exclude any passion from the theater," Mendelssohn writes in response to Lessing's claim that "admiration" was more suitable to heroic poetry than to tragedy. "As soon as the imitated passion can visibly convince us of the excellence of the imitation, it has deserved to be performed upon the stage." The success of the aesthetic illusion is all the justification required for dramatic propriety. Nicolai had made a similar claim for emo-

---

28. Lessing to Mendelssohn, 18 December 1756 and 29 March 1757, in Lessing, *Werke* IV, 194–95 and 208.
29. Mendelssohn to Lessing, January 1757, in Lessing, *Werke* IV, 196, 198.
30. Lessing to Mendelssohn, 18 December 1756, in Lessing, *Werke* IV, 185–90. See Michelson, "Die Erregung des Mitleids durch die Tragödie."

tional excitement in general. Mendelssohn complements Nicolai's *Discourse* by explaining, in accord with Wolff, the relation of the emotions to the reason. The purpose of the long-promised essay is to reveal how "aesthetic illusion is actually capable of temporarily silencing the reason."[31]

Although only the concluding section of Mendelssohn's essay is specifically entitled "On Illusion" ("Von der Illusion"), the first three sections provide the carefully formulated reply to Lessing's contention that illusion is a general aesthetic phenomenon not peculiar to the theater, and that in the theater sympathy alone is the vehicle for emotional and moral response.[32] Mendelssohn seeks to explain why Lessing has failed to perceive the rational judgment involved and has concluded that sympathy is capable of eliciting moral action independent of reason. He begins by positing a motive for action ("Bewegungsgrund," §1) in that concept which provides us with an impression of beauty or perfection: its presence provokes pleasure, its absence desire.[33] The greater the good in the impression, the stronger the longing in its absence. Mendelssohn describes a scale of measurement, from indifference to ardent desire, and a formula for the quantity of motivation as equal to the perfection of the impression, multiplied by the clarity of the perception, and divided by the time required to elicit the response. The point of this little exercise in the algebra of aesthetics (§2) is to emphasize the variable clarity and force of ideas (§§3–5) afforded, in accordance with the Leibniz–Wolff system, by the *cognitio symbolica* and *cognitio intuitiva*, the *cognitio distincta* and *cognitio obscura*. It is not that reason is excluded from certain motivating impressions, rather that, proportionate to clarity or quantity (§6), the time may be so reduced as to seem almost spontaneous. Habit ("Von der Gewohnheit," §7) may further increase the rapidity of response. Here Mendelssohn converts to the Leibniz–Wolff system Lessing's assertion that the purpose of tragedy is to exercise sympathy and to strengthen

---

31. Mendelssohn to Lessing, January 1757, in Lessing, *Werke* IV, 196: "Ästhetische Illusion ist wirklich im Stande, die obern Seelenkräfte auf eine Zeitland zum Schweigen zu bringen," IV, 198.

32. Mendelssohn's "Beykommende Blätter" are excluded from *Briefwechsel über das Trauerspiel*, in Lessing, *Werke* IV, 153–227, and only the section "Von der Illusion" is included in the notes, IV, 835–36. In his discussion of "Das Postulat der Illusion," Alois Wierlacher ignores the concern with illusion in Lessing's letters of 2 February 1757 and 29 March 1757 as well as Mendelssohn's "Beykommende Blätter"; he thus falsely declares that illusion is mentioned only by Mendelssohn, only in his letter of December 1756, and even then "ohne Nennenwertes auszuführen," *Das Bürgerliche Drama. Seine theoretische Begründung im 18. Jahrhundert*, 111.

33. Mendelssohn, "Beykommende Blätter" (= Von der Herrschaft über die Neigungen), in Lessing et al., *Briefwechsel über das Trauerspiel*, ed. Schulte-Sasse, 94–100.

the capacity of sympathy.[34] By exercising certain perceptual responses, Mendelssohn asserts, we can indeed educate any capacity of the mind to a degree of competency. In thus becoming accustomed to certain connections and judgments, we learn to make them so quickly that they seem intuitive and spontaneous.

In the third section of his essay ("Von der anschauenden Erkenntniß," §§8–10), Mendelssohn attempts to reconcile his position with Lessing's, not by granting that moral action can result immediately and directly through the excitement of the emotions (including sympathy), but by claiming that through habit and custom the judgment exercised by the higher faculty of symbolic cognition can be naturalized in the lower faculties as an acquired response of the intuitive or sensual modes of knowing. Thus transferred from the reason to the senses, the response is not only more rapid but more powerful, for it acts not through the judgment but directly on the will.[35] Moral sensibility is the result of cognitive authority delegated to the senses; it does, indeed, seem spontaneous and intuitive, because it receives rapid impressions of the true or apparent (aesthetic) good that may be encountered in an object. Discerning moral sensibility in the sympathetic response, Lessing mistakenly considered it a source of moral action. But moral sensibility provides no ground for moral action. It remains indifferent to the inclinations of virtue and vice because it operates independent of judgment. Without exercising rational judgment, an individual cannot act morally (the good that he might do is merely accidental, not moral).[36]

With this introduction to the problem, Mendelssohn then sets forth his theory of illusion ("Von der Illusion," §§11–14). With Lessing he agrees that illusion is an effect proper to all the imitative arts: The imitation is supposed to have enough in common with the original that our senses can persuade us, at least momentarily, that we behold the original itself. Thus aesthetic illusion arises from a deception of senses. Rhetoric, specifically the pathetic *pistis*, is the poet's means of deceiving the senses. The poet must address the senses through language; every speech, therefore, must involve

---

34. Lessing to Mendelssohn, 18 December 1756, in Lessing, *Werke* IV, 189–90.
35. Mendelssohn, "Beykommende Blätter," 97: "Wenn wir die symbolische Schlüsse der practischen Sittenlehre in eine anschauende Erkenntniß verwandeln, das heißt, wenn wäre sie von den abstracten Begriffen auf einzelne Begebenheiten in der Natur zurück führen, und die Anwendung derselben aufmerksam beobachten; so erlangen sie dadurch eine größere Gewalt, in den Willen zu wirken."
36. Lessing to Mendelssohn, 18 December 1756, in Lessing, *Werke* IV, 188–89, acknowledges "accidental" moral action.

us in aesthetic illusion (§11).[37] Aesthetic illusion requires the response of both the higher and lower faculties, sequentially, however, rather than simultaneously (§12). The response of the *cognitio intuitiva*, which occurs spontaneously, convinces us that "the representation is like the original" and we are thus involved in the illusion. The imposition of the *cognitio symbolica*, which may occur somewhat later, brings the contrary conviction that "the representation is not the original itself" and the illusion is thus disrupted.

Later, in his *Rhapsodie* (1771), Mendelssohn will grant the persistence, even in the midst of illusion, of "a secret consciousness that we have an imitation, and not the truth, before our eyes."[38] Conscious awareness, even in Mendelssohn's subsequent modification of his theory, must remain a latent factor, for rational judgment cannot intrude without disrupting the illusion. He must therefore separate aesthetic experience from aesthetic evaluation. The latter judges neither the intensity of the illusion nor the degree of pleasure it has afforded; rather, judgment attends to the skill of the artist ("Geschicklichkeit des Künstlers) required to produce a successful imitation (§13). Supporting Nicolai's objections to the obtrusive artificiality of stage decor, Mendelssohn considers stage decoration inessential to dramatic illusion and disruptive should the settings call attention to themselves, whether as especially beautiful or as obviously contradicting the illusion. Because the source of dramatic illusion is in the suasive rhetoric of the play, we need not see a performance to experience the illusion.

Negative emotions (anger, pain, sorrow, terror), Nicolai had asserted, produce pleasure because the body reacts only indirectly to the causes. With the positive emotions (love, laughter, happiness, delight), it is difficult to distinguish our response from the cause. Clearly in contrast to the pleasure with which, by means of dramatic illusion, we experience them, the negative emotions "convince us intuitively of the worth of the imitation" (§14). Again (as in §12), Mendelssohn describes a sequential response: the immediate sensory reaction is followed by the deliberated rational judgment. The actor makes us angry, sad, desperate, then we recall that "these affects are only imitated." Pleasure then leads to an appreciation of the illusion *as* illusion, that is, to our full recognition of the imitation that produced it.

Lessing, in his reply (2 February 1757), praises Mendelssohn's account of

---

37. Mendelssohn, "Beykommende Blätter," 99: "Der Dichter muß vollkommen sinnlich reden; daher müssen uns alle seine Reden ästhetisch illudieren."

38. Mendelssohn, "Rhapsodie, oder Zusätze zu den Briefen über die Empfindungen" (1761), in *Gesammelte Schriften*, ed. Elbogen et al., I, 381–424, 390.

the *cognitio intuitiva* and the principles of response, but he rejects the explanation of illusion as essentially superfluous to the aesthetic experience. Neither the response of the passions nor the evaluation of the judgment, as Mendelssohn has traced the dual causality, seem to require the mediation of illusion. Mendelssohn answers that, with Du Bos, he is merely trying to explain the pleasure in imitation (2 March 1757). Yes, complains Lessing, but the explanation is "at odds with your doctrine of illusion"; "if from these mere principles we may explain our pleasure in imitations of imperfections, then I cannot see why one must also call upon the pleasure of illusion."[39]

Lessing also answers Mendelssohn's algebraic formula by supplying his own mathematical ratios of illusion, reality, and emotional response (IV, 202–3). Unlike Mendelssohn's equations of intensity, Lessing's ratios indicate the diminishing affect when primary emotional response is translated into secondary aesthetic pleasure. If our initial fright at a "painted snake" is 10, then our pleasure upon discovering that it is only an image can be no more than 1. Appreciation of art is reduced to the judgment of pale shadows. Indeed, the process of discovery involves not only a diminution but perhaps even disappointment. Suppose, Lessing argues, I see in the distance a beautiful woman who seems secretly beckoning to me; I approach and discover that it is only a painting or a statue. The resulting disparity leaves no pleasure at all in art's deceit, only the sad memory of the initial anticipation.

As a preferable account of the aesthetic experience, Lessing once again puts forward his doctrine of sympathy. He uses the example of "sympathetic vibrations."[40] When two violins are placed next to each other and the *A* string of the one is struck, then the *A* string of the other will also vibrate. To extend the analogy to emotional response, Lessing grants the strings feelings and supposes that the vibrating is pleasing, yet being struck may be disagreeable. The first string, thus, may suffer, while the second string, vibrating sympathetically without having been directly touched, has only the pleasure of the response. This is the aesthetic experience, he tells Mendelssohn, that he has maintained since his first letters. The only affect

---

39. Lessing to Mendelssohn, 2 February and 29 March 1757, in Lessing, *Werke* IV, 202, 208: "Wozu brauchen wir nun hier die Illusion?" "Denn, wenn aus diesem bloßen Grundsatze das Vergnügen an nachgeahmten Unvollkommenheiten zu erklären ist, so sehe ich nicht, warum man das Vergnügen der Illusion erst zu Hülfe rufen müsse."

40. Bodmer, *Critische Briefe* 19, repeats the example of "sympathetic vibration" from Calepio, *Paragon della Poesia tragica d'Italia con quella di Francia* (1732).

crucial in tragedy is the sympathetic response—the experience of the affect *as* affect. All other responses, which require us to think of some object or to focus our attention on the affects experienced by others, are secondary and thus scarcely deserve the name.[41]

The *Correspondence concerning Tragedy* came to an impasse. Nicolai developed his conception of tragedy out of Du Bos's pleasure principle. Mendelssohn appropriated Du Bos to an aesthetic built upon the Leibniz–Wolff epistemology of sensual excitation and rational cognition. With Nicolai, he denied immediate moral effects. Lessing, however, turned to Shaftesbury and Hutcheson for the moral ground in instinctive sympathetic reactions. Mendelssohn appealed to illusion as the means by which tragedy could provoke emotional response in spite of rational awareness of the artificiality of theatrical representation. Through the power of illusion, he had to suppose, reason was temporarily displaced by emotional response. Then, to posit an evaluation of art, he had to set both illusion and emotion aside and take his criteria exclusively from the "imitation." The concern with illusion, Lessing objected, turns out to be irrelevant to the appraisal of the drama. While Mendelssohn attempted to avoid this seeming irrelevancy in subsequent revisions of his theory of illusion, Lessing, for his part, recognized the inadequacy of his exclusive reliance on sympathy and dismissal of illusion. He had not yet accounted for the mediation and modulation of emotional response: How were the sympathetic "vibrations" set in motion and what contributed to their variations in pitch and intensity?

Following *Correspondence concerning Tragedy*, Lessing began using the concept of illusion to discriminate possibilities and limitations among the various literary genre. We have already seen evidence of this in *Letters on Contemporary Literature*, no. 51 (16 August 1759). He also relies on the concept of illusion to explain our acceptance of talking animals in fables. In the commentary that accompanies his three-volume edition of *Fables* (1759), he argues that the fable is neither allegorical nor marvelous. It is essentially realistic and moralistic; its realism distinguishes it from such kindred moral narratives as the exemplum and the parable. The realism of the fable derives from coherent and readily identifiable characterization. The characters are not presented as mere types, but as individuals, and the action in which they are involved is narrated as having actually occurred. The fabulist, in the tradition of Aesop, relies on animal characters because certain traits and relationships (the wolf

---

41. Lessing to Mendelssohn, 2 February 1757, in Lessing, *Werke* IV, 203–4.

and the lamb, for instance) are commonplace and quickly discerned. As fictional characters, they also become familiarly human.

> Once we have granted them freedom and speech, we must also grant them at the same time all modifications of will and all intelligence which are consistent with these attributes, and upon which rests our sole and only advantage over them. Their individual character, as already stated, we must find consistent throughout the fable; and if we find it, then the illusion ensues that they really are animals, even though we hear them speak, and even though they are capable of such fine remarks and clever resolutions.[42]

We are not caught in dual perception in which the impossibility of talking animals militates against the fictive illusion. We accept the fiction on its own grounds, and we sustain the illusion so long as the characterization is consistent and coherent. As we shall see in his *Hamburgische Dramaturgie*, Lessing will argue in very similar terms to support his contention that such trespasses against enlightened reason as historical anachronism or supernaturalism need not be banished from the stage. No less than the talking animal in the fable, the ghost becomes perfectly acceptable upon the stage if the poet has properly prepared character and situation.

In the *Hamburgische Dramaturgie*, Lessing continues to affirm the principle of sympathy, but he describes sympathy as conveyed through the power of illusion wrought by the physical presence of the actor and the dramatic skill of the playwright. His first entry (1 May 1767) includes his declaration that, in order to evoke sympathy, the passions must be presented with the force and constancy of illusion. The passions must be visibly conjured "and allowed to grow, without a break, in such an illusory constancy, that the spectator must sympathize, whether he wants to or not." In no. 4 (12 May 1767) he describes how the language of gesture contributes to illusion. Because gesture attends and enhances our normal discourse in ways that we seldom consciously perceive, the actor or actress who masters the silent

---

42. "Abhandlungen über die Fabeln," in Lessing, *Werke* V, 403: "Haben wir ihnen einmal Freiheit und Sprache zugestanden, so müssen wir ihnen zugleich alle Modifikationen des Willens und alle Erkenntnisse zugestehen, die aus jenen Eigenschaften folgen können, auf welchen unser Vorzug vor ihnen einzig und allein beruhet. Nur ihren Charackter, wie gesagt, müssen wir durch die ganze Fabel finden; und finden wir diesen, so erfolgt die Illusion, daß es wirkliche Tiere sind, ob wir sie gleich reden hören, und ob sie gleich noch so feine Anmerkungen, noch so scharfsinnige Schlüsse machen."

communication of body movement is capable of lending an illusion of truth to the performance that is irresistible.[43] We respond to the body language without consciously recognizing and "translating" its meaning. Thus it persuades and convinces without our realizing the nature of the argument which it has forwarded and to which we have acquiesced. Fostered through physical presence and communicated through thoroughly habituated forms of social discourse, the illusion easily escapes detection as illusion.

In no. 11 (5 June 1767), Lessing raises the issue of illusion in connection with the supernatural. What is the place of the supernatural on the stage in an enlightened age? One might well assume, Lessing suggests, that the attempt to introduce a ghostly apparition would disrupt dramatic illusion by contradicting our rational convictions:

> Historic truth is not the end of the drama, but only a means to the end, which is to create illusion and through illusion to move us. If it is true that we no longer believe in ghosts; if this disbelief must necessarily hinder the illusion; if without illusion we cannot possibly sympathize with the action: then the playwright must obviously oppose his own purpose, should he nevertheless proceed to represent such an unbelievable tale; all his art would be in vain.[44]

Although such an argument would seem logical, Lessing maintains that our rational convictions have little to do with our theatrical experience. Fifty years later, in the *Biographia Literaria*, Coleridge proposes "a willing suspension of disbelief" as a way to attain a "poetic faith" in the literary use of the supernatu-

---

43. Lessing, *Hamburgische Dramaturgie* (= *HD*), no. 1 (1 May 1767): ". . . die Leidenschaften, nicht beschreiben, sondern vor den Augen des Zuschauers entstehen, und ohne Sprung, in einer so illusorischen Stetigkeit wachsen zu lassen, daß dieser sympathisieren muß, er mag wollen oder nicht: das ist es, was dazu nötig ist"; no. 4 (12 May 1767), in *Werke* IV, 248–53. The physical presence of the actor, the art of creating illusion through body movement, the resulting "subliminal" influence on the spectator, are topics of repeated concern in Lessing's deliberations on the drama; see "Beiträge zur Historie und Aufnahme des Theaters," no. 4, in *Werke* III, 355–510; "Abhandlungen von den weinerlichen oder rührenden Lustspiele," *Theatralische Bibliothek*, no. 1, in *Werke* IV, 12–58; "Der Schauspieler" ["Grundsätze der ganzen körperlichen Beredsamkeit"], in *Werke* IV, 723–33, 912; and *Literaturbriefe* V, Letter 81 (7 February 1760), in *Werke* V, 260–62.

44. *HD*, no. 11 (5 June 1767), in *Werke* IV, 282: "Die historische Wahrheit ist nicht sein Zweck, sondern nur das Mittel zu seinem Zwecke; er will uns täuschen, und durch die Täuschung rühren. Wenn es also wahr ist, daß wir itzt keine Gespenster mehr glauben; wenn dieses Nichtglauben die Täuschung notwendig verhindern müßte; wenn ohne Täuschung wir unmöglich sympathisieren können: so handelt jetzt der dramatische Dichter wider sich selbst, wenn er uns dem ohngeachtet solche unglaubliche Märchen ausstaffieret; alle Kunst, die er dabei anwendet, ist verloren."

ral. For Lessing, however, the supernatural may be introduced on the stage without any aesthetic conciliation or compromise of reason or will. The spectator neither deliberates nor chooses; the illusion is conjured through the dramatic art. Lessing, altering his earlier position, now endorses the mediation of sympathy through illusion; furthermore, he makes illusion—not imitation, as Mendelssohn had asserted—the ground for evaluation. The irresistible power of the illusion is the proof of the playwright's mastery of his art.

> But this sense of not believing in ghosts cannot and should not deter the playwright from making use of them. The seed of belief in the supernatural lies in us all, and most abundantly in those of us for whom he writes. It depends only upon his art whether these seeds can be made to grow; only upon a certain manipulation of circumstances to provide the grounds for the reality and to bring it rapidly into motion. If he has these in his power, no matter what we believe in our private lives, in the theater we must believe what *he* wants.[45]

Shakespeare is the master of his art in *Hamlet*, for the audience is fully caught up in the illusion of the encounter with the ghost. Voltaire, by contrast, makes us witness in *Eriphyle* not a ghost but the feeble deceit of "a cold playwright, who sought to frighten us with his illusion without knowing how to accomplish his purpose."

When he distinguishes between drama and fable, Lessing gives the advantage to drama. Narrative may borrow effectively from the drama the techniques of character interaction that allow for visual evocation of illusion; drama, however, must avoid the intent of the fable to deliver a moral exemplum.[46] Citing Favart's *Soliman II*, a play adapted from a tale by Marmontel, Lessing builds his case for the playwright's need to put aside all moral didacticism and turn his attention exclusively to engendering the illusion necessary to mediate a sympathetic response. Precisely because the

---

45. Ibid., 283: "Aber in diesem Verstande keine Gespenster glauben, kann und darf den dramatischen Dichter im geringsten nicht abhalten, Gebrauch davon zu machen. Der Same, sie zu glauben, liegt in uns allen, und in denen am häufigsten, für die er vornehmlich dichtet. Es kommt nur auf seine Kunst an, diesen Samen zum Käumen zu bringen; nur auf gewisse Handgriffe, den Gründen für ihre Wirklichkeit in der Geschwindigkeit den Schwung zu geben. Hat er diese in seiner Gewalt, so mögen wir in gemeinen Leben glauben, was wir wollen; im Theater müssen wir glauben, was *er* will." See Robertson, *Lessing's Dramatic Theory;* Daemmrich, "Illusion, Möglichkeit und Grenzen eines Begriffs."

46. Lessing, "Von dem Wesen der Fabel," in *Werke* V, 355–57.

illusion conjured by drama is more powerful, the audience is more attentive. For this reason, character and action in the drama must be more carefully developed than in a narrative tale.

> Since the illusion of the drama is much stronger than that of a mere tale, so the characters in a drama interest us far more than in a tale. We are not satisfied in seeing their fate resolved merely in terms of the immediate circumstances; rather, we want to know that an enduring resolution has been achieved.[47]

In a tale we are satisfied when moral purpose is served by the events of the moment. The illusion conjured through the drama, however, makes us witness a sequence of causes and effects. Our curiosity is aroused and we anticipate what is yet to come. It is not enough, therefore, to satisfy poetic justice yet leave the audience with loose ends. The resolution can be no makeshift circumstance: it must complete past action and leave the audience with the confidence that they know what may follow in the illusory dramatic world, beyond the play's end, after the curtain falls.

Voltaire failed in *Eriphyle* to sustain illusion because of inadequate dramatic preparation for the supernatural moment. The failure of dramatic illusion in Maffei's *Merope* Lessing attributes to the playwright's mistake in calling attention to the stage:

> The tragic poet should avoid everything which might remind the audience of the illusion, for as soon as the audience is reminded of the illusion, the illusion vanishes. Here (in *Merope*) it may seem as if Maffei wanted rather to strengthen the illusion by expressly suggesting that the theater is outside of the theater; nevertheless, the very mention of the stage and writing a play ("Con cosi strani avvenimenti uom forse / Non vide mai favoleggiar le scene"), undermines the illusion and confronts us with the very facts which should be concealed from us.[48]

---

47. *HD*, no. 35 (28 August 1767), *Werke* IV, 395: "Denn da die Illusion des Drama weit stärker ist, als einer bloßen Erzählung, so interessieren uns auch die Personen in jenem weit mehr, als in dieser, und wir begnügen uns nicht, ihr Schicksal bloß für den gegenwärtigen Augenblick entscheiden zu sehen, sondern wir wollen uns auf immer desfalls zufrieden gestellt wissen."

48. Ibid., no. 42 (22 September 1767), *Werke* IV, 427: "Der tragische Dichter sollte alles vermeiden, was die Zuschauer an ihre Illusion erinnern kann; denn sobald sie daran erinnert sind,

Schlegel and Coleridge both, as we shall see in the ensuing chapters, were to claim that Shakespeare heightened aesthetic illusion by calling attention to the play as play. This passage reveals that Lessing still held to the rationalist notion that illusion worked through the lower faculties and the higher faculties must be held in abeyance and not "reminded" of the illusory nature of the experience. In spite of Benjamin Bennett's argument to the contrary, Lessing did not endorse revelations of theatricality.[49] He did sanction self-reflexive allusions to the stage in comedy:

> It may more easily be granted to the comic poet to play in this manner and set representation against representation. To excite our laughter, the playwright does not need the same degree of illusion which he requires in order to arouse our sympathy.[50]

But Lessing makes it clear that he considers any reference to theatricality and the illusion-making process destructive of the aesthetic experience of illusion. The freedom may be given to comedy only because complete illusion is not required.

A certain freedom in plot development is necessary in tragedy as well as in comedy. Quoting from his own translation of Diderot, Lessing in no. 48 (13 October 1767) takes the side of Diderot in arguing that the spectator must be actively engaged in anticipating plot.[51] Surprise works upon the passive imagination; anticipation requires an active imagination. The effect of surprise is momentary; anticipation endures and may be incrementally height-

---

so ist sie weg. Hier scheinet es zwar, als ob Maffei die Illusion eher noch bestärken wollen, indem er das Theater ausdrücklich außer dem Theater annehmen läßt; doch die bloßen Worte, Bühne und erdichten, sind der Sache schon nachteilig, und bringen uns geraden Weges dahin, wovon sie uns abbringen sollen."

49. Bennett, *Modern Drama and German Classicism*, 58, 60–61, 65–72, 87–89. Haßelbeck, *Illusion und Fiktion. Lessings Beitrag zur poetologischen Diskussion über das Verhältnis von Kunst und Wirklichkeit*, 97–149, presents a more carefully documented case for Lessing's position on aesthetic illusion; the passages he cites, however, do not support the conclusion that for Lessing aesthetic illusion coexists with a rational awareness of its illusory quality. Schenkel, *Lessings Poetik des Mitleids*, finds self-reflexive play, inversion and negation of illusion in Lessing's dramatic exposition of sympathy; he compares Lessing's *Miss Sara Sampson* to Pirandello's *Sei personaggi in cerca d'autore*, Brecht's *Der kaukasische Kreidekreis*, and Handke's *Publikumsbeschimpfung*.

50. *HD*, no. 42 (22 September 1767), in *Werke* IV, 428: "Dem komischen Dichter ist es eher erlaubt, auf diese Weise seiner Vorstellung Vorstellungen entgegen zu setzen; denn unser Lachen zu erregen, braucht es des Grades der Täuschung nicht, den unser Mitleiden erfordert."

51. Ibid., no. 48 (13 October 1767), in *Werke* IV, 452–56. Lessing refers to the critique Diderot added to *Le Père de famille*.

ened. At odds with the prevailing notion of the passive reception of aesthetic experience through the senses, Lessing calls for an act of aesthetic complementation in which the spectator struggles against uncertainty and strives to know more than the characters about the course of events.

The performance of *Der Hausvater,* Lessing's translation of Diderot's *Le Père de famille* (1760), gave occasion for repeating Diderot's discussion of dramatic illusion in *Les Bijoux indiscrets* (1748). Mirzoza, the favorite of the Sultan's harem, delivers "an excellent academic lecture" on the drama in which she maintains that not the slightest detail should occur that might disturb the illusion. In its perfection, the dramatic *mimesis* should make the spectator think himself a witness to the events.[52] Selim, the Sultan's courtier, objects that illusion is never perfect; while the dialogue may succeed in sustaining illusion, every episodic shift in setting takes us out of the illusion. To Selim's claim that modern writers of tragedy understand this perfectly well, Mirzoza replies that their understanding has taken them "thousands and thousands of miles from nature":

> In vain the playwright seeks to conceal himself; he cannot hide from my perception. I see him constantly behind his characters. Cinna, Sertorius, Maximus, Aemilia, are in every moment the mouthpieces of Corneille.[53]

To demonstrate her point, Mirzoza posits an imaginary spectator who knows nothing of the theater and who is told that when the curtain rises he will witness events actually taking place in court. In spite of ideal conditions for illusion, even the uninitiated spectator will quickly see the counterfeit. Unsettled by Mirzoza's argument, Selim concedes the point but raises a final question. When we, in contrast to the uninitiated spectator, go into theater, do not we go "with the conviction that we will experience the imitation of an action, but not the action itself"? Mirzoza does not surrender the expectation of illusion. In her example, after all, it is the unnatural gesture and declamation of the actors that betray the counterfeit and inhibit the illusion. The conviction that the drama is but an imitation should not prevent "pre-

---

52. Ibid., no. 84 (19 February 1768), in *Werke* IV, 623.
53. Ibid., no. 85 (23 February 1768), in *Werke* IV, 624: "Umsonst sucht sich der Verfasser zu verstecken; er entgeht meinen Augen nicht, und ich erblicke ihn unaufhörlich hinter seinen Personen. Cinna, Sertorius, Maximus, Aemilia sind alle Augenblicke des Sprachrohr des Corneille."

senting the action in the most natural manner."⁵⁴ Whatever convictions the spectator may have upon entering the theater, successful imitation is still capable of exciting illusion.

Lessing continues in nos. 86–88 his exposition of Diderot, and in nos. 89–95, he contrasts Diderot's position with Aristotle's. Although he has turned to Diderot's *Le Fils naturel* (1758), Lessing does not pursue the problem of illusion, which, as we saw in the last chapter, provides the crux of the play as well as the major topic in the appended dialogue between the author and his character. Lessing addresses, instead, Diderot's account of character in tragedy and comedy. To be sure, Lessing certainly knew Diderot's account of the paradoxical nature of illusion. He had, after all, translated it into German.⁵⁵ A fictional character, according to this account, "bears the sign of its fictionality upon its brow, and we accept the illusion only upon the stage." However, this is not the problem of character and characterization that Lessing develops in the *Hamburgische Dramaturgie*. It may well be, as Otto Haßelbeck has argued, that Lessing recognized in Diderot's theory of the drama "an uncompromised consciousness of the fictionality of representation in the experience of dramatic illusion," but it does not follow that Lessing assumed the same position in his own theory.⁵⁶ Indeed, because the evidence is not to be found in the *Hamburgische Dramaturgie,* Haßelbeck can support his argument only in quoting from Lessing's translation of Diderot.

As Lessing has observed in no. 42, a greater degree of freedom is generally allowed the playwright in comedy, because the effect is not destroyed by lapses in illusion. When it comes to adapting historical manners and customs, a comedy need not adhere to historical fidelity. Indeed, a certain freedom with historical models is necessary to the wit and satirical attributes of comedy. If it is crucial that the spectators recognize and respond to social conventions, then the playwright must rely on those familiar to his immediate audience.

> The advantage which native customs contribute to the comedy derives from the intimate familiarity we have with them. The play-

---

54. Ibid., 626.
55. Lessing's translation, *Theater des Herrn Diderot* (1760), contains *Le Fils naturel* and *Le Père de famille,* as well as the appended discourses; in Lessing, *Werke,* ed. Petersen and Olshausen XI. See Mortier, *Diderot en Allemagne 1750–1850.*
56. Haßelbeck, 107.

wright need not first make us acquainted with them; he is thus relieved of all obligations to describe and signal their meaning; he can let his characters act according to manners and customs, without first having tediously to demonstrate their implications. The reliance on local customs therefore makes his task easier and also expedites illusion among the audience.[57]

Here, disagreeing with other critics, who insisted upon fidelity to classical sources, Lessing was prepared to grant the same freedom to tragedy as to comedy. Historical accuracy is more apt to strain the illusion than adherence to familiar, but perhaps anachronistic, manners and mores.

Why should the tragic poet surrender his claim to this effective double advantage? He too has reason to make the effort as easy as possible, and not waste his energies on secondary matters, but save them exclusively for the main purpose. For him, too, everything depends upon the illusion of the audience.—Perhaps one will answer here that tragedy has no great need for manners, that tragedy might completely dispense with them. But at the same time tragedy has no need of foreign manners; and of that little which a tragedy must have and show of manners, it will always be better if they are adapted from customs familiar to the audience, rather than from those which are remote and foreign.[58]

In contrast to his position in the *Correspondence concerning Tragedy*, where he argued exclusively in terms of sympathy and did not consider illusion necessary to his account of aesthetic experience, in his *Hamburgische*

---

57. *HD*, no. 97 (5 April 1768), in *Werke* IV, 676: "Der Vorteil, den die einheimischen Sitten in der Komödie haben, beruhet auf der innigen Bekanntschaft, in der wir mit ihnen stehen. Der Dichter braucht sie uns nicht erst bekannt zu machen; er ist aller hierzu nötigen Beschreibungen und Winke überhoben; er kann seine Personen sogleich nach ihren Sitten handeln lassen, ohne uns diese Sitten selbst erst langweilig zu schildern. Einheimische Sitten also erleichtern ihm die Arbeit, und befördern bei dem Zuschauer die Illusion."

58. Ibid.: "Warum sollte nun der tragische Dichter sich dieses wichtigen doppelten Vorteils begeben? Auch er hat Ursache, sich die Arbeit so viel als möglich zu erleichtern, seine Kräfte nicht an Nebenzwecke zu verschwenden, sondern sie ganz für den Hauptzweck zu sparen. Auch im kömmt auf die Illusion des Zuschauers alles an.—Man wird vielleicht hierauf antworten, daß die Tragödie der Sitten nicht groß bedürfe, daß sie ihrer ganz und gar entübriget sein könne. Aber sonach braucht sie auch keine fremde Sitten; und von dem Wenigen, was sie von Sitten haben und zeigen will, wird es immer besser sein, wenn es von einheimischen Sitten hergenommen ist, als von fremden."

Dramaturgie Lessing gives dramatic illusion primacy. Sympathy can be mediated and modulated only through illusion. Because illusion thus is crucial to dramatic effect, Lessing considers it more important than historical accuracy. As for rational conviction, Lessing's justification of the supernatural demonstrates his confidence that the emotional power of illusion overrides reason. Precisely because illusion operates through perception and feeling, however, Lessing objects to references to the stage and acting. If aroused from its passive acquiescence by the reminder of theatricality, the reason will destroy the illusory spell. While the reason must remain passive, the aesthetic engagement must be active, for the spectator should constantly add to the details supplied through the performance. Through the parts he endeavors to perceive the whole. The means for conjuring illusion do not belong exclusively to the poet's skill in developing plot and character through dialogue; a crucial factor in supporting the efficacy of dialogue is the silent but persuasive eloquence of body language (*körperliche Beredsamkeit*). The poet provides the materials; the actor performs the illusion.

In *Laokoön, or On the Boundaries of Painting and Poetry* (*Laokoon oder über die Grenzen der Malerei und Poesie*, 1766), written in Berlin before his move to Hamburg to oversee the new National Theater, Lessing had already come to terms with the province and boundaries of aesthetic illusion. Here he revised the position that he had assumed in the correspondence with Nicolai and Mendelssohn, but at the same time reinforced his argument on sympathy. Because his subsequent comments on theatrical illusion follow from the premises of his *Laokoon*, they have broad, significant implication, not just for his explanation of aesthetic experience, but also for his stand in relation to Mendelssohn and other critics of the late Enlightenment.

The key word in the title is *Boundaries*, for Lessing is concerned with clarifying distinctions that seemed to have blurred in contemporary aesthetics. "Painting and poetry," he begins, "both place before us absent things as present, the appearance as reality; both create illusion, and the illusion of both pleases."[59] Lessing attempts to delineate the boundaries that circumscribe painting and poetry by examining how each creates illusion. While the two are similar in their effects, they differ radically in their processes of artistic *mimesis*. They not only select different objects for representation, they also represent them differently. A painting offers visual space to the

---

59. Lessing, *Laokoon*, in *Werke* VI, 9: "Malerei und Poesie . . . stellen uns abwesende Dinge als Gegenwärtig, den Schein als Wirklichkeit vor; beide täuschen, und beider Täuschung gefällt."

104   Illusion and the Drama

beholder, who must then through his imagination lend temporality and movement to that space. A poetic narrative describes movement and action in the temporal medium of language, and the auditor must then use his imagination to visualize spatially what is narrated in temporal sequence.[60]

Both modes of artistic expression, therefore, must allow "free play" to the imagination. Illusion is not simply an engagement of what the artist has given, it is also an act of aesthetic complementation—the imagination engenders what has not been given. Lessing observes the differences in representing Laokoön's tragic plight in poetic narrative and in statue. Although it is time-bound, constrained to unchanging duration, the statue must allow us to imagine mobility and change. To accomplish this illusion of temporality, the artist must not give us the action at its height. If the sculptor had represented Laokoön in the extremity of his agony, the imagination would have been deprived of its free play. Laokoön's expression is not distorted with the horrible scream of utmost pain; rather, the mouth is open in a futile sigh amidst unrelenting struggle. Only the imagination can hear the scream which is yet to come.[61]

The narrative poet is not bound by time. With the temporal sweep of his epic verse, Vergil describes the rising agony and the tragic end. But his language can only hint at spatial attributes. If he describes Laokoön in his priestly robes, then the imagination must see through the garments to behold the swelling and straining muscles: "For the poet a robe is no robe; it covers nothing; our imagination sees through it." The poet can describe the serpent writhing around head and neck and torso; the imagination still sees Laokoön's mighty struggle. The sculptor, of course, must leave the body bare so that the imagination is capable of lending movement to the tensed muscles; too, the upper body must be left free so that the imagination sees active struggle rather than stifled entrapment.[62]

It should be noticed, here, that Lessing is using the word "freedom" in two different contexts: "freedom" in representation and "freedom" in response. Because the sculptor has represented spatially the "free" torso of Laokoön, the spectator has the freedom to imagine temporal movement. The reverse situation occurs in poetry. Because the artist is confined to a single moment, he must make this moment "as pregnant as possible, and

---

60. Ibid., 116–17: "Die Zeitfolge ist das Gebiete des Dichters, so wie der Raum das Gebiete des Malers."
61. Ibid., 26.
62. Ibid., 46–50.

develop it with all the illusion through which art, in representing visible objects, has the advantage over poetry." The poet, for his part, must emphasize those capacities of illusion which belong to poetry but not to painting: "The freedom to elaborate the single moment of the work of art in that which has past as well as that which is yet to come."[63]

Unlike the narrative poet, the dramatic poet must observe temporal as well as spatial boundaries. His medium has the advantages but also the limits of both verbal and visual representation. Because the actor works in and through visual space, he must, like the Laokoön statue, allow to his audience the freedom to imagine more than what is performed. If he reveals his agony or anguish, the audience must feel that a deeper pain still remains suppressed. As in the *Correspondence concerning Tragedy*, Lessing steadfastly holds to the principle of sympathy as the *sine qua non* of tragedy, but he also argues that the very nature of sympathetic response requires that the emotions expressed on the stage be authentic. He defends Sophocles' portrayal of the screaming Philocrates against the pedantic principle that the emotions must be tempered. If they become too vehement, others had argued, the spectator will notice the counterfeit and the illusion will be broken. Lessing, however, objects to concealing pain; stoicism is cold and untheatrical.[64] The sympathetic response to pain is dramatically effective. What is crucial is the character's struggle with his feelings.

Emotional struggle is a complex matter. Lessing disagrees with Adam Smith's simplistic example of sympathetic response: "If we see someone about to be struck on the arm or the shins, we naturally shrink back, and draw in our own arm or leg." Because it is impossible to trace the intricate weave of causes and effects that make up our feelings, Lessing rejects the account of sympathy as a stimulus-response mechanism.[65] We may wince at

---

63. Ibid., 124–25: "Der Künstler . . . kann sich auf einmal nicht mehr als einen einzigen Augenblick . . . zu Nutze machen. . . . Diesen einzigen Augenblick macht er so prägnant wie möglich, und führt ihn mit allen den Täuschungen aus, welche die Kunst in Darstellung sichtbarer Gegenstände vor der Poesie voraus hat. Von dieser Seite aber unendlich zurückgelassen, was kann der Dichter, der . . . mit Worten malen soll, und nicht gänzlich verunglücken will, anders tun, als daß er gleichfalls seiner eigentümlichen Vorteile bedienet? Und welches sind diese? Die Freiheit sowohl über das Vergangene als über das Folgende des einzigen Augenblickes in dem Kunstwerke auszuarbeiten."
64. Ibid., 16: "Alles Stoische ist untheatralisch."
65. Ibid., 35–36; in his account of sympathy, Lessing cites Adam Smith, *The Theory of Moral Sentiments*, then presents his own ideas on the sympathetic reaction to pain: "Nichts ist betrüglicher als allgemeine Gesetze für unsere Empfindungen. Ihr Gewebe ist so fein und verwickelt, daß es auch der behutsamsten Spekulation kaum möglich ist, einen einzeln Faden rein aufzufassen und durch alle Kreuzfaden zu verfolgen."

another's hurt. But when an actor howls his pain, rages his anger, we are apt to sense the comparative insufficiency in our own response. As a result, our sympathetic engagement ceases and we behold rant and bombast instead of the illusion of tragic pathos.

To arouse sympathy is "the sole purpose of the tragic stage." Precisely for this reason, Lessing objects to the pedantic notion that the tragic character must hold back the extremity of his feelings. Lessing wants the audience to have the freedom of sympathetic response and aesthetic complementation. "Only with difficulty, or not at all, can the actor sustain illusion in a representation of physical pain"; nevertheless, tragic heroes "must show their feelings, must express their pains, and allow mere nature to work its effects."[66] This end is better achieved through restraint than through display: The former prompts the audience to imagine more; the latter may seem forced and expose the pretense.

The "freedom" to imagine more is crucial to Lessing's account of aesthetic illusion. If "our eyes only want illusion," then "it may not matter to them, whence the illusion comes."[67] But there is more to illusion than a mere trick of perception. The imagination must take part in the illusion: "What we find beautiful in a work of art, is found to be beautiful not by the eye, but, through the eye, by the imagination."[68] Although Lessing emphasizes the function of the imagination in aesthetic experience, we must not make the mistake of reading the *Laokoon* as Romantic criticism. Lessing does not mean by the *imagination* what Coleridge, or Schelling, or Friedrich Schlegel meant. Indeed, his word—*Einbildungskraft*—must be seen as altogether different from that word as it was radically redefined in Kant's *Critique of Pure Reason* (1781). For Lessing, the imagination is constitutive and reproductive, but it is neither an organ nor an organon of reason. It operates spontaneously with the senses. From fragmentary data of the senses, the imagination assembles a completed picture. Since the natural task of the imagination is to constitute and complement the signs communicated through the senses, it serves an integral function in aesthetic experience.

66. Ibid., 30: "Hierzu füge man, daß der Schauspieler die Vorstellung des körperlichen Schmerzes schwerlich oder gar nicht bis zur Illusion treiben kann"; 37–38; "[Mitleid zu erregen] ist die einzige Absicht der tragischen Bühne.... Ihre Helden müssen Gefühl zeigen, müssen ihre Schmerzen äußern, und die bloße Natur in sich wirken lassen."
67. Ibid., 50: "Wollen unsere Augen nur getäuscht sein, und ist es ihnen gleich viel, womit sie getäuscht werden?"
68. Ibid., 52: "Was wir in einem Kunstwerke schön finden, daß findet nicht unser Auge, sondern unsere Einbildungskraft, durch das Auge, schön."

Illusion is wrought, then, in the imagination as a construct of signs. In discussing signs in relation to illusion, Lessing is aware of the attention to signs in contemporary hermeneutics. Breitinger's *Kritische Dichtkunst* (1740) and Meier's *Versuch einer allgemeinen Auslegungskunst* (1757) turn to semiotics to clarify a text.[69] Lessing acknowledges this function of semiotics in critical interpretation, "where the concern is not with illusion, where one addresses only the understanding of the reader."[70] Nevertheless, he sees the evocative power of the sign as accompanying, yet separable from its informational function. The poet's task is to exercise the former; the latter is the concern of prose writers.

In the verbal arts the signs are an arbitrary set of symbols; in the visual arts, the signs are appropriated directly from nature. Aesthetic illusion occurs when the sign is identified with the thing signified. This assumed identity is at work in the metaphor of the poet as well as in the visual image of the painter. We may see a scene in nature, see it again as represented by the painter, and yet again as described by the poet. Each time it is conveyed by our senses and reproduced in our imagination, whether by arbitrary or by natural signs; each time, therefore, "we must experience the same pleasure, even if not in the same degree." The poet may well imitate the painter in creating a verbal picture. If he succeeds, "the poet makes us perceive his object so sensually that we are more clearly conscious of his object than we are of his words." Thus a verbal description may bring us "closer to that degree of illusion which is the peculiar capacity of the material painting."[71]

In spite of the similarity of effect, the semiotic process is fundamentally different—different not just because the poet relies on one set of signs, and the painter on another; different, rather, because one set of signs is ordered in a temporal sequence and the other in a spatial array. How is the illusion

---

69. Breitinger, *Critische Dichtkunst;* Meier, *Versuch einer allgemeinen Auslegungskunst.*

70. Lessing, *Laokoon,* in *Werke* VI, 113: "Überall, wo es daher auf das Täuschende nicht ankommt, wo man nur mit dem Verstande seiner Leser zu tun hat, und nur auf deutliche und so viel möglich vollständige Begriffe gehet: können diese aus der Poesie ausgeschlossene Schilderungen der Körper gar wohl Platz haben."

71. Ibid., 52: "Das nämliche Bild mag also in unserer Einbildungskraft durch willkürliche oder natürliche Zeichen wieder erregt werden, so muß auch jederzeit das nämliche Wohlgefallen, ob schon nicht in dem nämlichen Grade, wieder enstehen"; 100: "Ein poetisches Gemälde ist nicht notwendig das, was in ein materielles Gemälde zu verwandeln ist; sondern jeder Zug, jede Verbindung mehrerer Züge, durch die uns der Dichter seinen Gegenstand so sinnlich macht, daß wir uns dieses Gegenstandes deutlicher bewußt werden, als seiner Worte, heißt malerisch, heißt ein Gemälde, weil es uns dem Grade der Illusion näher bringt, dessen das materielle Gemälde besonders fähig ist, der sich von dem materiellen Gemälde am ersten und leichtesten abstrahieren lassen."

accomplished? How can signs in temporal sequence (*nach einander*) express spatial arrangement (*neben einander*)? The signs of poetry, Lessing answers, do not follow each other in random sequence; they are arbitrarily ordered. Metrical arrangement and grammatical structure impose a necessary spatial configuration. Similarly, temporal awareness enters into our perception of a painting or a statue. Perception itself is a temporal process. We do not perceive a thing all at once; rather, we discover the "neben einander" only in terms of the "nach einander" of beholding.

Illusion, by this account, is an instinctive act of complementing the limited senses. It is a spontaneous and natural act of perception to assume both time and space. Verbal signs may be heard in temporal sequence, but they are also structured in arbitrary patterns. Thus they also command space and may express the body as it exists in space.[72]

> Since the signs of speech are arbitrary, so it is very well possible through signs to let the parts of a body follow one another, just as in nature they are found next to one another. Yet this is characteristic of speech and its signs in general, not, however in so far as they might best suit the intentions of poetry. The poet does not want merely to be understood; it is not enough that his representations should merely be clear and distinct; with this the prose writer might be satisfied. The poet, however, wants to make the ideas which he awakens in us so lively that we believe that we perceive in the rapidity the actual sensory impressions of their objects, and in this moment of illusion, we cease to be conscious of the means that he has used, even of his words.[73]

Lessing's concept of illusion as aesthetic complementation operates in the same manner as sensation and sympathy, spontaneous and independent of

---

72. Ibid., 109: "Die Zeichen der Poesie sind nicht bloß auf einander folgend, sie sind auch willkürlich; und als willkürliche Zeichen sind sie allerdings fähig, Körper, so wie sie im Raume existieren, auszudrucken."

73. Ibid., 109–110: "Da die Zeichen der Rede willkürlich sind, so ist es gar wohl möglich, daß man durch sie die Teile eines Körpers eben so wohl auf einander folgen lassen kann, als sie in der Natur neben einander befindlich sind. Allein dieses ist eine Eigenschaft der Rede und ihrer Zeichen überhaupt, nicht aber in so ferne sie der Absicht der Poesie am bequemsten sind. Der Poet will nicht bloß verständlich werden, seine Vorstellungen sollen nicht bloß klar und deutlich sein; hiermit begnügt sich der Prosaist. Sonder er will die Ideen, die er in uns erweckte, so lebhaft machen, daß wir in der Geschwindigkeit die wahren sinnlichen Eindrücke ihrer Gegenstände zu empfinden glauben, und in diesem Augenblicke der Täuschung, uns der Mittel, die er dazu anwendet, seiner Worte bewußt zu sein aufhören."

deliberate rational awareness. Indeed, in listening to poetry there is a shift of consciousness. "We are more clearly conscious of his object than we are of his words," Lessing tells us; "in this moment of illusion, we cease to be conscious of the means that he has used, even of his words." The rational attention to language subsides with the sensual engagement of illusion.

Just as Lessing revised his exposition of sympathy by appropriating the concept of illusion that he had originally denied in the *Correspondence concerning Tragedy*, Mendelssohn had still to answer Lessing's charge that his account of illusion was irrelevant to his explanation of aesthetic judgment. Aesthetic value, Mendelssohn maintained, was determined by the skill of the artist in creating an imitation. While the emotional excitement in experiencing the illusion might be taken as evidence of an effective imitation, the judgment is to be exercised totally independent of the emotional response. Aesthetic judgment is possible only in recognizing that "the fine arts are an imitation of nature, but not nature itself." The illusory response assumes an identity between art and nature; aesthetic judgment attends to the difference.

"What need do we have here for illusion?"[74] Lessing's question is given three different answers in Mendelssohn's subsequent attempts to develop a satisfactory theory of illusion. In his *Hauptgrundsätze* (1761), he adopts, as Lessing did in the *Laokoon*, the concept of signs and argues for a rapid alternation between illusion and reason. In his *Rhapsodie* (1771), he posits "a secret consciousness" ("ein heimliches Bewußtseyn") through which reason monitors, albeit passively, the effects of illusion. Finally, in his *Morgenstunden* (1785), he extends the semiotic ambiguity and defines illusion as interrupted induction, in which the sign is read only for its sensual meaning, that is, only in terms of the thing signified.

The theory of illusion presented in *Hauptgrundsätze* (1761) does not significantly depart from that in the *Correspondence concerning Tragedy*. Mendelssohn still argues that illusion is sensual, and that sensory/sensual illusion occurs in the response to art. By introducing the concept of signs, however, he can argue that the higher reason responds to the distinction between the sign and the thing signified, while the lower faculties perceive the sign as the thing itself. Art encourages this confusion by offering us "such an abundance of attributes . . . that we conceive the matter itself as more lively than the signs which express it; and to be sure, so much more

---

74. Lessing to Mendelssohn, 2 February 1757, in Lessing, *Werke* IV, 202: "Wozu brauchen wir nun hier die Illusion?"

lively, that our senses, at least for a moment, believe that they behold the matter itself." Aesthetic illusion is thus a semiotic confusion. Mendelssohn declares it to be "the highest degree of sensory cognition" (*cognitio intuitiva* or *anschauende Erkenntnis*).[75]

Mendelssohn has altered his earlier position by limiting the effects of illusion to a momentary dominance of the senses over the reason. Too, a certain complexity of representation ("an abundance of attributes") is necessary to illusion. For that reason, aesthetic experience remains an observation and evaluation of the artist's skill in imitation; aesthetic illusion is a brief interruption of the rational response. In spite of his quibbles with Lessing's account of the temporal and spatial limits of visual and verbal signs,[76] Mendelssohn offers virtually the same explanation of illusion as presented in *Laokoon*. Compare Lessing's "The poet ... wants to make the ideas that he awakens in us so lively that we believe that we perceive in the rapidity the actual sensory impressions of their objects, and in this moment of illusion, we cease to be conscious of the means that he has used, even of his words" and Mendelssohn's "The means of making a speech sensual consists in the choice of such expressions as evoke in the memory an abundance of attributes all at once, in order to make us feel the thing signified more lively than the signs.... The objects appear to the senses as if immediately represented and our lower faculties experience illusion, in that they often forget the signs and believe they behold the matter itself."[77] Mendelssohn, how-

---

75. Mendelssohn, "Über die Hauptgrundsätze der schönen Künste und Wissenschaften," in *Philosophische Schriften*, part 2 (Berlin, 1761), in *Gesammelte Schriften*, I, 286: "Die Gegenstände können entweder in der Natur anzutreffen, oder erdichtet seyn. In beiden Fällen muß der Ausdruck, dessen sich die Kunst bedienet, unsere Sinne täuschen. Das heißt, wir müssen eine solche Menge von Merkmalen auf einmal Wahrnehmen, daß wir die Sache selbst uns lebhafter vorstellen, als die ausdrückenden Zeichen; und zwar um so viel lebhafter, daß unsere Sinne, wenigstens einen Augenblick, die Sachen selbst vor sich zu sehen glauben. Dieses ist der höchste Grad der anschauenden Erkenntniß, den man die ästhetische Illusion nennet." Werner Strube, "Ästhetische Illusion. Ein kritischer Beitrag zur Geschichte der Wirkungsästhetik des 18. Jahrhunderts," 85–142, has investigated Mendelssohn's theory of illusion in terms of an irreconcilable conflict between a hedonistic aesthetic and a rationalist ethic.

76. Mendelssohn, "Zu einem Laokoon-Entwurf Lessings," in *Gesammelte Schriften*, ed. Elbogen et al. (Berlin: Friedrich Fromann, 1929–32), II, 233–58; on signs, 234–35. Mendelssohn provides a further account of signs in "Über die Quellen und die Verbindungen der schönen Künste und Wissenschaften," in *Gesammelte Schriften* I, 174–75. Christian Garve's "Laokoon-Rezension," prompted Lessing to elaborate his aesthetic of signs in his letter to Nicolai (26 May 1769); see Rudowski, *Lessing's Aesthetica in nuce*.

77. Mendelssohn, *Philosophische Schriften*, part 2, in *Gesammelte Schriften* I, 291. "Das Mittel eine Rede sinnlich zu machen, besteht in der Wahl solcher Ausdrücke, die eine Menge von Merkmalen auf einmal in das Gedächtnis zurück bringen, um uns das Bezeichnete lebhafter

ever, now presents the experience as brief and fleeting, although it may recur repeatedly.

The subject of negative emotions had been deliberated in the *Correspondence concerning Tragedy*. Mendelssohn returns in his *Rhapsodie* (1771) to the seeming paradox of our attraction to the repulsive. In the context of discussing how we can feel aesthetic pleasure in what we know to be morally repugnant, he proposes that a conscious distancing takes place, in which we "distinguish the relation to ourselves from the relation to the object." Such aesthetic distance, however, can be achieved only through a rational act. Aesthetic illusion, according to his earlier account, works through the senses, the emotions, the lower faculties. Has Mendelssohn changed his mind? Has he brought about a marriage between the higher and lower faculties? No, not even a cohabitation. The higher faculties, however, have been granted a voyeur's privileges. Even while the lower faculties are engaged in aesthetic intimacy or immediacy, the reason may look on, quietly keeping aesthetic distance.

Frightening events may become pleasing, Mendelssohn argues, as imitated through art, for "a secret consciousness, that we have an imitation and not the truth before our eyes, tempers the strength of objective repulsion and at the same time heightens the subjective conception."

> It is true, that the senses and the desires are tricked by the illusion of art, and the imagination so captivated that we at times forget all signs of imitation, and believe that we see the true nature. Yet this magic endures only as long as is required to give our conception of the objects the necessary life and fire. We have accustomed ourselves, to our great pleasure, to turn our attention away from everything which might disturb the illusion, and to direct it exclusively toward that, through which it is entertained. However, as soon as the relation to the object begins to be displeasing, we are reminded by the multitude of evidence, which immediately springs into sight, that we are witnessing a mere imitation.[78]

---

empfinden zu lassen, als das Zeichen. . . . Die Gegenstände werden unsern Sinnen, wie unmittelbar vorgestellt, und die untern Seelenkräfte werden getäuscht, indem sie öfters der Zeichen vergessen, und der Sache selbst ansichtig zu werden glauben."

78. Mendelssohn, *Gesammelte Schriften* I, 390–91: "So bald wir in den Stand gesetzt werden, die Beziehung auf uns von der Beziehung auf den Gegenstand zu trennen; so ist die Kenntniß des Übels, die Mißbilligung desselben, und die Äußerung des Abscheues für das Böse, eine sehr

Even though the reason may provide "a secret consciousness" that an illusion is only an illusion, Mendelssohn still confirms the overwhelming power of the sensual experience. While at times we deliberately hold our reason in passive abeyance in order to focus our attention on the illusory experience, our lower faculties (senses, desires, imagination) may become so enthralled that we "forget" to discriminate between art and reality.

We have seen how the debate over illusion in the *Correspondence concerning Tragedy* became stifled by the strictures of the Leibniz–Wolff psychology, as well as by the failure of Mendelssohn and Nicolai to come to terms with the doctrine of sympathy Lessing had adapted from Shaftesbury and Hutcheson. In his *Laokoon*, Lessing sought to simplify the task of explaining illusion by avoiding the psychological problems of perception and cognition and by reinforcing his doctrine of sympathy with an argument of aesthetic complementation and the interpretation of natural and arbitrary signs. We may recognize in the *Laokoon*, then, a turn to phenomenology and semiology to explain illusion.

A similar turn takes place in Mendelssohn's *Morgenstunden* (1785). Mendelssohn continues to use the vocabulary of rationalist psychology. Illusion is still seen to arise from the senses overwhelming the reason; the cause, however, is no longer attributed to the sheer power of sensual excitation. There is a shortcoming in the reason: "Incomplete induction is the primary source of all sensory delusion."[79] The reading of signs, natural and arbitrary, is the inductive task by which reason deciphers sensory perception. We acquire certain "habits," Mendelssohn explains, that prompt us to suspend the inductive process.

---

anziehende Beschäftigung der Seelenkräfte, die nicht ohne Wohlgefallen seyn kann. Ein anderes Mittel die schrecklichsten Begebenheiten zärtlichen Gemüthern angenehm zu machen, ist die Nachahmung durch die Kunst, auf der Bühne, auf Leinwand, im Marmor, da ein heimliches Bewußtseyn, daß wir eine Nachahmung, und keine Wahrheit vor Augen haben, die Stärke des objektiven Abscheues mildert, und das Subjektive der Vorstellung gleichsam hebt. Es ist wahr, die sinnliche Erkenntniß und Begehrungskräfte der Seele werden durch die Kunst getäuscht, und die Einbildungskraft so mit fortgerissen, daß wir zuweilen aller Zeichen der Nachahmung vergessen, und die wahre Natur zu sehen wähnen. Allein dieser Zauber dauert nur so lange, als nöthig ist, unserm Begriffe von dem Gegenstande des gehörige Leben und Feuer zu geben. Wir haben uns gewöhnt, zu unserm größten Vergnügen, die Aufmerksamkeit von allem, was die Täuschung stören könnte, abzulenken, und nur auf das zu richten, wodurch sie unterhalten wird. So bald aber die Beziehung auf den Gegenstand unangenehm zu werden anfängt; so erinnern uns tausend in die Augen fallende Umstände, daß wir eine bloße Nachahmung vor uns sehen."

79. Mendelssohn, *Morgenstunden oder Vorlesungen über das Daseyn Gottes* (1785), in *Gesammelte Schriften* III-2, 29: "Unvollständige Induction ist eine Hauptquelle des Sinnenbetrugs."

All illusions of the fine arts derive from the same source. They all are grounded in the connection between the sign and the thing signified, and result from the conclusion which we are wont to draw from incomplete induction. If, through repeated indulgence in our early years, incomplete induction should become a habit, if the association of ideas directly excites the feelings, so our senses will continue unhindered to accept the sign as the thing signified, and will expect the latter whenever they perceive the former. The rational cognition of the real may convince us of the opposite, but sensory illusion has its own way to connect and conclude, and the imitation succeeds in its effect even though the reason recognizes that it is only an imitation.[80]

Mendelssohn had first argued that illusion results when the emotions overwhelm the reason; next he posited a rapid alternation of emotional and rational response; then he proposed a secret monitoring of emotional response by the passive reason. In the *Morgenstunden,* he clearly asserts the copresence of the rational and the emotional response. We experience the illusion even though we know that it is only an illusion. This dual consciousness, however, is achieved through an apparently pathological self-indulgence. Consciousness is rendered virtually schizophrenic, and reason is helplessly at odds with the senses and feelings.

Mendelssohn immediately corrects the implications of a pathological self-indulgence. Not all self-indulgence is overindulgence. The pleasure principle of Du Bos is still present, and Mendelssohn is trying to draw moral boundaries between a healthy and a depraved voluptuary. In the position he had assumed with Nicolai, aesthetic experience was amoral precisely because the reason was not involved. If reason is to be a coconspirator or fallible partner in the illusion, it must assume moral responsibility:

---

80. Ibid., 32–33: "Alle Täuschungen der schönen Wissenschaften und Künste fließen aus derselben Quelle. Sie gründen sich alle auf die Verbindung zwischen dem Zeichen und dem Bezeichneten, und auf den Schluß, den wir aus unvollständigen Induction zu ziehen pflegen. Wenn diese, durch öftere frühe Wiederholung, zur Gewohnheit worden sind; wenn die Ideenfolge gleichsam zur unmittelbaren Empfindung wird; so schließ unsere Sinne von dem Zeichen auf das Bezeichnete ungehindert fort, und erwarten dieses, so oft sie jenes wahrnehmen. Die deutlichere Erkenntniß des Würklichen, mag uns immer von dem Gegentheile überführen, die sinnliche Täuschung hat ihren eigenen Weg, zu schließen und zu folgern, und die Nachahmung hat ihre Würkung gethan; obgleich die Vernunft erkennt, daß es bloß Nachahmung sey."

114   Illusion and the Drama

> We know that this marble Laocoön does not feel the bite of the snake, the effect of which the artist has made visible throughout even to the toes of the feet. If only we bring the intention to allow ourselves the pleasant experience of illusion, then the sensual faculties will play their usual game, letting us imply the passion from the sign of the passion, purpose and determination from the sign of free choice, and thereby making us interested in persons who are not present. We take actual part in feelings and actions that are not real, because, for our own pleasure, we so effectively abstract from this not-reality.[81]

Mendelssohn devotes five chapters (3–7) of *Morgenstunden* to the problem of distinguishing illusion from truth. While we must recognize that the argument here is leading toward his *a priori* proof of the existence of God, it is important to see that he now gives to reason the full responsibility over the sensual indulgence of illusion. The limited capacity of the senses frequently produces perceptual illusions; reason provides the corrective. Should error, habit, or weakness limit the reason as well, then pathological illusions will abide. Accepting *often* for *always*, *many* for *every* exhibits the same inductive fallibility as in accepting *illusion* for *reality*. The incomplete inductive process leaves us abstractions which we take to be facts.

If his purpose were to explore psychology, Mendelssohn says, he could demonstrate the caprices of "this mental capacity for separating and isolating and show you through many examples, how our sensual faculties are combined with many accomplishments, which one usually attributes exclusively to reason." This is a crux in Mendelssohn's argument. The Leibniz–Wolff system labeled the activity of the sensual faculties as *cognitio obscura* and *cognitio confusa*, obviously confounding and distorting the *cognitio intuitiva*. The sensual and sensory responses are now fully educable. The bad habits of incomplete induction can be countered by good habits of rapid inductive reasoning. In many respects this is a refinement of the aesthetic

---

81. Ibid., 33: "Wir wissen es, daß dieser marmorne Laocoon die Schlangenbisse nicht fühlet, deren Würkung der Künstler bis in den äußersten Zähen seiner Füße hat zu bemerken gegeben; bringen wir nur den Vorsatz mit, uns auf eine angenehme Weise täuschen zu lassen, so treibt die sinnliche Erkenntniß ihr gewohntes Spiel; sie läßt uns von Zeichen der Leidenschaft auf Leidenschaft, von Zeichen der freywilligen Handlungen auf Vorsatz und Bewegungsgrund schließen, und uns solchergestalt für Personen interessieren, die nicht vorhanden sind. Wir nehmen würklichen Antheil an nicht würklichen Empfindungen und Handlungen; weil wir von dem Nichtwürklichseyn, zu unserm Vergnügen, vorsetzlich abstrahieren."

algebra in the *Correspondence concerning Tragedy*. The essential difference is that the higher reason not only operates spontaneously and effortlessly, but also remains (in the wings, as it were) to enjoy the aesthetic illusion that it denies yet allows to persist: "A sound human understanding, which alone seems to effect the pleasure in the beautiful, presupposes the operation of reason, which must take place in us without conscious awareness."[82]

In reviewing the account of illusion in the works of Lessing and Mendelssohn, I have given particular attention to their changing notions on the role of rational awareness. From his early position of defining illusion as a product of the lower faculties, dispelled by the presence of reason, Mendelssohn gradually adopts a notion of copresence in which reason can monitor the lower faculties and even witness the illusion, which it knows to be a deception. Later in the Romantic period, some poets and critics continue to see reason and illusion as opposing forces. Hazlitt, for example, asserts "the progress of knowledge and refinement has a tendency to circumscribe the limits of the imagination, and to clip the wings of poetry"; and Keats renders the same idea poetically: ". . . all charms fly / At the mere touch of cold philosophy" and "Philosophy will clip an Angel's wings."[83] Throughout the Enlightenment and the Romantic period, however, there is a countermovement, persistent and growing, to convert reason from antagonist to benefactor of the imaginative and the visionary.

Because illusion was supposed to be fostered exclusively by the lower faculties, when in 1750 Karl Wilhelm Ramler discovered that his aesthetic experience persisted in spite of his attempts to abjure the illusion through reason, he regarded his wayward tears as a paradoxical oddity. He wrote to Gleim confessing his emotional response to Richardson's *Clarissa:* "I shed a thousand tears, and all notions of the poetic invention and deception were not able to prevent them."[84] Ramler found his experience at odds with the

---

82. Ibid.: "Wenn hier meine Absicht mehr auf das Psychologische ginge; so würde ich von dieser Betrachtung Gelegenheit nehmen, euch von dem sinnlichen Absonderungsvermögen zu unterhalten, und euch durch mehrere Beyspiele zeigen, daß unsre sinnliche Erkenntnisse mit mancherley Seelenverrichtungen vermischt sind, die man gemeiniglich nur der Vernunft zuzutrauen pflegt. Der gesunde Menschenverstand, welcher beym Genuß des Schönen allein zu würken scheint, setzt Operationen der Vernunft voraus, die ohne Bewußtseyn in uns vorgehen müssen."

83. Hazlitt, "On Poetry in General," in *Collected Works* V, 1–18; Keats, "Lamia" (ll. 229–37), in *Poems*, 472–73.

84. Ramler to Gleim (7 November 1750), in Gleim, *Briefwechsel zwischen Gleim und Ramler*, I, 206f.: "Ich habe tausend Thränen vergossen und alle Vorstellugen der Erdichtung und des Betruges haben es nicht verhindern können."

account of illusion that continued to prevail in rationalist aesthetics until the end of the eighteenth century. For, while Lessing and Mendelssohn had tried to develop an adequate understanding of the nature of illusion, other important deliberations taking place during this period contributed to the radical reformulation of aesthetic experience in the works of Kant and Hegel.

Heinrich Wilhelm Gerstenberg's *Letters on the Curiosities of Literature* (*Briefe über Merkwürdigkeiten der Literatur*, 1766–67) are indeed remarkable and curious, partly because of his refusal to endorse the mainstream of rationalist aesthetics, but also because of the irony and insight derived from deliberately decentering the discussion. Letter 20 is devoted to explaining illusion, the experience that "overpowers and carries us away," that "leaves a fire burning in our soul," that "lifts us above ourselves." Gerstenberg calls illusion by a base name: deceit (*Betrug*)—to which he adds a lofty modifier, deceit of a higher inspiration (*Betrug einer höheren Eingebung*). Illusion sustains inspiration through lively scenes, actions, fictions, and makes us feel as if we were present as witnesses. It is powerful (Gerstenberg refers to its heat, strength, force); it is continuous (*anhaltend*) and uninterrupted (*beständig*); it is experienced (*Erfahrung*) as well as felt (*Gefühl*); this means, that illusion involves the understanding (*Verstand*) as well as the emotions (*Herz*). In avoiding the schemes of the Leibniz–Wolff school, he does not pause to consider the significance of simultaneous rational and emotional awareness; he simply takes the dual responses for granted. He also sets his definition of "Imagination" apart from "the concept of the metaphysicians and a few Swiss poets and critics" (Bodmer and Breitinger) and redirects such basic aesthetic terms as imitation (Baumgarten) and enthusiasm (Cramer). It is useless, Gerstenberg argues, to define aesthetic terms as principles or effects. We know from experience what the effects are; and learning the theoretical principles does not explain the artist's methods. How is illusion attained?

As critical advocate of the new cult of genius, Gerstenberg emphasizes the poet's mental processes in creating illusion: *imagination*, a sensitivity to the images received through the senses and a capacity to think in images; *observation*, an ability to perceive details as well as relationships, parts as well as the whole, and to reconstruct what one has observed; *cleverness*, the skill in expression and ability to affect the reason and emotions. The true power of illusion, therefore, must be understood as poetic illusion, "the deceit of a higher inspiration." Illusion, as Gerstenberg defines it, is distinguished from a narrowly conceived mimetic representation that merely tricks the external senses. Theatrical illusion may succeed briefly in deluding the senses and arousing the emotions. If the inspiration and genius are missing, however, we promptly notice the shallow and tawdry nature of the performance. Poetic illusion, by contrast, endures; the performance is transformed into a presence, the audience into witnesses. The poetic illusion of "presence" is achieved because the action has been embued with "the colors of poetic genius."[85]

Friedrich Just Riedel, in his *Theory of the Fine Arts and Belles Lettres* (*Theorie der schönen Künste und Wissenschaften*, 1767), did not ignore the rationalists; rather, he turned to Longinus for an answer to the reason-emotion dilemma. In his chapter on "Imitation and Illusion" ("Nachahmung und Illusion"), he reviews contemporary theories and tries to bring them into order. He identifies four modes of artistic representation: "Copy of nature, selection of beautiful nature, combination of beautiful parts from many individuals, [and] personal creation." All four may evoke illusion, the first and second because they imitate nature, the third and fourth because they seem to imitate nature. From Longinus, Riedel adapts the concept of *fantasia* to explain the difference between actual and seeming appearances. In the philosophical language of the Greeks, Riedel points out, *fantasia* did not refer to delusion. He cites Cicero to demonstrate that the Latin *visum* translated the Greek *fantasia;* the word meant, that is, *sensation*, the impression or the image that is excited by an external object or the remembrance left in its place. Sensation produces an image. The image, as replacement (*Stellvertreter*) for the real, is an illusion. To the extent that it is accepted as real, any image may provide an illusion. Illusion, therefore, results from imagination (an inward-picturing or *Einbildung*).[86] In Riedel's formulation sensation may arouse a process of inward-picturing; the acceptance of the picture as real is illusion. Following Longinus on the sublime in art, Riedel claims that art attempts to intensify sensation. All sensation may lead to illusion; aesthetic illusion differs only in regard to the modes of representation involved.

---

85. Gerstenberg, *Briefe über Merkwürdigkeiten der Literatur.* On Gerstenberg's concept of illusion, see Gerth, *Studien zu Gerstenbergs Poetik*, 162ff; on Gerstenberg and the cult of genius, Schmidt, *Die Geschichte des Genie-Gedankens in der deutschen Literatur, Philosophie und Politik 1750–1945* I, 78, 167–68.

86. Riedel, *Theorie der schönen Künste und Wissenschaften. Ein Auszug aus den Werken verschiedenen Schriftsteller*, 150–52; see also the review in *Neue Bibliothek der schönen Wissenschaften und der freyen Künste.*

The popularity of the domestic tragedy, as Christian Heinrich Schmid explained to the readers of his literary chronicle in 1768, derives from the apparent intimacy between stage and home: "Virtues, vices, situations, all appear to us more probable, because they come from the sphere of our own experience." This appraisal of the illusion of domestic tragedy is repeated by Theodor Gottlieb von Hippel in 1778: "We are, so to speak, among ourselves, and we take a greater part in the events, because that which we are watching could occur to our relatives, friends, our selves."[87]

Christian Felix Weiße also emphasized intimacy and familiarity as the source and power of illusion in historical drama. In his preface to *Das Fanatismus, oder Jean Calas* (1780), Weiße claimed to have followed his historical sources so meticulously that the very dialogue was taken from the court transcriptions. Weiße advocates documentary fidelity as more effective than any poetic adaptation in securing the intended audience response: illusion and pathos.[88] The difference that art should bring to the imitation of nature, crucial to the critical precepts of Bodmer in 1736, has been utterly dissolved in the assumption of documentary realism. The history play and the domestic tragedy work their illusion by disallowing the artist's indulgence of imagination.

So close does it mimic reality, fiction ceases to remain fiction. Weiße, as editor of the *Kinderfreund*, found himself caught up in the paradox of multiple reflections—art imitating life imitating art. He described a fictional family in various episodes. Presuming these were accounts of his own family, readers addressed letters and gifts to Weiße's fictional family. The confusion worked in both directions. His real family began to find themselves cast

---

87. Schmid, "Über das bürgerliche Trauerspiel" (1768), in *Litterarische Chronik* III, (1788), 212: "Tugenden, Laster, Begebenheiten, alles ist uns wahrscheinlicher, weil sie aus der Sphäre unserer eignen Erfahrung genommen sind." Theodor Gottlieb von Hippel, quoted in Schneider, *Theodor Gottlieb von Hippel*, Appendix, 16: "Wir sind sozusagen unter uns, und nehmen an dem, was vorgeht, um so mehr Anteil, als das, was wir sehen, unseren Anverwandten, unsern Freunden—uns selbst begegnen kann."

88. Weiße, Preface: in *Das Fanatismus, oder Jean Calas. Ein historisches Schauspiel in fünf Aufzügen, Samt einer kurzen Geschichte von seinem Tode*, 2; "So hat sich der Verfasser so strenge an die Geschichte gehalten, daß kein historischer Zug, ich möchte fast sagen, kein Ausdruck darinnen ist, den er nicht aus dem Processe selbst und aus den Schutzreden für die Unschuld des Calas vor den Gerichten in Paris, gezogen hätte"; 3: "Uebrigens sehe ich diese strenge Anhänglichkeit an der Wahrheit für nichts weniger, als für ein Verdienst meines Stückes an: nur glaube ich durch sie besser, als durch alle Dichtungen, den Endzweck meines Drama, Täuschung und Rührung, zu erreichen." See also "Rezension: Trauerspiele von C. F. Weiße," in *Allgemeine deutsche Bibliothek* (1782), and Schmitt, "Christian Felix Weißes *Jean Calas*—Dokumentarisches Theater im 18. Jahrhundert."

into the roles of their fictive counterparts, and the fictional episodes began to reflect more and more the real family.[89] The aesthetic of domestic drama is absorbed into the practice of daily life.

The illusion of "a real family situation," writes Johann Friedrich Schink in his *Dramaturgische Fragmente* (1781–82), is so perfectly wrought by Marchand in the title role of Diderot's *Le Père de famille* that one completely "forgets" actor and stage and sees only the duress of the family. The actor disappears into his role. Illusion is experienced through the emotions, not through the reason—it "speaks to the heart." Unless an actor should play so badly that "he tears me with force out of the illusion," Schink declares that he ceases to be in the theater and is emotionally present in the family home. With Diderot, Schink defines illusion as an involuntary response, but unlike Diderot, he claims illusion can be complete and enduring—the affects are still felt even after one leaves the theater. To achieve total illusion, mere appearance is not enough. Appearance is no substitute for reality. Schink would rephrase Aristotle: he does not want *mimesis*, an imitation of human action; he wants a realization of human emotions. What is "real," according to Schink, is feeling. When emotional interest is aroused, when "the heart is affected," the performance becomes real. At that point, the illusion is complete: we "forget" poet and player; we no longer sit before a stage but "live in a real world."[90]

In 1792, Idelfonso Valdastri submitted his essay on dramatic illusion to the Academy of Science and Belles Lettres in Mantova. In examining the differences between domestic tragedy and comedy, he claimed the advantage of comedy because it was free to exploit illusion, while tragedy had to intensify and, at the same time, protect against any possible disruption of illusion. Lessing, as we saw in *Hamburgische Dramaturgie* No. 42, had similarly granted comedy a greater freedom with illusion. Valdastri, however, provided a defense for the general dramatic function of self-reflexive modes and revealed illusion. Further, he described the affect of illusion as an exchange of identity: "The spectators must experience illusion so that they are completely in the situation of the characters." Metadramatic devices in the play thus restore self-awareness, causing the spectators to confront their own play acting. When Valdastri's arguments appeared in

---

89. Weiße, *Selbstbiographie*, 184–86.
90. Schink, *Dramaturgische Fragmente*, 758, 420, 881–82, 699–700, 650, 699, 728, 458, 15–20; see Wierlacher, "Das Postulat der Illusion," in *Das Bürgerliche Drama*, 111–15.

German,[91] they contributed to the reappraisal of illusion already under way. The pleasure principle, as forwarded by Du Bos, was no longer accepted as a simple hedonism; nor was it enough that illusion simply mediate emotional response, as had been argued by Nicolai and Mendelssohn. Illusion no longer seemed limited to the spectator's response; rather, its origin was claimed to reside in the poet's perception. For the playwright especially, illusion is a means as well as end. Illusion does not follow from, but precedes, directs, and ultimately contains all other elements with which the playwright composes his play.

Kantian philosophy argued that illusion brought about neither a loss of identity nor an intermittent alterity, but rather a discovery of identity. As discussed above in the introduction, aesthetic experience was being redefined, following Kant, in terms of sensually "disinterested" responses that stimulated the inquiry of intellect and imagination, giving rise to an exploration of the mind's own processes. The comparison of illusion to dream, however, was developed by a number of critics not at all interested in Kantian subjectivity. As we saw in chapter 1, the similarity between aesthetic illusion and dream was introduced into English criticism during the latter half of the eighteenth century. Lord Kames in his *Elements of Criticism* (1762) had suggested that a theater audience experienced a play as in a "waking dream." Erasmus Darwin in *The Botanic Garden* (1789) had proposed that, because the dreamlike state was repeatedly interrupted by waking reason, we "alternately believe and disbelieve, almost every moment, the existence of the objects represented before us."[92]

When Johann Gottfried Herder, in his essay "Shakespear" (1773), first forwarded the dream analogy, he used it not to explore the nature of illusion, but to argue the irrelevancy of the unities of space and time. Drama, no less than dream, creates its own peculiar experience of space and time. Herder insists, first, that all experience of space and time is relative, that our perception of time and space is subordinate to other circumstances that command our attention. While boredom or excitement may alter our perception of time and space, the dream makes time and space follow utterly in accord

---

91. Valdastri, "Dissertazione," 3–90; "Valdastri Preisschrift," in *Neue Bibliothek der schönen Wissenschaften und der freyen Künste*. "Welche Vorzüge hat das bürgerliche Trauerspiele und dem Lustspiel? Warum steht es dem Letztern nach? Und welches sind die ihm ausschließlich zukommenden Eigenschaften?" Also, "Die Zuschauer müssen so getäuscht werden, daß sie sich gänzlich in der Lage der handelnden Personen versetzen."

92. Home, *Elements of Criticism* (1762); Darwin, *The Botanic Garden* (1789).

with the appearance of its images. The same reversal of priority is the privilege of the playwright, whose task is to put the spectator into a dream.[93]

Twenty-seven years later, in his *Kalligone* (1800), Herder attempted to develop a full account of aesthetic experience. His explanation of illusion reaffirms the dreamlike substitution of poetic time and space: "I should forget myself, forget even my own time and place, and be carried on the wings of poesy into the dramatic action, into its time and place."[94] However, this "forgetting' now depends upon specific psychological conditions. The dreamlike state is no mere analogy; rather, Herder is describing a complex act of mental participation. His understanding of Galvani's "animal electricity" and his "metacritical" response to Kant[95] have both been absorbed into his account of play and illusion. He rejects the definition of "play" as "idle game," of "illusion" as "deception."

When Gadamer establishes his ontology of play, he repeats, without mention of Herder, Herder's discussion of the connotations of the word *Spiel*. Play (*Spiel*) is "a light movement," as we use the word in referring to play of wind through the trees, the play of light upon the water, the play of flames, or the play of color. The actions and passions of the drama are real and true; what is meant by "play" is the transformation of deadly struggles into "light movements." What is physically threatening is thereby suspended, but even in transformation the endeavors remain earnest. Play is competitive, and the competition must be true and just. There is no place for deception and deceit. In dramatic play we expect a free competition, according to rules, between the characters. Whatever is falsified deserved to be hated and rejected by the audience. Illusion, then, has to be clearly distinguished from deception. In Herder's etymology, illusion (*Täuschung*) involves an exchange (*Tausch*); just as Valdastri had defined it, the spectator exchanges his own manner of thinking and accepts the author's. Similar to the popular account of the mesmeric trance, illusion is a mental state willingly accepted by the participant:

---

93. Herder, "Shakespear" (1773), in *Werke* V, 227–28.
94. Herder, *Kalligone* (1800), in *Werke* XXII, 155: "Vergessen soll ich mich selbst, vergessen sogar meine Zeit und meinen Raum, auf den Flügeln der Dichtkunst in die dramatische Handlung, in ihre Zeit, ihren Raum getragen."
95. Herder, "Verstand und Erfahrung. Eine Metakritik zur Kritik der reinen Vernunft. Erster Theil" (1799), "Vernunft und Sprache. Eine Metakritik zur Kritik der reinen Vernunft. Zweiter Theil" (1799), and "Metakritik zur Kritik der Urtheilskraft" (1799), in *Werke* XXII, 1–190, 191–339 and XXII, 333–41. For Herder's reference to Galvani's experiment, see XXII, 331.

> From exchange [*Tausch*] comes illusion [*täuschen*], and in effect the poet has me in illusion when he has transposed me into his manner of thinking, into his acting and feeling; I exchange with him my own, or, so long as his is working on me, I leave my own in slumber; I forget my self. The dramatic-narrative poet I follow willingly wherever he leads me; I see, hear, believe, whatever he makes me see, hear, believe; if he cannot accomplish this, he is no poet.[96]

Through this exchange of thoughts and feelings, the spectator surrenders his intellectual being, his imagination and his feelings, to the author; nevertheless, he maintains control of his physical being. Should the author trespass against conditions of his own representation and urge facts inconsistent with his own fiction, an instinctive physical reaction against the deceit awakens the self and annuls the exchange.

Johann Georg Sulzer had described dream consciousness as early as 1758 when his paper on the processes of reason was recorded in the *Mémoires de l'Academie Royale des Sciences et Bélles Lettres*. In 1774—just a year after Herder's "Shakespear" and long before his *Kalligone*—Sulzer dismissed the mere analogical reference to dream in explaining aesthetic illusion and formally proposed the psychological relevance of dream consciousness. He argued that aesthetic experience elicits a mental state similar to dream consciousness and that aesthetic illusion replicates the mode of response in dreaming. The senses, which in waking excite our perception of those external circumstances affecting our person, in sleep are weakened and feeble. Images still play through the mind in sleep, and the mind persists in interpreting them as if they were the product of the senses, as if they revealed conditions in which we were actually involved. Whatever random image might drift from feeble sensation or memory into the dream consciousness will then agitate the mind to engender other images to interpret the first, and soon we have in dream a complete scenario—time, place, circumstance—in which our imagination has involved us. Complete illusion has no admixture of external awareness but

---

96. Herder, *Kalligone* (1800), in *Werke* XXII, 152–54 and 154–55: "Von Tausch kommt täuschen, und allerdings täuscht mich der Dichter, wenn er mich in seine Denkweise, in seine Handlung und Empfindung versetzt; ich tausche mit ihm die meine, oder lasse sie, so lange er wirkt, schlummern; ich vergesse mich selbst. Dem darstellend-erzählenden Dichter folge ich willig, wohin er mich führet; ich sehe, höre, glaube, was er mich sehen, hören, glauben macht; vermag er dies nicht, ist er kein Dichter." On the usage of "Spiel," see Gadamer, *Wahrheit und Methode*, 99.

elaborates only the inner scene. There are gradations of dream consciousness, as in reverie or daydreams, in which the senses are partially revived and contribute other perceptions that may merge with, or detract from, the attentive imagination.

In order to seduce the mind into dream consciousness, the dramatic performance must focus our attention exclusively upon stage, so that we gradually lose all awareness of immediate exterior circumstance and our senses no longer register surrounding details in the audience. Not everyone, Sulzer grants, is capable of this mental transfer from normal waking attention to dream consciousness. The artist can prompt illusion only in those who possess a responsive sensibility and lively imagination. To the extent that he succeeds in directing our attention exclusively to the performance, he has us in that dreamlike spell which he stimulates, and seeks to hold, by avoiding any distracting inconsistencies, contradictions, improbabilities. The "imitation of nature" is a useful rule for art, Sulzer affirms, just as it is useful in describing dreams; the artist, that is, is not bound to external nature, but to sustain illusion he must make sure that his images conform to our perception of nature.[97] It is worth noting that Sulzer has no concept of the subconscious or unconscious; dream consciousness is merely inward-directed consciousness. Also missing from Sulzer's theory is a tolerance of paradox, or an allowance for multiple "levels" of illusion.

When Schiller relates dream to illusion, he refers to an essentially empty or negative aesthetic experience. Thus Schiller's "On the Use of the Chorus in Tragedy" ("Über den Gebrauch des Chors in der Tragödie," 1803) has been cited as an Anti-Illusionist argument.[98] But to make Schiller a spokesman for Anti-Illusionist aesthetics is problematic indeed. The play theory developed in his "Kallias" (1793) and "On the Aesthetic Education of Humanity" ("Über die ästhetische Erziehung des Menschen," 1795) depended on appearance as opposed to reality. Art is not free, but it must seem free. Because of the constraints of the artistic medium (whether the sculptor's marble, the painter's oils and canvas, the poet's language), there are certain material and formal obstacles confronting the expression of the artistic idea. During his apprenticeship, the artist learns to confront these obstacles; once he has mastered his skills, he no longer exposes his own

---

97. Sulzer, "Täuschung." Sulzer's work went through three editions during the first decade of publication (Leipzig, 1771–74; 2d ed. 1773–75; 3d ed. 1778–79).

98. Strube, "Ästhetische Illusion," 181–83.

struggle with his media. Art is "freedom in appearance" ("Freiheit in der Erscheinung").[99]

To be sure, Schiller does say that the chorus may be an "external thing," a "foreign body," which merely "disrupts the course of action" and "destroys the illusion." But these negative consequences follow only when the chorus is without its proper function. That lesser mode of art which merely provides an "escape from the constraints of reality," "a pleasing madness for the moment," "a transitory illusion," Schiller distinguishes from the more earnest endeavor of art, which is not content with "a momentary dream of freedom" but actually strives to make man free. There are, then, two modes of illusion: one, a passing fantasy wrought by engaging the senses in mimetic play; the other, an educative process that allows the spectator to see through the sensual matter and discover the "free working of the mind." The illusion of art that Schiller endorses, then, is not that it seems real, but rather that it reveals the very freedom by which idea informs matter.

If one went no further than his claim that "art must never content itself merely with the illusion of reality," Schiller might indeed sound like an Anti-Illusionist. His argument, however, is that art must achieve a far more significant illusion by revealing the very freedom of the creative process. Because the tragic chorus mediates between the ideal and the sensual, appearing to step between the two planes of dramatic action and to interpret their interaction, Schiller defends its use in contemporary drama.[100] "Fantastic scenes lined up together do not achieve the ideal, and bringing back imitations of reality does not represent nature." Both misdirected efforts fail to realize that the ideal and nature are not opposite poles; rather, they are one and the same: "Art is thereby true only when it completely abandons reality and becomes purely ideal." Since "nature itself is only an idea of the mind," art represents nature in becoming ideal. Thus the drama is made to serve false purposes when it is supposed to create a convincing imitation of reality; in this error, "one demands *illusion*, which, even if it were really to be achieved, would always be a poor charlatan's fraud."[101]

99. Schiller, "Kallias," in *Sämtliche Werke* V, 394–433; "Über die ästhetische Erziehung des Menschen," in *Sämtliche Werke* V, 570–669; Wenzel, *Das Problem des Scheins in der Ästhetik: Schillers Ästhetische Briefe.*
100. According to Crabb Robinson (28 January 1811), "Coleridge seemed willing to censure Schiller's and Schlegel's ideas concerning the German idea of the Greek chorus, but he did not fix any reproach upon them that I could comprehend. Neither did he show the analogy between the chorus and the Fool [in Shakespeare's *King Lear*]," *Henry Crabb Robinson on Books and their Writers* I, 21.
101. Schiller, "Über der Gebrauch des Chors in der Tragödie," in *Sämtliche Werke* II, 815–23.

The autonomy of mind must be brought into play and replicated in art as *heautonomy*. Schiller identifies three basic drives in human creativity: the *Stofftrieb* is the delight in raw material, the impulse for physical contact and sensual interaction; the *Formtrieb* is the drive to give shape, order, harmony to experience; the *Spieltrieb* brings the two former drives together in free play, so that, instead of form becoming subservient matter, or *vice versa*, the two are engaged together. The purpose of play is to bring the rational and the sensual, the formal and the physical attributes of human being into balance. That balance, expressed as "living shape" (*lebende Gestalt*), is what we recognize as beautiful. At the end of the "Kallias" letters Schiller defined the beautiful in poetry as the "free self-determination of nature in the chains of language." In the letters on "Aesthetic Education," he works out the paradox through the facility of play. Man has his freedom because he can balance, play with, his mental and physical inclinations. Schiller developed his play theory to counter the Kantian exclusion of sensual participation in the intellectualized aesthetic moment of "disinterestedness." Schiller's concept of play restores interested involvement of the whole human being: man "is only completely man, when he plays." This means that art cannot be reduced to the merely sensual, nor made the instrument of political or moral doctrine: "With the beautiful one should only *play*, and one should play *only with the beautiful*."[102] Through play we come to the ultimate illusion of art: The inanimate appears animated and freedom becomes visible as "living shape."

The next two chapters are devoted to unraveling a problem that has long complicated the discussion of the Romantic reception of Shakespeare. Coleridge in his lectures of 1811–12 began to intersperse a number of ideas that were borrowed from Schlegel's lectures (published in 1809 and 1811). Like Coleridge, Schlegel too had read widely in the theories of the drama reviewed in these first three chapters. Many of Schlegel's basic tenets were adapted from Lessing, Herder, and Schiller. Coleridge delved into these very same sources. Although Schlegel is generally hostile to French theory, again like Coleridge, he covertly absorbed many of their arguments.[103] It is

---

102. Schiller, *Sämtliche Werke* V, 433, 618; for commentary on this mediation in relation to Hegelian dialectic, see Pillau, *Die fortgedachte Dissonanz. Hegels Tragödientheorie und Schillers Tragödie*, 27–32, 155–68.

103. Coleridge, *Lectures 1808–1819: On Literature* I, lix–lxiv; A. W. Schlegel, *Vorlesungen über dramatische Kunst und Literatur*, in *Kritische Schriften und Briefe* V, 5–6. See also Bate, *Shakespeare and the English Romantic Imagination*, 9–16.

important, therefore, to keep the debate over illusion, as it had been fostered during the Enlightenment, well in mind while reading Schlegel and Coleridge. Only by giving very close attention to their discussion of specific plays is it possible to observe how radically different they are in their critical interpretation. Schlegel stresses the thematization of illusion. Coleridge emphasizes the poetic imagination.

4

Illusion and the Play: A. W. Schlegel

While it is helpful to study August Wilhelm Schlegel's theory of the drama in terms of his response to the aesthetics of the Enlightenment and his involvement in the Romantic "school," so many of his literary concepts have been identified as borrowings from Lessing or Herder, from Friedrich Schlegel or Caroline Schlegel, that his practical and theoretical criticism has been called an extended exercise in reception and variation.[1] Nevertheless, his *Vorlesungen über dramatische Kunst und Literatur* remains the major statement on the drama in the Romantic period and an important clearinghouse for critical ideas. Coleridge relied on Schlegel as a source for his own lectures on Shakespeare, borrowing the distinction between *mechanic* and *organic* form, and between the *plastisch* and *pittoreske*.[2] De Quincey borrowed

---

1. Gebhardt, *Schlegels Shakespeare-Übersetzungen. Untersuchungen zu seinem Übersetzungsverfahren am Beispiel des Hamlet*, 11.
2. That Coleridge took, among many passages from Schlegel, the distinction between mechanic and organic form has been repeatedly documented—see note 21 below; for Coleridge's account of dramatic illusion, see chapter 5.

them too, then perversely praised himself for being the first to point out Coleridge's plagiarism.[3]

The factor of unacknowledged sources and influences also complicates any attempt to explain Schlegel's contribution to the prevailing discussion of dramatic illusion. Chapters 2 and 3 traced several different accounts of illusion in the latter eighteenth century: Diderot's paradoxical mediation of the players; Mendelssohn's audience affected through emotional excitation; and Lessing's audience affected through sympathy. This chapter will describe how the effects of illusion became distinguished and separated from emotional excitation or sympathy. The power of the drama, for Schlegel, resides in the play itself, or, rather, in the way in which the thematic conjuring of illusion elicits audience participation. Dramatic illusion, as Schlegel defines it, is a thorough engagement of perception and an active participation in the dialogic interchange; its elements are *Teilnahme* and *Täuschung*.[4] In the theater, the spectator does not merely respond in emotional sympathy, he is called to witness the dramatic plotting of illusion.

In describing the spontaneous sensual experience of dramatic illusion, Schlegel returns to the eighteenth-century questions: How does aesthetic illusion work upon the mind? How are its effects discriminated from "real" experience? Schlegel resolves the mystery of illusion in terms that clearly anticipate Coleridge's formula for "poetic faith" as the "willing suspension of disbelief for the moment." Coleridge, discussed in the next chapter, gives more importance to the volitional commitment. Therefore, in examining Coleridge's idea of illusion, it is not necessary to trace cause and effect throughout his exposition of Shakespeare's plays. For Schlegel, however, illusion pervades plot, character, and dialogue. The illusions that characters have about themselves, as well as the dissimulation and disguise that so often becomes a part of their role playing, are inseparable from the illusions conjured by the playwright. Schlegel emphasizes how readily we respond to the compelling enchantment of the theater. Just as natural instincts prompt a protective suspicion when we confront an optical illusion, the spectator assumes an alert caution, testing the causality of his experience as it occurs. Literary criticism should pursue a similar cautious testing, Schlegel asserts, as it attempts to explain and enhance the intellec-

---

3. Jordan, *Thomas De Quincey, Literary Critic*, 104–13, 190–91; De Quincey, *Selected Essays on Rhetoric*, xvii–xxi, 163–67, 315.

4. As discussed in chapter 2 above, Ludwig Tieck had also utilized the concepts of *Täuschung* and *Teilnahme* in his essay, "Shakespeare's Behandlung des Wunderbaren" (1793).

tual awareness of art even while it celebrates the power of the imagination to engender illusion.

Schlegel's theory of the drama builds upon a set of basic premises: Drama is poetic dialogue; as poetry, it develops through the imagination, not through the reason. The theater grows out of cultural traditions and national values; therefore, each country must encourage its own playwrights rather than relying on foreign models. From these same premises, Schlegel derived his most often cited distinctions: the classic and the romantic, the plastic and the picturesque, the organic and the mechanic. Classical art, as it emerged in ancient Greece, values the ideal, the simple, the finite; romantic art, as evident in Christian Europe, prefers the mystical, the complex, the infinite. The forms of classical art are plastic: the artist approaches his material as the sculptor his marble. In the plays of Aeschylus, Sophocles, and Euripedes, dramatic character is shaped with the same exterior constraint as in Attic sculpture. Romantic art, however, is picturesque, attending more to content than to form.[5] Both the classic and the romantic are organic, for they grow naturally out of the cultures in which they are engendered. That art is mechanical which appropriates the forms of another culture, defines them according to rational principles, advocates imitation, and opposes imaginative play. The French pretensions to the classic, then, are mechanic rather than organic.

While the basic premises of Schlegel's theory are clearly set forth in his *Vorlesungen*, delivered in Vienna in 1808 and published in Heidelberg in 1809 (vols. 1 and 2) and 1811 (vol. 2, part 2), he had been nourishing his ideas on the drama since he began translating Shakespeare a dozen years earlier. In preparing the Viennese lectures for publication, the text grew and grew, especially the commentary on Shakespeare. Schlegel wrote to his publisher to apologize for the delay in revising the lectures: "I wanted to comply to some degree with the expectations which one might assume from a writer, who has occupied himself for many years of his life with this poet."[6]

---

5. A. W. Schlegel, *Kritische Schriften und Briefe* (=*KSB*), repeats the comparison of classical poetry to sculpture and modern poetry to painting: II, 86, 101, 104–8; V, 45, 69–71, 73, 79, 99, 209–10; VI, 28, 112–13. The comparison derives from Lessing's *Über das Laokoon* and was appropriated by Jean Paul Richter in his *Vorschule der Ästhetik* as well as by both August Wilhelm and Friedrich Schlegel (Kluckhohn, *Das Ideengut der deutschen Romantik*, 163–68).

6. "Ich wünschte einigermassen der Erwartung zu entsprechen, die man von einem Schriftsteller hegen kann, der sich mehrere Jahre seines Lebens mit diesem Dichter beschäftigt hat." Letter to Johann Georg Zimmer, 6 August 1810, *August Wilhelm Schlegels Briefwechsel mit seinen Heidelberger Verlegern*, 64.

In his previous essays and lectures, Shakespeare had become both the organ and the organon for his exposition of the drama. Whether he is surveying the history of the drama, explaining its aesthetic effects, or analyzing specific plays, Shakespeare is his everpresent critical touchstone. Before we turn to the *Vorlesungen*, then, it will be useful to examine the formative ideas on aesthetic process in Schlegel's earlier work.

In his essay, "Etwas über William Shakespeare bei Gelegenheit Wilhelm Meisters" (1796),[7] Schlegel takes the popular reception of Goethe's novel as an occasion to set forth his notions on the drama and, in none too subtle a justification of his own efforts, to call for a new translation of Shakespeare. Wilhelm Meister's initiation into the theater and acting, especially his account of *Hamlet*, provides Schlegel an appropriate context to define the crucial importance of poetic language in conjuring dramatic illusion. The difficulties in acting Hamlet, explains Wilhelm Meister, have led to his discovery of a method for studying a character.[8] The task is to enter fully into the character and to be able to portray every subtlety and nuance. The method is to recreate the prehistory of the character, to imagine, that is, the growth of the character prior to the circumstances that he confronts upon the stage. In contrast to earlier accounts of the "sympathetic imagination" in acting, which tended to rely on vaguely emotional processes by which the actor was to feel his way into a part,[9] Goethe offers a concrete approach to the study of character. In illustrating his case, he has Wilhelm Meister sketch Hamlet's character before the death of his father. Following his account, the troupe of players applaud this manner of penetrating both the "spirit of the role" ("Geist der Rolle") and the "Spirit of the writer" ("Geist des Schriftstellers"), and each of them immediately picks up a play in order to practice the method.

Although he is willing to concede that Wilhelm Meister's method may help prepare an actor to perform a complex character, Schlegel also emphasizes that the actor need only address the exterior attributes of characterization:

> He may therefore be quite capable of accommodating himself within the prescribed outlines, and to animate the character through the

---

7. Schlegel, *Kritische Schriften und Briefe* (=*KSB*) I, 88–122. Subsequent references to this edition will be given parenthetically in the text. German quotations are provided in the footnotes to accompany translations in the text. For Schlegel's *Vorlesungen*, I use Black's translation in *Lectures on Dramatic Art and Literature;* other translations are my own.

8. Goethe, *Wilhelm Meisters Lehrjahre*, book 4, chap. 3.

9. Wasserman, "The Sympathetic Imagination in Eighteenth-Century Theories of Acting."

richest and most beautiful coloring of his person, his voice, his gestures; indeed, he may bring a perfect harmony to the expression of a character without being able to penetrate the most secret and primal ground why each attribute is thus or so. Does this mean that an actor might conceive Hamlet in accord with Wilhelm Meister's explanation, without knowing it and without being able to express it himself? Precisely so.[10]

Nor is it necessary for the actor to understand more than the external manifestations of character:

> The poet spares him from the concern with finding a great inner coherence in all of this. So long as the actor does not destroy what has been given, the spectators, in accord with the measure of their abilities, will feel it more or less darkly, until a more profound intellect helps to bring their presentiment into the light of understanding.[11]

The player can play Hamlet without comprehending the inner motives of his character. The spectator, again with no complete understanding of the inner motives, can respond to Hamlet's tragedy. Nor is it the philosopher whom Schlegel would call forth to explain to actors and audience the meaning of Hamlet's dilemma. Even for the philosopher, the human mind is too complex to be reduced to concrete explanation: "Still less is it his task to guess with sheer luck or through a bold stroke try to tie together at one juncture, where they happen to touch at a common point, those relationships which frequently cross and extend in an incomprehensible maze."[12] A

---

10. *KSB* I, 92. "Er kann daher sehr gut imstande sein sich treu in die vorgezeichneten Umrisse zu fügen, und sie durch das kräftigste und schönste Kolorit seiner Person, seiner Stimme, seiner Gebärden zu beleben, ja er kann eine vollkommene Harmonie in die Äußerungen eines Charakters bringen, ohne doch die geheimsten und ersten Gründe, warum jedes so oder so ist, zu durchschauen. Also könnte wohl gar ein Schauspieler den Hamlet übereinstimmend mit Wilhelm Meisters Erklärung vorstellen, ohne von dieser zu wissen und ohne imstande zu sein, sie selbst zu geben? Nicht anders."

11. Ibid. "Der Dichter überhebt ihn der Sorge für einen großen, innigen Zusammenhang in allem diesem. Wenn er derselben nur nicht zerstört, so werden ihn die Zuschauer nach Maßgabe ihrer Fähigkeiten mehr oder weniger dunkel fühlen, bis ihnen einmal ein überlegener Geist hilft, die Ahnung bis zur Erkenntnis aufzuhellen."

12. Ibid. "Desto weniger ist es seine Sache, glücklich kühn zu erraten, und Verhältnisse, die sich vielfach durchkreuzen und unübersehlich auseinanderlaufen, durch einen raschen Griff bei dem einzigen gemeinschaftlichen Berührungspunkte aller zu fassen."

reductive explanation of character will lead actor and spectator alike into misinterpretation. How then is one to know Hamlet? Through an ever deeper penetration into the illusion of his being. For Schlegel, this is a hermeneutic task. One has already begun to trace the hermeneutic circle with the "presentiment" of Hamlet's human being. Hamlet is not simply a character: he has character.

The hermeneutic process attempts first to identify and then to cast light upon the "dark passages" of a text. Rather than reiterate eighteenth-century explanations of what causes an impenetrable text,[13] Schlegel formulates his own account of negative and positive obscurity. There are, he says, three sources of literary obscurity. The first two are lethal to aesthetic experience; the third, however, contributes to its fullest consummation. The first derives from the author's incapacity to express his thoughts; his ideas may be sound, but his language omits the best part. The second derives from the author's inability to fathom his own imagination; his fantasy may be productive but enveloped in confusion, "which hinders it from ever giving its offspring a proper shape" (*KSB* I, 92). The third source of darkness lies in the very capacity of reason and imagination to peer into the mystery of being, "the unfathomable abyss of creative nature."[14] Life, says Schlegel, is the great secret of nature, and it is the task of the dramatic artist not to solve its riddles but to imitate its inscrutable power. The darkness does not dissipate as the artist seeks to penetrate the abyss of being in creating human character; indeed, the darkness grows more intense the more he succeeds in revealing the depths. Those aspects of character, however, which are revealed to our perceptions must fit together as parts within the whole. Even that spectator whose perception is guided more by "presentiment" than by "understanding" must recognize the dramatic character as fellow man.

Because the response to character cannot be explained by critical explication, it really does not matter whether Shakespeare conceived of Hamlet in the same, or even similar, terms as those deduced by Wilhelm Meister. One must distinguish, Schlegel asserts, between "evident perceptions" ("anschauliche Wahrnehmung") and "derived conceptions" ("entwickelte Begriffe"). The conceptual is never adequate to the task of explaining the perceptual, and it is very probable that Shakespeare knew more about his Hamlet than he

---

13. Chladenius, *Einleitung zur richtigen Auslegung vernünfftiger Reden und Schrifften*, §179, 96–103.
14. *KSB* I, 92–93, "welche sie hindert, ihre Geburten jemals recht auf Reine zu bringen," "die Unergründlichkeit der schaffenden Natur."

consciously thought he knew (*KSB*, I, 94). Schlegel does not give explicit formulation here to his later distinction between the organic and the mechanic, but he clearly privileges an intuitive and perceptual access to the meaning of human nature over the most refined efforts of logic:

> Although man's science cannot claim to have fathomed the essence even of a single atom, it persists in dissecting the dead products of the physical world into their simple constituent parts; it can attentively investigate all the vital elements of an organized being in terms of structure and components. But has it ever discovered that living energy, the effects of which we see everywhere around us and which we feel within ourselves?[15]

While the discursive understanding can only explicate through a dissection of the constituent parts, the perceptions at once engage and sympathetically replicate the essential human feelings, the very life and being of the character. Thus Schlegel calls for a literary interpretation that begins with the natural responses.

It is by no means a mere nod to cultural relativism that leads him to postulate the importance of national and cultural manners to the drama. Among the many forms of literary expression, the drama is most thoroughly a social phenomena. The theater is not simply a building in which people gather to witness a play; the theater is itself a product of historical tradition and social ritual, akin to church or senate or marketplace, where people gather with certain socially defined expectations to participate in a communal event. The characters who appear on the stage must therefore share prevailing notions of good and evil if they are to excite the passionate involvement of the theater audience. Through an extensive affinity with the language as well as with the manners and mores, Schlegel insists, the Germans have readily accepted Shakespeare as their own poet. Shakespeare is so perfectly at home on the German stage that the German spectator immediately recognizes the play as a public rendition of his own private thoughts

---

15. Ibid., 93. "Obgleich sich die menschliche Wissenschaft nicht rühmen darf, das Wesen eines einzigen Atoms erschöpft zu haben, so kann sie doch die toten Erzeugnisse der Körperwelt in ihre einfacheren Bestandteile zerlegen; sie kann an organisierten Geschöpfen alle Werkzeuge des Lebens nach ihrem Bau und ihren Bestandteilen sehr genau untersuchen. Allein hat sie jemals die lebendigen Kräfte selbst erhascht, die wir überall um uns her wirkend sehen, deren eine wir in uns fühlen?"

and feelings: "The extravagances of his fantasy and his feelings (which can be compared to nothing else) are exactly those, which we are most often inclined to indulge, and his characteristic virtues seem to be most particularly intended for the high-minded German."[16] In its exhibition of human nature and social conditions, the world of Shakespeare's plays is coextensive with the real world familiar to any German theatergoer (*KSB* I, 105).

As he acknowledges in his 1827 editorial note to this essay (*KSB* I, 118–22),[17] the argument on the proper German rendition of Shakespeare's plays was written in justification of his own translation. Because he intended to retain in his translation Shakespeare's use of poetry and prose as well as the shifts in high and low diction, he had felt in 1796 that a certain polemical stance was called for to defend the dramatic propriety of blank verse on the stage. Indeed, so much of the essay is devoted to a defense of blank verse that Schlegel may seem to belabor the obvious. In 1827, the battle had been won to restore poetry as dramatic language. But in 1796 poetry was effectively banned. The pompous declamation of hexameters in the classical French style had prompted Lessing to lead the campaign to purge the theater of dramatic verse. J. J. Engel, as theater director in Berlin, continued the zealous prohibition of metrical language in the drama.[18] In taking up the defense of Shakespeare's use of blank verse and its potential advantage even in contemporary performance, Schlegel emphasizes the conjuring power of poetry and its contribution to dramatic illusion.

In his note "Über den dramatischen Dialog. 1796," Schlegel argues that the essence of the drama resides in its dialogic action. What, he asks, distinguishes the theater from the marketplace? Both are places where crowds flock and where man has occasion to observe the deliberations and actions of his fellow man. Admittedly, the marketplace also serves a commercial function as a place where farmers and tradesmen sell their wares and people come to buy. The theater may, in contrast, seem to be a palace of vanity where man beholds the portrayal of his own image and thus merely gratifies a sense of his own importance. The theater, however, gives man the

---

16. Ibid., 100, "Die Ausschweifungen seiner Phantasie und seines Gefühls (gibt es anderes dergleichen) sind gerade die, denen wir selbst am meisten ausgesetzt sind, und seine eigentümlichen Tugenden gelten einem edlen Deutschen unter allen am höchsten."

17. Schlegel provided notes and commentary when editing his *Kritische Schriften*, 2 vols. (Berlin: Georg Reimer, 1828).

18. Lessing, *Hamburgische Dramaturgie*, no. 15, in *Werke*, ed. Göpfert, et al., IV, 298–303; Engel, *Über Handlung, Gespräch und Erzählung*.

rare opportunity to witness a fine distillation of human experience. The tedium, the boredom, the humdrum routine of daily experience are removed in order to reveal the essence of human character. By concentrating attention on the decisive moments of life, the playwright can expose the secret motives and the inner workings of mind in less time than is normally required to take stock of a person's external appearance and social mannerisms. Plot, according to Schlegel's conception of the drama, is always subservient to character. Events must be selected and disposed in such a way as to develop or reveal character (*KSB* I, 107). For the same reason, plot is also subservient to dialogue. Dialogue is the playwright's sole means of presenting character (*KSB* I, 108).

The drama, then, is an exhibition of human character and it works through dialogue. Schlegel provides two sets of critical conditions, the first for defining, the second for evaluating the dialogue. First, he defines its structure: the interchange of reflection and speech, action and reaction. Dialogue comprises not only speaking but also those silences in which each character broods on what he hears and what he has to say; it consists, therefore, of the interdependency of speaker and auditor. As speaker and auditor exchange roles, we witness in the continuum of cause and effect a progressive unfolding of character. Monologue, too, becomes dialogue when we see a character truly talking to, and answering, himself; soliloquy, that is, becomes dramatic only when it involves the dialogic action and reaction in speaking and deliberating. Secondly, Schlegel suggests that the dialogue may also be usefully studied in terms of the perfection attained: its generic perfection as dialogue; the affective perfection of its content and expression. Perfection, here, means a complete revelation of the subjective through the dialogic interchange; perfection also means the complete participation of the auditor and the speaker. The audience, Schlegel says, is caught up in that participation. Proportionate to the playwright's success in dialogue, the aesthetic response of the audience is heightened (*KSB* I, 109–10).[19]

Granting the structural conditions that are necessary to dialogue, he points out that the playwright may choose to undermine those conditions. The imperfect dialogue, or nondialogic dialogue, can also provide a telling dramatic effect, as in the French farce, *Le Babillard*, where two characters, each too preoccupied to listen to the other, nevertheless pretend to engage

---

19. Jauß, "Der dialogische und der dialektische *Neveau de Rameau* oder: Wie Diderot Sokrates und Hegel Diderot reziptierte" and "Anmerkungen zum idealen Gespräch."

in conversation (*KSB* I, 109 and note). Whether or not the characters fully participate in the dialogue, the audience is an active partner alert to even those aspects of the interchange which the characters on the stage might miss or misconceive. Dramatic irony rests on precisely this sort of disparity between the dialogue on the stage and the audience participation in the dialogue. The task of the playwright is to develop the dialogue in such a way as to draw out character through the interaction of the participants.

The interchange of speaker and auditor conveys the intellectual and emotional excitement of the moment. Asserting the same argument that Lessing forwarded in *Briefe, die neueste Literatur betreffend*, no. 51 (16 August 1759), Schlegel emphasizes the illusion of spontaneity as crucial to the dramatic effect of the dialogue. The seeming spontaneity of dialogue, in fact, is the primary source of all theatrical illusion. The illusion rests on perfectly natural social conditions. We all are familiar with those individuals who try to make a spontaneous inspiration sound as if it were a carefully deliberated and well-rehearsed opinion, or those who privately memorize witticisms and clever phrases which they then seek to insert into an evening's conversation as if they were conceived impromptu. The playwright may have the actor play with either pretension in dialogue. If we see the actor simply reciting lines, however, the dialogue ceases and the dramatic illusion is disrupted (*KSB* I, 110–12). Nevertheless, the power of the aesthetic experience rests fully in the appreciation of the drama as illusion: "To promote pleasure in any entertainment, illusion is more important than truth; in drama, moreover, it is already understood that the appearance of spontaneity in dialogue is pure illusion."[20]

When all the artifice of the drama would seem to oppose the effort, what, we may well ask, enables the playwright to engender and sustain the illusion of spontaneity? In answering this question, Schlegel appropriates Aristotle's argument that "probable impossibilities" serve the drama more effectively than "improbable possibilities." As an example of improbability, he cites the use of metrical language, and he repeats Lessing's objections. Are we to believe that Brutus and Cassius deliberated their plot to murder Caesar in carefully modulated blank verse? For that matter, Schlegel asks, are we

---

20. *KSB* I, 111. "Für das Vergnügen der Unterhaltung entscheidet hierbei der Schein mehr als die Wahrheit; im Drama versteht es sich ohnehin schon, daß das Ansehen des Unvorbereiteten in den Reden bloßer Schein ist." For Lessing's argument that illusion depends upon the apparent spontaneity of dialogue, see *Briefe, die neueste Literatur betreffend*, no. 51 (16 August 1759), in *Werke* V, 184.

supposed to believe that Brutus and Cassius have abandoned their native Latin and stand before us, eighteen centuries after the deed, upon some stage in London, speaking perfect English and pretending to repeat their act even though the Roman capitol is far away and Caesar lies long dead? (*KSB* I, 113) Shakespeare himself could play with the improbabilities inherent in dramatic illusion. In *All's Well That Ends Well*, we follow Bertram and Parolles from Paris to Florence and are privy to the plot of the French lords to trap Parolles, the "damnable both-sides rogue" who "hath a smack of all neighboring languages." Confident that we, his audience, have thoroughly accepted the illusion that we, too, understand the languages of the Continent, Shakespeare treats us to the game of the French soldiers in Italy speaking a mock language:

> Second Lord. Throca movousus, cargo, cargo, cargo.
> All. Cargo, cargo, cargo, villianda par corbo, cargo.
> Parolles. O, ransom, ransom! do not hide mine eyes.
>   [They seize and blindfold him.]
> First Soldier. Boskos thromuldo boskos.
> Parolles. I know you are the Muskos' regiment:
> And I shall lose my life for want of language:
> If there be here German, or Dane, Low Dutch,
> Italian, or French, let him speak to me; I'll
> Discover that which shall undo the Florentine.
>   (IV.i.71–80)

Desperately grasping for an apt *parole*, Parolles reveals that his quick tongue may be facile enough to delude Bertram, but that his *lingua franca* is a hybrid of opportunism, cowardice, and lies. For the alert spectator, of course, the game of language both exposes and enhances the dramatic pretenses of language. Illusion neither overwhelms our reason with emotion, nor persuades it with convincing replication of reality. As Schlegel seeks to demonstrate, we fully appreciate the conditionality of illusion. Thus we savor the paradox of the transformed player when we observe Hamlet instructing the players. We accept the representation because he has engaged our imagination in the play of possibilities:

> Theatrical illusion need not adhere to that probability, among many possible consequences, attributed to the one course of events most

abundantly grounded and perhaps even arithmetically determined; rather, theatrical illusion depends on the appearance of truth to the senses. What may be unlikely, completely wrong, almost impossible in terms of probability, may nevertheless appear to be true so long as the grounds for impossibility are left out of the circle of our comprehension or are cleverly veiled from our attention.[21]

Although reason and illusion, as Schlegel observes, never seem to tolerate one another, they do coexist. Just as darkness is necessary to the definition of light, reality is necessary to the definition of art. The engagement of illusion is conditioned by the knowledge of its artifice; the aesthetic experience is sustained by the simultaneity of "observing and forgetting" ("beobachten und vergessen" *KSB* I, 113–14).

Although he is consistent in defining the theater as a product of national culture, this concept takes on immediate social and political significance when he examines the contemporary contexts of art in his essay, "Über Literatur, Kunst und Geist des Zeitalters" (1803), published in Friedrich Schlegel's *Europa*. While social causes can direct and unify a people, faction and political turmoil disrupt and divide. The drama, because it is the most public of the arts, is also the most sensitive in responding to, and potentially the most powerful in influencing, the "Spirit of the Age" ("Geist des Zeitalters"). The want of effective national consciousness in contemporary theater, Schlegel complains, has allowed originality to be usurped by translations and bad imitations of French, English, and Italian plays. The influence of Diderot, through Lessing, has brought the stage under the domination of a false doctrine of "naturalness," which is, in fact, no more than a lack of art.[22] The problem is not easy to correct, because bad theater perpetuates itself. So, too, does good theater, which might be restored if playwrights, actors, and audience would reflect more attentively on the nature of their mutual experience in the theater:

21. *KSB* I, 113. "Bei der theatralischen Täuschung kommt es gar nicht auf jene Wahrscheinlichkeit an, die man unter mehreren möglichen Erfolgen demjenigen zuschreibt, welcher die meisten Gründe für sich hat, und die sich in vielen Fällen sogar arithmetisch bestimmen läßt, sondern auf den sinnlichen Schein der Wahrheit. Was in jener Bedeutung unwahrscheinlich, völlig falsch, ja fast unmöglich ist, kann dennoch wahr zu sein scheinen, wenn nur der Grund der Unmöglichkeit außer dem Kreise unserer Erkenntnis liegt, oder uns geschickt verschleiert wird."

22. Schlegel, "Über Litteratur, Kunst und Geist des Zeitalters," 12.

Through reciprocal influence, playwright, player, and public naturally find themselves in harmony; just as they mutually develop in response to one another, so too they can pervert the relationship in a faulty circle which is ever again the cause of its own corruption. Incrementally, then, the most talented minds abandon the stage, and good plays remain unwritten, for no one is left who knows how to perform them properly, nor even how properly to listen or see.[23]

To restore the arts to the people, the people must realize their own community as a people. Because the aesthetic experience of the drama is so fully the experience of community, the restoration of the harmonic circle of playwright, player, and spectator is the most obvious arena in which to begin the general redirection of the "Spirit of the Age."

In his *Vorlesungen über dramatische Kunst und Literatur,* Schlegel reasserts his conception of the drama as dialogue, but he now explains dramatic action in three aesthetic contexts: the human, the poetic, and the theatrical. Human activity is the primal source of pleasure and provides the stimulating effects in dramatic art. Schlegel does not mean by activity the basic animal behavior of man in nature; activity is never solitary but is excited through social intercourse:

> The highest object of human activity is man, and in the drama we see men, measuring their powers with each other, as intellectual and moral beings, either as friends or foes, influencing each other by their opinions, sentiments, and passions, and decisively determining their reciprocal relations and circumstances.[24]

The action, then, is an interaction that not only involves one character with another but also engages the anticipation and response of the spectator.

---

23. Ibid., 14. "Dichter, Schauspieler und Publikum setzen sich natürlich durch gegenseitigen Einfluß in Harmonie, wie sie sich selbst einander zubilden, so können sie sich auch wieder verbilden; ein fehlerhafter Zirkel, in welchem das Verderben dann immer wieder Ursache von sich selbst wird. So entziehen sich die besten Köpfe der Bühne immer mehr und mehr, und gute Stücke bleiben deswegen ungeschrieben, weil man nicht mehr versteht, sie gehörig aufzuführen, noch auch sie gehörig zu hören."

24. *KSB* V, 29. "Der höchste Gegenstand menschlicher Tätigkeit ist der Mensch, und im Schauspiele sehen wir Menschen in freundlichem oder feindseligem Verkehr ihre Kräfte aneinander messen, als verständige und sittliche Wesen durch ihre Meinungen, Gesinnungen und Leidenschaften aufeinander einwirken und ihre Verhältnisse gegenseitig entscheidend bestimmen."

"Closet drama," for Schlegel, is a contradiction in terms. Drama, after all, is the presentation of action through dialogue. Unless the dialogic action can excite the mimetic tendencies of the spectator, an attempt at drama cannot succeed on the stage. Nor can one read a play with an appreciation of its dramatic effectiveness without being familiar with stage production. The reader who has the capacity of "thinking" the production ("die Aufführung hinzuzudenken" *KSB* V, 30) draws from his experience in the theater, which, in turn, rests upon primal mimetic behavior.

The theater as a cultural phenomenon is merely the maturation and formalization of the natural tendency to mime, which is everywhere evident in the play of children. From the mimetic play of children to the development of the theater is but a simple step, a step which has been taken in most cultures throughout history. The mimetic tendency to act out the fragments of social life assumes a ritualistic significance as it is brought before a mass of people. Joys and fears, laughter and tears, otherwise suppressed or privately indulged, are revealed collectively and without shame as the emotions of a community (*KSB* V, 35). In the theater an audience expresses shared values and feelings.

Schlegel's whole course of lectures is concerned with distinguishing the cultural elements that contribute to the particular characteristics of the Greek drama in contrast to the Roman, the ancient in contrast to the modern, and the French and Italian in contrast to the Spanish, English, and German. While it is possible to glean sundry references to the peculiarities of the dramatic illusion within a given culture, the important point is that dramatic illusion is promoted by the sense of community:

> Almost inconceivable is the power of a visible communion of numbers to give intensity to those feelings of the heart which usually retire into privacy, or only open themselves to the confidence of friendship. The faith in the validity of such emotions becomes irrefragable from its diffusion; we feel ourselves strong among so many associates, and all minds and hearts flow together in one great and irresistible stream.[25]

---

25. Ibid., 37. "Es ist unglaublich, welche verstärkende Kraft die sichtbare Gemeinschaft vieler für ein inniges Gefühl hat, das sich sonst gewöhnlich in die Einsamkeit zurückzieht oder nur in freundschaftlicher Zutraulichkeit offenbart. Der Glaube an dessen Gültigkeit wird durch seine Verbreitung unerschütterlich, wir fühlen uns stark unter so vielen Mitgenossen, und alle Gemüter fließen in einen großen unwiderstehlichen Strom zusammen."

The evocation of illusion, however, can be easily abused; its positive manifestation as aesthetic experience can be turned to that negative end often called "mass hysteria."

As noted in the first chapter, no critics have argued the power of dramatic illusion more emphatically than those who also hold that the theater is a dangerous and immoral institution. Schlegel has such arguments in mind when he addresses the abuse of the theater.

> As one may disinterestedly animate them [the assembled crowd], for the noblest and best of purposes, so another may entangle them in the deceitful meshes of sophistry, and dazzle them by the glare of a false magnanimity, whose vainglorious crimes may be painted as virtues and even as sacrifices. Beneath the delightful charms of oratory and poetry, the poison steals imperceptibly into ear and heart. Above all others must the comic poet (seeing that his very occupation keeps him always on the slippery brink of the precipice,) take heed, lest he afford an opportunity for the lower and baser parts of human nature to display themselves without restraint. When the sense of shame, which ordinarily keeps these baser propensities within the bounds of decency, is once weakened by the sight of others' participation in them, our inherent sympathy with what is vile will soon break out into the most unbridled licentiousness.[26]

No wonder, then, that lawmakers in all lands have looked with caution upon the theater and have often imposed censorship in the effort to control its demagogic powers for good and evil. The same wary concern, Schlegel reminds us, prompted Plato to ban the poets from his ideal Republic.

Because the drama is a performing art, it must be regarded in two additional contexts, as poetic and as theatrical expression. By *poetic* Schlegel is

---

26. Ibid. "Wie man sie [die versammelte Menge] für das Edelste und Beste uneigennützig begeistern kann, so läßt sie sich auf die andern Seite auch in sophistischen Truggeweben verstricken und von dem Schimmer falscher Seelengröße blenden, deren ehrgeizige Verbrechen als Tugend, ja als Aufopferung geschildert werden. Unter den gefälligen Einkleidungen der Redekunst und Poesie schleicht sich die Verführung unmerklich in die Ohren und Herzen ein. Vor allem hat sich der komische Dichter zu hüten, da er vermöge seiner Aufgabe immer an dieser Klippe hinstreift, daß er nicht dem Gemeinen und Niedrigen in der menschlichen Natur Luft mache, sich zuversichtlich zu äußern: ist durch den Anblick der Gemeinschaft auch in solchen unedlen Neigungen die Scham einmal überwunden, welche die gewöhnlich in die Grenzen der Anständigkeit zurückdrängt, so bricht das Wohlgefallen am Schlechten bald mit zügelloser Frechheit los."

not referring to metrical and ornamental language, but rather to the unity of form and content. As poetic form, the drama should be "a coherent, self-contained and satisfying whole." Poetic content must not merely reflect transcendental ideas (necessary and eternally true thoughts and feelings), it must also bring them before the senses as perceivable images. By *theatrical* Schlegel understands the aesthetic experience, the affective attributes of the stage performance. The purpose of the drama is to move the audience, to heighten their attention, to excite their participation. Just as the orator relies on clarity, timing, and emphasis to keep his audience from being distracted, the playwright, too, is concerned with holding the interest within the circle of the dramatic performance (*KSB* V, 34–35).

A crowd is a buzzing chaos of mutually stimulated distraction and becomes an audience only when the attention of the mass is attracted in one direction. Even then, attention will be readily scattered again unless there is an unrelenting appeal to eye and ear. From the moment the curtain rises, the playwright must command his audience. The appeal must be physical, engaging the senses. The audience must be taken out of themselves ("aus sich heraus versetzen") and made to participate in the action of the drama. Here the poetic and the theatrical come together. There is a kind of poetry that plays upon the sensations and draws forth an emotional response, Schlegel says, as from an Aeolian harp. Such poetry, however, usually works in solitary moments upon a reader who has deliberately sought privacy for this pleasure. The poetic appeal of the drama, as Schlegel repeatedly emphasizes, is a public affair and it works through bold stimulation of community response (*KSB* V, 35–36).

The spectator enters the circle of the dramatic performance as a member of a community. With the entire audience he attains identity in the dramatic action. Personal identity becomes redefined in terms of participation in the dialogue upon the stage. This is not to say that the spectator sacrifices his own identity as he becomes involved with the characters on the stage. Schlegel reminds us that the individual spectator is not alone in his involvement, rather he merges with the group consciousness of the audience. Each spectator communicates his emotions and each feels his own response to action on the stage charged synergistically by the mass of people surrounding him: his spirits rise or fall with the tides of laughter or sadness that move the entire audience. The more he is caught up in the collective experience, the less he is conscious of his own individual identity.

The poetic aspects of the drama work through dialogue to engage our involvement in character and action. The theatrical aspects solicit our sensory participation in the physical environment. Schlegel describes a complex accumulation of effects: The individual spectator responds to the community of spectators. The audience interacts with the dialogue on the stage. The emotions are stimulated by the dramatic action. The senses are teased by the stage setting. Dramatic illusion is produced, then, through an ensemble of poetic and theatrical effects, "where the magic of several arts may work in union." Although dramatic illusion does not depend upon the optical tricks of lighting and stage decoration, nor upon sound effects nor the mood-stirring accompaniment of music, the total ensemble of artistic efforts combine to enhance the conjuring power of the drama (*KSB* V, 38–39).

Up to this point Schlegel has only hinted at the duplicitous nature of dramatic illusion, the need not just to observe and forget its artifice (*KSB* I, 113–14) but also to resist as well as acquiesce to its spell. As he commences his history of the drama, however, he finds it necessary to propose a conscious awareness of illusion in order to explain specific plays.

Schlegel begins his history, of course, with the drama of ancient Greece. Continuing to develop his analysis of the poetic and theatrical contexts, he describes in detail the architecture of the amphitheater in order to explain the staging of the Greek drama. The very fact that this is an open-air theater contributes to the mingling of real and ideal that is an essential attribute of both comedy and tragedy. When Electra steps forward in the opening scene and speaks, "O thou pure sunlight, and thou air, earth's canopy, how often have ye heard the strains of my lament," her appeal is directed to the very real presence of the sun and the sky. The dramatic action visibly presumes the controlling forces of nature. Greek drama insists upon this copresence or coexistence of ideal and real: history and myth are fully integrated traditions. While human endeavor may be aggrandized to heroic dimensions, it still remains subject to the lusts, rivalries, jealousies, and petty drives. In tragedy, corporeal nature is subsumed within ideal aspirations (*KSB* V, 61–62). In comedy, the relationship is reversed: animal nature dominates, but only because man chooses to ignore the ideal harmony with higher nature and to enslave his reason and understanding in base servitude to the senses (*KSB* V, 133).

While some critics condemn such mixing of real and ideal, reality and artifice, as undermining the development of illusion, Schlegel objects that they merely misunderstand the true nature of illusion ("das Wesen der

Täuschung") as the deliberate effect of artistic representation. Art requires a conditional, rather than a complete illusion. Illusion is complete only when all contrasting elements are hidden from perception, when the senses are totally engulfed in illusion.

> If we are to be truly deceived by a picture, that is, if we are to believe in the reality of the object which we see, we must not perceive its limits, but look at it through an opening; the frame at once declares it for a picture.[27]

Many an artist has thus disguised his frame as a wall cabinet or window that contains or reveals his *trompe l'oeil*. If painted scenery cannot be completely integrated, it is far better *not* to insist upon the optical illusion. The amphitheater tended to dissolve the distinction between outside and inside, surrounding nature and the stage; similarly, the Greeks relied on stage props and painted scenes that were either completely deceptive in detail or merely suggestive and symbolic. After acknowledging the frames and borders one is still free to move imaginatively beyond the boundaries. Schlegel argues that the Greeks had developed the illusions of theatrical perspective to a high art, so that the machinery and scenery could effectively enhance the dramatic illusion (*KSB* V, 51, 198–223). Nevertheless, he distinguishes between the optical illusion wrought through stage decoration and the dramatic illusion evoked though performance. Dramatic illusion does not depend upon optical illusion.

Having defined the drama as the presentation of action through dialogue, Schlegel is obviously concerned with the dialogic structure of the Greek drama. The audience participation in the dialogue, Schlegel argues, is manipulated through the chorus, for the chorus is the vocal proxy of the audience. As the idealized representative of the spectator, the chorus had its seat on the *thymele* where the radii of all the seats in the amphitheater merge. While the chorus thus provided commentary on the action, it could also join in the dialogue, sometimes in unison, more often through one speaker. Through *strophe, antistrophe,* and *epode,* the song and dance provided the chorus a dialectic instrument to ponder the antagonism of the real

---

27. Ibid., 52. "Soll ein Gemälde eigentlich täuschen, d.h. das Gesicht betrügen als wirklich, so muß man seine Grenzen nicht sehen, sondern es durch irgendeine Oeffnung erblicken; der Rahmen erklärt es gleich für ein Gemälde."

and the ideal (*KSB* V, 54, 65). In speaking for the audience, the chorus could mediate the sympathies with the natural human passions that beset the tragic hero.

If the playwright presented his character as morally perfect, no tragic conflict could occur. Some human fault (*hamartia*) must undermine nobility and dignity. The conflict depends on the opposition between desire and destiny. The character thus strives against the necessary constraints of his own physical impulses. Schlegel's formula: "Inner freedom and outer necessity, these are the two poles of the tragic world."[28] He applies this formula not only to tragic conflict but also to audience participation. In discussing Aristotle's account of audience response to tragedy, Schlegel objects primarily to eighteenth-century interpretations of *catharsis* as a moral *Heilkur*.[29] Even if one grants that a tragedy can arouse sensations of pity and fear and thus purge the body of extreme passions, that still does not explain how these negative effects coexist with the pleasure derived from the aesthetic experience.

Why should an audience expose itself to an aesthetic experience that opposes the desires and needs of sensual nature and provokes, in their stead, feelings of pity and fear? Schlegel considers several attempts to explain the apparent paradox of positive and negative effects. The spectator takes pleasure in tragedy, according to one explanation, because he is reassured of his own peaceful contentment in contrast to the storm and confusion of the passions. Were such the case, answers Schlegel, one could only talk about aesthetic detachment, not about *Täuschung* or *Teilnahme*. According to another explanation, the pleasure derives from moral improvement. The spectator who learns his first lessons of good and evil in the theater must be a poorly educated individual, Schlegel replies, and is more apt to feel humiliation than exaltation. Furthermore, tragedy does not always provide clear lessons in "poetic justice." Many tragedies end with no exhibition of virtue rewarded or vice punished. Still another explanation would attribute the cause of our aesthetic pleasure in tragic representation to the power of shocking events to excite us out of the dull routine of daily existence (*KSB* V, 62–63). Schlegel does not deny the excitement produced by brutal scenes. The Spaniard's enthusiasm for the bullfight or the Roman's excite-

---

28. Ibid., 61. "Innere Freiheit und äußere Notwendigkeit, dies sind die beiden Pole der tragischen Welt." Schlegel repeats this formula in "Über die dramatische Poesie der Griechen," in *KSB* III, 267.

29. Lessing, *Hamburgische Dramaturgie*, no. 19 in *Werke* IV, 317–21.

ment at the battle of gladiators derive from such response to bloody stimuli. If the aesthetic effect of the tragic drama is no different than that of bullbaiting, then the genius of Sophocles and Shakespeare was wasted on tragic art.

Rather than trying to ignore or resolve the paradoxicality of pleasure and pain, Schlegel grounds his own explanation of tragic *catharsis* in the opposition of positive and negative effects. The aesthetic experience is an exaltation of the basic human conflict between reason and passion. We participate in the suffering of the tragic hero or heroine as an extension of our own struggle to assert freedom over the tyranny of mere physical existence.

> The satisfaction, therefore, which we derive from [our participation in] the representation, in a good tragedy, of powerful situations and overwhelming sorrows, must be ascribed either to the feeling of the dignity of human nature, excited in us by such grand instances of it as are therein displayed, or to the trace of a higher order of things, impressed on the apparently irregular course of events, and mysteriously revealed in them; or perhaps to both together.[30]

While tragedy makes us feel the frailty of the flesh and thus stirs our sensations of pity and fear, at the same time it confirms the human capacity to struggle against the demeaning conditions of mere physical being.

Schlegel calls attention to the similar opposition in Kant's analysis of the sublime. Kant describes an alternating inhibition (*Hemmung*) and effusion (*Ergießung*). While the star-filled sky (Kant also names the pyramids in Egypt and St. Peter's Cathedral in Rome) prompts the imagination to exult in its perception of and participation in such grandeur, the imagination suffers, as well, utter frustration and failure before the incomprehensible vastness.[31] The negative (the feeling of incapacity) thus accompanies the positive (the striving to extend the limits of the imagination) in a manner essentially identical to Schlegel's explanation of the tragic *catharsis*. Indeed,

---

30. *KSB* V, 63–64. "Was in einem schönen Trauerspiel aus unsrer Teilnahme an den dargestellten gewaltsamen Lagen und zerreißenden Leiden eine gewisse Befriedigung hervorgehen läßt, ist entweder das Gefühl der Würde der menschlichen Natur, durch große Vorbilder geweckt, oder die Spur einer höheren Ordnung der Dinge, dem scheinbar unregelmäßigen Gange der Begebenheiten eingedrückt, und geheimnisvoll darin offenbart, oder beides zusammen."

31. Kant, *Kritik der Urteilskraft* §23, in *Werke* V, 328–31.

Schlegel readily admits that Kant's account of the aesthetic experience is missing only the application to tragedy.

The contrasts between comedy and tragedy, which seem to penetrate every dimension of the aesthetic experience, Schlegel attributes especially to the sensual aspects of the spectator's participation in dramatic illusion. Both Euripedes and Aristophanes dramatize, even to excess, the sexual urges. Hecuba, for example, reminds Agamemnon of his sexual delight with Cassandra in order to persuade him to punish Polymestor. Euripedes develops the wild passion of Medea and the unnatural passion of Phaedra as moving forces in his tragedies. He seduces the audience through the sensual stimulus of physical pleasure and pain to an encounter with the ideal (*KSB* V, 105–7). Although Aristophanes, too, constantly reminds his audience of the sexual impulses, the moral virtues remain but an abstract ideal within the drama. Every attempt to rise above the base animal drives, to assume the ideal, fails. A character may rally against, but will inevitably fall victim to, his or her natural weakness, be it lechery, vanity, cowardice, laziness, or any other of the multitude of human vices. Evoked but unattained, the ideal is thus present only through its absence within the drama. Aristophanes assumes, however, a shared sense of the ideal among his spectators (*KSB* V, 133–34). His audience therefore enjoys a sense of superiority to his characters. It is this externality of the harmonic order that allows the comic playwright to move in and out of the dramatic illusion.

Because the theater was such an important cultural institution, the Greek audience were keen judges of the drama and possessed a virtually comprehensive knowledge of form and content (*KSB* V, 141). Both tragedy and comedy could appeal to an extensive familiarity with the historical and mythic traditions and with the complexities of social and moral law. While one tragedy could build upon another (as in the case of the trilogies), comedy could also parody the tragedy. The audience, Schlegel asserts, would have to know the plays almost as well as the actors, for the allusions sometimes turned on the subtle and ironic twisting of a phrase. Aristophanes allows his characters to soar in poetic flight then lets them fall like Icarus: "With capricious wantonness he lavishes it [the high elevation of the Dithyrambic ode] only to destroy at the next moment the impression he has made" (*KSB* V, 140). As an example of Aristophanes' comic appropriation of the tragic poetry of Euripedes, Schlegel offers a scene from *The Acharnians* (*KSB* V, 151–56). The scene also reveals the self-reflexive attention to dramatic illusion in dialogue.

The Acharnians, an Attic people suffering under oppression, are angry at Dicaeopolis and threaten to execute him because he has accepted peace with the enemy. He agrees to address the Lacedaemonians, but the Acharnians require that he put his head on the block while he delivers his speech. If he fails to persuade them, he shall lose his head. Dicaeopolis, in whom we recognize Aristophanes himself, goes to Euripedes to beg from him the pitiful appearance in which his tragic heroes always appeal for sympathy. The scene takes place in the street before Euripedes' house. Euripedes is writing a tragedy and his servant refuses to disturb his master in the midst of his creative transport. Dicaeopolis continues shouting for Euripedes until the playwright, much disturbed at the interruption, appears at the upstairs window. Although he replies that he has no time, Dicaeopolis insists: "Have yourself wheeled out." Calling attention to the artifice of stage illusion, Aristophanes puns here on the *eccyclema* (*KSB* V, 198, 256n.), a turntable upon which an exterior facade may be rotated to reveal the interior. "Well, let them roll me out," Euripedes consents, "as to coming down, I have no time." Dicaeopolis pleas for the "miserable tragic rags" he needs to help him win his appeal and save his neck.

As the dialogue proceeds, Euripedes recalls various tragic characters: the aged Oeneus, the blind Phoenix, the beggar Philoctes, the lame Bellerophontes. Dicaeopolis keeps calling for an even more miserable and pitiful figure. When Euripedes names Telephus, the exchange begins. In putting on the ragged costume of Telephus, Dicaeopolis also puts on the rhetorical manner, echoing lines from Euripedes' tragedy. With his newly acquired suasive skill, he persists in begging while Euripedes laments ever more loudly that the intruder robs his dramatic devices: "You are stealing a whole tragedy.... it is all over with my plays!" The *eccyclema* rolls Euripedes back in again, and Dicaeopolis, swelling with the rhetoric of tragic pathos ("fully steeped in Euripedes"), prepares to confront the Lacedaemonians—and put his head on the block. More than just a parody, this dialogue requires attention to the artifices of staging and language as it demonstrates the differences in comic and tragic style.

Like the chorus in tragedy, the chorus in comedy also represents the audience and voices the pervasive sense of participation (*Teilnahme*). In tragedy, the chorus turns its attention inward, engaging in the dialogue and commenting on the tragic action. In comedy, however, the chorus turns its attention outward, directly addressing the audience and disrupting the dramatic illusion. This disruptive intrusion, the *parabasis*, is appropriate to comedy, Schlegel argues, even though it would destroy the effects of tragedy. In comedy, the audience welcomes the play with form as well as the play with subject matter. Too strict an adherence to the formal principles of the drama would be at odds with the celebration of laughter. Schlegel reminds us that in contemporary European theater, a comic character often plays to the audience with winks and gestures as well as verbal asides. Yet many a critic maintains that the drama, whether comic or tragic, should remain a closed circle; neither the playwright nor the actor should trespass the boundaries of the stage and interact directly with the audience (*KSB* V, 135–36).

Because he advocates audience participation, we would expect Schlegel to object to this principle of exclusion. He has already argued that the audience belongs within the circle of the dramatic performance (*KSB* V, 35). Unfortunately, he raises no counterargument here and seems content to leave his audience as idle voyeurs outside the circle. The very plurality of a company of voyeurs changes the nature of voyeurism into something of a conspiracy.[32] Should a player step out of his role and address the audience in terms of their collective identity and shared experience, the theatrical experience remains intact. As it is usually defined, the concept of *destroyed illusion* (*Illusionzerstörung*)[33] misrepresents the dramatic situation: The primary dramatic illusion is not destroyed, it is merely suspended for the moment (*aufgehoben*); in its place, the playwright introduces a secondary illusion. The character, after all, may have stepped out of one role but he has stepped into another. Schlegel might well have reasserted, at this point, his argument on the illusion of spontaneity (*KSB* I, 110–12). The fundamental principle of all dramatic illusion is spontaneity. The actor should never seem to be speaking lines he has learned by rote. By having a character step out of his role and speak as a player, perhaps directly to the audience, perhaps to the other players, the playwright has enhanced, not destroyed, the illusion of spontaneity. The deviation from his role is seen as a spontaneous intrusion, not as another part that the actor has learned.

The advantage of the *parabasis*, then, is not simply that it disrupts the illusion but rather that it calls attention to the imaginative process of creating illusion. Schlegel, however, offers no other justification of the *parabasis* than the authorial play with form. He even suggests that the *parabasis* was introduced into comedy to make up for a deficiency of material in the comic

---

32. Bergson, "Laughter."
33. Nef, "Das Aus-der-Rolle-Fallen als Mittel der Illusionszerstörung bei Tieck und Brecht."

action (*KSB* V, 136, 150). Schlegel promises to return to the problem of disrupting the illusion. As we shall see, his promise is kept when he comes to discuss kindred modes of irony in Shakespeare (*KSB* VI, 136–39, 146–49). Although he would not have considered Tieck's *Prinz Zerbino* (1796–98), *Der gestiefelte Kater* (1797), and *Die verkehrte Welt* (1798) in the same class with Shakespeare's comedy, he recognizes Tieck's ability to exploit the ironic manipulation of illusion (*KSB* III, 265).[34]

When Schlegel turns from the classic to the romantic, Shakespeare commands his attention. In France and Italy, the drama became stifled by a doctrine of *mimesis* that set imitation of the classical Greek models in the stead of imitation of human nature. In Spain and England, however, the drama developed with little dependency on classical models or foreign influences (*KSB* V, 235–36; VI, 110–11). Schlegel begins with the reemergence of the theater during the Italian Renaissance; he passes rapidly, however, to the Italian theater of the eighteenth century. Here he sees a contest of contrasting trends that prompt him to reflect on the meaning of irony. In tragedy he observes the opposing manners of Alfieri and Metastasio; in comedy he discusses Goldoni and Gozzi.

Because his plays were composed for operatic performance, Metastasio is able to escape the dullness of mechanical rule mongering. Schlegel praises his drama for purity, clarity, delicacy, grace, and lyric tenderness of language. Passion expressed through song is an attribute of the performance that ceases to seem unnatural and excessive as soon as the spectator has accepted the conventions of the opera. The musical context allows a display of feeling that well suits the courtly mannerisms of the opera. Although Schlegel dislikes the politics of courtly affectation and intrigue, he still argues the opera is a more appropriate vehicle for courtly drama than the tragedy (*KSB* V, 241). Metastasio's muse is a concupiscent nymph; Alfieri's muse an aggressive Amazon. What he praises in Alfieri is the rejection of courtly mannerisms. The dialogue is stark and constrained; the action is a stoic encounter with catastrophe. In dismissing the softer emotions, Alfieri has also deprived his tragedy of the subtler appeals to the fantasy. The audience is given a world that is gloomy and repulsive (*KSB* V, 243).

34. In his review, "Ritter Blaubart und der gestiefelte Kater, von Ludwig Tieck," *Jenaische Allgemeine Litteratur-Zeitung*, no. 333 (1797), Schlegel had praised the play with illusion as a sublime joke on the critics and theoreticians (Schlegel, *Kritische Schriften*, 2 vols. [Berlin: G. Reimer, 1828], I, 311–21).

Schlegel draws a similar contrast in comedy between Goldoni and Gozzi. Goldoni he sees as the Italian master of neoclassical purity. The concept of purity, however, is of dubious value in the drama. Presumably, purity would serve to enhance the dramatic illusion by removing all extraneous and distracting effects. Schlegel argues that purity and unity have little to do with the evocation of illusion and may well result in monotony and superficiality. Goldoni purchased his purity at the expense of the vitality of cultural tradition. Just as Gottsched had banned *Hanswurst* from the German stage, Goldoni brought about the expulsion of the *commedia dell'arte*. To be sure, Arlequin, Brighella, and Pantalon still appear in Goldoni's plays, but utterly deprived of their lusty antics and spontaneity. Gozzi wins Schlegel's praise for restoring the *commedia dell'arte*. Schlegel is quick to point out that Gozzi was less talented as a playwright than Goldoni. Having challenged his rival to a dramaturgical duel, with the public to decide who had produced the better comedy, Gozzi succeeded in arousing popular interest, and he secured his triumph over Goldoni through a particularly romantic combination of *fiabe* and *commedia dell'arte*. What elements could more appropriately contribute to a truly national theater? Gozzi takes his characters from the traditional masked players and his plot from the folk tale. Because the *commedia dell'arte* is improvisational, Gozzi had to do little more than sketch the outlines for adapting the folk tale to dramatic performance. In the Sacchi troop of Venice he had the most skilled improvisational players of the day, and his choice of folk tales especially excited an audience long deprived of stage enchantment. In spite of the success of *The Love of the Three Oranges* and *The Blue Monster*, Gozzi grew tired of setting the *fiabe*, and he tried his hand at adapting Calderón for performance with the *commedia dell'arte*. The results were disastrous. Calderón's lyrical vision of reality became crude and coarse in Gozzi's adaptation.

In explaining why Gozzi was able to attain such an intimate juxtaposition of the natural and supernatural with the *commedia dell'arte* and *fiabe*, Schlegel argues that the opposition was a perfect balance of extremes. The grotesque masked players exaggerate social manners as a thin disguise for the natural passions; the fairy tale exaggerates the rites of living and loving with the touch of magical enchantment.

> The wonderful extravagance of the masked parts serves as an admirable contrast to the wild marvels of fairy tale. Thus the character of

these pieces was, in the serious part, as well as in the accompanying drollery, equally removed from natural truth.[35]

Gozzi's comedy thus involves the audience in a peculiar province of ironic contrasts. Freely improvising from Gozzi's prosaic text, the masked players create an ironic bond with the poetic fantasy of the fairy tale. Schlegel tells us that he will elaborate further on irony when he comes to the plays of Shakespeare and Calderón; here, in the context of Gozzi's paradoxical combination, he must give further attention to how irony contributes to dramatic illusion.

> What I here mean by irony, I shall explain more fully when I come to the mixture of the tragic and comic in the romantic drama of Shakespeare and Calderon. At present I shall only observe, that it is a sort of confession interwoven into the representation itself, and more or less distinctly expressed, of its overcharged one-sidedness in matters of fancy and feeling, and by means of which equipoise is again restored.[36]

Similar to his earlier promise to elucidate the momentary disruption of illusion in the comedy (*KSB* V, 136), this promise to explain the province of irony is fulfilled in his account of juxtaposing, or superimposing, alternate possibilities (VI, 136). Indeed, both promises seem to refer to kindred dramatic phenomena: the player's aside to the parterre and the subtle avowal of one-sidedness. Schlegel refers here to a "lightly hinted admission" ("leise angedeutetes Eingeständnis") and later to a "secret agreement" ("verstohlnes Einverständnis"); both phrases suggest a direct but subtle, even secret, relationship between player (or author) and spectator. This privileged relationship involves a dramatic shift from one level of response to another: from the participation in the illusion to the conscious awareness

---

35. *KSB* V, 248. "Dem abenteuerlichen Wunderbaren der Feenmärchen diente die ebenso stark aufgetragene Wunderlichkeit der Maskenrollen vortrefflich zum Gegensatz. Die Willkür der Darstellung ging in dem ernsthaften Teile wie im beigesetzten Scherz gleich weit über die natürliche Wahrheit hinaus."

36. Ibid., 248–49. "Was ich unter Ironie verstehe, werde ich zur Rechtfertigung des dem Tragischen beigemischten Komischen im romantischen Drama des Shakespeare und Calderon näher entwickeln. Hier nur so viel, daß es ein in die Darstellung selbst hineingelegtes mehr oder weniger leise angedeutetes Eingeständnis ihrer übertriebenden Einseitigkeit in dem Anteil der Phantasie und Empfindung ist, wodurch also das Gleichgewicht wieder hergestellt wird."

of the illusion-making processes of the drama. We have seen his account of the dual nature of the aesthetic response. Although he never offers, even when he later returns to the task, a clear explanation of dramatic or romantic irony, he apparently sees this duality exploited. Just as irony juxtaposes comic with tragic, it also sets the imaginative in opposition to the emotional response.

His discussion of French theater hurries through the early history to dwell on the neoclassicism exemplified in Corneille, Racine, and Molière. The long-standing debate over the "three unities," he declares, has been waged, both pro and con, with a faulty set of premises. Instead of appealing to "authority," one should consider what contributes to effective drama. Aristotle and, after him, Seneca provide the principal "authority" cited by Boileau and other French critics of the drama. If the playwright could actually succeed in conjuring a more complete and powerful dramatic illusion by adhering to unity of time, place, and action, then the arguments of the French critics ought to be given full credence. In investigating the dramatic function of the three unities, Schlegel elaborates his definition of dramatic illusion:

> This idea of illusion has occasioned great errors in the theory of art. By this term there has often been understood the unwittingly erroneous belief that the represented action is reality. In that case the terrors of Tragedy would be a true torture to us, a nightmare oppressing the fancy. No, the theatrical as well as every other poetical illusion, is a waking dream, to which we voluntarily surrender ourselves. To produce it, the poet and actors must powerfully agitate the mind, and the probabilities of calculation do not in the least contribute towards it. This demand of literal deception, pushed to the extreme, would make all poetic form impossible.[37]

37. Ibid., VI, 22–23. "Der Begriff der Täuschung hat in der Kunsttheorie große Irrungen angerichtet. Man hat oft darunter den Unwillkürlich gewordenen Irrtum, als ob das Dargestellte wirklich sei, verstanden. Dann würde sie bei den Schrecknissen des Trauerspiels eine wahre Plage sein, ein Alpdrücken der Phantasie. Nein, die theatralische Täuschung, wie jede poetische, ist eine wache Träumerei, der man sich freiwillig hingibt. Um sie hervorzubringen, müssen Dichter und Schauspieler die Gemüter lebhaft hinreißen; die berechneten Wahrscheinlichkeiten helfen nicht im mindesten dazu. Jene Forderung der buchstäblichen Täuschung, aufs Äußerste getrieben, würde alle poetische Form unmöglich machen." Black mistranslates "ein Alpdrücken der Phantasie" as "an Alpine load on the fancy"; I have amended the phrase to "a nightmare oppression of the fancy."

This passage has such marked similarities to Coleridge's definition of stage illusion that it has been mistakenly assumed that, as on many other occasions in preparing his Shakespeare lectures, Coleridge once again helped himself to Schlegel's ideas. Because previous studies of Coleridge's debt to Schlegel have erroneously identified supposed parallels and have not acknowledged the actual indebtedness in Coleridge's analysis of dramatic illusion, we will return in the following chapter to examine Coleridge's borrowing.[38] Illusion, Schlegel states, is neither involuntary misapprehension, nor a confusion of the represented with the real. If either were the case, then the scenes of horror in tragedy would work as a nightmare upon the fantasy. Instead, like all poetic illusion, theatrical illusion is a waking dream in which we engage voluntarily.

In investigating how the "three unities" contribute to dramatic illusion, Schlegel begins with the unity of action. From Plato one might have adapted the principle of "rhapsodic vision" ("anschauende Begeisterung" *Ion*, 536, 542; see also, "vision presented to waking sight" *Epistles* VIII, 357); from Aristotle one has only the constituent parts, the beginning, middle, and end of the causal structure (*Poetics*, 1450b). Schlegel accepts Aristotle's definition of human action as both *proairesis* and *praxis;* the tragic hero must respond, deliberate, choose, then act. "Its unity will consist in the direction toward a single end; and to its completeness belongs all that lies between the first determination and the execution of the deed."[39] But he quickly points out that this definition by no means accounts for all Greek tragedy and it ill suits modern tragedy. The problem is that action is not confined to one character, and that tragic circumstances may allow no freedom to choose. For example, one can follow the unity of action in *Antigone* from the heroine's decision to perform the funeral rites for her unburied brother. That action is completed without difficulty; but the tragic complications begin only in the aftermath when she must confront the punishment for her action. The tragic plot is most often constructed not out of unity of action, but out of action and reaction. If we try to hold to the Aristotelian concept of action as deliberation and deed, most tragedies will be seen to have not unity but plurality of action. Which action, Schlegel asks, is the major action in *Antigone?* Creon's decision to uphold his dignity by maintaining the death

38. See below, chapter 5, note 17. Coleridge, *Lectures 1808–1819: On Literature* I, 129–36.
39. *KSB* VI, 16–17. "Ihre Einheit wird in der Richtung auf ein einziges Ziel bestehen; zu ihrer Vollständigkeit gehört alles, was zwischen dem ersten Entschlusse und der Vollbringung der Tat liegt."

sentence against any person who should attempt to bury Polyneices is no less important to the drama than Antigone's decision, and its consequences are equally tragic for it brings about the utter ruin of the house of Creon.

How much more complicated is the supposed unity of action when we try to trace *proairesis* and *praxis* in French tragedy. Schlegel cites Racine's *Andromache* as example:

> Orestes wishes to move Hermione to return his love; Hermione is resolved to compel Pyrrhus to marry her, or she will be revenged on him; Pyrrhus wishes to be rid of Hermione, and to be united with Andromache; Andromache is desirous of saving her son, and at the same time remaining true to the memory of her husband. Yet nobody ever questioned the unity of this piece, as the whole has a common connexion, and ends with one common catastrophe. But which of the actions of the four persons is the main action?[40]

Even as a description of Greek tragedy, Aristotle's concept of unity of action ignores the contest or opposition of will between characters and fails to recognize the idea of destiny, the exercise of human will within a scheme of determined causality. Too, the containment of action as a "whole," with a beginning, middle, and end, is a matter of aesthetic perception, for the chain of causality has no empirical beginning or end. What is involved in creating dramatic illusion is not a replication of a single causal sequence, but the ordering of human action into a unified aesthetic experience.

Because "unity of action" has led to a mechanical schematization of plot, Schlegel prefers to adopt from de La Motte the concept of "unity of interest."[41] The attempt to reduce the vast complexity of cause and effect to a single chain of events imposes a mechanical unity that unnecessarily limits dramatic illusion. The "unity of interest," as Schlegel defines it, is an organic unity that enlarges the scope of participation beyond the destiny of a single character and allows a total engagement of the audience in the dra-

---

40. Ibid., 18. "Orest [will] die Hermione zur Gegenliebe bewegen; Hermione will den Pyrrhus nötigen, sich mit ihr zu vermählen, oder will sich an ihm rächen; Pyrrhus will die Hermione los sein, und sich mit der Andromache verbinden; Andromache will ihren Sohn retten und zugleich dem Andenken ihres Gemahls treu bleiben. Dennoch hat niemand diesem Stücke die Einheit abgesprochen; weil alles ineinander greift und mit einer gemeinschaftlicher Katastrophe endigt. Welche unter den Handlungen der vier Personen ist nun aber die Haupthandlung?"

41. Houdar de La Motte, "Preface à *Oedipe*" (1730) and "Réponse à M. de Voltaire," in *Les Paradoxes littéraires de La Motte*, 50–77.

matic situation. For Schlegel, unity is a meaningful criteria only in reference to the spectator's sense of a total impression ("Gesamteindruck"). A logical cohesion of cause and effect is a means not an end. The drama should excite the response of all the "Geisteskräfte." If the understanding should balk at some causal improbability, the imagination and the feeling are not apt to follow. The "unity of interest" is never pulled along by a single thread of dramatic action, however, and the cumulative effect may well overwhelm the skeptical reason. Schlegel likens it to a river fed by many tributaries that continues to increase its turbulent strength until it pours forth into the vast sea (*KSB* VI, 21).

Illusion requires, then, a certain probability, but neither a "unity of time" nor a "unity of place" are useful assets. Our bodies may be bound to time and place, but our imagination is free to roam. The argument that a shift in scene will destroy dramatic illusion is based on the simplistic notion that expects the drama to counterfeit the passive apprehension of reality. The spectator, however, is quite content to accept the slightest architectural hints and to complement the illusion within his own imagination. As for the radical shifts of time and place, Schlegel cites from Samuel Johnson (a critic from whom he expects a strict adherence to "rules") the defense of Shakespeare's *Antony and Cleopatra:* If "the spectator really imagines himself at Alexandria," why balk at the move to Rome? "Surely he that imagines this may imagine more."[42] The ability of the mind to make vast leaps through time and space, Schlegel adds, is a familiar phenomenon of the thought process. The pliable imagination of the spectator is ready to follow the playwright wherever he shall lead (*KSB* VI, 31). The poet should not be required to abstain from the full exercise of his art, but should be allowed to conjure with "all the magic of genuine illusion" (*alle Zaubermittel der echten Täuschung*) (*KSB* VI, 26).

Schlegel calls attention to shifts in time and place in classical drama, but he also argues that it is characteristic of romantic drama to extend time and place even more freely than classical drama. Indeed, he derives his contrast between the plastic and the picturesque from the respective treatment of time and place. The plastic relies on the externality of time and place; the picturesque on the internalizing of temporal and spatial effects. A scene from Aeschylus or Euripides, as Schlegel describes the effect in an open-air theater, was posed as a three-dimensional grouping which

---

42. Johnson, "Preface to Shakespeare," in *The Works of Samuel Johnson* XII, 8–9.

could be viewed from the wide semicircle of spectators. Romantic drama, however, he imagines as viewed through the frame of the proscenium arch. Not Shakespeare's Globe Theater, but the stage of the seventeenth and eighteenth centuries provides the defining attributes. Just as expression of time and space are crucial to the romantic drama, so, too, a more articulate stage design, lighting and perspective, become essential to its particular magic (*eigentlicher Zauber*). Even in the matter of setting, then, the confinement of time and place in French theater deprives the stage of the very qualities that seduce the perceptions. A rational unity (*Verstandeseinheit*) usurps the place of the requisite gratification of imagination and feeling (*KSB* VI, 28–31).

Schlegel is alert to how changes in social mores and manners influence taste. One should be cautious in trying to establish moral boundaries between what is suitable and what is unfit for the stage. He appeals to history to affirm that moral boundaries are necessary. At its worst, as in some *commedia dell'arte*, the drama may lapse into obscene antics. "The dramatic effect of the visible may, it is true, be liable to great abuse; and it is possible for a theatre to degenerate into a noisy arena of mere bodily events, to which words and gestures may be but superfluous appendages."[43] Still, the opposite extreme of moral censorship that allows "the eye no conviction of its own" is just as destructive to the drama. So dictated by refined courtly manners that it hides all impulses of the body, the theater becomes impotent. He praises Voltaire (a rare occurrence in the *Vorlesungen*) for his efforts to return physical vitality to the stage (*KSB* VI, 32).

In his commentary on French tragedy, from Corneille and Racine through Voltaire, he objects to the substitution of courtly intrigue for tragic action and to the constraints imposed by unity of time on the proper maturation of motives. In his review of comedy, from Molière to Marivaux, he accepts intrigue and the unity of time, not as necessary but as compatible with the development of comic plot and character. Although he complains that unity of place has inhibited the imaginative range of French comedy, the monotony of character and situation arouse Schlegel's more adamant objections. He praises Molière's appropriations from the type-characters of Latin comedy, but he notes that Molière did not always succeed in furnish-

---

43. *KSB* VI, 32. "Es ist wahr, die dramatische Wirksamkeit des Sichtbaren kann sehr mißbraucht werden und das Theater kann in einen lärmenden Tummelplatz bloß körperlicher Ereignisse ausarten, wo alsdann Worte und Gebärdenspiel eine fast überflüßige Zugaben sind."

ing his borrowed characters with manners fitting to contemporary satire. The character of Phormio in *Les Fourberies de Scapin*, adapted from Terence, is a peculiar anomaly, estranged from the comic world of the Romans and utterly out of place on the French stage (*KSB* VI, 82–83).

The French playwright most successful in creating comic illusion is Marivaux. Although his illusion depends on his own highly wrought mannerism, *Marivaudage*, he conjures for his audience an effective irony of situation and character.[44] According to Schlegel's definition, the *esprit d'observation* is most enjoyed in comedy, "when a peculiarity or property shows itself most conspicuously at the very time its possessor has the least suspicion of it, or is most studious to conceal it" (*KSB* VI, 94). In applying this principle to the passions, the playwright must give his comic character a certain naiveté, for an unsuspecting naiveté is required for the involuntary exposure or self-betrayal. Herein lies the peculiarity of Marivaux's manner: his characters are all too conscious of their own supposed naiveté. Naiveté becomes, paradoxically, an artifice and affectation:

> It is like children in the game of hide and seek, who cannot stay quiet in their corner, but keep popping out their heads to see whether someone is about to find them; nay, sometimes, which is still worse, it is like the squinting over a fan held up from affected modesty. In Marivaux we always see his aim from the very beginning, and all our attention is directed to discovering the way by which he is to lead us to it.[45]

We recognize, here, that once again Schlegel is addressing the presence of self-reflexive irony in which a character knowingly hints at his own simple-mindedness or the one-sidedness of the situation (*KSB* V, 136; V, 249). What Schlegel observes in the comedy of Marivaux is not that the dramatic illusion is momentarily exposed, rather that it remains peculiarly transparent throughout. The illusion becomes a *coquetterie* sustained only through the player's flirtation with the audience. Not surprisingly, then, the development

---

44. Cf. Lambert, *Réalité et ironie. Les jeux de l'illusion dans le théâtre de Marivaux.*
45. *KSB* VI, 94. "Es ist wie das Versteckenspielen der Kinder, die in ihrem Winkel keine Ruhe halten können, sondern immer mit dem Kopfe hervorgucken, ob man sie nicht bald entdecken wird; ja zuweilen, was noch schlimmer, wie das Schielen durch einen Fächer, den man sich aus gezierter Sittsamkeit vorhält. Das Ziel sieht man bei Marivaux immer vom Anfang an voraus, die ganze Aufmerksamkeit wird also auf den Weg gelenkt, worauf er uns bis dahin führen wird."

remains superficial. The plot seldom depends on anything more than a vow of love; tension is maintained by stratagems to elicit the declaration and the coy or obstinate reluctance to speak it (*KSB* VI, 95).

What had been a survey of Shakespeare in a one-hour lecture in 1808 grew to be the major section of the *Vorlesungen:* 240 printed pages of volume 2, part 2, published in December 1810.[46] Schlegel begins by recapitulating his distinctions between the organic and mechanic (*KSB* VI, 109–10), classic and romantic (VI, 111), plastic and picturesque (VI, 112). He then discusses the involvement of the imagination in dramatic illusion (*KSB* VI, 113). Because these passages are preparatory to his introduction of Shakespeare as the quintessential romantic poet, Schlegel's rhetoric is charged with enthusiasm and reverberates with echoes from brother Friedrich's *Athenäum* fragments on romantic poetry:

> Romantic poetry . . . is the expression of the secret attraction to a chaos which lies concealed in the very bosom of the ordered universe, and is perpetually striving after new and marvelous births; the life-giving spirit of primal love broods here anew on the face of the waters. . . . [Romantic poetry], notwithstanding its fragmentary appearance, approaches more to the secret of the universe. (VI, 112)[47]

While classical poetry reflects the external, objective order of nature, the romantic seeks to reveal the internal, subjective process of creation. The evocation of illusion in romantic art depends not upon an imitation of the world of things, but rather upon the repetition of the way in which the senses, the reason, the emotions, respond to, and thus recreate, the world of things. In contrast to classical sculpture, romantic painting attends only indirectly to solid form while it emphasizes the mediating atmosphere: "Its particular charm, in short, consists in this, that it enables us to see in bodily

---

46. Schlegel, *Vorlesungen uber dramatische Kunst und Literatur.* Edgar Lohner bases his text of Schlegel's *Vorlesungen* on the posthumous 3d edition in *Sämtliche Werke,* ed. Eduard Böcking (Leipzig, 1846–47); for the 2d edition (1817), see *Vorlesungen,* ed. Amoretti.

47. *KSB* VI, 112. "Die romantische ⟨Poesie⟩ . . . ist der Ausdruck des geheimen Zuges zu dem immerfort nach neuen und wundervollen Geburten ringenden Chaos, welches unter der geordneten Schöpfung, ja in ihrem Schoße sich verbirgt: der beseelende Geist der ursprünglichen Liebe schwebt hier von neuem über den Wassern. . . . [die romantische Poesie], ungeachtet ihres fragmentarischen Ansehens, ist dem Geheimnis des Weltalls näher." Cf. Friedrich Schlegel, *Athenäum-Fragmente,* §§116 and 252, in *Kritische Ausgabe,* ed. Behler, II, 182–83, 207–8.

objects what is least corporeal, namely, light and air."[48] What we anticipate, then, in romantic art is the revelation of the imagination. Far from dissipating under scrutiny, its illusion is heightened as we grow consciously alert to its effects.

The same freedom of dramatic movement that makes the "unities" of time and place irrelevant to romantic drama also renders the strict discrimination of tragedy and comedy inapplicable. *Scherz* and *Ernst* commingle in experience. The free movement—temporal, spatial, and emotional—is possible only because a perceptual awareness and an engagement of the sensibilities is an accompanying attribute of the movement. Even as the playwright brings one scene into theatrical perspective, the spectator is allowed to entertain a continuing awareness of alternatives: this time or place is experienced only at the exclusion of other possibilities (*KSB* VI, 113). Every revealed presence necessarily conceals another.[49]

As Walter Jackson Bate has pointed out, the antecedents of Keats's poetic dicta of *negative capability* and *no identity* are abundant in the aesthetics of the later eighteenth century.[50] In explaining that achievement "which Shakespeare possessed so enormously," and in declaring that "the poetical Character" takes "as much delight in conceiving an Iago as an Imogen," Keats clearly agrees with Schlegel. In Schlegel's formulation, Shakespeare succeeds as dramatic poet because he fully exercises the power of the imagination to assume identity: "It is the capability of putting himself so completely into every type, even the most unusual" ("Es ist die Fähigkeit, sich so vollkommen in alle Arten zu sein, auch die fremdesten, zu versetzen") (*KSB* VI, 129). Because of the playwright's accomplishment in creating identity, the spectator is able to sustain the illusion of spontaneity in dialogue. The character must speak out of his or her identity, so that the dialogue seems to arise out of a natural causality. The playwright is fully invisible, and the actors never seem to be reciting their lines for the benefit of the spectator. Even the most unnatural characters—the witches in *Macbeth,* Caliban and Ariel in *The Tempest*—thus assume a natural reality. The fantastic is so

---

48. *KSB* VI, 113. "Ihre ⟨die Malerei⟩ eigentlicher Zauber liegt endlich darin, daß sie an körperlichen Gegenständen sichtbar macht, was am wenigsten körperlich ist, Licht und Luft."
49. Lobsien, *Theorie literarischer Illusionsbildung,* 22–23, argues that the logic of alternatives is the only significant logic underlying narrative probability.
50. Bate, *Negative Capability: The Intuitive Approach in Keats,* 25–78; Bate, "The Sympathetic Imagination in Eighteenth-Century English Criticism"; Keats to George and Thomas Keats, 21 and 27 December 1817, and to Richard Woodhouse, 27 October 1818, in *Letters 1814–1821.*

completely translated into the dramatic realm of nature that the spectator experiences an intimacy even with "the extraordinary, the wonderful, the unheard-of" (*KSB* VI, 130–31).

Although dramatic illusion depends on the engagement of the imagination rather than on the excitation of the emotions, the emotional response is still very much a part of the ensemble of dramatic effects. Citing Lessing's argument that the emotional effect should insinuate itself subtly and increase gradually until it usurps all control over the passions, "until it becomes the sole tyrant of all our desires and fears,"[51] Schlegel agrees that the spectator may accept even painful impressions, but he argues that the pleasure we take in the agonies of tragic action depends on the accompanying sense of an elevating and strengthening power (*KSB* VI, 132–35). Our emotional response to the tragic circumstances exists within our larger appreciation of the art of tragedy. Our perception of tragedy involves, then, an essential paradox, and Shakespeare fully exploits the various dimensions of this paradox: in character, in dialogue, in plot, even in his own elusive identity. Our problem in trying to define his authorial identity is that his presence is chameleonic:

> He unites in his soul the utmost elevation and the utmost depth; and the most opposite and even apparently irreconcilable properties subsist in him peaceably together. The world of spirits and nature have laid all their treasures at his feet: in strength a demigod, in profundity of view a prophet, in all-seeing wisdom a guardian spirit of a higher order, he lowers himself to mortals as if unconscious of his superiority, and is as open and as unassuming as a child.[52]

Schlegel's analysis of this paradoxical copresence of knowledge and naiveté takes us into a further examination of irony. The irony of character is not to be distinguished from the irony of dialogue, for Shakespeare delineates character through the interaction with other characters. Because we learn about a character through dialogue, through what he says to one and to

---

51. Lessing, *Hamburgische Dramaturgie*, no. 15 in *Werke* IV, 298–303.
52. *KSB* VI, 135–36. "Er verknüpft alles Hohe und Tiefe in seinem Dasein, und die fremdartigsten, ja scheinbar unvereinbarsten Eigenschaften bestehen in ihm friedlich nebeneinander. Die Geisterwelt und die Natur haben all ihre Schätze in ihn niedergelegt: an Kraft ein Halbgott, an Tiefblick ein Prophet, an überschauender Weisheit ein Schutzgeist höherer Art, läßt er sich zu den Menschen herab, als wüßte er nicht um seine Überlegenheit und ist anspruchlos und unbefangen wie ein Kind."

another, and what they say to him and to others about him, we also learn to juggle contradictions, ambiguities, dissemblings, and deceits: "Ill-advised should we be were we always to take men's declarations respecting themselves and others for sterling coin." This means that we listen to dramatic dialogue with alert suspicion, for Shakespeare will have us hear how declarations of noble purpose may be misconstrued and perverted, how devious purpose may speak the language of trustworthy honesty.

Shakespeare is uncannily accurate in delineating that most pervasive of all deceits, self-deceit, "the half self-conscious hypocrisy towards ourselves, with which even noble minds attempt to disguise the almost inevitable influence of selfish motives in human nature." This irony of characterization, Schlegel admits, is the death of enthusiasm. It is as if Shakespeare had the misfortune to look into the core of humanity and discover the sad truth that virtue and dignity were neither pure nor genuine. Our admiration is undermined, and we are forced into an uneasy ambivalence. Dramatic illusion, were it sustained only by the emotional bond of a sympathetic identification, would certainly be disrupted by such irony. The illusion, however, is heightened, not destroyed, by the intrusions of irony. Schlegel observes that irony may reside, not merely in dialogue and characterization, but may penetrate the entire plot.

Because the drama, as Schlegel defined it at the very beginning of his *Vorlesungen*, is the expression of national values, it inevitably becomes an instrument of ideological faction. Most playwrights, when they take sides and use the dialogue to argue their own convictions, would presume the audience utterly convinced. In practice, however, an audience quickly recognizes when a character is being used as a covert medium for propaganda. But what if a shrewd playwright should subtly expose, at least to the more clever spectators, his purpose? He would thus show them that he is no mere dupe of faction or opinion, that he respects their intelligence, and that he has anticipated their objections. Although it would seem that those who perceive this irony, a secret agreement ("verstohlenes Einverständnis") as countertext, would therefore be liberated from the narrow opinions of the main text, the playwright has in fact succeeded in initiating his clever spectators into a conspiracy. The playwright seems to say that he is not committed to his own representations, that he could unrelentingly annihilate ("unerbittlich vernichten") the beautiful and irresistibly compelling illusion ("den schönen, unwiderstehlich anziehenden Schein") that he has just produced (*KSB* VI, 137). The illusion is that through irony's shared secret, playwright and spectator have transcended some set of ideological constraints. But, of course, the *Schein* persists; the text remains intact.

Schlegel recognizes that irony plays with the very process of illusion making, even when it threatens to destroy illusion. Not all dramatic dialogue can make room for this superimposed dialogue between the playwright and the audience. The tragic confrontation requires that the dialogue be totally absorbed in the character's anger or desperation. The dialogue of a tragedy can sustain irony and comic wit, however, until the moment when tragic circumstances overwhelm the action. Except for these moments when mortal agony must be heard, irony may freely speak its part. The Fool, no less than Kent, is a proper companion for King Lear. Schlegel considers irony to be a discourse of alternatives as well as an alternate discourse. It can bring dark overtones into the midst of levity as well as comic mockery into scenes of sorrow. But even while it is the art of trespassing across the boundaries between comic and tragic, good and evil, or merely between pro and con, it is an art that can subsist only through the reconfirmation of boundaries (*KSB* VI, 137).

In order to play with an alternative, beyond the boundary, the ironist must have a sure sense of the line he is trespassing, and his irony can be sustained only in its constant reference to the realm that has been left behind. Thus in claiming its alterity, irony often sets a mirror upon the boundary, the distorting mirror of parody or burlesque. With Stephano and Trinculo in *The Tempest*, for example, the audience is treated to a parody of the serious plot. While the concept of comic relief seems to endorse a moment of frivolity to ease the mounting tensions of tragic passion, Schlegel advises us to look at such scenes—the gravediggers in *Hamlet* or the porter in *Macbeth*—with an awareness of ironic alterity. Parody, or the mere revelries of the fantasy ("eine leichte Gaukelei der Phantasie"), remind us that there are, in fact, alternatives to the tragic conception of mortal destiny.

Johnson's defense of the mixture of tragic and comic in Shakespeare may seem reasonable, for Johnson appeals to verisimilitude.[53] Just because sadness and gaiety are seldom sorted out and separated in real life, Schlegel objects, is no reason for declaring that the playwright ought to mix them together in his play. Where he needed only to explain why comic and tragic elements *may* be combined in the drama, Johnson argues, instead, that they *should* be combined. Art is not life. While the mixture of comic and tragic

---

53. Johnson, "Preface to Shakespeare," in *Works* XI, 334–37.

may satisfy the conditions of theatrical probability (*KSB* VI, 138), art has its own justifications. It may serve the playwright's purpose to separate the comic from the tragic; or, should he choose to bring them together, he may well be more interested in irony than in verisimilitude. The argument that art imitates reality would offer no sanction for the manifold irony Shakespeare is able to manipulate through the doubling of Antipholus and Dromio in *The Comedy of Errors*. Certainly, too, it is the logic, or the illogic, of irony, not the dictates of verisimilitude, that better explains the purpose of Shakespeare's fools (*KSB* VI, 139).

In the ensuing discussion, Schlegel comments on thirty-five plays; first the comedies, then the tragedies, concluding with the history plays.[54] The commentary follows no formula: He usually sketches the plot; sometimes he focuses on character; sometimes on dramatic development. Generally, he returns to ideas developed in the preceding lectures. Thus he continues to consider aspects of dramatic illusion. Too, he seeks out instances of Shakespeare's *Absichtlichkeit*, the deliberate attention to the art of the drama. He often refers to the tension between imagination and emotion. The more profound effects of Shakespearean drama, he emphasizes, derive from the engagement of the imagination rather than from even the most tumultuous excitement of the emotions. Among the dramatic occasions for calling attention to the illusion-making process, he refers to the obvious self-reflexiveness of the play-within-a-play. Also, he observes the repeated use of *Verkleidung* (disguise) and *Verstellung* (feigned attitudes). When Shakespeare has a character assume another identity, or disguise his or her actual motives, the audience must exercise a dual perception of the character, constantly adjusting the words and actions of the "revealed" character in order to fathom the "concealed" character. This dual perception is not merely a complication of dramatic illusion, it repeats the primary engagement of illusion; we see a replication of the actor playing a character, as that character plays another character.

Julia, in *The Two Gentlemen of Verona*, gives us some anticipation of the irony of disguise that Shakespeare later elaborates in Viola and Imogen. The audience delights in knowing what the fickle Proteus does not know, that the handsome young page, Sebastian, who accompanies him on his

---

54. Schlegel discusses all the plays acknowledged by scholars, with the exception of *Pericles* and *Titus Andronicus*, to which he refers in his appendix on the spurious plays, *KSB* VI, 204–10. The "Anhang über die angeblich Shakespeare untergeschobenen Stücke" is apparently derived from Tieck; see Sauer, *A. W. Schlegel's Shakespearean Criticism in England, 1814–1846*, 52, 164.

amorous misadventure is his true and constant love, Julia. The disguise has its own peculiar enticement as we shift our perception of sexuality and our way of listening to the dialogue. In the midst of the banter between Proteus and Sebastian we witness a modest young lady in a daring predicament. Schlegel has already pointed out that young men played all the female parts in Shakespeare's time, so his audience was treated to an added transvestite shift, a man playing a woman playing a man. In doubling the joke of Plautus's *Menaechmi*, Shakespeare's *Comedy of Errors* also doubles the improbability: "But when once we have lent ourselves to the first, which certainly borders on the incredible, we shall not perhaps be disposed to cavil at the second; and if the spectator is to be entertained by mere perplexities they cannot be too much varied" (*KSB* VI, 146).

In *The Taming of the Shrew* Petruchio dons the invisible disguise, the feigned attitude. Schlegel ignores the *Verkleidung* of the suitor Lucentio and the *Verstellung* of her sister, Bianca, who shows her true inclinations only after marriage. Katherina and Petruchio receive sole attention. Petruchio's *Verstellung* is nothing more than an exaggerated masculine parody of Katherina's behavior as the female termagant. In the church, on the ride home, in their country house, even in their wedding bed, Petruchio plays the obstinate and petulant male in order to cure Kate of her wild and defiant antics. Throughout, Shakespeare reminds us of the role playing of his character (*KSB* VI, 147). Indeed, the ironic counterillusion is ever present, for an audience is on the stage to cheer the performance. *The Taming of the Shrew* is one large play-within-a-play. The Induction initiates the audience into the play as prank, then has them join the players as audience to another ruse, Petruchio's wooing-game. Schlegel sees the Induction as the opening half of a dramatic frame and assumes that the concluding scene has been lost, or perhaps that Shakespeare merely left the task of returning the drunken tinker to the alehouse steps to be performed *ex tempore* by the player-audience at the end of the play.[55]

The hoodwinking of Christopher Sly is, in itself, a study in the ironies of dramatic illusion. As a whim to amuse himself, a British Lord has the tinker Sly, in a drunken stupor, carried to his splendid chambers, dressed in the finest clothes, and served by a retinue of players, who, costumed in appropri-

---

55. Craig, in *The Complete Works of Shakespeare* (Chicago: Scott, Foresman, 1959), 155, cites the suggestion of Adams, *A Life of William Shakespeare* (1923), that the clowns might return Sly to the alehouse steps at the play's close; Schlegel had proposed the possibility a century earlier.

ate livery, pretend that he is a wealthy nobleman just revived from a fifteen-year fit of insanity. The Lord's instructions to the players are simple and direct: They are to play the jest in earnest without "over-eying his odd behaviour" or smiling at his antics. As with Hamlet's speech to the players, the audience is reminded of the artifice of acting. Although Hamlet's stage audience, the King and Queen, react and depart, the Lord keeps his audience captive. Sly himself must play out the role that is given him. He neither forgets that he is Sly the tinker, nor readily accepts the tale of his long lunacy; yet, pleased by a finer illusion of self, he believes even in his disbelief. He is willingly seduced by the deception, for the staged scene is compelling. A "wife" is brought to him and he is titillated by promised pleasures. Sly may not think that seeing is believing, but he is offered the chance to prove each perception and gratify all the senses, to "smell sweet savours" and "feel soft things." Thus he acquiesces to the illusion, declaring himself "a lord indeed / And not a tinker nor Christopher Sly." Just as he is ready to bed down with his lady, he is told that such excitement might provoke a relapse into madness. Instead, his "wife" settles him down to watch the players "play a pleasant comedy" designed to "frame your mind to mirth and merriment." The audience in the theater joins the audience on the stage—Sly and his lady, the Lord and his players—to watch as the scene opens in Padua (*KSB* VI, 148).

Love's Labour's Lost is another play that Schlegel considers highly self-reflexive, a play about playacting. It openly displays its illusions as "a high-spirited charlatanry," and its dialogue is the rapid and relentless jesting of "passing masks at a carnival." Shakespeare employs his major devices for calling attention to artifice and provoking a dual perception of illusion: feigned actions, disguises, and even a play-within-a-play. In the very opening scene, Shakespeare sets forth the circumstance for the feigned actions: The young King of Navarre and three of his courtiers swear a grand oath to devote themselves to study and live in strict celibacy, banning all women from court. Their pompous vows are no more than pronounced, when the Princess of France arrives with her retinue of ladies to request the return of a province pledged to Navarre's keeping. The King meets with the Princess and immediately falls in love with her. His courtiers are likewise smitten by the ladies, and all oaths are soon broken.

The comedy of feigned actions consists, then, in pretending to keep the broken oaths. One by one, the King and his courtiers are exposed, till only the mock-virtuous Biron is left "to whip hypocrisy" and chide his companions for perjuring their vows. His complaint against their deceit, however, is deflated when Costard arrives with Biron's love letter to Rosaline. In his verbal maneuvering to redeem himself, Biron exonerates his companions as well. The oath, he declares, was ill-conceived, for celibacy cannot be forced on youth. The pledge to study they shall honor by devoting themselves to their ladies, for a woman's eyes are "the books, the arts, the academes, / That show, contain and nourish all the world." As Schlegel observes, the play could well end with this scene, "der Gipfel des Ganzen," at the end of act 4.

One might object, Schlegel grants, that the masque and masquerades of act 5 are too long; that the death of the Princess's father, the King of France, is an unwarranted tragic note; indeed, that the whole of act 5 is anticlimactic. Schlegel justifies act 5 by arguing that it fittingly resolves the raillery and comic pretensions of playacting that have dominated the play (*KSB* VI, 148–49). The folly of pretension is once more elaborated in the reception of the disguised lovers by the disguised ladies. The masque of the Nine Worthies echoes the pompous self-delusion of the opening oath. And the news of the King's death forces a seriousness upon the merriment: "The characters could not return to sobriety, except under the presence of some foreign influence." The play closes with the trial imposed upon the lovers. Not three years, but one they must wait for the fulfillment of their love. In calling for a year of constancy, till the Princess returns from her period of mourning, all oaths and vows are deliberately avoided. What is sworn is too easily forsworn. Mere words will not take the place of the fidelity and commitment of true love. The conclusion thus resolves the self-delusions and false pretensions of the opening. Like *Hamlet* or *Midsummer-Night's Dream*, *Love's Labour's Lost* is a play that sustains the awareness of playing. When the lovers must bid each other farewell at the end, Biron laments "Our wooing doth not end like an old play; / Jack hath not Jill." And when the King reassures him that with "a twelfthmonth and a day" the play will have a proper ending, he glumly responds "That's too long for a play."

All's Well That Ends Well is a play that few critics claim to enjoy. Schlegel cites Dr. Johnson's frank declaration of his dislike for Bertram, who comes out at the end with no other punishment than a passing shame and is still rewarded by the undeserved reunion with his virtuous bride.[56] Schlegel offers a manifold defense. Like the tale of patient Griselda, this play draws

---

56. Johnson, "General Observations on the Plays of Shakespeare," in *Works* XII, 62.

from the cultural mores of folklore in defending the loyalty and devotion of the woman against the tyranny and abuse of the man. As a folktale heroine, Helena heals the sick king and requests a husband as her boon. As in folktale, too, the heroine must fulfill impossible conditions: to present her husband with the ring from his finger, which he declines to remove, and the child of her body, which he refuses to father. The play must be understood, then, as drawing from sources very different from those exhibited in a comedy of manners. Still, it is a play to be enjoyed for rich characterization: "the plain honesty of the King, the good-natured impetuosity of old Lafeu, and the maternal indulgence of the countess to Helena's passion for her son." All characters and all sympathies are directed against the haughty pride of Bertram and the deceitful tongue of Parolles. Shakespeare absolves Bertram from the full burden of cruelty by giving a share of the guilt to Parolles, the "manifold linguist" and "double-meaning prophesier," who would rank among the finest of comic characters, Schlegel says, were he not eclipsed by Falstaff. The dialogue is necessarily sententious rather than rich in imagery, for "the radiant colors of fantasy would not be appropriate to this matter." Nevertheless, the play has its compelling scenes of *Verstellung* and *Verkleidung:* Helena disguising herself as another woman in order to embrace her husband, a "wicked meaning in a lawful deed"; the French soldiers acting out a "Mystification" in order to expose the cowardice and deceit of Parolles (*KSB* VI, 150–51).

Failing to understand the symmetry of illusion (*Symmetrie der Täuschung*), one critic of little insight, whom Schlegel does not name, has charged Shakespeare with a paucity of imagination in *Much Ado About Nothing* because he twice resorts to the same trick in trapping Benedick and Beatrice. It is said that a stage magician should not repeat his illusions lest he expose his trickery. Stage illusion, when it derives from plots to deceive, may be enriched by the repetition, for the audience learns to anticipate both the deception and the character's response. In *Much Ado,* Shakespeare challenges his characters and his audience with the task of interpreting. Appearances are not what they seem; reports are misleading; covert messages are lies. While others fail in uncovering truth, the bungling interrogators, Dogberry and Verges, succeed simply because they are not distracted or deluded by their own motives or passions. The accusation of the bride at the altar is a bold theatrical stroke that might well have seemed too tragic, had not Shakespeare already prepared the way for redeeming Hero from the false charges. The preceding scene closes by having the nightwatchmen arrest Borachio and Conrad. Borachio has been bragging of his part in the villainy, wooing Margaret, while Claudio and Don Pedro watch from a distance convinced that the lady is Hero. Since the nightwatchmen have already heard his confession, the audience expects that the truth will out. Shakespeare heightens the dramatic effect with agonizing delays; the truth is long hindered and baffled before it emerges.

The symmetry of illusion is accomplished in the major plot through the two scenes at the altar. The second bold theatrical stroke balances the first. Believing that Hero is dead, the mourning and repentant Claudio is married to a masked bride who is, of course, his lost Hero. A similar repetition of action provides the symmetry of illusion in the minor plot. Just as Don John plots to destroy the union of Claudio and Hero, Don Pedro plots to bring the ever-quarreling Benedick and Beatrice together. Don Pedro and Claudio tell Benedick how Beatrice secretly loves him even though another admirer insists that Benedick abuses her love. Knowing that Beatrice eavesdrops, Hero and Ursula describe the devoted passion of Benedick, which Beatrice cruelly scorns. The *Symmetrie der Täuschung* increases the dramatic effect in the major plot and the comic effect in the minor plot; further, by having Benedick and Beatrice drop their quarreling and jesting and seek to revenge the wronged Hero, Schlegel argues, Shakespeare cleverly links the two plots together.

The resurrection of the dead bride is a motif that Schlegel observes in the roles of Hero in *Much Ado* and Helena in *All's Well*. The cold condemnation and punishment of Hero and Helena links these comedies with *Measure for Measure*, which also gains its dark overtones from the presence of death. As did most of his Romantic contemporaries,[57] Schlegel sees the play as a confirmation of goodness and grace:

> But yet, notwithstanding this agitating truthfulness, how tender and mild is the pervading tone of the picture! The piece takes improperly its name from punishment; the true significance of the whole is the triumph of mercy over justice; no man being himself so free from errors as to be entitled to deal it out to his equals.[58]

---

57. On *Measure for Measure*, see *Charles Lamb on Shakespeare*, 50, 65; *Hazlitt on Theatre*, 78–82.
58. *KSB* VI, 153. "Aber wie schonend und milde ungeachtet der ergreifenden Wahrheit ist alles gehalten! Sinn des Ganzen ist eigentlich der Triumph der Gnade über die strafende Gerechtigkeit, weil kein Mensch sicher genug vor Fehltritten ist, um sich zu deren Verwalter unter seinesgleichen aufzuwerfen."

When Schlegel later discusses Calderón, he notes the dramatic tension created through the opposition of physical and spiritual passion, social and religious order (*KSB* VI, 258–60). In *Measure for Measure* he observes a similar opposition: the action here is more involved with criminal law and the judicial process than elsewhere; further, religion and providence are more directly integrated into the course of events than in any other play. Isabella wears the robes of a novice as if she were "a very angel of light." The Duke, on the other hand, plays his role as monk with full awareness of his *Täuschung*. The irony, of course, is that neither social law nor divine providence is allowed to operate. Angelo corrupts the law, and the Duke has usurped providence. The Duke may seem to unite the wisdom of church and state, "Only in his wisdom he is too fond of roundabout ways; his vanity is flattered with acting invisibly like an earthly providence."

Again, things are not what they seem. Isabella's piety disguises a prude. Angelo's stiff judicial manner disguises his sadistic lechery. And the Duke is the master of disguise who attempts to manipulate people as well as illusions. Because he has been too lenient a governor, his laws have become "more mock'd than fear'd." To Angelo he has entrusted the task of restoring legal authority. For loving Juliet prior to marriage, Claudio is sentenced by Angelo to be executed as a fornicator. When Isabella pleads for her brother's life, Angelo offers his pardon if she will repeat with him Claudio's crime with Juliet. She visits the prison to tell Claudio of Angelo's hypocrisy and is further outraged to hear her brother urge her to save him and thus make a virtue of the sin. In *All's Well*, Helena arranged the bed trick, substituting herself for Diana, to capture her own errant husband. In *Measure for Measure*, the Duke arranges the bed trick, putting Mariana in the place of Isabella, to trap Angelo. When he tells how Angelo has loved and abandoned Mariana (III.i), the Duke reveals that he has not, after all, blindly misjudged Angelo's character. He also reveals a curious vanity in controlling others. Schlegel argues that we thus always see the Duke playing the Monk, and that we especially savor Lucio's slanderous account of the Duke (III.ii). He may not be the whoremonger and the drunkard that Lucio describes, but the charges that "the duke had crotchets in him" and could be "a very superficial, ignorant, unweighing fellow" cannot be dismissed as groundless.[59] While much of the

---

59. Ibid., 154. Schlegel observes that Shakespeare does not indulge the Protestant stereotype "von den schwarzen tückischen Mönch." The monk or friar in *Romeo and Juliet* and *Much Ado About Nothing*, as well as the Monk/Duke in *Measure for Measure*, may have their fallibilities but they are not villains.

irony in *Measure for Measure* derives from the Duke's efforts to manipulate illusion, a crucial ingredient of that irony is Shakespeare's revelation of the Duke's fallibilities and ineptitudes as "stagemanager."

Portia is a more proficient stagemanager, manipulating not only the action in the guessing game of the three caskets played in the idyllic setting of Belmont but also the action in the trial of the flesh-bond staged in the competitive world of Venice. In calling attention to the contrast between the two plots of law and love (*der Rechtshandel* and *der Liebeshandel*) Schlegel notes that both are fables: in the victimization of Antonio the purported "facts" remain highly improbable; in the testing of Bassanio the fairy-tale motif nevertheless excites the imagination as "true." Although both are irreal, each makes the other more believable. The two plots are connected through immediate cause and effect: "Bassanio's preparations for his courtship are the cause for Antonio's subscribing the dangerous bond." They also complement each other aesthetically: the terror of Antonio's impending fate is alleviated by the romantic adventure of the three suitors. Most importantly, the two plots are united through Portia's skill in directing the outcome of events (*KSB* VI, 155).

Because of the difficulties in creating a role that transcends the stock character of the Jew, Schlegel appraises Shylock as one of Shakespeare's masterpieces of characterization. Shylock possesses "a well-defined, developed, and original personality." Although he rises to dramatic power as the most fully wrought character of the play, he nevertheless lapses into a mere caricature as comic villain. His intelligence and the complexity of his personality are undercut, Schlegel observes, in one matter: his morality is predicated on his utter disbelief in human virtue and nobility. Greed and revenge impel his cunning, but they also strip him of sympathetic identity and reduce him to comic meanness. The full power of his dramatic character is at work when he speaks of the lot of the Jews ("Prick us, do we not bleed?"), but he becomes an ineffective foil when his desire for revenge causes him to scorn Portia's appeal to mercy.

Like *Love's Labour's Lost*, *The Merchant of Venice* has a plot that is dramatically complete at the close of act 4. At the close of act 3, Portia has Bassanio perform the ritual of the caskets to win her as his bride. In the trial scene of act 4, Portia enters disguised as a Doctor of the Law and turns the words of the bond against Shylock. What need, then, of act 5? As in *Love's Labour's Lost*, Shakespeare chooses to purge the lover's self-delusion that provided the comic elements in the earlier scenes (*KSB* VI, 156). With the union of

Jessica and Lorenzo, the ill will against Shylock is absolved. Producing the ring that she had given her husband and he then surrendered as the fee demanded by the unknown Doctor, Portia lets Bassanio squirm while she confesses that "by this ring, the doctor lay with me." The sexual teasing, again as in *Love's Labour's Lost,* exposes the empty pretension of verbal oaths and, when Portia admits the disguise, reinforces the lovers' bond of trust and fidelity.

It is difficult, Schlegel observes, to summarize *As You Like It* in terms of its story; what happens is less important than what is said. The play is about the ways in which the characters construct and perceive illusory situations. Self-delusion and disguise are once more crucial elements. Although banishment or flight from the hostile politics of court has brought the characters into the Forest of Arden, the play deals but little with the illusions of court. The characters are caught up in "the illusions of love" (*KSB* VI, 157). Disguised as the shepherd Ganymede, Rosalind has the task of altering the illusions not only of the pastoral pair, Silvius and Phebe, but of her own beloved Orlando. Shakespeare also introduces two clowns to counter the illusions of love: Touchstone, who sees love as physical and carnal, and Jacques, who sees no love at all in his melancholy view of the world. Rosalind's task is not to dispel illusions, *per se,* but to sort out and abjure harmful or vicious illusions.

In his commentary to *Twelfth Night,* Schlegel again emphasizes the dialectic of the theatrical and the poetic elements of the drama. Intrigue, character, and situation are developed poetically. Because of Shakespeare's attention to the "color magic of an aethereal poesie," the comedies typically treat love more as a matter of the imagination than of the feeling (*KSB* VI, 157). Since eighteenth-century critics based their analysis of dramatic illusion on the appeal to the emotions, the difficulties in their discussions of Shakespearean comedy may well derive from the playwright's inattention to sentimental evocation. Indeed, the merely emotional and sentimental aspects of love are the subject of comic ridicule. The word *fancy,* Schlegel reminds us, referred to both *Phantasie* and *Liebe.* As Duke Orsino makes clear in the very opening scene, Shakespeare's concern is with the illusion-making powers of love. The Duke's love for Olivia is not merely *Phantasie,* it is *Einbildung* (*KSB* VI, 158). The dramatic complications derive from the compounding of illusion through self-preoccupation and conceit.

In her disguise as Orsino's page, Viola is merely the agent rather than the cause of illusion. The cause dwells in the mind of the beholder. The dilemma is not that the love is unrequited, but that it is a solipsism. Just as the Duke nourishes a self-engendered love for Olivia, Olivia becomes ensnared in illusory love for Viola as Cesario. Olivia is then caught up in a second illusion, for she cannot distinguish Viola in her male disguise from Viola's twin brother Sebastian. The high-flown folly of the major plot is mirrored in the bald pranks of the subplot (*KSB* VI, 158). Malvolio, Olivia's steward, is also the victim of illusory love. In contrast to the Duke, who has persuaded himself that he loves Olivia, Malvolio is convinced that Olivia loves him. While the other members of Olivia's household, the fun-loving Maria and genial Uncle Toby Belch, plot to make Malvolio the victim of his own conceit, the characters in the major plot are released from their *Einbildung* in the grand revelation scene in act 5. Olivia discovers that she has married not Cesario, but Sebastian, and Duke Orsino learns that Cesario is Viola, a maiden who loves him with loyal devotion.

In the comedies Schlegel has been discussing, the play within a play and disguised attitudes or appearances are repeatedly cited as evidence of Shakespeare's concern with revealed illusion. When he comes to *Midsummer Night's Dream* and *The Tempest*, he names a fourth dramatic element, magic. To *Verstellung* and *Verkleidung*, Shakespeare adds *Verwandlung*, and a powerful device it is, for it not merely dramatizes, it demonstrates the illusion-making process. In both plays, the multiple plot joins the magic world to the courtly world and the rustic world. Because the combination of the supernatural, the natural, and the comic belongs to both plays, they have often been compared by the critics. Schlegel disagrees with those critics who, persuaded by the notion of Shakespeare's maturation as a dramatic artist, assume that the later play is vastly superior to the earlier play.

In spite of structural and thematic similarities, Schlegel argues that the two plays are developed according to very different dramatic premises and must be judged accordingly. The magical conjuration of illusion in *A Midsummer Night's Dream* is a game. Oberon's plan to resolve the confusion of the lovers may go awry, but the prank involves no intrigue, no subversion, no disguise, no self-conscious manipulating. Prospero, far more in control as a "stagemanager" than Rosalind, Portia, or even Duke Vincentio, knows the potential dangers of the power he wields. Prospero is no Oberon. Instead of the open effusion of enchantments, the machinations of *The Tempest* are wrought in conspiracy. The magical, the courtly, and the rustic worlds do not peacefully coexist; they are caught up in rebellious and deceitful power struggles. The earlier comedy merely plays with illusion: "The most extraordinary combination of the most dissimilar ingredients seems to have been brought about without effort by some ingenious and lucky accident, and the colors are of such clear transparency that we think the whole of the variegated fabric may be blown away with a breath." In the later play, however, Shakespeare works with concealment rather than transparency: "As a whole we must always admire the masterly skill which he has here displayed in the economy of his means, and the dexterity with which he has disguised his preparations—the scaffoldings for the wonderful aerial structure."[60]

In Schlegel's interpretation, the dramatic illusion of *Midsummer Night's Dream* is thematized as dream. Thus the emotions have no substantial reality: angry conflicts dissolve into playful teasing; passionate desires, removed from the physical context, are merely seductive fancies. The dream, nevertheless, must reflect waking experience. *Verwandlung* becomes the dramatic means of giving substance to fancy, making its images as palpable as reality. While the flower juice works its capricious magic on the eyes of Lysander, Demetrius, and Titania, the audience, too, is treated with a dual perception of love, "presented as a poetic enchantment, which through an opposing magic can be suspended and made to appear again at any moment" (*KSB* VI, 159). The dream, as well as reality, has its extremes of ridiculous and sublime. The *Verwandlung* of Bottom, Schlegel argues, merely translates a metaphor into its literal sense. The courtly world of Theseus and Hippolyta serves as the highly ornamented and decorative frame for the fantastic vision of fairy and the grotesque performance of "Pyramus and Thisbe." The bungling comic rendition of the tragedy, Schlegel observes, aptly parodies the tryst of Lysander and Hermia.

Magic in *A Midsummer Night's Dream* is a fickle plaything; in *The Tempest* it is a moral and political tool. The plays are to be understood, then, in terms of contrary attitudes toward the power and purpose of illusion. Just as accident links the succession of events in the earlier play, the latter is directed by Prospero's overriding causal authority. Under his control are all the varied events of the drama: the shipwreck, the union of the lovers, the assassination of King Alonso plotted by Sebastian and Antonio, and the

---

60. Ibid., 158–59. *Midsummer Night's Dream:* "Die außerordentlichste Zusammenstellung fremdartiger Bestandteile scheint durch einen sinnreichen Zufall ohne Mühe entstanden zu sein, und die Farben sind von einer so hellen Durchsichtigkeit, als ließe sich die ganze bunte Gaukelei mit einem Hauche wegblasen"; *The Tempest:* "Man muß an dem Ganzen eine tiefsinnige Kunst bewundern, die ihre Mittel weise ausspart und ihre Anstalten, das Gerüst zu dem luftigen Wundergebäude, geschickt zu verkleiden weiß."

insurrection against himself plotted by Caliban, Stephano, and Trinculo. As Schlegel phrases it, the resolution is already present in the exposition. What we witness, then, is illusion not as the display of capricious fancy, but illusion as the revelation of a social as well as an individual *psychomachia*. Herein lies, too, the limitation of Prospero's, and the playwright's, illusion making: he can reveal character, but he cannot change it. He seeks to alter perception (his brother's, his daughter's), but he can accomplish his ends only within the limited time and place of these hours upon the island. The power of his magic, like the very illusion on the stage, is transitory.

The Good and Bad Angels who speak to Faustus in Marlowe's play belong to the same tradition that informs Shakespeare's creation of Caliban and Ariel, but good and evil are not the applicable epithets for these contrasting creatures of earth and air. Caliban is wild and earthy, "half demonic, half bestial nature"; he is human consciousness represented under the dictates of purely animal instincts. Under Prospero's tutelage he has acquired language and reason, but not understanding and judgment. Although the agent and instrument of the imagination, Ariel, it should be remembered, also resists Prospero's authority. Shakespeare may engage the allegorical tradition, but he has created definite individual beings, not mere allegorical personifications. Whenever we encounter the supernatural in Shakespeare's plays, here no less than in the magical scenes in *Macbeth*, the purpose is to translate superstitious belief into a revelation of the inner life of nature and its hidden causes (*KSB* VI, 161).

The marvelous in *Winter's Tale* and *Cymbeline* prompts Schlegel to discuss these plays, too, in comparison. Though akin to magic, the marvelous reveals still another aspect of dramatic illusion. The truth of the illusion, here, resides in representation of the characters and the passions. Critics who insist on deriving dramatic truth from adherence to probabilities can only vent their frustration and exasperation over the course of events in these plays. The plays are developed with deliberate artifice, Schlegel argues, and they address, dramatically and thematically, the relation between nature and art. Shakespeare's plays, Schlegel maintains, attempt to reenact the dual perception of art within nature (accompanying, of course, the perception of nature within art). Although Shakespeare made use of this Renaissance conceit, he also complicated it. Schlegel refers to a passage from *The Winter's Tale*:

> Yet nature is made better by no mean,
> But nature makes that mean: so, over that art

> Which you say adds to nature, is an art
> That nature makes. You see, sweet maid, we marry
> A gentler scion to the wildest stock,
> And make conceive a bark of baser kind
> By bud of nobler race: this is an art
> Which does mend nature, change it rather, but
> The art itself is nature.
>
> (IV.iv.89–97)

Aware of his son's attraction to a shepherd's daughter, King Polixenes, in his botanical metaphor, reduces love to a mere breeding when he proposes, as master gardener, to "marry / A gentler scion" and "bud of nobler race" to "the wildest stock" and "bark of baser kind." There is nothing flattering to Perdita in this proposal, nor is the breeding a proper marriage; rather, she is told to "make your garden rich in gillyvors, / And do not call them bastards." Perdita agrees that art is nature, but she utterly rejects the prostitution of nature (and, by implication, of herself) in the name of higher art:

> I'll not put
> The dibble in earth to set one slip of them;
> No more than were I painted I would wish
> This youth to say 'twere well and only therefore
> Desire to breed by me.
>
> (IV.iv.99–103)

Such dramatic situations, for Schlegel, entangle the dual perception required of the audience. The *double entendre* of the dialogue, with its simultaneous reference to Perdita's garden and to her relationship with Florizel, at the same time relates to the presumed differences between the nobility and mere rustics. Furthermore, on the literal level, the discussion of art and nature calls attention to the players and the play.

A motif of fairy tale and romance is the royal child reared by peasants. Banished or kidnapped, the child may grow up unaware of his or her identity, but the noble blood still manifests itself in mind and manner. As Polixenes must admit of Perdita, "nothing she does or seems / But smacks of something greater than herself, / Too noble for this place" (IV.iv.157–59). Thus the marvelous tale provides another circumstance similar to

Verstellung and *Verkleidung*. The audience, here too, must observe the duality of the character, the highborn princess coincident with the lowborn lass.

In Miranda and Perdita, we see the advantage of the natural over the acquired ("die Überlegenheit des Angeborene über das Erlernte"). In interpreting Shakespeare to mean that "the art which enriches nature" exists within "a higher art created by nature herself," Schlegel, according to the note in the English translation, errs: "Shakespeare does not here mean to institute a comparison between the relative excellency of that which is innate and that which owes to instruction."[61] Although the English translation is competent, this statement misunderstands Schlegel, misunderstands his concern with Shakespeare's "tiefe Absichtlichkeit"—which might, after all, have been translated as "intentionality" (as Coleridge translated it) rather than as "depth of purpose" (Black's translation).[62] In spite of Polixenes' crude innuendoes, which Perdita clearly understands, she readily grants that "art itself is nature." Such an argument happily supports Schlegel's emphasis on the organic over the mechanic. When he celebrates the natural in art, as represented in Perdita or Miranda, Schlegel does not mean that there is no artifice. Of course there is artifice, and we should be fully conscious of it, too. His point is that artifice is not an end in itself; rather, it mediates the perception of nature and reveals the natural in human activity. Schlegel's formulation of the primacy of the innate over the acquired simply follows Kant; we behold the ordering powers of the mind. Art, as defined in the mimetic tradition, pretends to be nature; the mimetic activity, however, is itself nature.[63]

Because Florizel courts Perdita disguised as a shepherd, the audience witnesses contrasting presumptions of duality, deliberate and natural. A similar situation occurs in *Cymbeline*, when Imogen, disguised as a boy to escape her husband's jealous wrath at her supposed adultery, encounters Guiderius and Arviragus, her long-lost brothers.

> As Miranda's unconscious and unstudied sweetness is more pleasing than those charms which endeavour to captivate us by the bril-

---

61. Schlegel, *A Course of Lectures on Dramatic Art and Literature*, 398.
62. Sauer, *Schlegel's Shakespearean Criticism*, 67, approves Black's translation of "tiefe Absichtlichkeit" as "depth of purpose" (rather than "deep purposefulness"). Coleridge seems to have the concept of "Absichtlichkeit" in mind when he discusses the "consciousness and intentionality" in Falstaff's wit, *Literary Remains* II, 180.
63. *KSB* V, 64, VI, 273; on "imitation," see also Kant, *Kritik der Urteilskraft*, §§46–49, in *Werke* V, 405–20; Schelling, "Über das Verhältnis der bildenden Künste zu der Natur" (1807).

liant embellishments of a refined cultivation, so in these two youths, to whom the chase has given vigour and hardihood, but who are ignorant of their high destination, and have been brought up apart from human society, we are equally enchanted by a naive heroism which leads them to anticipate and to dream of deeds of valour, till an occasion is offered which they are irresistibly compelled to embrace. When Imogen comes in disguise to their cave; when, with all the innocence of childhood, Guiderius and Arviragus form an impassioned friendship for the tender boy, in whom they suspect neither a female nor their own sister; when, on their return from the chase, they find her dead, then "sing her to the ground," and cover her grave with flowers:—these scenes might give to the most deadened imagination a new life for poetry.[64]

What stimulates the imagination is not merely the romantic pathos of the scene, but the incremental complication of the multiple roles, culminating in the seeming death of the seeming adulteress become a seeming boy.

The "death" of Hermione (*The Winter's Tale*) and the "death" of Imogen (*Cymbeline*) reminds Schlegel of the resurrection of the dead bride as a motif in *Much Ado* and *All's Well*. In contrast to his tragedies, where he dramatizes death with full emotional impact, the seeming deaths of these comedies Shakespeare represents with an emphasis on the funereal ritual rather than on the agony of a dying person. What happens on the stage—the bride feigns death, is merely reported dead, or seems dead because of a drugged trance—may be revealed, or at least hinted, to the audience. Furthermore, the grief is alleviated by shifting attention from individual response to ceremonial mourning. Consistent with the manner of romance, artifice predominates over nature.

Schlegel has shown how Shakespearean comedy exploits the duality of perception so that the audience is persistently aware of the fictive pretenses

---

64. *KSB* VI, 163–64. "Wie Mirandas unbewußte und ungesuchte Anmut mehr gefällt als Reize, die im glänzenden Putz der feinsten Ausbildung zu gefallen streben, so entzückt an den beiden, bloß durch die Jagd abgehärteten, sonst von ihrer hohen Bestimmung und der menschlichen Gesellschaft fern gehaltnen Jünglingen ein naiver Heldenmut, der sie Taten ahnen und träumen läßt, bis der erste Anlaß sie unwiderstehlich dazu hinreißt. Wie Imogen verkleidet in ihre Höhle kommt, wie Guiderius und Arviragus für den zarten Knaben, in dem sie weder Weib, noch ihre Schwester vermuten, eine kindlich leidenschaftliche Freundschaft fassen, ihn bei der Zurückkunft von der Jagd plötzlich tot finden und mit Gesang unter Blumen bestatten: diese Auftritte könnten eine ganz erstorbne Einbildungskraft neu zur Poesie beleben."

in the dramatic experience. Can tragedy, however, sustain the same sort of play with illusory situations? Does not the very presence of death (that is, the dramatic representation of an actual rather than a feigned death) radically alter the nature of dramatic illusion? When Schlegel turns to the tragedies, he points out Shakespeare's concern with keeping the manipulation of illusion a moving force in dialogue and plot. Neither the elements of composition, nor the manner of their dramatic exposition, but simply the direction given to the whole determines the play as tragedy (*KSB* VI, 164–65). No less than their comic counterparts, the characters in the tragedies display their ingenuity at dissimulation and disguise. The comic aspects of manipulating illusion are far more pervasively and subtly interfused in Shakespearean tragedy than can be explained by referring to the supposed need for "comic relief."[65] The mixture of comic and tragic is dramatically justified not because of their copresence in reality nor because the playwright must alleviate the spectator's emotional anguish; rather, as we have already seen Schlegel argue, the comic and tragic interchange heightens awareness of ironic alterity and thus enriches the aesthetic experience. Tragedy may fully exploit irony and comic wit until the very moment when tragic circumstances overwhelm the action (*KSB* VI, 137–38).

In the death scene from *Romeo and Juliet* Shakespeare offers a revealing variation on the motif of the resurrected bride that Schlegel observed in the comedies: Hero, Helena, Hermione, and Imogen all are assumed dead, yet are resurrected and reconciled with their respective lovers. Friar Laurence's stratagem manipulates illusion much in the same manner. In this case, however, the audience is fully aware that the death is counterfeit while Romeo and the other characters at the tomb are caught up in grief. The illusion of death gives way to more agonizing confrontations with death: the duel and the suicides. Opening her eyes as from a dream, the resurrected bride may expect to dissolve the illusion in a happy reconciliation but beholds instead the two corpses and chooses, as her lover did before her, death as her "restorative."

Schlegel offers no detailed comparison of dramatic illusion in comedy and tragedy; he does, however, observe that mediated, as opposed to immediate, audience participation is a distinguishing factor. Shakespeare dis-

---

65. On the comic in tragedy and "comic relief," see Lessing, *Hamburgische Dramaturgie*, no. 55, in *Werke* IV, 487–89; Richter, *Vorschule der Ästhetik* (1804) §§28, 32–33, in *Werke* II, 110, 125–32; De Quincey, "On the Knocking at the Gate in *Macbeth*" (1823), in *Collected Writings* X, 389–94.

tances the idea of death in comedy by emphasizing the funereal ritual while he nurtures its full emotional impact in tragedy by eliminating all self-exposing pretenses of illusion. In his earlier essay, "Über Shakespeares Romeo und Julia" (1797), Schlegel spent several pages on the deviations from the source.[66] Shakespeare's most telling change in the story is the meeting of Paris and Romeo at Juliet's grave. Although he closely follows his source, the dramatization of the narrative verse makes full use of the dramatic capacities of the dialogue. The lovers become lyrical. And the audience is drawn into the intensity of their love. Where the verse narrative stifled aesthetic participation (*Teilnahme*), Shakespeare engages the audience by holding to the very simplicity of the plot and heightening the elements of anticipation and suspense (*KSB* I, 124–25; VI, 165). Romeo's initial infatuation for Rosaline is another illusory pretense ("willig gehegte Täuschung") effectively setting off the sudden power of true love when Romeo meets Juliet (*KSB* I, 126–27). Thus, too, the bawdy anecdotes of the Nurse contrast with the lyric language of the lovers (*KSB* I, 133–34). Schlegel similarly defends the witty raillery of Mercutio. The comic provides counterpoint in this tragedy which Schlegel typifies as a play of opposites and contradictions brought together in the unity of effect (*KSB* VI, 166).[67]

In his discussion of *The Winter's Tale* and *Cymbeline*, Schlegel has already referred to the common ground these comedies share with the tragedy of *Othello* (*KSB* VI, 162–64). Leontes and Hermione, Posthumus and Imogen, no less than Othello and Desdemona, dramatize the rage of the jealous husband and the persecution of the innocent wife. And for cunning *Verstellung*, Iago has a counterpart in Iachimo. Again it is in the distancing that Schlegel finds the crucial differences. In *The Winter's Tale*, for example, we witness no incremental rise of the jealous madness, none of the "motives, symptoms, and intensifications"; dramatic attention is given not to immediate cause and effect, but rather to the consequences and resolution in the love of Florizel and Perdita. From the very outset of *Cymbeline*, we see Posthumus and Imogen caught up in the machinations of the wicked Queen. The focus is not on Posthumus but on the romance: the wrongly

---

66. Schlegel, "Über Shakespeares Romeo und Julia" (1797), in *KSB* I, 123–40; among the sources, Schlegel cites da Porto, *Istoria novellamente ritrovata di due nobili amanti*, but gives particular attention to the verse narrative of Arthur Brooke, *The Tragicall History of Romeus and Juliet* (London, 1562).

67. Schulz, *Literaturkritik als Form der ästhetischen Erfahrung*.

accused bride, the wicked stepmother, the long-lost brothers, and the epic contest of the British valiantly defending their country against Roman invaders. The jealousy, murderous as it is, is merely an added torment besetting the banished husband and persecuted wife.

In *Othello*, however, our attention is focussed on the rising passion of jealousy, and our participation is intensified as we witness Othello split into two beings: spiritual and sensual, virtuous and vicious. Before his mind is ravaged by Iago's insinuations and incriminations, we see Othello as the noble, heroic, loyal servant of his country and as the tender, doting husband of Desdemona. Just as he described *The Tempest* as social *psychomachia*, Schlegel considers this play a study in the individual crisis of body and soul. Othello is a divided being pulled in opposite directions by a Good Angel and an Evil Demon. The physical and sensual attributes of his character, Schlegel points out, are sufficiently delineated in the opening scenes for the audience to perceive the flaw that enables Iago to crack him in two, the higher and lower impulses are divided and set into conflict. Othello is thus made to suffer "as a double man" (*KSB* VI, 167). The tragedy is about illusion and delusion, the exaltation and perversion of perception. The audience must participate in Othello's experience to understand and reject his shifting perception of Cassio and Desdemona. Too, Othello's guilt must be largely absorbed in the evil of Iago as the insidious manipulator of illusion.

Iago manipulates *Täuschung;* Desdemona mediates *Teilnahme*. Whereas the wickedness of Iago's purposes would elicit only repugnance, the audience is inevitably distracted by a fascination with his methods. In spite of the negative emotional response, the reason becomes preoccupied with this master of dissimulation. Stirred by no other emotions than those he excites within himself, Iago knows how to arouse emotions in others and turn them to his own ends. Although he sees in everything only an ugly side, he knows how to stimulate the imagination with his crude and debasing perception of the sexes. In contrast to this Evil Demon, Desdemona is the Good Angel. Her innocence harbors no notion of ugliness or depravity. Her devotion to Othello, the goodness and nobility that she honors in him, directs the aesthetic response to his jealous rage as well as to his despair, killing himself "to die upon a kiss."

Because of its power to provoke the audience to reflection and deliberation, Schlegel calls *Hamlet* a "Gedankentrauerspiel." He studies its attributes as thought-tragedy not simply in Hamlet's brooding character, but in his questioning. The problems he mulls are perplexing and profound, entangled in moral and metaphysical paradoxes. Whether or not he is merely toying with Rosenkrantz and Guildenstern in asserting that "there is nothing either good or bad, but thinking makes it so" (II.ii.255), Hamlet confronts the audience with the same solipsism that Satan proclaims in *Paradise Lost:* "The mind is its own place, and in itself / Can make a heaven of hell, a hell of heaven" (*PL* I, 253–54). Hamlet not only challenges social and moral order; no less than Satan, he doubts the primacy, even the possibility, of divine order. This is no introspective liberation, as Byron would affirm of the inner province in *Manfred.*[68] Because perceptions deceive and judgment falters, thinking unmakes what it makes, and the mind is left a very unstable place.

Shakespeare introduces this dilemma of perception and judgment in the opening encounter with the ghost of Hamlet's father. Hamlet's belief in the vision as "an honest ghost" soon is subjected to doubt: The devil may be preying on "my weakness and my melancholy" (II.ii.630). First, he believes in the copresence of all things visible and invisible; then, he denies the mortal access to the spiritual. While he still perceives the Ghost, he declares: "There are more things in heaven and earth, Horatio, / Than are dreamt of in your philosophy" (I.v.166–67). But when he contemplates death, in his "To be, or not to be" soliloquy, he has no confidence in an afterlife, only the "dread" that the possibility imposes on the living. If there is "something after death" it is an "undiscover'd country from whose bourn / No traveller returns" (III.i.79–80). Reminding us of what Hamlet seems to have forgotten (i.e., that his Father is a returning traveler), Schlegel argues that the purpose of these paradoxical turns is to show Hamlet bereft of the conviction needed to give him firm footing in his dilemma. Fending off the spying and prying of Rosenkrantz and Guildenstern, he rehearses the metaphors of divine order only to deny that man is the godlike image: "Yet to me what is this quintessence of dust?" (II.ii.320) Only as the threat of death closes upon him does Hamlet reassert belief in an absolute order. When Horatio warns him to be wary, just before the duel with Laertes, Hamlet dismisses augury and confirms faith, "a special providence in the fall of a sparrow" (V.ii.231).

Awful metaphysical uncertainties, then, accompany the "antic disposition" that Hamlet puts on in his effort to escape suspicion himself even

---

68. Thorslev, "The Romantic Mind Is Its Own Place."

while he endeavors to confirm his uncle's guilt. In his earlier essay (*KSB* I, 88–106), Schlegel had not directly opposed the interpretation of Hamlet in *Wilhelm Meister*.[69] Here he dismisses Goethe's explanation of character and motives as oversimplified. Acknowledging Hamlet's madness as another instance of dramatic *Verstellung*, Schlegel emphasizes that the dissimulation is prompted more by natural predilection than by circumstantial necessity. The very attributes of mind that prompt his wavering speculations also lead Hamlet to pursue devious ways (*KSB* VI, 170). The King and courtiers manipulate illusion in their intrigue of hypocrisy and deceit; Hamlet conjures illusion as a game of survival and a means for revenge. Not just in his role of madness, but in his plot with the players Hamlet seeks to expose hidden evil through illusion.

The play within a play assumes the efficacy of illusion making. Hamlet gives a special turn to the power of dramatic illusion. If emotional response can be so effectively wrought "in a fiction, in a dream of passion," what might not a player accomplish, asks Hamlet, "Had he the motive and the cue for passion / That I have?" By this formula, the more closely the play reflects human experience, the more powerfully it can work upon the feelings. Thus Hamlet has his scheme: "the play's the thing/ Wherein I'll catch the conscience of the king" (II.ii.633–34). Schlegel comments on the rhetoric of antithesis and balance that Shakespeare uses in the play within a play as a theatrical artifice to reinforce his own illusion of spontaneity. Hamlet not only speaks this "theatrical" language when he invites the player to recite the tale of Pyrrhus, Priam, and Hecuba, he goes on, in his advice to the players, to insist that artificiality will disappear if the player can "suit the action to the word, the word to the action" (III.ii.1–40).

The performance has all its intended efficacy, for Claudius rises distraught when he witnesses the repetition of his own crime. Yet Hamlet's success is also a failure; as stagemanager and manipulator of illusions he has not the control of a Prospero or a Duke Vincentio, of a Rosalind or a Portia. Hamlet's failure, of course, is thematic: "the native hue of resolution / Is sicklied o'er with the pale cast of thought." In other plays, Shakespeare may argue that difficulties may be resolved through illusion. In *Hamlet*, however, Shakespeare shows us the limitations of illusion. It is a play about the inability to reach resolution: "This enigmatical work resembles those irratio-

---

69. Schlegel "Etwas über William Shakespeare bei Gelegenheit Wilhelm Meisters" (1796); Goethe, *Wilhelm Meisters Lehrjahre*, book 4, chap. 3.

nal equations in which a fraction of unknown magnitude always remains, that in no way admit of solution" ("Diese rätselhafte Werk gleicht jenen irrationalen Gleichungen, in denen immer ein Bruch von unbekannten Größen übrigbleibt, der sich auf keine Weise auflösen läßt" *KSB* VI, 169). Caught up in the manifold acts of deception, the spectator, no less than the protagonist, participates in the dramatic struggle to free perception from delusion and deceit.

In contrast to the emphasis on judgment in *Hamlet,* both *Macbeth* and *King Lear* engage imaginative participation through the emotions: terror in *Macbeth,* pity in *King Lear.* Schlegel does not relinquish the argument, here, to those eighteenth-century critics who explained dramatic illusion completely in terms of the emotional response. The powerful emotional effects, he argues, are excited through a careful dramatic exposition of causes. Schlegel begins his discussion of *Macbeth* with an account of the supernatural. What is crucial here is not whether Shakespeare or his audience believed in the supernatural, but the very fact of superstition as an attribute of human culture and individual consciousness. Superstition has its origins in man's dread of the unknown, in his intimations of a spirit world and a haunted "Nightside of Nature."[70] Shakespeare does not merely represent the supernatural, he creates a philosophy of its meaning, not an empirical philosophy, proclaiming reason and ridiculing the irrationality of superstition; rather, a natural philosophy, seeking out causes and effects. Where Hamlet questions the demonic or divine origin of the apparition, Macbeth becomes entangled in the evil auguries.

Ugly, grotesque, repulsive, the witches are images of evil power, yet before we can turn away in disgust, the imagination is stimulated ("der geistige Schauer überwiegt der sinnlichen Abscheu" *KSB* VI, 173). Although Schlegel ridicules the attempt on the German stage to represent the witches in *Macbeth* as if they were the Erinyes or Furies of Aeschylus's *Eumenides,* he does see them as kindred forces. Indeed, the action of *Macbeth* moves under a fatal destiny similar to that of Greek tragedy. In thoroughly Christian terms, however, evil manifests itself in the causality of sin—from tempting desires to tormenting guilt. The witches are merely the instruments of the fatal power: they do not cause evil, they reveal it. The evil is set loose in a most atrocious crime: Macbeth murders a generous, noble, aged man—his king and his guest—while he sleeps. Hamlet and Lear are sinned against;

---

70. Schlegel alludes to Schubert, *Ansichten von der Nachtseite der Naturwissenschaft.*

Othello and Macbeth are sinners. Shakespeare allows us to keep our sympathy for Macbeth by depriving him of all the criminal hardness necessary to the perpetrator of so vile a crime. Just as Iago takes on a major share in the murder of Desdemona, Lady Macbeth is made to absorb much of the responsibility for Duncan's death. While Lady Macbeth seems ruthless before the deed, we witness her character utterly destroyed as moral anguish drives her to madness. Macbeth suffers such hellish guilt that when the discovery of his crime brings Birnam Wood to Dunsinane, the retribution, dealt by man not born of woman, is met as a release from self-inflicted agony.

Because the witches seem to promise Macbeth invulnerability, we are compelled to share in his surprise as the impossible conditions are fulfilled and he finally recognizes "the equivocation of the fiend, / That lies like truth" (V.v.43–44). We are also thrilled by his fatal yet heroic turn to action as he confronts Macduff. The dramatics of terror fill scene after scene: the witches, the murder of Duncan, the dagger appearing before Macbeth's eyes, Banquo's appearance at the banquet, Lady Macbeth's nocturnal wanderings (*KSB* VI, 175). The dramatic illusion resides in the enactment of guilty delusions. The terror is made to fascinate even as it repulses. Participation does not flag or fail, for it is carried forward by the universal experience of guilt and dread.

In emphasizing the evocation of pity in *King Lear*, Schlegel again avoids returning dramatic illusion to emotional or sympathetic response. Just as he has argued that a philosophy of superstition mediates the elements of terror in *Macbeth* (*KSB* VI, 172), he refers to the science of *pathos* informing *King Lear* (VI, 176). Both plays require conscious attention to causes, the processes of arousing the emotions, as well as to effects, the mind struggling to cope with emotional extremes. Schlegel fully acknowledges that the poet storms the passions in his drama of manifold suffering, but he emphasizes the studied contrasts that require our rational attention to troubled and tormented reason. In Ophelia and Hamlet, we have already seen the dramatic contrast of true and pretended madness. In contrast to other modes of *Verstellung* and *Verkleidung*, the boundaries between reason and madness are subtle, elusive, perhaps even self-deceptive. *King Lear* takes us back and forth across the boundaries. The Fool becomes a wise man, the noble son a mad beggar: "This goodhearted fool clothes reason with the livery of his motley garb; the highborn beggar acts the part of insanity; and both were they even in reality what they seem, would still be enviable in comparison with the King, who feels that the violence of his grief threatens to overpower his reason" (*KSB* VI, 176).[71] In dramatizing perverse reason and multiple villainy (Goneril and Regan against Cordelia and Lear; Edmund against Edgar and Gloucester; Edmund against Cordelia and Lear; Goneril against Regan and Edmund), Shakespeare does not merely reinforce a plot with a parallel subplot. He forces us to discriminate.

The similarities are obvious: a deluded father fails to recognize the truly devoted child, while the perverse children repay his love and trust by robbing him of his fortune and happiness. The two plots may seem alike in their appeal to the emotions, but the circumstances are so different, Schlegel argues, that to the imagination they must be seen as opposites. Edgar rescues his blind father from suicide. After being reunited with his son, Gloucester hears from Kent "the most piteous tale of Lear . . . / . . . which in recounting / His grief grew puissant, and the strings of life / Began to crack" (V.iii.214–17). Lear is rescued by Cordelia, but both are imprisoned by Edmund. Before Edmund, vanquished by Edgar, can rescind the death sentence, Cordelia is hanged, and Lear dies in grief. Rather than merely surrendering emotionally to the drama of suffering, the spectator is challenged to compare and contrast, to discriminate and evaluate. As the one complements the other, plot and subplot merge aesthetically; more importantly, they merge dramatically, for the two are interwoven in the conclusion: Gloucester participates in the fate of Lear; Edmund joins with Goneril and Regan; in their adulterous lust for Edmund, Goneril and Regan destroy each other; attempting to restore his father and the king, the outcast Edgar defeats his brother, yet too late to halt the inexorable tragic doom (*KSB* VI, 176–77).

There is more on dramatic illusion to be gleaned from the Roman plays and the English history plays. In *Antony and Cleopatra*, for example, Schlegel celebrates the expansion of time and place so that what, within the narrow constraints of the "three unities," might only have moved the emotions, is given the grand dimensions to captivate the imagination (*KSB* VI, 181). And in *Henry IV,* he is especially attracted to the opposition and complementation of rational purpose and sensual indulgence, comic irony and high seriousness. Schlegel observes a juncture and balance in Prince Hal and Falstaff. Dissimulation, disguise, and the play within a play all take on new signifi-

---

71. *KSB* VI, 176. "Dieser guthertzige Narr kleidet die Vernunft in seine buntscheckige Tracht, der edelgeborne Bettler spielt den Wahnsinn, und beide, wenn sie wirklich wären, was sie scheinen, würden noch beneidenswert im Vergleich mit dem König sein, der es fühlt, wie ein zerreißender Schmerz seine Vernunft zu überwältigen droht."

cance within the historical context. The challenge is to perceive and interpret correctly the historical moment. Superstition deludes Glendower's perception, effeminacy Mortimer's, impetuosity Hotspur's. Even King Henry lacks the insight to read correctly the motives of his own retinue, overprizing Hotspur and undervaluing his own son.

Prince Hal alone has the gifts of perspicuity and perspicacity. Hal's shrewdness in playing the games of *Verstellung* and *Verkleidung* in the tavern suggest a schooling for the more dangerous games of intrigue in court and battlefield. Schlegel calls particular attention to the adventure in which the Prince, disguised as a robber, compels Falstaff to surrender the booty he has just taken, and to the exchange of roles in which Falstaff and Prince Hal take turns acting the King interrogating the Prince. Although related to similar scenes of playacting in the comedies, this mode of conscious role playing provides for a revealing dialogue of acute observation and penetrating judgment uniquely appropriate to the historical drama (*KSB* VI, 191).

In surveying the history of Spanish theater, Schlegel notes the emergence of formative conventions identical to those which shaped the drama in England, specifically in the handling of scene changes. When the stage was left empty for a moment and another set of characters appeared through another entrance, the audience was prepared to imagine a complete change in time or place. Before stage design was introduced and elaborated, spectators were accustomed to rely on their own imagination in order to fill in a lapse of time or to provide a different setting. The act of aesthetic complementation (or, as Schlegel calls it, "die ergänzende Phantasie") underlies all the pleasures of *Teilnahme* and *Täuschung* in our response to the drama. In aesthetic complementation, the spectator is called upon to join the playwright as a fellow poet in coauthoring the dramatic effects. Thus the response cannot be passive; it must be active and conscious. It must also be concentrated and focused:

> That is the true illusion, when the spectators are so completely carried away by the impressions of the poetry and the acting, that they overlook the secondary matters, and forget the whole of the remaining objects around them.[72]

---

72. Ibid., 217. "Die wahre Täuschung besteht eben darin, wenn man durch die Eindrücke der Dicht-und Schauspielkunst so hingerissen wird, daß man die Nebensachen übersieht und die ganze übrige Gegenwart vergißt."

Schlegel notes that these priorities are often turned about: the misdirected fascination with costumes and settings results in treating the primary concerns—good plays and good players—as if they were secondary. He goes on to lament the plight of the spectator who suffers from an impotent imagination, who sees only the holes in the fabric of illusion. Lacking the power of aesthetic complementation, he learns to take a perverse pleasure as an unbelieving skeptic at the shrine of the imagination. He preys upon the imperfections and inadequacies of the performance, not realizing that the sublime effects of the drama can never be fully represented on the stage. An impotency of the imagination thus results in an inability to engage illusion ("die Unfähigkeit getäuscht zu werden"). A vocal skeptic does not simply deprive himself of pleasure, he may well disenchant others as well. Just as illusion is enriched through the mutual contagion among the spectators, so too a prosaic disbelief ("prosaische Unglaube") can undermine the conditions favorable to dramatic effects (*KSB* VI, 216–17). As we shall see in the next chapter, Schlegel's objections against the destructive effects of a "prosaische Unglaube" is directly related to Coleridge's insistence upon "a willing suspension of disbelief" to attain the "poetic faith" in illusion. Indeed, this was the very passage from which Coleridge quoted in his second lecture at Bristol (2 November 1813)—and which has not been identified either by Raysor or by Foakes.[73]

The critics of the eighteenth century equated illusion with emotional response. In appealing to the doctrine of sympathy, they saw their premises broadly imitated in social mannerisms, in the prevailing cult of sensibility, and in the popularity of sentimental comedy. With the Kantian conception of the *Einbildungskraft*, the Romantics began to define illusion as an act of the creative imagination. For Schlegel and Coleridge (following Kant, but long before Gombrich), illusion is distinguished from delusion.[74] As Gombrich has explained it, the perceiver is conscious of the illusory nature of his perception: he perceives the *painting* of the mountain or the *mountain* in the painting; he does *not* ignore or lose perception of the painting and think that he perceives a mountain.[75]

---

73. Coleridge, *Biographia Literaria* II, 6; *Shakespeare Criticism* I, 70–71; *Lectures 1808–1819: On Literature* I, 528. The unidentified quotation, "Das spottische auflauern ob nicht ein umstand der wirklichkeit widerspricht," is from Schlegel, *KSB* VI, 217: "Das spöttische Auflauern hingegen, ob nicht irgendein Umstand der scheinbaren Wirklichkeit widerspricht."
74. Kant, *Anthropologie in pragmatischer Hinsicht*, §§11–14, in *Werke* VI, 440–47.
75. Gombrich, *Art and Illusion: A Study in the Psychology of Pictorial Representation*, 5–7.

Because he was arguing the same point, Schlegel had already postulated that illusion is attained consciously. As he studied it in the plays of Shakespeare, Schlegel found illusion a recurrent theme. The reality we perceive in a play is constructed out of illusion. The confounding effects of deception and disguise turn illusion to irony. Schlegel demonstrates that it is neither fragile nor brittle: irony may momentarily alter our perception, but we easily reassemble the dramatic action. The art of illusion is a reflexive, often ironic, attention to the process of illusion making. Thus the characters in a play, without losing the illusion of spontaneity, may remind the audience that they are acting. Our awareness of our own perception (that is, of our own engagement of and contribution to illusion) enhances the experience of dramatic illusion. Schlegel documents the conditions of illusion as they are dramatically and thematically implicated on the stage. Coleridge, as we shall see in the next chapter, emphasizes these conditions as they operate within the mind.

5

Illusion and the Poetic Imagination: Coleridge

On 6 November 1811, just twelve days before he began his second series of lectures, Coleridge wrote to Crabb Robinson: "I am very anxious to see Schlegel's *Werke* before the Lectures commence."[1] John Payne Collier, in his notes to the lectures, records Coleridge's statement a month later in lecture 9: "Yesterday afternoon a friend had left for him a Work by a German writer, of which Coleridge had time only to read a small part, but what he had read he approved and should praise the book much more highly, were it not that in truth it would be praising himself, as the sentiments contained in it were so coincident with those Coleridge had expressed at the Royal Institution [in 1808]" (16 December 1811).[2] As Anna Helmholtz pointed out in her study of Coleridge's debt to August Wilhelm

---

1. Coleridge, *Collected Letters of Samuel Taylor Coleridge* (= *CL*) III, 343.
2. Coleridge, *Lectures 1808–1819: On Literature* (= *LL*), in *The Collected Works of Samuel Taylor Coleridge*, I, 353–54. *Coleridge's Shakespearean Criticism* (= *Sh C*) I, 164, rev. ed. (London: Dent, 1960), I, 126.

Schlegel, the most extensively "coincident" passages actually begin in Coleridge's lecture 9.[3]

Most of what has been written on Coleridge's plagiarism from Schlegel's *A Course of Lectures on Dramatic Art and Literature* has addressed the commentary on *The Tempest* and the distinction between "mechanic" and "organic" form. I am referring here to the work of René Wellek, Gian Orsini, Thomas McFarland, Norman Fruman, M. M. Badawi, and Reginald Foakes.[4] Coleridge himself, however, was more chary of other debts. He takes pains in the *Biographia Literaria* (1817) to date his insight into Shakespeare's "consummate judgment" from his first lecture series, which began in January 1808, before Schlegel had delivered his lectures in Vienna later that same year.[5] In Schlegel's lecture 12, the major source for the borrowings in Coleridge's lecture 9, Schlegel had grounded Shakespeare's creative principle in his "tiefe Absichtlichkeit."[6] In this chapter, it will become clear that, despite specific debts to Schlegel, Coleridge's concerns in his lectures on Shakespeare are very different from Schlegel's. Where Schlegel was fascinated by Shakespeare's making illusion a part of the plot, Coleridge attempts to explain illusion in terms of the poetic imagination.

Reginald Foakes, in his commentary to *Lectures 1808–1819: On Literature*,[7] calls our attention to Coleridge's reaction to Richard Payne Knight's *Analytical Inquiry into the Principles of Taste*. Foakes, however, does not go on to examine the marginalia, probably because most of the notes are in Wordsworth's hand. Because Wordsworth and Coleridge annotated this work at the very time Coleridge was preparing his 1808 lectures, we may well anticipate a relation to the lectures.[8] The arguments raised in the marginalia

---

3. Helmholtz-Phelan, *The Indebtedness of Samuel Taylor Coleridge to August Wilhelm Schlegel*. As evidence of plagiarism, Lewes printed four parallel examples from Coleridge's *Literary Remains* and Black's translation in his review of the French edition of Schlegel's *Essais Littéraires et Historiques*. Sara Coleridge, in her edition of Coleridge's *Lectures upon Shakespeare and other Dramatists* (London, 1849; New York, 1854), 457–88, attempted to document all similarities to Schlegel.

4. Wellek, "Coleridge"; Orsini, "Coleridge and Schlegel Reconsidered"; Orsini, *Coleridge and the German Idealists;* McFarland, *Coleridge and the Pantheist Tradition;* Fruman, *Coleridge: The Damaged Archangel;* Badawi, *Coleridge: Critic of Shakespeare;* Foakes, "Repairing the Damaged Archangel"; McFarland, "Coleridge's Plagiarisms Once More: A Review Essay"; Sauer, *A. W. Schlegel's Shakespearean Criticism in England, 1814–1846*, 81–100; Foakes, "Coleridge and A. W. Schlegel," *LL* I, 172–75.

5. Coleridge, *Biographia Literaria* (=*BL*) I, 34.

6. Schlegel, *Vorlesungen über dramatische Kunst und Literatur* II, ii, 52.

7. *LL* I, 31.

8. Coleridge and Wordsworth, marginalia in Knight, *Analytical Inquiry into the Principles of Taste*. Marginalia transcribed with commentary by Shearer and Lindsay.

against Knight's discussion of illusion subsequently shaped Coleridge's corrections to Schlegel's account of illusion. On the one hand, Coleridge objected to the passive nature of aesthetic response in Knight's associationism; on the other hand, he saw that Schlegel, in grounding aesthetic illusion in imagination rather than in emotion (as in most eighteenth-century discussions), had failed to give an adequate explanation of the will. In 1808 he had not yet made the act of will the crucial factor in desynonymizing *delusion* and *illusion*.[9] But he had, before he turned to Schlegel in his lectures of 1811–12, already considered the simultaneous attention to artifice and illusion in the aesthetic response.

Between 1808 and 1819, Coleridge delivered eight series of lectures on literature in London and Bristol. Following the publication of John Black's English translation of Schlegel's *Lectures on Dramatic Art and Literature* (1815),[10] Coleridge became more insistent in his claims of precedence,[11] and the reference to Schlegel in the *Biographia* has been cited, again and again, as proof of his integrity and candor (if we agree with Raysor, Foakes, Badawi) or as evidence of disingenuous and self-serving defensiveness (if we accept Wellek or Fruman). Somehow in the discussion of plagiarism, the significance of the critical idea, "judgment" or "intentionality" (*Absichtlichkeit*), has been neglected,[12] and with it, one of the crucial arguments in the history of aesthetics: the problem of art and illusion.

---

9. The distinction, of course, is already present in Immanuel Kant, *Anthropologie in pragmatischer Hinsicht* (1798), in *Werke* VI, 412–58, and 526–29. See esp. §11, "Von dem künstlichen Spiel mit dem Sinnenschein" (VI, 440ff). For other sources and antecedents to Coleridge's analysis of self-consciousness in aesthetic experience, see Greiner, "Deutsche Einflüsse auf die Dichtungstheorie von Samuel Taylor Coleridge: Eine neue Untersuchung über den Einfluß von Tetens, Kant und Schelling auf Coleridge."

10. Schlegel, *A Course of Lectures on Dramatic Art and Literature*.

11. Coleridge claims precedence to Schlegel: lecture 9 (16 December 1811) *LL* I, 353–54; letter, mid-December 1811, *CL* III, 359–60; *BL* (1817) I, 22n; letter to James Perry, 5 February 1818, *CL* IV, 831; *Courier* (13 February 1818), in *Essays on His Times* III, 320–21; letter to William Mudford, 18 February 1818, *CL* IV, 839; lecture 1 (17 December 1818) *LL* I, 263–64; report on lecture 1, *Courtier* (18 December 1818), *CL* IV, 898–99; lecture 3 (7 January 1819) *LL* II, 293–94; letter to J. Britton, 28 February 1819, *CL* IV, 924.

12. Coleridge's claim of precedence, *Courier* (18 December 1818), was challenged in the *Morning Chronicle* (29 December 1818): "Though Mr. Coleridge was long in Germany, and is well acquainted with German Literature, it does not follow that he is indebted to Schlegel for any part of his ideas; but unless he can shew that in Lectures or publications of so early a date as 1801, he advocated the judgment displayed by Shakespeare in the composition of his works, it will be somewhat difficult for him to establish the claim to the title of a *discoverer*" (*CL* IV, 898–900). His prior claim to the principle of "judgment" (*Absichtlichkeit*) was precisely what Coleridge defended in the *BL* I, 22n, 102–3. See Orsini, "Coleridge and Schlegel Reconsidered," 105; Sauer, 86–87, 180n; *LL* I, lv.

The parallel passages on the nature of *theatralische Täuschung* (stage illusion) have received but little attention in the many commentaries on Schlegel and Coleridge. Out of the concern with illusion, Coleridge drew his explanation of the "willing suspension of disbelief." In essays devoted to the exposition of Coleridge's theory of "stage illusion," Earl Leslie Griggs, J. R. de J. Jackson, and R. A. Foakes make no mention of Schlegel.[13] Coleridge's claim that illusion is experienced through the spectator's "voluntary contribution" to a state of "half-waking, half-sleeping," Raysor claims in a note to this passage, is derived from Schlegel's assertion that illusion "is a waking dream, to which we voluntarily surrender ourselves."[14] Raysor points out, however, that the 1805 watermark of the Coleridge manuscript seems to suggest a date earlier than the commencement of the 1811–12 lectures.

Foakes, in the new edition of the *Lectures,* persuasively denies the influence of Schlegel. The passage, he demonstrates, was indeed drafted before Schlegel had delivered his lectures.[15] Further evidence in support of Foakes's dating of the "Desultory Remarks on the Stage, & the present state of the Higher Drama," which he places in the Shakespeare lectures of April 1808, can be drawn from the annotations to Knight. In bringing forth still another source, my purpose is not to undermine Coleridge's contribution to the continuing debate over aesthetic illusion. Rather, I intend to clarify his explanation of illusion, how it has been misunderstood, and how, in fact, his response to Knight as well as to Schlegel led to his own "true Theory of Stage Illusion." By the time Coleridge turned to Schlegel, he had already set forth his own concern with the problem and defined the necessary mediation of the will.

The passage that Raysor and Foakes cite from the Schlegel's *Vorlesungen* is but one of many attempts at definition in a work persistently concerned with manifestations of dramatic illusion. In discussing French neoclassicism, as exemplified in Corneille, Racine, and Molière, Schlegel takes up the "three unities." Obedience to traditional precepts, he objects, has replaced attention to what might actually be effective in dramatic performance. If the playwright could actually succeed in conjuring a more com-

13. Griggs, "The Willing Suspension of Disbelief"; Jackson, "Coleridge on Dramatic Illusion and Spectacle in the Performance of Shakespeare's Plays"; and Foakes, "Form to his Conceit: Shakespeare and the Uses of Stage Illusion." Morrill, "Coleridge's Theory of Dramatic Illusion," observes the parallel in Schlegel's *Vorlesungen,* but attempts to relate Coleridge's discussion of "a suspension in the power of comparison" to Kant's analysis of the sublime in *Kritik der Urteilskraft,* §25—a passage which Schlegel cited as particularly relevant to his account of the effects of tragedy (*KSB* V, 64).
14. *Sh C* I, 201.
15. *LL* I, lv–lvii, 128–29.

plete and powerful dramatic illusion by adhering to unity of time, place, and action, then the critical position of the French critics ought to be given full credence. To answer the claims that dramatic illusion depends on adherence to the three unities, Schlegel elaborates his own definition of illusion:

> This idea of illusion has occasioned great errors in the theory of art. By this term there has often been understood the unwittingly erroneous belief that the represented action is reality. In that case the terrors of Tragedy would be a true torture to us, a nightmare oppression of the fancy. No, the theatrical as well as every other poetical illusion, is a waking dream, to which we voluntarily surrender ourselves. To produce it, the poet and actors must powerfully agitate the mind, and the probabilities of calculation do not in the least contribute towards it. This demand of literal deception, pushed to the extreme, would make all poetic form impossible.[16]

As we observed in the preceding chapter, this passage has marked similarities to Coleridge's definition of stage illusion. Did Coleridge, as happened on other occasions in preparing his Shakespeare lectures, once again "lift" a paragraph from Schlegel's text?

In contesting the presumption of the French critics, Schlegel denies that the probability provided by the "three unities" is necessary. Illusion, he argues, is neither involuntary misapprehension, nor a confusion of the represented with the real. If either were the case, then the scenes of horror in tragedy would work as a nightmare upon the fantasy. Instead, like all poetic illusion, theatrical illusion is a waking dream in which we engage voluntarily. Coleridge, too, counters the French critics, distinguishes illusion from delusion, stresses the voluntary over the involuntary, and compares the experience to a waking dream.

---

16. Schlegel, *Lectures on Dramatic Art and Literature*, 246; *Vorlesungen über dramatische Kunst und Literature*, in *KSB* VI, 22–23. "Der Begriff der Täuschung hat in der Kunsttheorie große Irrungen angerichtet. Man hat oft darunter den Unwillkürlich gewordenen Irrtum, als ob das Dargestellte wirklich sei, verstanden. Dann würde sie bei den Schrecknissen des Trauerspiels eine wahre Plage sein, ein Alpdrücken der Phantasie. Nein, die theatralische Täuschung, wie jede poetische, ist eine wache Träumerei, der man sich freiwillig hingibt. Um sie hervorzubringen, müssen Dichter und Schauspieler die Gemüter lebhaft hinreißen; die berechneten Wahrscheinlichkeiten helfen nicht im mindesten dazu. Jene Forderung der buchstäblichen Täuschung, aufs Äußerste getrieben, würde alle poetische Form unmöglich machen." Black mistranslates "ein Alpdrücken der Phantasie" as "an Alpine load on the fancy"; I have amended the phrase to "a nightmare oppression of the fancy."

The parallels are striking. Nevertheless, Coleridge formulated this position while preparing his notes on Shakespeare for his first lecture series (15 January to 8 June 1808)—before Schlegel delivered his lectures in Vienna (31 March to 10 May 1808). In the last chapter, we saw how the concern with illusion informs Schlegel's interpretation of Shakespeare. In spite of his extensive debt to Schlegel's *Vorlesungen,* Coleridge owes virtually nothing to Schlegel's fascination with illusion, for the analysis of *Teilnahme* and *Täuschung* would have to be modified and made to serve his own emphasis on the controlling will in the aesthetic experience of illusion. Because it is always subservient to the will of the spectator, Coleridge does not pursue, with Schlegel, Shakespeare's thematic concern with illusion. When he draws from Schlegel, repeatedly and extensively, for his demonstration of Shakespeare's "excellent judgment," it is important to recognize that Coleridge could and did refer to "intentionality" and "purpose" when he translated *Absichtlichkeit,* and that "judgment," the necessary complement to "genius," was intended to refer to the shaping and control of art as "imitation."

In his preparatory notes for the 1808 lectures, Coleridge discussed a "temporary Faith which we encourage by our own Will" and a "suspension of the Act of Comparison" that brings the spectator into a "negative Belief."

> Stage Presentations, are to produce a sort of temporary Half-Faith, which the Spectator encourages in himself & supports by a voluntary contribution on his own part, because he knows that it is at all times in his power to see the thing as it really is. . . .
> The Subject of Stage-Illusion is so important, and so many practical Errors & false criticisms may arise, and indeed have arisen, either from reasoning on it as actual Delusion—(the strange notion, on which the French Critics built up their Theory, and the French Poets justify the construction of their Tragedies—) or from denying it altogether, (which seems the butt of Dr Johnson's reasoning and which, as Extremes meet, would lead to the very same Consequences by excluding whatever would not be judged probable by us in ⟨our⟩ coolest state of feeling with all our faculties in even balance) that a short digression will, I hope, be pardoned, if it should serve either to explain or illustrate the point.[17]

17. *LL* I, 129–36; from British Museum, Add Ms 34225 f56.

What follows is Coleridge's digression on dreams. He distinguishes "*ordinary* Dreams" from "the Night-mair": in the former, the comparative power is suspended and the will is inactive; in the latter "the waking state of the Brain is re-commencing" so that in "a rapid alternation, a *twinkling* as it were of waking and sleeping," the action of the will, partially aroused, torments the mind with false images which cannot yet be properly weighed by the judgment. Because Coleridge was fascinated with dream images and filled his notebooks with the records of his own hallucinations, it is understandable that the critics have become distracted here from attention to essential attributes of Coleridge's account of aesthetic illusion. While pursuing the analogue of the dream, they neglect Coleridge's concern with the will.

As antecedents to Coleridge's reference to illusion as "half-waking, half-sleeping," commentators have cited Erasmus Darwin's *The Botanic Garden* and Lord Kames's *Elements of Criticism*.[18] Reference to the "waking dream" is such a commonplace in eighteenth-century criticism that we can scarcely exclude any of the major accounts of aesthetic illusion: Diderot and Rousseau in France; Lessing, Nicolai, and Mendelssohn in Germany. It was elaborated, as well, by Herder and Sulzer.[19] Yet to affirm the conscious and mediating presence of the active will is not merely new and different, but also profound in its ramifications. To be sure, Schlegel talks about a "voluntary surrender," and even Erasmus Darwin said that we "permit ourselves to relapse into the delusion, and thus alternately believe and disbelieve." But can we engage illusion without a "relapse" or "surrender" of the will?

Coleridge, it should be recalled, had an intense personal interest in affirming the active power of the will. Thus in his notebooks, he was much concerned with discovering and asserting the capacity of a sane mind to wield control over delusions.[20] In the detailed account of phantom images he saw during his stay in Malta (12 May 1805), for example, he wrote: "Often and often I have had similar Experiences, and therefore resolved to

---

18. Home (Lord Kames), *Elements of Criticism* II, 418; Darwin, *The Botanic Garden* II, 87; cited in Schneider, *Coleridge, Opium, and Kubla Khan*; *BL* II, 6–7n.; *LL* I, lvi–lvii.

19. Diderot, "Entretiens sur le Fils naturel" (1757), in *Oeuvres complètes* VII, 85–168; *De la poésie dramatique* (1758), in *Oeuvres complètes* VII, 299–394; Herder, "Shakespear" (1773) and *Kalligone* (1800), in *Werke* V, 227–28, and XXII, 155; Sulzer, "Täuschung."

20. I have dealt with this problem previously; see Burwick, "Coleridge, Schlegel, and Animal Magnetism," 283–84; and *The Haunted Eye: Perception and the Grotesque in English and German Romanticism*, 114–15.

write down the Particulars . . . / as a weapon against superstition."[21] The delusions were upon him again at the very time of the 1808 lectures. The second lecture of 1808 was postponed for two weeks, and the third lecture had to be put off for another six weeks. Again despairing in his opium addiction and afraid that he was losing his sanity,[22] he describes "a fact of Vision" that occurred in his little bedroom at the *Courier* office (23 March 1808). He "was thinking of something introversely," he writes, and gazing at the wall. In the narrow space, less than a foot, between the bed and the wall he suddenly sees the pattern on the wallpaper grow larger and more vivid. The narrow space widens so that "a pair of Friends might walk arm in arm through the Interstice." His introverse thinking is interrupted, and he is completely entranced by his delusion of expanding space. He wants to repeat the vision, to make the delusion subject to his voluntary control:

> I again voluntarily threw myself into introversive Reflections, & again produced the same Enlargement of Shapes & Distances and the same increase of vividness—but all seemed to be seen thro' a very thin glaceous mist—thro' an interposed Mass of Jelly of the most exquisite subtlety & transparency. But my reason for noting this is—the fact, in my second & voluntary production of this Vision I retained it as long as I like, nay, *bent over* with my body, & looked down into the wide Interspace . . . without destroying the Delusion/ —then started my eyes & something . . . of the Brain behind the eyes started or jirked them forward, and all was again as in common. / The power of acting on a *delusion*, according to the Delusion, without dissolving it/—Carry this on into a specific Disease of the Kind—Prophets, &c—[23]

This "second & voluntary production" is important to Coleridge, for it transforms his role from passive victim into active agent. The delusion becomes a kind of mental experiment that he controls. Or is the "voluntary production" merely a part of the delusion? Perhaps Coleridge has caught himself here in that same kind of paradoxical predicament he described in his lecture on Hamlet's feigned madness as a *"half-false"* pretense. While he

---

21. Coleridge, *The Notebooks of Samuel Taylor Coleridge* (= *CN*) II, 2583.
22. Ibid. III, 3277n; Coburn notes that Coleridge began expressing his fears of impending "madness" in 1794; see *CL* I, 107ff, letters 62, 63, 65, 67, 68, 73, 74.
23. *CN* III, 3280.

means to reassert voluntary control by "acting on a delusion," he can only do so "according to the Delusion."

After Mary Lamb wrote to the Wordsworths confirming the sad plight of "poor Coleridge," Wordsworth hastened from Grasmere to London on 23d February.[24] Lamb wrote to Crabb Robinson on March 12th that Wordsworth was so occupied in attending to Coleridge that "we cannot have him in an evening."[25] When Coleridge recommenced his lectures, Wordsworth wrote to Sir George Beaumont that he "heard Coleridge lecture twice [30 March and 1 April] and he seemed to give great satisfaction; but he was not in spirits and suffered much during the course of the week both in mind and body."[26] Wordsworth left London on April 3d. During the previous month, Wordsworth assisted Coleridge in annotating Knight's *Analytical Inquiry into the Principles of Taste*. Most of the marginalia are in Wordsworth's hand, but content and style suggest that these notes were dictated by Coleridge for use in his lectures. At several points the notes reveal the manner of the public lecturer. Too, we must remember that Wordsworth was not in the habit of annotating works for himself.

There were both opportune and polemical reasons for turning to Knight for these lectures. First, the book was at hand, for in his opening lecture Coleridge had introduced a long passage on beauty from "a writer on the subject of Taste, whose work has excited no ordinary degree of attention." In spite of the "many undoubted Truths" in Knight's account of the beautiful, Coleridge proceeds to examine "the Error" in its failure to discriminate differences in aesthetic apperception or to acknowledge "that a ⟨certain⟩ distinct faculty or modification of the human mind has a real existence."[27] In his first lecture, Coleridge read six pages (pp. 9–15) from Knight's commentary on the beautiful. The marginal notes commence with the discussion of the sublime (pp. 93–94), and the most capacious notes provide a counterargument to Knight's explanation of aesthetic illusion (pp. 319–20, 331–34).[28]

---

24. Dorothy Wordsworth to Lady Beaumont, (approx.) 20 February 1808, *The Letters of William and Dorothy Wordsworth* II. *The Middle Years*, part 1. 1806–11, 197.
25. Robinson, *The Correspondence of Henry Crabb Robinson with the Wordsworth Circle* I, 51.
26. William Wordsworth to Sir George Beaumont, 8 April 1808, *The Letters of William and Dorothy Wordsworth* II, *The Middle Years*, part 1, 208.
27. *LL* I, 31–35. Foakes (nn. 10, 16, and 17) relates Coleridge's commentary to this passage from Knight to the objections raised in the *Friend* I, 11n, and to the arguments in "On the Principles of Genial Criticism," and in the first lecture of the 1811–12 series. He does not acknowledge, however, any use of the marginalia in the lectures.
28. Wordsworth and Coleridge, Marginalia in Knight, *Analytical Inquiry into the Principles of Taste*.

Drawing from associationist doctrine, Knight constructs his analysis of aesthetic response in terms of sensory stimulations of pleasure and pain. In Gothic architecture, for example, a vaulted roof supported by slender columns "may offend the eye of a person, who suspects it to be inadequate to its purpose, and therefore associates ideas of weakness and danger with it" (p. 176). Aesthetic experience is thus reduced to behavioral response with no more involvement of reason or imagination than was exercised by Pavlov's dog in salivating at the ring of a bell. With scoffing reference to Knight's book on phallic worship,[29] Coleridge declares that the author of the *Inquiry into the Principles of Taste* "is just as ignorant *in head* of Taste, and its Principles, as the Author of the Priapus &c must needs have been ignorant *in heart* of Virtue & virtuous feelings." Coleridge's principal objection to empiricist, mechanist, and associationist theories is that they define mind as passive.[30] Knight claims support from Burke's *On the Sublime*[31] in asserting that "the nearer tragedy approaches the reality and the further it removes us from all idea of fiction, the more perfect is its power." The marginal note declares this assertion a "wretched trifling" because it ignores the active involvement of the mind:

> Supposing that it were possible to represent a tragedy in such a manner that the delusion during the representation would be perfect, then suppose when it is proposed to repeat this tragedy that at the same time an event resembling it in its main outline, or at least the catastrophe of such an event is to be exhibited in the public execution of some King, princess or other eminent person. We are then to ask to which spectacle the person would repair. But there is in the essentials of the case no similitude; for whatever may be our sensations when the attention is recalled to a scenic representation how farsoever we may then lose sight of its being a mimic show, we know perfectly at the time, when we are going to see it, or when assembled at the Theatre in expectation; that it is nothing better or

---

29. Knight, *A Discourse on the Worship of Priapus and its connections with the Mystic Theology of the Ancients* (London, 1786).

30. Coleridge to Thomas Poole, 23 March 1801, *CL* II, 709: "*Mind* [in the materialist system of Newton] is always *passive*—a lazy *Looker-on* on an external world." *BL* I, 111: In the associationist system of Hartley, "our whole life would be divided between the despotism of outward impressions, and that of senseless and passive memory."

31. Burke, *A Philosophical Enquiry into the Origin of our Ideas of the Sublime and the Beautiful. The Second Edition, With an introductory Discourse concerning Taste*, part 1, sec. xv "Of the effects of Tragedy," 75–79.

> worse. It is possible, that the mind during the representation of a tragedy may have its fits of forgetfulness and deception and believe the fiction to be the reality, but the moment you suppose it in a condition to make a choice of this kind, all sense of such delusion vanishes. Therefore however perfect according to Burke's notion of perfection a tragedy may be unless you suppose the delusion indestructible the cases can admit no comparison, nor if you do can they admit of any for then they are identical, both becoming realities. But these absurdities are too gross for notice. (gloss to Knight 319–20)

The juxtaposition of reality and illusion, here, accomplishes little more than what the concluding line remarks: the supposed confusion of the two results in absurdities. But Schlegel, in his essay "On Dramatic Dialogue" (1796), had observed that in spite of the opposition between reality and illusion, they do coexist. The reality of dramatic dialogue is that the text is written; the illusion is that dramatic dialogue is spoken spontaneously. Because the spectator's engagement of illusion is conditioned by the knowledge of its artifice, his aesthetic experience is sustained by the simultaneity of "observing and forgetting" (*beobachten* and *vergessen*).[32] But in terms of the gloss to Knight's text, the "fits of forgetfulness and deception" do not—indeed, cannot—occur simultaneously with the conscious awareness of artifice. As soon as the will is active, "all sense of such delusion vanishes." The aesthetic experience, as determined in this pronouncement, is an either/or proposition. The spectator cannot choose to believe.

The very next marginal note, however, grants the possibility of simultaneous awareness of artifice and illusion. Knight's assertion is in accord with the eighteenth-century accounts of illusion as excited through emotional sympathy.[33] In insisting upon the difference between the response to fictive and to real distress, the note begins with the assumption that fiction "subdues the mind to a passing belief" and goes on to posit "various degrees of continuous belief in the truth of fictitious stories."

> The most extravagant Arabian Tale that ever was formed if it be consistent with itself and does not violate our moral feeling, subdues

---

32. *KSB* I, 113–14. "Über den dramatischen Dialog" was first published with "Etwas über William Shakespeare bei Gelegenheit Wilhelm Meisters" in Schiller's *Horen* (1796).

33. Bate, "The Sympathetic Imagination in Eighteenth-Century English Criticism"; Wasserman, "The Sympathetic Imagination in Eighteenth-Century Theories of Acting."

> the mind to a passing belief that the events related really happened. In reading Hamlet or Lear, though we are frequently sensible that the story is fictitious, yet in other moments we do not less doubt of the things having taken place than when we read in History about Pompey or Julius Caesar, we question the truth of the general story. Yet in Lear and Hamlet we have the ⟨almost⟩ arealizing accompaniment of Metre. Nevertheless we believe: Our situation at a Theatre is undoubtedly very different, and the question before me now is to determine whether (as there can be no doubt that we have various degrees of continuous belief in the truth of fictitious stories in verse) whether by the helps which representation supplies the delusion can be carried still further, and we may be made to believe even for a moment that the scene before us is not the [p. 332] representation of a transaction, but the transaction itself, is not a shadow or reflexion but a substance. (gloss to Knight 331–32)

The presumption was already put forward in an earlier note (to Knight 319–20) that delusion, or belief in fictive representation, could occur as temporary "fits," a flickering or alternating of belief and disbelief. Here, however, the question is pondered whether a "passing belief" may be raised to a "continuous belief." The "various degrees" of aesthetic illusion, it is argued, do involve a simultaneous consciousness of artifice. Note, however, that the word is still *delusion*. The opposition between real and fictive is partially resolved in the very task of reading a text. A historical text, no less than a literary text, requires the imaginative animation of events, events that "we do not less doubt" as "having taken place." The drama, because of the artifices of metrical language, calls attention to its own artificiality. "The question before me now," the marginal note continues in podium rhetoric appropriate to Coleridge's lecture, is whether the arts of staging and acting can make us "believe even for a moment that the scene before us is not the representation of a transaction, but the transaction itself." This is, indeed, the crux: Does the spectator lose his conscious awareness of "representation"?

Continuing in podium style ("In our attempt to answer this question . . ."), the note counters Knight's argument that through sympathy emotion overwhelms reason. While the very artifice of drama effectively bars the imagination from generating that "degree" of illusion experienced in reading, "another species of delusion" is "occasionally superinduced."

> In our attempt to answer this question let us first ask if there be anything in the representation of a play that will tend to strengthen the first species of delusion which undoubtedly exists in reading it, viz that of the facts represented or feigned having actually occurred. I believe the answer will be no; the Playhouse, the audience, ⟨the persons of the actors,⟩ the lights, the scenes all ⟨tend⟩ interfere with that de⟨lusion⟩[ception] and above all the persons, gestures, and voices of the actors which ⟨so⟩ immediately tell us that it is Mr or Mrs Such a One. These matters of fact, while consciously before us, are insuperable bars to the Imagination. Here there is a mighty loss; & If ⟨then⟩ during the progress of the Piece another species of delusion were not in its stead occasionally superinduced ⟨viz that⟩ and by the very reason which had destroyed the ⟨former⟩ former, viz that the scene before us is a *reality* I do not see how it is possible that we should be *affected* to the degree ⟨that⟩ to which a fine tragedy exquisitely represented often does affect us. (gloss to Knight 332)

In order to define the nature of this "superinduced" perception of a dramatic scene as "a *reality*," the note appeals to the maturation of the imagination and the differences between the response of the child and the adult.

> Whence is it that after the first inexperience of Childhood and youth has ceased we are so languidly moved by the representations of imaginative Tragedies, such as Lear, Macbeth & Hamlet, and the most languidly by those parts which are most imaginative, whence but because it is utterly impossible here to appro[xi]mate to either species of delusion: there is such disproportion betw[een] [p. 333] ⟨between the means and the end⟩ the Powers of Nature, Storms &c, and the means employed to represent them and in like manner, with respect to the supernatural agencies. But in the looks, the gestures, and tones of a genuine actor, aided by the knowledge of Nature displayed in the words of the Poet, there is no such disproportion or unfitness; and the representation I confess appears to me not only to approach to reality but often for a short while to be wholly merged or lost in it. (gloss to Knight 332–33)

The argument, at this point, is identical to that developed in Coleridge's lecture 4 and in the "Desultory Remarks on the Stage," which Foakes has identified as introductory to one of the lectures on Shakespeare given in April 1808.³⁴ The child, it is argued here and in the "Desultory Remarks," readily suspends the comparison between artifice and reality. Because the adult persists in exercising comparative judgment, the adult finds both "species of delusion" (rendering the fictive "real," as in reading a story; accepting a "representation" as the "transaction itself," as in watching a play) made difficult with increasing demands imposed upon the imagination. Where the imagination is expected to accept radical disproportion between reality and representation, as with a violent storm or the appearance of a ghost, the spectator may well experience a detachment from the stage events. By contrast, the purely human aspects of dramatic performance may be so effectively performed by the actor that the representation may appear "for a short while to be wholly merged or lost in" reality.

In his "Desultory Remarks," Coleridge complains that "a ⟨Forest-⟩Scene is not presented to the Audience as a Picture ⟨of a Forest⟩, but as a Forest." The advantage of a "picture" over a "scene" is that in a picture the means serve the end, so that the art is experienced as "an harmonious Whole, having an End of its own, to which the peculiar ends of its components (taken separately) are subordinated and made subservient." We see, that is, art "imitating reality under a semblance of reality." We are not expected to see a forest, but, rather, a forest in a picture or a picture of a forest. In contrast, Coleridge argues, stage scenery is not regarded as a separate artifact. Its purpose is to indicate place. If the playwright has sent his players into Arden wood, then the stage scenery of a forest is to be seen as a forest. The gloss note to Knight pursues this same problem of the visual presumption of stage scenery:

> The scenery and machinery with which our ⟨modern⟩ theatres are decorated may heighten the delusion for simple minds, but they produce a contrary effect in those that are cultivated; and so far are injurious to their pleasure. Stage suns and moons and stage thunder and lightning are ludicrous to the refined spectator; nor does he even look with much pleasure on the groves of Ardennes in As You Like it: yet still if Jacques and Orlando be exquisitely represented, the imperfect consciousness which the spectator may have of the

---

34. *LL* I, 128–29; for parallels see esp. I, 133–35.

> presence of these scenic helps as they are intended to be, may not materially impair, nay perhaps may in some instances assist the delusion which the skill of the actors is I think enabled to produce. The fact, I think is, that we *know* the thing to be a ⟨dec⟩ representation, but that we often *feel* it to be a reality. Though to this is to [be] referred but a small portion of the pleasure which fine acting gives. (gloss to Knight 333)

The statement, here, that stage props fool only "simple minds" is similar to Coleridge's claim in lecture 4 that delusion in the theater is "a gross fault" indulged in only by "low Minds" who cannot engage the higher activity of "heart or head" and thus "endeavor to call forth the momentary affections." The word "⟨dec⟩[eption]," promptly corrected into "representation," reveals a hesitation in defining the contrary aspects of the aesthetic experience. The spectator is presumed to experience an antagonism between what he knows (rational awareness of the play as play) and what he feels (sympathetic emotional response to the dramatic action). No vacillation, however, is presumed here; the feeling of reality, while not persistent (it "often" occurs), is not claimed to usurp or replace the opposing knowledge.

After having worked out an argument for a conscious awareness of artifice, it is surprising that the note, in the continuation on the next page, returns to the argument of short "fits" of delusion:

> I have said above that the machines the scenes the actors &c destroy that sort of delusion with which the mind is overcome in reading a good fictitious narrative, and this being taken away, on the opening of the piece by such obtrusive images, is it ever likely to be restored by the same agency. ⟨I do not see how it is possible⟩ To lose the man in the impersonation ⟨seems⟩ is indispensable to the highest pleasure given by acting. ⟨And if we forget the actor &c⟩ It seems much more easy to pass into a delusion that the things ⟨they are⟩ represented are actually performed, than that such forgetfulness of the Actors ⟨professions names⟩ persons & names &c should take place and have no other effect than to impress a belief that the whole is merely a mode of telling a true story. The senses have too strong impressions made on them for the imagination to have liberty to rest in that species of faith. An acted play approaches too nearly to the reality to affect us in that manner, and therefore I think no other supposition

> will account for the degree to which we are affected, saving that of short fits of belief that scene before us is a real affliction, or action. (gloss to Knight 334)

The conflict between the mechanics and the aesthetics of illusion is deemed so "obtrusive" that a special focus of attention is necessary in order to achieve the kind of imaginative engagement that one more readily experiences "in reading a good fictitious narrative." Rather than enhancing illusion, stage machinery distracts the spectator. Worse, even the actors inhibit our access to the characters enacted. We do not see Coriolanus, but Kemble playing Coriolanus. Schlegel, we may recall, made the illusion of spontaneous dialogue the foundation for dramatic illusion. The argument, here, that we must "forget the actor" and "lose the man in the impersonation," is very different from the earlier equation of "forgetfulness and deception," and does indeed involve that simultaneity of "observing and forgetting" posited in Schlegel's account of illusion (*KSB* I, 113–14). This studied act of forgetting "is indispensable to the highest pleasure given by acting." The advantage of such "forgetfulness" to the aesthetic experience is that it would "have no other effect than to impress a belief that the whole is merely a mode of telling a true story." Nevertheless, as the note concedes to Knight's text, the senses might well dictate the response. The spectator is more likely "to pass into a delusion" than to "forget the actor" in conscious attention to the representation: "The senses have too strong impressions made upon them for the imagination to have liberty to rest in that species of faith." The act of will necessary to poetic faith, then, is subdued by the impact on the senses and the emotions. The note concludes by resorting to the notion that what we experience in the theater consists in alternating "fits" of belief and disbelief.

To Knight's account of the aesthetic response to *Othello*, a subsequent note again attempts to restore the simultaneity of knowing and feeling. Since we know that in this play Othello is going to kill Desdemona, and that both are only acting, it is impossible—Knight declares—that we should feel either apprehension or pity. The note counters:

> We know it no doubt but do we in every part of the piece, *feel* it. If we do what is the meaning of those phrases with which we consummate our praise of a good actor; that he was *lost* in the character; he appeared and *became* the very man . . . ? (gloss to Knight 342)

There is a shrewd inversion of terms in this reply: Even if we "know" that we witness players in a play, the question remains whether we also "*feel*" only the acting and not what is enacted. Even if the actor may be said to have "*lost*" himself in the character, the transformation must also take place in the spectator's perception. Should we falter in feeling what we know, and begin to feel in terms of the enacted fiction, then on the level of feeling the response may be defined as "fits." But is what we "know" constant and continuous? Knight argues that "Fiction is known to be fiction, even while it interests us most" (p. 358). The note declares "this is false—it is not *felt* to be fiction when we are most affected" (gloss to Knight 358). Knowledge and feeling, it would appear, are again made to interchange in "fits," but the note also asserts that the affective response overrides Knight's restriction to "interest."

Because Knight substitutes associational response for aesthetic engagement, the mimetic and reflexive excitement of the drama becomes virtually irrelevant. Stage machinery, therefore, cannot possibly distract; to the contrary, it provides all that is "absolutely necessary to support the dignity of tragedy." An adequate display of "splendid dress, rich scenery, and pompous ceremony," Knight concludes, may "serve as a universal substitute, and compensate for the want of every other merit" (p. 366). Pointing a rhetorical question to the barren stage in Shakespeare's time, the marginal note challenges the claim that decoration and ritual satisfies the intellect (and, at the same time, mocks Knight with Duke Vincentio's ironic comment on Angelo):

> Was this the case in Shakespears time, to an intellectual mind such a substitute as he got who asked for *bread* and received a *stone*.
>
> (gloss to Knight 366)

> Duke: Lord Angelo is precise;
> Stands at a guard with envy; scarce confesses
> That his blood flows, or that his appetite
> Is more to bread than stone: hence shall we see,
> If power change purpose, what our seemers be.
>   (*Measure for Measure*, I.iii.50–54)

After wrestling with the problem of aesthetic illusion in the marginalia, as recorded by Wordsworth in the copy of Knight's *Inquiry* that Coleridge had used in his first lecture of 1808, Coleridge went on to draft his "Desultory Remarks." I have already called attention to some of the topics repeated from the marginalia: Coleridge's comments on the aesthetic response of the child and on the distinction between picture and scene. Just as the more extensive annotations to Knight, the "Desultory Remarks" are primarily concerned with stage illusion. These "Remarks" were apparently not appropriated in lecture 4, the last which Wordsworth attended before he left London, but their introductory and theoretical character makes it probable that they were used in one of the lectures immediately thereafter.

In lecture 2 (5 February 1808), Coleridge had already begun to trace the development of dialogue out of responsorial hymns. The responsorial became individuated to the point that a singer would assume dramatic character: "Gradually, it would suggest itself that the interest would increase with the Delusion, and the Delusion would be aided by ⟨Dresses or⟩ some mark of dress."[35] From this account of the rise of drama, Coleridge recommenced, after the long delay, with a discussion of Shakespeare as poet in lecture 3 (30 March 1808). In his notes to *Venus and Adonis*, Coleridge refers to "Humanizing Imagery" and "Activity of Thought" in the opening stanza, then goes on to discuss stanzas 6, 7, and 8 in terms of "the poetic Power of making every thing present to the Imagination / both the forms, & the passions that modify these forms." The attributes of aesthetic illusion, then, are once more present in this examination of how inanimate forms can be animated when "seen by the mind in moments of strong excitement." The purpose of "poetic Power" is to communicate "poetic feeling." Poetry is thus defined in terms of its effect: "the power of producing or reproducing" its own engendering excitement. The concluding notes to lecture 3 promise to develop the principle of "Energy, depth, and activity of Thought" in terms of Shakespeare's drama, "the subject of my next lecture."[36]

In lecture 4 (1 April 1808), Coleridge asserts that, in addition to "the requisites of Poet—namely, deep Feeling & exquisite sense of Beauty," Shakespeare possessed the special capability of the dramatic poet—"That these feelings were under the command of *his own Will*—that in his very first productions he projected his mind out of his own particular being, & felt and made others feel." Nor is it enough that he can make others feel, he

---

35. Ibid., 40, 45. The text for lecture 2 Foakes has taken from manuscript notes in the Berg Collection, New York Public Library, ff. 6–7 and Egerton 2800, ff. 15–18, British Museum.
36. *LL* I, 60, 66, 68; lecture 3, from Berg, ff. 8–9, and *CN* III, 3242, 3246, 3247.

must also have "the power of so carrying on the Eye of the Reader as to make him almost lose the consciousness of words—to make him *see* every thing." This is Coleridge's version of the principle of "judgment" or "intentionality" that he would later find in Schlegel's *Vorlesungen*. Acknowledging the "gross fault" of delusion, the kind of hysteria of "momentary affections" indulged by "low Minds," Coleridge launches his analysis of true aesthetic experience by distinguishing a *copy* from an *imitation*. A copy merely mirrors and reproduces, an imitation reveals the conscious artistry involved. Although "the consciousness of the Poet's Mind must be diffused over that of the Reader or Spectator," it must be *"always in keeping."* To the extent that this "consciousness" pervades of the work of art as an inherent and integral attribute, it successfully "prevents us from perceiving any strangeness."[37]

In the subsequent lectures of April 1808, Coleridge built his case against the notion of passive sympathy. Aesthetic experience requires voluntary engagement. Just as he had rejected the philosophical materialism of Locke or Newton for describing the mind as "always *passive*—a lazy *Looker-on*,"[38] he scorns the passive mode of aesthetic response, "a sort of beggarly Daydreaming, in which the mind furnishes for itself only laziness and a little mawkish sensibility, while the whole *Stuff* and Furniture of the Doze is supplied *ab extra* by a sort of spiritual Camera Obscura, which (*pro tempore*) fixes, reflects, & transmits the moving phantasms of one man's Delirium so as to people the barrenness of a hundred other trains under the same morbid Trance, or '*suspended Animation*', of Common Sense, and all definite Purpose."[39] In the same terms as set forth in the marginalia to Knight, Coleridge continues in the "Desultory Remarks" the discrimination of copy and imitation. In contrast to the landscape painting, the stage scenery involves an *"analogon* of deception, a sort of temporary Faith which we encourage by our own Will." No trace is left here of the earlier speculation that the

---

37. *LL* I, 72, 80, 82–84, 86–87; lecture 4, from *CN* III, 3286, 3288, 3289, 3290, and Egerton 2800, ff. 21–22. The distinction between copy and imitation, crucial to Coleridge's theory of illusion, is frequently repeated in his lectures and in the *Biographia Literaria;* the passage from Schelling, *Sämtliche Werke*, VII, 293, which has been identified as his "source," has less in common with his formulation than the versions he would have known from Aristotle or Petrarch.

38. Coleridge to Thomas Poole, 23 March 1801, *CL* II, 709.

39. *LL* I, 124. British Museum Ms Egerton 2800, ff. 89–90. Acknowledging that the opening section was reworked in *BL* I, 48–49, Foakes places these notes at the beginning of the supplementary records to the 1808 lectures. Foakes's arrangement, it should be observed, is further supported by the logical sequence; the statement on the active will in reading appropriately introduces the argument on stage illusion in the "Desultory Remarks."

spectator might experience alternating "fits" of belief and disbelief. Instead, Coleridge now affirms complete volitional control over stage illusion: "We know that it is at any time in the power of our will to see it as it is."[40] In this formulation, intellectual awareness neither disrupts nor destroys aesthetic illusion. As a matter of deliberate choice, the spectator holds in abeyance the mind's impulse to judge and compare. Thus volitional participation becomes a necessary condition in all aesthetic illusion.

During the lectures of 1811–12, Coleridge began to adapt Schlegel's argument on the imaginative participation in illusion to his own concern with the decisive act of will. Illusion depends not only on the volitional acceptance of the spectator; the artist must also have the necessary volitional control over his own creative genius. What this means to his commentary on Shakespeare is that Coleridge can demonstrate Shakespeare as the consummate master of stage illusion only by attending to the evidence of his judgment. In his *Vorlesungen,* Schlegel was preoccupied with Shakespeare's attention to illusion, but Coleridge found that he needed to correct Schlegel's explanation. Where Schlegel posited an awareness of Shakespeare's "intentionality" (*Absichtlichkeit*), Coleridge insisted on the decisive act of will in Shakespeare's judgment. The act of will in the artist's imitation becomes for Coleridge the key factor in the spectator's act of will in accepting the illusion.

The passage in which Schlegel defines illusion as "a waking dream, to which we voluntarily surrender ourselves" is the only context in which the action of the will is specifically linked to the experience of illusion, and even then it acts only to "surrender." In his other pronouncements on theatrical illusion, Schlegel simply tells us that it "need not adhere to probability," that it "depends on the appearance of truth to the senses," that even the impossible may be accepted "so long as the *grounds* for impossibility are left out of the circle of our comprehension or are cleverly veiled from our attention." For Schlegel, the imagination is the arena of aesthetic experience, while the will operates in the separate arena of practical experience. In "true illusion," Schlegel argues, "the spectators are so completely carried away by the impressions of the poetry and the acting, that they overlook the secondary matters, and forget the whole of the remaining objects around them."[41]

40. *LL* I, 128–36; the two drafts of "Desultory Remarks" are from British Museum, Add Ms 34225, ff. 54–55 and f. 56.
41. *KSB* VI, 22–23; see also I, 113: "Bei der theatralischen Täuschung kommt es gar nicht auf jene Wahrscheinlichkeit an, die man unter mehreren möglichen Erfolgen demjenigen zuschreibt,

Already in 1808, just as Coleridge later claimed, he had denounced the argument that Shakespeare "was a great Dramatist by a sort of Instinct," "a delightful Monster—wild indeed, without taste or Judgment," and had gone on to describe the judgment pervasively evident in Shakespeare's plays:

> That these feelings were under the command of *his own Will*—that in his very first productions he projected his mind out of his own particular being, & felt and made others feel, on subjects no way connected with himself, except by force of Contemplation—& that sublime faculty, by which a great mind becomes that which it meditates on.

Schlegel makes a very similar point in his lectures when he praises Shakespeare for his "capability of putting himself into every type, even the most unusual." Coleridge, however, also attempts to explain the meditative process. To understand why the "psychologic portraiture" he achieves in his characters is "characteristic" in relation to humanity, yet "characterless" in relation to the poet, one must recognize "the living Balance" he sustains between meditation and observation. Shakespeare develops a character not by simply copying what he observes, but by imitating the psychological veracities discovered through meditation.[42]

Coleridge returns to this argument in his second lecture (21 November

---

welcher die meisten Gründe für sich hat, und die sich in vielen Fällen sogar arithmetisch bestimmen läßt, sondern auf den sinnlichen Schein der Wahrheit. Was in jener Bedeutung unwahrscheinlich, völlig falsch, ja fast unmöglich ist, kann dennoch wahr zu sein scheinen, wenn nur der Grund der Unmöglichkeit außer dem Kreise unserer Erkenntnis liegt, oder uns geschickt verschleiert wird" (Theatrical illusion need not adhere to that probability, among many possible consequences, attributed to the one course of events most abundantly grounded and perhaps even arithmetically determined; rather, theatrical illusion depends on the appearance of truth to the senses. What may be unlikely, completely wrong, almost impossible in terms of probability, may nevertheless appear to be true so long as the grounds for impossibility are left out of the circle of our comprehension or are cleverly veiled from our attention); and *KSB* VI, 217: "Die wahre Täuschung besteht eben darin, wenn man durch die Eindrücke der Dicht- und Schauspielkunst so hingerissen wird, daß man die Nebensachen übersieht und die ganze übrige Gegenwart vergißt" (If we are to be truly deceived by a picture, that is, if we are to believe in the reality of the object which we see, we must not perceive its limits, but look at it through an opening; the frame at once declares it for a picture).

42. *LL* I, 80–81, and 126–28 (BM Add Ms 34225, ff. 47–48). This idea of Shakespeare's "characterless" creation of characters anticipates Keats's account of Shakespeare's "Negative Capability." In his *Vorlesungen*, Schlegel refers to Shakespeare's "Fähigkeit, sich so vollkommen in alle Arten zu sein, auch die fremdesten, zu versetzen" (VI, 129).

1811) of the 1811–12 series. Granting Shakespeare's many other "extraordinary powers," Coleridge claims that "his judgment was the most wonderful." Here, too, he elaborates his crucial distinction between the copy as a replica of the real, and the imitation as the imaginatively created ideal. Theatrical representations, in contradistinction to the real, became "fit & true" only because they were perceived by the imagination as ideal. The effects of reality are tied to the moment: "If mere pain for the moment were wanted, could we not go to our hospitals: if we required mere pleasure could we not be present at our public fêtes." As Du Bos and Bodmer had argued a century earlier, Coleridge attributes the aesthetic experience to an awareness of difference: "This was not what was required from dramatic exhibition; we wanted a continual representation of it before our eyes." Without calling for adherence to the unities, as his eighteenth-century predecessors had done, Coleridge repeats their claim that this difference involves our sense of space and time. In Coleridge's reformulation, drama provides that experience of illusion that gives us pleasure in the power of our own imagination: "The real pleasure derived from knowing that the scene represented was unreal and merely an imitation."[43]

Lecture 3 (25 November 1811) goes on to clarify why only an imitation, not a copy, can produce "the great total effect." A copy reflects only the accidents of the moment. An imitation reveals the informing presence of the mind. The word *imitation*, Coleridge explains, "means always a combination of a certain degree of dissimilitude with a certain degree of similitude." It is our recognition of the difference that delights us. Even if the poet or artist has selected the "purest parts" of his material, they must still be blended with the mind. Poetry results from "blending the nobler mind with the meaner object." It is "not the mere copy of things, but the contemplation of mind upon things." Thus the effect of art can never be, and should never be, a confusion with reality. Our willing acceptance of the "truth" of art never lapses into a belief that it is real: "The height of delusion, the utmost point to which it can arrive is that we do not think about its being real or false, but are affected only by the vividness of impression, independent of the thought of reality." Although Coleridge here refers to "delusion" (if Tomalin has accurately recorded the word), he clearly means a conscious awareness of the difference. Indeed, he amplifies this crucial aspect of

---

43. *LL* I, 210–11. Du Bos, *Réflexions critiques sur la poésie, la peinture et la musique;* Bodmer, *Brief-Wechsel von der Natur des poetischen Geschmackes.*

imitation by defining various degrees of illusion that result from the exposition of difference. Domestic tragedy and opera provide the two extremes of the scale. In domestic tragedy, the difference is minimal and the effects may be "too real to be compatible with pleasure." In opera, the sense of reality is minimal, but the use of music and dance in "explaining some tale" can "deeply affect and delight an audience." On this scale of reality and difference, Shakespeare achieves true balance; he "seems to have taken the due medium, & to gratify our senses from the imitation of reality."[44]

In achieving dramatic illusion, Shakespeare depended on the imagination of the spectator unsupported by the decorations of stage. Although this fact is generally ignored or forgotten by Schlegel,[45] Coleridge found it important to remind his auditors that in Shakespeare's day, "the Theatre itself had no artificial, extraneous inducements—few scenes, little music, & all that was to excite the senses in a high degree was wanting." To document Shakespeare's own recognition that illusion was addressed to imagination rather than sensation, Coleridge was fond of quoting the Prologue to *Henry V*:

> But pardon, gentles all,
> The flat unraised spirit that hath dar'd
> On this unworthy scaffold to bring forth
> So great an object: can this cockpit hold
> The vasty fields of France? or may we cram
> Within this wooden O the very casques
> That did affright the air at Agincourt?
> O, pardon! since a crooked figure may
> Attest in little place a million;
> And let us, ciphers to this great acompt,
> On your imaginary forces work.[46]

The disadvantages in present-day theater Coleridge attributes to dependence on stage machinery and the "endeavour to make everything appear reality." Although he would have responded to the new techniques of stag-

---

44. *LL* I, 224–27.
45. *KSB* VI, 28–31, 130–36; see above, chapter 3, 37.
46. *LL* I, 228; after introducing the quotation from the Prologue to *Henry V* in this lecture (24 November 1811), he used it in subsequent lectures in the same context of discussing Shakespeare's barren stage and his appeal to imagination rather than sensation: *LL* I, 519 (28 October 1813); *LL* II, 267 (17 December 1818).

ing, we should nevertheless be grateful, Coleridge asserts, that Shakespeare had no "conception of that strong excitement of the senses" and that he therefore addressed his plays so completely to the imagination.

In lectures 6 (5 December) and 9 (16 December 1811), he further develops the ramifications of copy vs. imitation: A copy is the result of strict observation; an imitation requires the interest of meditation; the modern stage of mechanical contrivance attempts to copy, making everything appear reality; the Shakespearean stage relied on imitation, "and the Actor as well as the author were obliged to appeal to the imagination & not to the senses."[47] In lecture 9, of course, passages from Schlegel suddenly abound: mechanical and organic form, the sculpturesque Greek drama and the picturesque Shakespearean drama. Even previously formulated ideas take on fresh nuance under the stimulation of Schlegel's analogical thinking. In appropriating Schlegel's idea of the "painterly" (*malerisch*), for example, Coleridge describes an illusion that is no longer simply the "difference" projected by the mind, but a momentary realization of what even art cannot achieve. Shakespeare's characters, however, are not confined by the painterly moment: "They have the union of reason perceiving, & the judgment recording actual facts and the imagination diffusing over all a magic glory."[48] Too, his earlier assertion in 1808, of illusion as "half-faith" gains new and richer dimension.

Schlegel, it should be recalled, does not speak of illusion as "faith" or "belief"—these are Coleridge's terms. From Schlegel's account of *The Tempest*, Coleridge makes use of the description of Caliban and Ariel.[49] Too, Schlegel's appreciation of Prospero's magic as kindred to the playwright's illusion making has quite apparently impressed Coleridge, for he finds the "Power of Poetry" revealed in Prospero's "supernatural agency." The discussion of *The Tempest* is introduced by an account of two sorts of dramatic illusion (Collier's notes give the word as "delusion"): "those where the real is disguised in the ideal & those where the ideal is hidden from us in the real." *The Tempest* exemplifies the former. In giving predominance to the ideal, Shakespeare can use "magic" as a metaphor for the imagination. From Prospero's tale to Miranda of their banishment from Milan, "Me and thy crying self" (I.ii.132), Coleridge points to "crying" as a word capable of

---

47. Ibid., I, 289, 349–50.
48. Ibid., 349.
49. *KSB* VI, 161.

producing such "energy in the mind as compels the imagination to produce the picture." Although narrative rather than dramatic, Prospero's recollection not only provides necessary background for the events about to unfold, it also prepares the spectator "to exert his imagination." Shakespeare, in other words, has made the audience wish for a "supernatural agency" to aid the lovely Miranda, even before Prospero calls upon his magic to grant her sleep. This state of mind, says Coleridge, is "Poetic Faith," which he defines with a phrase borrowed from *Henry IV,* Second Part (IV.v.93): "The wish was father to the thought."[50]

With the concept of "Poetic Faith," Coleridge has brought his theory of illusion a very important step forward. The mind is involved in anticipating an imaginary event. Because the usual conditions of probability or cause-and-effect have nothing to do with this act of faith, "our common notions of philosophy give way." The engagement of illusion now rests upon an intuitive confidence in the logic of the imagination. Once established, it involves us in a more comprehensive aesthetic experience than is afforded by that illusion which builds only upon historical facts. In the marginalia to Knight, we have already seen the earlier claim that "in reading Hamlet or Lear, though we are frequently sensible that the story is fictitious, yet in other moments we do not less doubt of the things having taken place than when we read in History about Pompey or Julius Caesar."[51] Coleridge is now prepared to define a "stronger" conviction. In poetic faith, he identifies a "feeling . . . much stronger than historic faith in as much as by the former the mind was prepared to exercise it."[52] This is the argument that Coleridge repeats in the *Biographia Literaria,* not only in the *locus classicus* on "the willing suspension of disbelief" (chap. 14), but also in the subsequent affirmation of "A faith, which transcends even historic belief" (chap. 22).[53]

"Poetic Faith" is similar to religious faith. In order to explain this act of faith more fully, Coleridge turns briefly from *The Tempest* to the Bible and *Paradise Lost* (the example he again uses in *Biographia Literaria,* chap. 22). *Genesis* gives but a brief version of the story Milton amplified in *Paradise Lost,* but we do not respond "that what was not scripture appeared not to be true," or that "it seemed like mingling lies with the most sacred truths." We

---

50. *LL* I, 357, 362.
51. Wordsworth and Coleridge, Marginalia in Knight, *Analytical Inquiry into the Principles of Taste,* 331.
52. *LL* I, 362–63.
53. *BL* II, 6, 134.

discover, instead, such a confluence and harmony between the scriptural text and the poetic amplification, that from our faith in the former we not only accept but we begin to anticipate the latter: "The Poet has substituted the faith of the mind to regard as true what would otherwise have appeared absurdity."[54] As an act of faith, we willingly accept authorial judgment in lieu of personal judgment.

The thinking that prompted him to convert "half-faith" into a fully active "Poetic Faith" had been tentatively explored in his essay "On Certainty" (August–September 1809). Certainty cannot be attained through "the logical completeness of my Intuitions, Notions, Judgments, and Elementary Positions in themselves and in relation to my particular conviction." An act of faith is required. In presuming "the universal and necessary truth of the principles of Logic," the mind acts according to a "Confidence" rather than according to its achieved state of knowledge. Even the skeptic must believe in some absolute criterion to be reached through negative reduction. Coleridge may have the Cartesian "cogito" in mind. Without some *pou sto*, some "fixed Scale," understanding and comparison is impossible. Thus the intellectual faculties are driven in an "Instinctive Pursuit of a sufficient ground." Although the ground is unattained, "the sense of Power supplies the conviction, that there *is* a certain ground." This faith is evident in our response to art.

> This is so true, that even in the Imitative Arts, that are supposed to have their being in fiction, a well-disciplined mind is offended by actual Delusion. To exclaim, that we had actually mistaken the picture for reality, is an hyperbole of a clumsy flatterer—and to have been gratified by an actual Cheat, the pleasure of a bad and vulgar Taste . . . the meanest Taste finds its pleasure in a painted marble Apple or Peach exhausted after it has been once or twice seen and handled—while the Fruit-piece of some eminent Dutch painter which had never appeared to him other than a picture will give him increased pleasure in proportion as he can be induced to look at and think of it.[55]

In contrast to delusion, which is self-contained as counterfeit, illusion presumes a relation of object to subject—the very certainty missing from our

---

54. *LL* I, 363.
55. *CN* III, §3592 (August–September 1809).

experience. The Bible, with its "strong and very frequent eulogies on Truth,"[56] intends to teach the intuitive act of beholding an all-pervading intimacy between object and subject. Philosophers, too, (Coleridge cites Plato, Aristotle, Epicurus, Malebranche, and Berkeley) are compelled by the same instinct to derive from mere "representations & notions of Things" a universal and necessary ground. The compelling instinct is not prompted by "the desire of attaching *Outness*, an *externality* to our representations"; rather, the desire to externalize our representations is prompted by the instinct ("this very attachment of Outness originates in this Instinct"). Certainty is an act of faith in which we seem "to possess *a ground* to know a fixed Cause generating a certain reason." As an example, Coleridge refers to the intimate link between idea and thing, between "Clouds mountain-shaped & Mountains," which Wordsworth establishes in his sonnet.[57]

Shakespeare, Coleridge goes on to declare in his lecture on *The Tempest*, conjures poetic faith by engaging his audience in the moment of perception. We do not merely see, we anticipate the very act of beholding. When Ariel leads Ferdinand into their presence, Prospero arouses Miranda from her reverie:

> The fringed curtains of thine eye advance
> And say, what seest yond?
> (I.ii.408–9)

These lines are not a flowery amplification of "Look what is coming." The censure, in *The Art of Sinking in Poetry* (1727), of Prospero's magical language as "a piece of the grossest bombast" has misconceived the conjuror's art. Prospero, whose art is much like the playwright's, has set the stage "to produce a strong impression on Miranda at the first view of Ferdinand," and he bids the curtains to rise.[58]

The concept of illusion does not seem to have been further developed in Coleridge's six "Lectures on the Drama" (19 May–5 June 1812). He does, however, relate dramatic illusion to the visual referentiality of language. "Bookish & pedantic words" are inappropriate to drama because they fail to conjure visual images. Thus it is that a mediocre playwright may succeed on

---

56. *CN* III, §3592n. Coleridge intended to quote passages from St. Paul.
57. *CN* III, §3592n. Kathleen Coburn suggests Wordsworth's "With how sad steps, O Moon, thou climb'st the sky . . . Running among the clouds."
58. *LL* I, 366–67.

the stage simply because he manages to address the audience with familiar words and risks nothing "unusual above or absurd below mediocrity." Coleridge distinguishes between a language of nature and a language of symbols. The former refers to objects, the latter appropriates the former but shifts the reference to feelings or ideas. The latter is far richer, but must always "return to the dominant Idea" of the former. Such words "are judged of by *authority*, not by actual experience." The language of symbols derives its power of visual evocation from the language of nature, but acquires a wide ranging freedom. The visual power which words possess through virtual identity with the thing represented is liberated in symbols that become "self-manifestations" of that visual power: they "have infinite advantages from their ⟨very nothingn⟩ess per se; but the Language of Nature is a subordinate Logos, that was in the beginning, and was with the Thing, ⟨it⟩ represented, & was the Thing represented."[59] Coleridge relates this distinction to Shakespeare. Repeating his formulation of Shakespeare's judgment as balance between observation and meditation, he now shows us why a mere language of things would restrict the playwright to observation and entrap his play "as a Counterfeit" within the confines of the copy.

As Foakes acknowledges in his account of the twelve "Lectures on Belles Lettres" (3 November 1812–26 January 1813), Coleridge was increasingly preoccupied during this period with the preparations for the production of *Remorse* at Drury Lane—which opened 23 January, just before the final lecture. Foakes surmises that Coleridge, especially in lectures 4 through 7, relied heavily on Schlegel's *Vorlesungen*. Coleridge himself confesses: "I never once thought of the Lecture, till I had entered the Lecture Box." Nevertheless, the very excitement of the production kept his spirits high and apparently the enthusiasm was evident in his delivery, for Henry Crabb Robinson confirms that he received "great applause" at the concluding lecture.[60] The success of *Remorse* at Drury Lane may owe much to Coleridge's attention to illusion as a major thematic interest while revising *Osorio*. In chapter 7, I will return to *Remorse* to show how the play puts into practice Coleridge's theory of illusion.

For the Shakespeare lectures delivered the following year in Bristol (28 October–23 November 1813), Coleridge wrote to Mrs. Morgan specifically requesting his edition of Schlegel as well as his notebooks. These lectures

59. Ibid., 428–29.
60. Ibid., 482–83, 497.

follow rather closely the arguments which he had already developed for his previous series. The ideas of Schlegel may be more prevalent, but they are also more fully integrated. In the first lecture, he again quotes Shakespeare's appeal to the imagination from the Prologue to *Henry V* and links the idea of illusion to Shakespeare's "exquisite judgment."[61] In the second lecture (2 November 1813), he borrows, apparently for the first time, Schlegel's critique of "disbelief." Those who achieve "true illusion," Schlegel asserts, are so attentive to "the poetry and the acting, that they overlook the secondary matters, and forget the whole of the remaining objects around them." Schlegel goes on to denounce fault-finding critics who are preoccupied with details that might conflict with the reality. Such critics suffer from "prosaic disbelief," a symptom of deficient imagination and an incapacity for illusion.[62] A paradox observed in criticism from Diderot through Stendhal and Hugo, the argument on the impossibility "perfect illusion" had already been raised in Coleridge's marginalia to Knight.[63] Here Coleridge adapts from Schlegel's version:

> Das spottische auflauern ob nicht ein umstand der wirklichkeit widerspricht—which is yet never obtainable—and if attainable would disappoint the very purposes and ends of the Drama, demonstrates not good sense, but an utter want of all Imagination, a deadness to that necessary pleasure the being innocently—shall I say deluded? No! but drawn away from ourselves into the music of noblest thoughts in harmonising sounds.[64]

When he comes to the word *getäuscht* in Schlegel's text, Coleridge asks "shall I say deluded?" He decides, of course, that illusion is the preferable word. He then turns to *Macbeth* and examines the problem of illusion and

---

61. Ibid., 519–20.
62. *KSB* V, 217.
63. Wordsworth and Coleridge, Marginalia in Knight, *Analytical Inquiry into the Principles of Taste*, 319.
64. *LL* I, 528–29. Coleridge's source, not identified by Raysor or Foakes, is the following passage from Schlegel: "Die wahre Täuschung besteht eben darin, wenn man durch die Eindrücke der Dicht-und Schauspielkunst so hingerissen wird, daß man die Nebensachen übersieht und die ganze übrige Gegenwart vergißt. Das spöttische Auflauern hingegen, ob nicht irgendein Umstand der scheinbaren Wirklichkeit widerspricht, die, strenge genommen, doch niemals vollkommen zu erreichen steht, beweist die Ohnmacht des Einbildungskraft und die Unfähigkeit getäuscht zu werden" (*KSB* VI, 217).

delusion as an aspect of dramatic characterization. As we saw in the previous chapter, Schlegel constantly attends to the illusion of characters. Fully independent of Schlegel's *Vorlesungen*, Coleridge analyzes how a character creates, or falls prey to, illusion in terms of psychological process.

Coleridge observes that Macbeth indulges the "sophistry of self-delusion" only "previous to the dreadful Act." Afterward, he began to project "the terrors of Remorse into Fear from external dangers—like delirious Men, that run away from the Phantoms of their own Brains." In lecture 3 (4 November 1813), he continues to emphasize the problems of self-wrought illusions and delusions in discussing the character of Hamlet. He begins by reasserting his conception of Shakespeare's judgment as observation, meditation, and self-projection. The character of Hamlet expresses this very process—gone awry:

> Shakespear's mode of conceiving characters out of his own intellectual & moral faculties, by conceiving any one intellectual or moral faculty in morbid excess and then placing himself thus mutilated and diseased under certain circumstances. . . . In Hamlet I conceive him to have wished to exemplify the moral necessity of a due Balance between our attention to outward objects, and our meditation on our inward Thoughts—a due Balance between the real and the imaginary World—In Hamlet this Balance does not exist—his Thoughts Images & Fancy far more vivid than his Perceptions, and his very Perceptions instantly passing thro' the medium of his contemplations, and acquiring as they pass, a form and color not naturally their own. Hence great enormous intellectual activity, and a consequent proportionate aversion to real action.

Hamlet exhibits "judgment" perverted by a loss of "Balance" and a consequent introspective "Habit of brooding over the world within." Hamlet confounds perception with "the half embodyings of Thought." His pretense to madness becomes entangled in his own "shadowy approach to the Images and Movements within." The illusion he feigns for others leaves him teetering dangerously close to delusion. "Hamlet's Wildness is but *half-false*—O that subtle trick to pretend to be *acting* only when we are very near to *being* what we act." Coleridge closes this lecture by returning from illusions of self to stage illusion. He again praises "scanty Scenery" in requiring playwright and audience to draw upon "the Strength of inward Illusion," a strength which Coleridge advocates as a moral advantage for the "Actor on the Stage of real Life."[65]

Whether the two lecture series of 1814, on Milton and Cervantes and on the French Revolution, provided occasion for further investigation of dramatic illusion cannot be determined, for no notes survive and contemporary reports are scanty. The combination of biblical and fictive matter in *Paradise Lost* might well have prompted him to expand upon "poetic faith." In the preceding lectures, Coleridge had elaborated the ideas originally formulated in 1808 and had begun to discuss the interrelationships with language and imagination. The concern with "poetic faith," evident in Coleridge's note "On Certainty" in 1809, and in his lecture on *The Tempest* in 1812, is again stressed in his letter to Daniel Stuart (13 May 1816). Here he attempts once more to provide a comprehensive definition of dramatic illusion. In setting forth the "will" as instrument and "faith" as agent, Coleridge has little in common with Schlegel, whose use of these terms are negative or passive rather than positive and active. Schlegel, we should remember, argues that we engage illusion by *suspending* the will, and he refers not to a dynamic "poetic faith" but only a "prosaic lack of faith" ("prosaische Unglaube") that disrupts the engagement.[66] In his letter to Stuart, Coleridge explains how the mind could voluntarily engage illusion:

> The truth is, that Images and Thoughts possess a power in and of themselves, independent of that act of Judgement or Understanding by which we affirm or deny the existence of a reality correspondent to them. Such is the ordinary state of the mind in Dreams. It is not strictly accurate to say, that we believe our dreams to be actual while we are dreaming. We neither believe or disbelieve it—with the will the comparing power is suspended, and without the comparing power any act of Judgement, whether affirmation or denial, is impossible. The Forms and Thoughts act merely by their own inherent power: and the strong feelings at times apparently connected with

---

65. Ibid., 539–43.
66. Ibid., lvii. Although Foakes seems unaware of Schlegel's position on volitional "Teilnahme" and the negative effects of "poetische Unglaube," he is correct in stating that, in the 1808 notes, "Coleridge's formulation of a 'temporary Half-faith', with his sense of his power to abstract himself at any moment, marks a considerable advance in subtlety and understanding of any of the earlier discussions, and for that matter on Schlegel's later account. It looks forward to the masterly and satisfying summation of the process in *Biographia Literaria* as 'that willing suspension of disbelief for the moment, which constitutes poetic faith.' "

them are in point of fact bodily sensations, which are the causes or occasions of the Images, not (as when we are awake) the effects of them. Add to this a voluntary Lending of the Will to this suspension of one of its own operations (i.e. that of comparison & consequent decision concerning the reality of any sensuous Impression) and you have the true Theory of Stage Illusion.[67]

This passage, which clearly follows from the position already assumed in 1808, provides an apt corrective to the misunderstandings or misrepresentations of Coleridge's argument on the purpose and the action of the will in aesthetic illusion.[68] "Images and Thoughts" are granted a primacy in the mind. In practical experience it is the task of judgment to link our ideas and impressions to an external reality. Where we succeed, we create understanding. In dreams that process is inactive. Aesthetic experience has something in common with both dream experience and practical experience. As in dream experience, "Images and Thoughts" are allowed to sustain mental primacy and "act merely by their own inherent power." As in practical experience, the will is alert and ready to compare and judge. Aesthetic experience involves the conscious appreciation of art as art. "Suspending disbelief" does not mean that we suspend the will; quite to the contrary, it means that the will consciously acts in *not* engaging its usual tasks of comparing and judging. Once the mind chooses not to disbelieve, it prepares the way to engage, even to anticipate, ideas and impressions in terms of a deliberate act of faith.

Before looking into the *Biographia*, let us summarize the developments in his theory of dramatic illusion. The major elements are all in the first deliberations of 1808. In reaction to Richard Payne Knight's associationist account of illusion as passive response, Coleridge argued that the aesthetic experience depended upon a willing and active awareness of illusion as illusion. Knight described the mind reacting in sympathy with increasing emotional stimulation until the reason surrenders to the force of the passions. Coleridge argues that dramatic illusion is not a passive response, nor even a voluntary surrender to illusion. It involves, rather, a deliberate choice *not* to compare and contrast, but to accept the experience in the

---

67. *CL* IV, 641–42.
68. Brinker, "Aesthetic Illusion"; Walton, "Appreciating Fiction: Suspending Disbelief or Pretending Belief?"

artist's own terms; *not* to judge, but to witness the judgment of the artist. Judgment is a balance of observation and meditation. It appeals primarily to the imagination, rather than merely to the senses. The spectator engages the work as "waking dream" or "half-dream." Through a "half-faith" or "temporary Faith which we encourage by our Will," we arrive at "a negative Belief" in illusion. As Thomas McFarland has shown, Coleridge's effort to revise Hume's analysis of belief into an argument of faith led to his decisive formulation of "poetic faith" as "the willing suspension of disbelief."[69]

What is desired, as Coleridge already recognized in 1808, is not a "Perfect illusion" but a willing and alert pleasure in the illusion of art as imitation rather than copy. As these elements are reiterated in subsequent lecture series, Coleridge calls attention to varying degrees of aesthetic engagement, which may be defined on a scale from the realistic to the fantastic. Coleridge sees this polarity in parallel processes: observation and meditation, copy and imitation, the senses and the imagination. In 1812, "half-faith" or "temporary Faith" is transformed into the anticipatory and abiding "Poetic Faith." He also attends to the visual power that is transferred from the language of things to the language of symbols.

Although vaguely hinted in his earlier discussions, in the *Biographia Literaria* (1817) Coleridge explicitly extends his definition from stage illusion to aesthetic illusion *per se*. The scale described by contrasting the realism of domestic tragedy with the rich imaginary context of opera (lecture 3 in the 1811–12 series) may be recognized as similar to the contrast he draws between Wordsworth's poetry of "ordinary life" and his own poetry of the supernatural. It is Coleridge's poetry that departs from observation and the language of nature in order to delve more deeply into meditation and the language of symbol:

> The incidents and agents were to be, in part at least, supernatural; and the excellence aimed at was to consist in the interesting of the affections by the dramatic truth of such emotions, as would naturally accompany such situations, supposing them real. And real in *this* sense they have been to every human being who, from whatever source of delusion, has at any time believed himself under supernatural agency. . . . it was agreed, that my endeavours should be directed

---

69. McFarland, *Shapes of Culture*, 114–45; see also McFarland, *Originality and Imagination*, 52.

to persons and characters supernatural, or at least romantic; yet so as to transfer from our inward nature a human interest and a semblance of truth sufficient to procure for these shadows of the imagination that willing suspension of disbelief for the moment, which constitutes poetic faith.[70]

Here the word "delusion" does indeed refer to that aberration of mind in which hallucination is seen as reality. The cause may be hallucination, but the effect upon mind and body is real; the physical reaction may be observed, then, as external symptom of the mental duress. If the poet succeeds in conveying the psychological process, the audience will respond to the "dramatic truth." Not confined to the drama, such "dramatic truth" may also be recreated in any medium that permits the exposition of psychological action and reaction. Meditation is the crucial ground, for the poet must communicate "inward nature." But he must also provide that fidelity to nature gained only through observation.

The idea of "poetic faith," as Coleridge explained it in lecture 9 of the 1811–12 series, involves an intuitive confidence in the logic of the imagination. In his discussion of Wordsworth's poetry (chap. 22), Coleridge seems to be substituting this faith in the logical coherence of illusion for the classical precepts of *representative* and *probable*. While he does not endorse Samuel Johnson's caveat against numbering "the streaks of the tulip," he does acknowledge the validity of the general and the representative in art. In poetry, the characters, "amid the strongest individualization, must still remain representative." The validity of the "representative," as set forth in Horace's *Ars poetica*, is derived from the "nature both of poetry and of the human mind." If the poet radically departs from the general and representative, his fictive circumstances may seem all the more improbable. It is the probability of the general that solicits "poetic faith." Deviations into the particular not only perplex "the reader's feelings," they also "divide and disquiet his faith." As well as Horace's "decorum," we can recognize in this discussion Aristotle's recommendation that a probable impossibility is better than an improbable possibility. But in the context of Coleridge's argument on faith in illusion, the representative and the probable are made to serve the logic of the imagination. Already in 1808, we were informed that Johnson's insistence on the probable is irrelevant ("Desultory Remarks"), that

---

70. *BL* II, 6.

what is required, if a tale is to subdue "the mind to a passing belief," is that "it be consistent with itself" (gloss to Knight 331–32).

As in lecture 9 of the 1811–12 series, Coleridge refers to the success of Milton's *Paradise Lost* in fostering poetic faith, which he contrasts with the failure of Klopstock's *Messiah* or Cumberland's *Calvary: or the Death of Christ*:

> That *illusion*, contradistinguished from *delusion*, that *negative* faith, which simply permits the images presented to work by their own force, without either denial or affirmation of their real existence by the judgment, is rendered impossible by their immediate neighbourhood to words and facts of known and absolute truth. A faith, which transcends even historic belief, must absolutely *put out* this mere poetic Analogon of faith, as the summer sun is said to extinguish our household fires, when it shines full upon them. What would otherwise have been yielded to as a pleasing fiction, is repelled as a revolting falsehood. The effect produced in this latter case by the solemn belief of the reader, is in a less degree brought about in the instances to which I have been objecting [in Wordsworth's poetry], by the baffled attempts of the author to *make* him believe.[71]

What Coleridge has been objecting to in Wordsworth is a failure to subsume the particular observation within his poetic narrative. In describing the plan for the *Lyrical Ballads* in chapter 14, he first defined *novelty* and *familiarity* as the "two cardinal points of poetry" and then referred to the natural and the supernatural as the two sorts of poems to be contributed by Wordsworth and himself respectively. The "two cardinal points" were to be neglected by neither poet: Wordsworth was to enhance the ordinary with the "meditative and feeling mind," so as "to give the charm of novelty to things of every day, and to excite a feeling analogous to the supernatural"; Coleridge was to lend to the supernatural "a semblance of truth" that would make the strange seem familiar. In chapter 22, he lists among the defects of Wordsworth's poetry a failure to blend observation and meditation. As a result, unwanted particularization disrupts the illusion of verisimilitude; or, to use the terms of the lectures, the copy intrudes upon the imitation.

Again in chapter 23, Coleridge refers to the balance of opposites in art. It

---

71. Ibid., 133–34.

should here become apparent that the oppositions that poetic judgment is to resolve in creating illusion are essentially the same as those which are set forth at the end of chapter 14 in his definition of poetry as "the balance and reconciliation of opposite or discordant qualities." He has referred to qualities in Tirso de Molino's Don Juan and Milton's Satan that render the abstraction of wickedness or evil palpable and intelligible to the imagination. Of primary importance is the balance of the real and the ideal.

> The poet asks only of a reader, what as a poet he is privileged to ask: viz. that sort of negative faith in the existence of such a being, which we willingly give to productions *professedly ideal*. . . . The ideal consists in the happy balance of the generic with the individual. The former makes the character representative and symbolical, therefore instructive; because, *mutatis mutandis*, it is applicable to whole classes of men. The latter gives it its *living* interest; for nothing *lives* or is *real*, but as definite and individual.

The failure to sustain proper balance produces the same disruptive incongruity which Coleridge objected to in Wordsworth's poetry: the copy intrudes upon the imitation.

> To understand this completely, the reader need only recollect the specific state of his feelings, when in looking at a picture of the historic (more properly of the poetic or heroic) class, he objects to a particular figure as being too much of a *portrait;* and this interruption of his complacency he feels without the least reference to, or the least acquaintance with, any person in real life.[72]

Aesthetic illusion as the "negative faith" that we "willingly give" to the poet, as the "willing suspension of disbelief . . . which constitutes poetic faith," is not a naive act. Suspending personal judgment in aesthetic experience requires that we sustain confidence in authorial judgment. No poet can succeed without judgment, and his most carefully wrought creation will fail if the reader or spectator discerns a lapse of balance. The successfully sustained illusion is the proof of the artist's judgment.

Following the publication of the *Biographia Literaria*, Coleridge delivered

---

72. Ibid., 214–15.

several series of lectures: fourteen lectures on the principles of judgement (1818), six lectures on Shakespeare (1818–19) and, immediately following, seven lectures on Shakespeare, Milton, Dante, Spenser, Ariosto, and Cervantes (1819), which were given on alternate evenings along with the series of fourteen philosophical lectures (1818–19). He was not yet content with the theory of illusion which he had been evolving for ten years. When he reworks his notes on the dialectics of judgment, there is a major innovation to be observed. The new element is play: the imagination not in free play, but in the structured play of game. If we are to entertain improbability, Coleridge decides, then "there must be Rules respecting it."

Coleridge's rules for representing in art the scenes and creatures of the imagination have been described by Thomas McFarland in terms of the "the *meontic* mode." In the *meontic* mode, as opposed to the *mimetic*, "the imitation is not of what is there, but of what is not there." In Coleridge's account of the artistic process, McFarland observes, the representation of nature is always rendered in terms of the mind's own shapings. "Examine nature accurately," Coleridge stated, "but write from recollection." Not letting this formulation lapse into the Wordsworthian dictum, he immediately added his *meontic* emphasis, "and trust more to your imagination than to your memory."[73]

Copy and imitation, real and ideal, observation and mediation remain, as before, the essential attributes of that art which elicits our voluntary engagement of illusion. Coleridge rehearses these points, for example, in lecture 4 of 1818. When we exclaim, " 'How natural Shakespeare is'," we surely cannot mean he copies nature, for "a *mere* copy never delights us." In fact, we cannot "read but a few detached lines," without recognizing the author. His characters become "true to nature" because they are mediated through his own experience. The term "nature," we should notice, appears in a context where we might have expected "imitation." Coleridge has not dropped "copy and imitation" from the set of oppositions; rather, he is rethinking his argument on the representative and the probable. In 1811, Coleridge had opposed the notion of Shakespeare's *natural* genius as implying some kind of wild "Monster." As will become apparent in the final lecture series of 1818–19, he seeks to *naturalize* genius as the revelation of judgment. Here, however, he simply tells his audience that they must enter a

---

73. McFarland, *Romanticism and the Forms of Ruin. Wordsworth, Coleridge, and Modalities of Fragmentation*, 384–418. Coleridge, *Table Talk*, 109 [22 September 1830], quoted in McFarland, 387.

kind of contract with the author. To appreciate the "exquisite judgement" of Shakespeare, they must "conceive a stage without scenery," and they must be prepared to attend to the playwright who promises illusion to those who "will listen to me with your minds—& not with your eyes to scene & assist me with your imagination."[74]

The argument deliberated in the annotations to Knight, developed and polished in the lectures of 1808 and subsequent lecture series, is brought forth for the last time in lecture 1 of 1818–19. A proper understanding of the words "probable" and "natural," he declares, is "the indispensable Condition not only of just and genial criticism, but of all consistency in our opinions." These words, in their "ordinary meaning," cannot be applied to the drama. Before he begins to unfurl the ambiguities in these words to locate the meanings he wants, he presents his familiar distinction of *copy* and *imitation*. But something new has been added. *Imitation* is now said to be "contra-distinguished" from *copy* because of "a certain quantum of Difference." Rhetorical imitation as *idem in alio* would seem to be echoed here, but Coleridge radically shifts the significance of the classical formula. "Difference" becomes the ground into which he transplants "natural" and "probable."[75]

Because we have willingly set aside comparison and contrast, "our sense of Probability" no longer involves reference to the causal conditions of the external world. By the criteria of comparison and contrast, we may be confronted with any number of incongruities and improbabilities that do not "disturb or disentrance us from all illusion." Because they are accepted as a part of the fictive "groundwork of the story," or because they are internally consistent with other elements of the drama, "they do not contravene or interrupt the Illusion"; they are improbable only when related to conditions outside the play. The choice to be deceived requires an attentive commitment to the mental state "in which the Images have a negative reality." We are brought to this state gradually through the arousal of interest and excitement afforded "by the Art of the Poet and the Actors." Then, "with the consent and positive Aidance of our own Will," we take the essential step: "We *chuse* to be deceived." The one abiding rule in this game of illusion is that the improbable must *appear* probable.

74. *LL* II, 115, 120, 122.
75. Coleridge's "rule" for transforming the improbable into the probable may have been adapted from Schlegel, *KSB* I, 113 (quoted in note 41 above). See also the discussion of "Wahrscheinlichkeit" and "Natürlichkeit" in chapter 3.

Strict causal probability is, then, a misleading doctrine, for it may lead the playwright to represent actions that fail to avoid internal improbability. The poor playwright thus prevents us from "producing and supporting this willing Illusion." Shakespeare enlarges our capacity. As evidence of the conditionality of illusion and the need for conscious awareness of the illusion-making process, Coleridge quotes from *The Merchant of Venice*. When Shakespeare has us under the spell of his illusion, convinced that we listen to the dialogue between a lady of Venice and her maid, he has Portia deny her ability to speak English:

> Nerissa. What say you then to Falconbridge, the young baron of England?
> Portia: You know I say nothing to him; for he understands not me, nor I him: he hath neither Latin, nor French, nor Italian: and you will come into the court and swear that I have a poor pennyworth in English. (I.ii.71–77)

Obviously, an alert spectator would not miss the incongruity of such a disclaimer. Indeed, Coleridge argues, it is at such moments that the playwright makes us aware of his art. The improbable becomes probable. We are neither lost in delusion nor committed to a mere "copy" of reality. Art offers us "a certain quantum of Difference," and in this "Difference" we find the "indispensable condition and cause of the pleasure, we derive from it."[76]

Coleridge, like Schlegel, cites evidence of Shakespeare's deliberately exposing illusion to his audience. Neither the above passage from *The Merchant of Venice* nor the opening chorus from *Henry V*, however, are passages which Schlegel put forth in his exposition of self-reflexive and metadramatic moments in Shakespeare's use of illusion as a part of the plot. Coleridge recognized a parallel concern in Schlegel's account of Shakespeare's *tiefe Absichtlichkeit*, but he was more interested in demonstrating an informing judgment in Shakespeare's imitation of character than in his plots. In the illusory "imitation" Coleridge discovers the capacities of poetic imagination.

---

76. *LL* II, 263–67, 277.

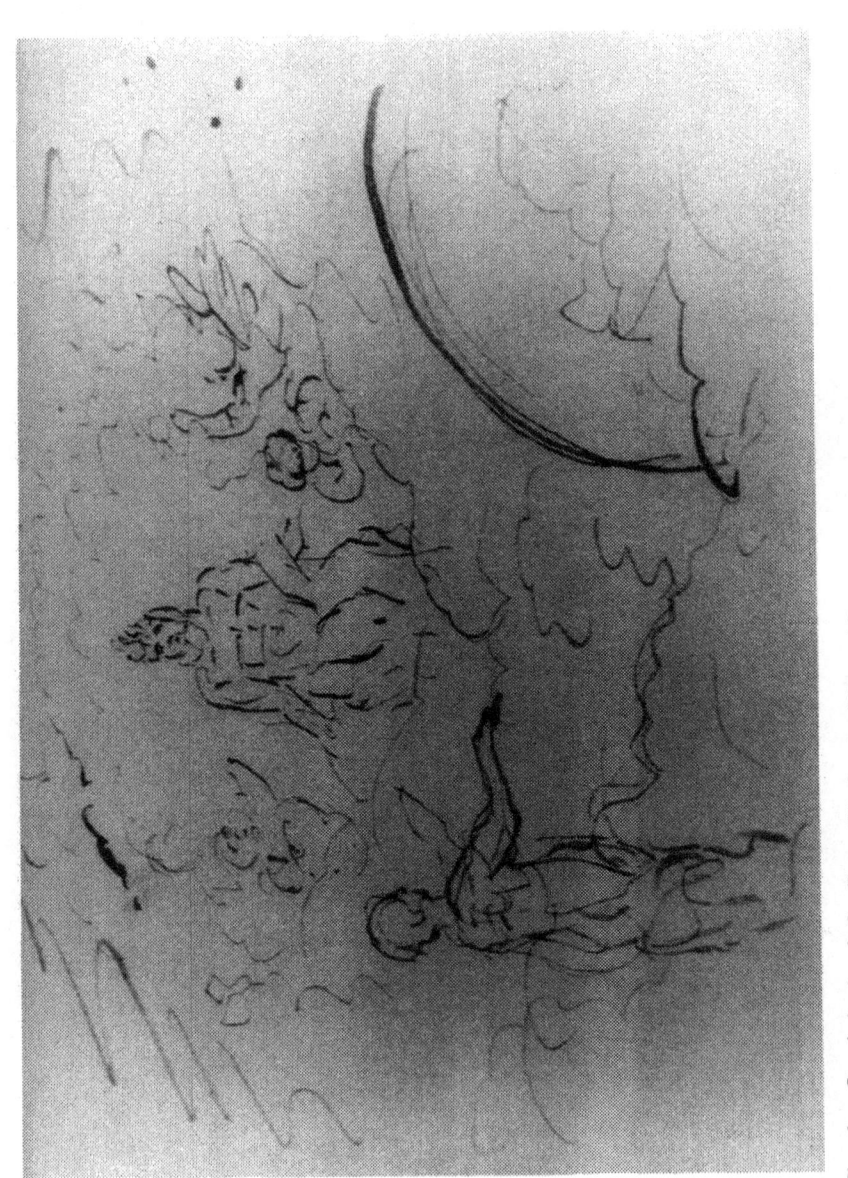

FIG. 1. Goethe's sketch for *Faust*: "Prolog im Himmel."

FIG. 2. *Faust* (as performed at the Lyceum), engraved by R. Taylor.

FIG. 3. Faust and Mephisto (as performed at the Comédie français, Paris), illustrating the *trappe anglais*.

FIG. 4. Goethe's sketch for *Faust:* "Erscheinung des Erdgeistes."

Fig. 5. Goethe's sketch for *Faust:* "Studierzimmer. Pudelbeschwörung."

FIG. 6. Goethe's sketch for *Faust:* "Hexenküche."

FIG. 7. "Hexenküche," line engraving by Moritz Retzsch (1816).

Fig. 8. Goethe's sketch for *Faust:* "Auf dem Brocken."

Fig. 9. Goethe's sketch for *Romeo and Juliet,* Act V.

FIG. 10. Goethe's sketch for the witches in *Macbeth*.

FIG. 11. Hugo's sketch for *Les Jumeaux* (1839).

FIG. 12. *Hernani*, Act II (first performance: Comédie française, 25 February 1830; Michelot as Don Carlos, Firmin as Hernani, Mlle Mars as Dona Sol).

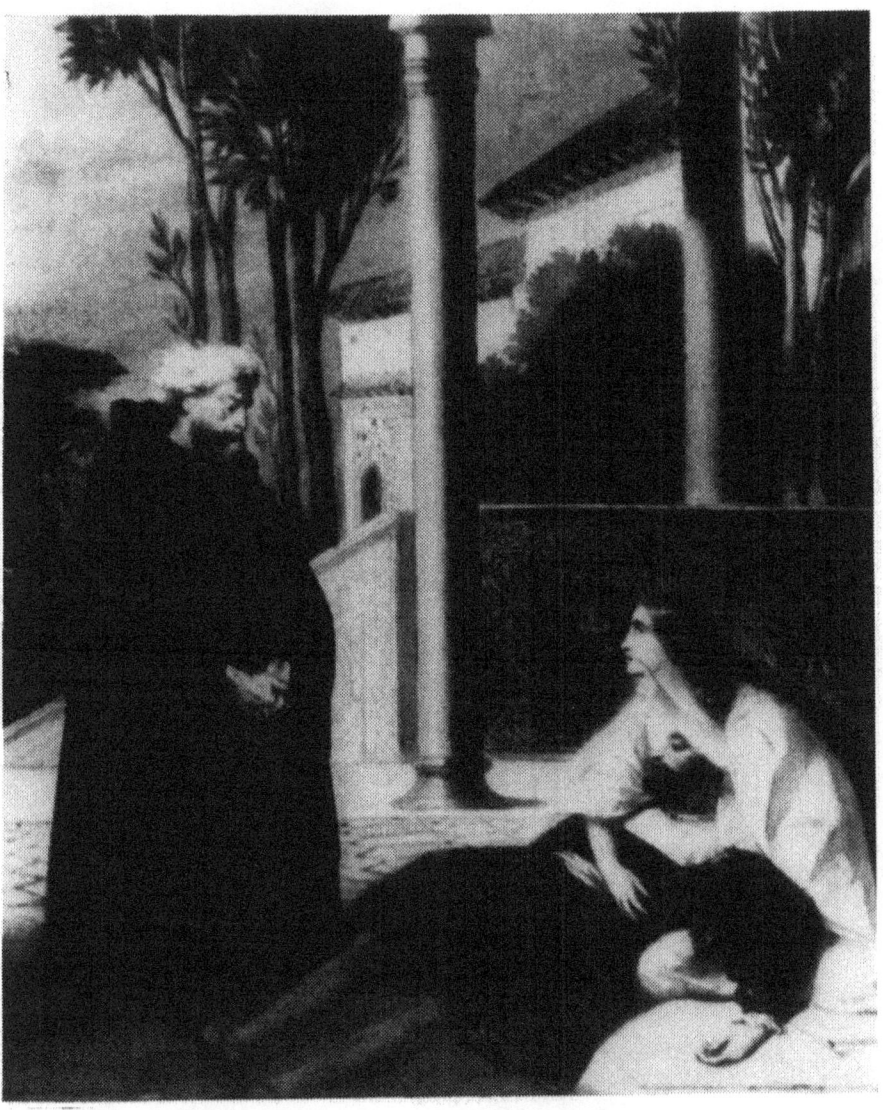

FIG. 13. The death scene from *Hernani* (Joanny as Don Ruy Gomez), Act V, by Louis Boulanger.

Fig. 14. "La Bataille d'Hernani," by Granville.

Fig. 15. Hugo's sketch for *Le Roi s'amuse*, Act II.

Fig. 16. Hugo's sketch for *Ruy Blas*, Act I.

FIG. 17. *Ruy Blas*, Act V (first performance: Théâtre de la Renaissance, 8 November 1838; Frédérick Lemaître as Ruy Blas, Atala Beauchêne as Dona Maria, Queen of Spain).

Fig. 18. Hugo's sketch of "Le Burg à la Croise."

FIG. 19. Hugo's sketch for *Les Burgraves*, Act I.

6

Illusion and the Stage: Goethe and Hugo

The entire history of the drama could be studied in terms of the opposition of two basic elements: *spectacle* and *mime.* Certainly there have been periods in history when one or the other dominated. Shakespeare's Globe, as Coleridge reminded his auditors, provided only a naked stage with the barest minimum of props. The gimmicks of stagecraft, which began to overwhelm the theaters in the Baroque era, have continued to exert tremendous influence on the drama, often forcing playwright, player, and the play itself, into subservience. The very effort to create stage illusion seems sometimes to have inhibited it. The visual enchantment of stage effects may become an end rather than a means.[1] Staging and acting, of course, are not incompatible constituents of drama. Nevertheless, dramatic theory and practice attest to the tension that persists between them. In the Romantic age, this tension between staging and acting was unusually high, and the debate over the nature of stage illusion raged at all levels: among actors, directors, playwrights, and critics. The Ro-

---

1. Frenzel, *Geschichte des Theaters. Daten und Dokumente* 50–151.

mantic rebellion against neoclassical rule also led to experiments in the drama that have been labeled nonmimetic or anti-illusionist.

In looking back to the theater of ages past, critics have found in Goethe's "world theater" and Hugo's "word opera" plays that belong to a historical tradition of anti-illusionist drama. Goethe's *Faust* and Hugo's *Les Burgraves* have both been considered Romantic contributions to Anti-Illusionist theater.[2] Still there is illusion even in the pretense of anti-illusion. Although the various constituents of the theatrical experience make different demands upon perception, the play, the acting, and the staging all contribute to stimulating illusion in the mind of the beholder. The playwright conjures primarily through the language and action of the play; he may stipulate, as well, specific directions for staging and acting. The stage manager is concerned with effects of a particular production in a specific theater, given proper application of available technology. Hugo and Goethe both enjoyed privileged circumstances that enabled them to carry out their own ideas for translating text into performance. Since both Goethe and Hugo have left us notes and sketches for staging, it is possible for us to trace their concern with illusionist effects as well as an "anti-illusionist" departure from the mimetic tradition. Goethe, as we shall see, became fascinated with the magic lantern and the techniques of the popular phantasmagoria. Hugo, for his part, was partial to a decor of hidden passages, reversals of onstage and offstage events, and above all a dynamic interaction between character and stage setting.

The opposition between the mechanics and the aesthetics of stage illusion and the tension between mimetic reality and poetic imagination are not only pertinent to the Romantic drama, they are thematic and, as my examples from Goethe and Hugo will show, fully integrated into the plays themselves as challenges to audience expectations. Their art is certainly anti-illusionist if we accept that definition involving a *reflexive* (ironic) attention to the process of illusion making. In the drama, the characters are caught up in their own illusory perceptions, and they "escape" only to remind the audience that they are acting. Contrary to the argument forwarded by several recent critics,[3] this act of "falling out of the role" (*aus der Rolle fallen*) reinforces rather than disrupts the spontaneity of stage

---

2. Brown, *Goethe's Faust. The German Tragedy*, 16–20; Affron, *A Stage for Poets. Studies in the Theatre of Hugo and Musset*, 62–82.
3. Nef, "Das Aus-der-Rolle-Fallen als Mittel der Illusionszerstörung bei Tieck und Brecht."

illusion. If a character falls out of one role, after all, he inevitably falls into another.

Goethe and Hugo were intrigued with the effects of lighting and stage design. Developments in gas-lighting early in the nineteenth century, the advent of the limelight in 1825, and the stage trickery of mirrors and the magic lantern, stirred a fascination with optical effects.[4] Of particular significance on the Romantic stage is the use of optical effects in representing the subjective and the supernatural. Hugo emphasized *chiaroscuro* effects on stage, and preferred to use light to emphasize shadowy darkness. Instead of a realistic setting with "natural" overhead lighting, Hugo would create stark effects with angled light, hand-held lanterns, and torch or candle processions.[5]

Goethe, in *Literature and Truth* (*Dichtung und Wahrheit*, 1811–14), distinguishes between the illusion of a "higher reality" and the misdirected attempt in domestic drama to reproduce common everyday reality on the stage: "The highest task of every form of art is to produce through its appearance the illusion of a higher reality. It is a false endeavor, however, to carry the appearance of the real to such a length that finally only a common reality remains."[6] In an earlier essay, "On the Truth and Probability of Art" ("Über Wahrheit und Wahrscheinlichkeit der Kunstwerke," 1797),[7] Goethe sought to refute what he considered to be Diderot's false doctrine of illusion. The ideas that he attributes to Diderot, however, are not the ideas that we examined in our study of Diderot in chapter 2. In his misunderstanding of Diderot,[8] Goethe reveals his own stage-oriented approach to drama.

Imitating Diderot's use of dialogue, Goethe takes the side of the artist in arguing with a spectator who represents Diderot. The spectator wants a perfect illusion, so that he may forget all imitation and believe in the reality of what he sees. The spokesman for the artist answers that it is not the purpose of the performance to appear real, rather it must have the "appear-

---

4. Brewster, *Letters on Natural Magic, Addressed to Sir Walter Scott* 37–97; see also Burwick, "Romantic Drama: From Optics to Illusion."
5. Barrère, "Le Lustre et la rampe. Petite note sur la conception de la scéne selon Victor Hugo."
6. Goethe, *Dichtung und Wahrheit*, book 11, in *Werke*, division 1, vol. 28, 65: "Die höchste Aufgabe einer jeden Kunst ist, durch den Schein die Täuschung einer höheren Wirklichkeit zu geben. Ein falsches Bestreben aber ist, den Schein solange verwirklicht, bis endlich nur ein gemeines Wirkliche übrig bleibt."
7. Goethe, "Über Wahrheit und Wahrscheinlichkeit der Kunstwerke" (1797), in *Werke*, div. 1, vol. 47, 254–66; "Diderots Versuch über Malerei" (1798/99), in *Werke*, div. 1, vol. 45, 245–322.
8. Jauß, "Diderots Paradox über das Schauspiel (Entretiens sur le Fils naturel)," 400–401.

ance of truth." It is only a want of an informed and mature aesthetic sensibility, Goethe declares in behalf of the artist, that prompts the inexperienced to seek a replication of reality; the connoisseur looks for the revelation of artistic genius in the total ensemble, in the performance as a work of art. The "appearance of truth" is achieved when the artist reveals the "higher reality" within the imitation of nature in such a way as to lend to the represented "reality" a unity and dignity. Although Goethe has perceived the paradox of Diderot's *Entretiens sur le Fils naturel* and has provided a resolution of his own, he has utterly missed Diderot's contention that the artist's perception of the beautiful is possible only because the ideal (Goethe's "higher reality") is already present in the real.

Unlike Diderot, who saw illusion in the *modèle idéal* realized through the player's total control, Goethe saw illusion as the harmony of performance. Without slighting the role of the player, or ignoring the importance of audience participation,[9] Goethe addressed his critical attention to the total effect of the stage. Significantly, when he indulges his metadramatic jests in *The Triumph of Sensibility* (*Der Triumph der Empfindsamkeit*, 1778),[10] the artifacts of illusion are all stage props. Prince Oronaro, Goethe's "man of sensibility," is so sensitive that he must guard himself from the harshness of the world and surround himself with the beauties of nature. Real nature being full of such discomforts as inclement weather and pesky insects, the prince has contrived his own "beauties of nature"—not only in the artificial woods, bowers, and grottoes with which he has decorated his palace, but in the portable "beauties of nature" he takes with him on his journeys.

Merkulo, cavalier of Oronaro's court, explains these wonders to two inquisitive ladies: in one chest is a bubbling spring, in another the song of birds, a third is filled with moonlight. When the ladies beg to see these wonders displayed, Merkulo answers that he would be pleased to show them, "if only the decorations in this room were in any way commensurate with the Nature that's imprisoned in these chests." As if taking her cue from the critical debate of the Enlightenment, one of the ladies responds, "You can't ask illusion to be as perfect as that." To render the setting more appropriate for the display of the "beauties of nature," the ladies call for the court upholsterer to lower suitable decorated tapestries. With a flourish of

---

9. For Goethe's attention to audience participation and the spectator's contribution to the total production of theater, see his letters on *Iphigenia*, also the Lauchstädt *Was wir bringen* (1802), in *Werke*, div. 1, vol. 13, 72–73; *Werke*, div. 4, vol. 15, 15–16; vol. 16, 75, 79, 83–86.

10. Goethe, *Der Triumph der Empfindsamkeit* (1778), in *Werke*, div. 1, vol. 17, 3–73.

music, the stage—or, in terms of the dramatic fiction, the court hall—is transformed into a splendid forest scene. With this maneuver, stage and fictive setting become identical. That is, they look exactly alike. As the dialogue continues, the ladies and the cavalier scrutinize and praise the "effects." One of the ladies observes that the prince must be a lover of theater. "Quite so," replies the cavalier, "for theater and our nature are closely related to one another." After thus introducing a metadramatical conceit in which the artificial nature of stage props are redefined as the improved nature of the exquisitely sensitive prince, Goethe prepares for the entrance of the prince as a consummate actor who can improvise his role according to the setting and circumstance. The distinctions between theater and reality merge into the metadramatic exposition of illusion making.[11]

Goethe aptly expresses his concern with the illusion-making process in his review of Calderón's *The Daughter of the Air*.[12] Calderón is "thoroughly theatrical, even stagy (*bretterhaft*)." Furthermore, he is utterly free of "what we call illusion, especially that sort which excites the emotions." His plays are set forth with a rational plan; the scenes follow an artistic necessity like a perfectly choreographed ballet. The delight is in the aesthetic execution similar, Goethe says, to the pleasure in the "technique of our most recent comic operas." His plots always develop the same *leitmotifs:* "conflict of duties, passions, circumstances, deriving from the opposition of characters and from the recurrent situations." While the major plot follows a course that is poetic, "the interludes, which move in dainty figures like minuets, are rhetorical, dialectical, and sophistic." Because he represents "all elements of humanity," even the Fool is included: "Should any illusion lay claim to our inclination and participation, the fool's homely reason threatens to destroy it immediately if not sooner."[13]

Goethe's comments on illusion, here, deserve close attention, for they have much to do with dramatic oppositions in *Faust*. He dismisses from his consideration of Calderón that sort of illusion "which excites the emotions," not that which engages the imagination. He dismisses, that is, Enlightenment not Romantic aesthetics. He goes on to observe in Calderón a deliber-

---

11. Prudhoe, *The Theatre of Goethe and Schiller*, 72–74.
12. Calderón, *La Hija del Aire*.
13. Goethe, "Die Tochter der Luft," in *Über Kunst und Altertum*, vol. 3, Heft 3 (1822), in *Werke*, div. 1, vol. 41, 351–55. Brown, *Goethe's Faust. The German Tragedy*, 19–21, refers to Goethe's review of Calderón in distinguishing illusionist and non-illusionist drama. See also Hardy, *Goethe, Calderon, und die romantische Theorie des Dramas*.

ate and self-conscious artistry that gives his drama a technical polish akin to the ballet or the opera. The human elements, however, are still at work, but the dramatic illusion is not allowed to overwhelm our sympathy. The Fool provides that sort of ironic intrusion which, as Goethe says, "threatens to destroy" illusion, but which, in fact, reminds the audience not to rely on a merely emotional response. Ironic intrusion heightens attention to the dramatic illusion.

Goethe goes on, in this same review, to contrast Calderón with Shakespeare: The former gives attention to artifice, the latter to nature.[14] The point of the contrast is to identify two different dramatic modes: the one elicits audience response through the imitation of nature, the other through artistic manner and convention. Along with Calderón's theater of artistic manner, Goethe lists the ballet and the comic opera. This is the sort of performance, again in contrast to Shakespearean or mimetic drama, that has traditionally called for the most elaborate stage settings and technical accoutrements. The theater of masques requires high ornamentation; the theater of mimetic action is self-sufficient on a barren stage.

Goethe certainly did not see as mutually exclusive the contrasts that he draws here. Indeed, the opposing elements might well interchange dialectically, so that stylized pomp and ritual could interact with a simple imitation of human action. Goethe not only experiments with this possibility throughout *Faust*, he introduces his audience to the dialectic opposition in his "Prelude" and "Prologue" to the play. The "Prelude in the Theater" is used to introduce the "Prologue in Heaven," which in turn introduces the "Tragedy." We are to understand that Poet, Director, and Merry Person are witnesses to the wager between God and Mephistopheles, and that God himself becomes a spectator to the "Tragedy." In *The Taming of the Shrew*, Shakespeare also made his play a vast play within a play by introducing it as an entertainment intended to distract Christopher Sly.[15] Petruchio's stratagem to cure Kate is seen as part of the prank that the Lord plays on the drunken tinker. Goethe has added to the complexity, then, by presenting a play within a play within a play.

In the "Prelude in the Theater," we witness on the stage three characters arguing about the nature of the stage and about the play that is to be

---

14. Goethe, *Werke*, div. 1, vol. 41, 353.
15. Schlegel, *KSB* VI, 146–48, discusses *The Taming of the Shrew* as an example of Shakespeare's ironic play with illusion; see chapter 4 above.

performed.[16] What is "to be hoped for," the Director asks, "from this effort / In countries of the German tongue?" (35–36). As we would expect, the Director thinks in terms of box-office receipts (54–56). Pleasing the crowd is what he emphasizes; therefore, he wants a play that will amaze, caress the taste, engage, and work its wondrous sway (43–44, 48, 57). Rather than astonish the perceptions or excite the physical passions, the Poet aims at lofty ideals in the "nook of heaven's stillness" (64–65). The Poet rejects the Director's crowd-pleasing tactics; the audience he seeks to please is "posterity" (74). The Merry Person is a Player, a Hanswurst drawn from the tradition of German comedy. Posterity is a meaningless goal for the Merry Person. He emphasizes the "Now" (75–80).

Even if the Poet longs for "a broader audience," his appeal must be to the moment. The Poet may want to address the ideal, but to do so he must also engage the complete human being:

> Show Fancy in her fullest panoply:
> Sense, understanding, sentiment, and passion,
> And mind you, last not least, some foolery.
> (86–88)

The Director agrees with the Merry Person's advice to the Poet, and recommends "above all . . . plot." Plot, however, he understands as "a solid eyeful," something at which the audience "can gasp and marvel" (90–93). Plot means *action*, not necessarily the Aristotelian "imitation of human action," but variety and excitement. For the Director, the best plot is episodic: it can be served in "pieces" like a "stew" (99–100). The Poet responds directly to the Director's metaphor, calling it a degradation of "true art" to equate it with a "charlatan's ragout of tricks and bawdry" (105–6). The Director, however, holds to his position. It is pointless to "daydream on your poet's eminence" if the audience is not satisfied. The way to please an audience, the Director repeats, is to "give more, and ever, ever more" (129). The Poet need not enlighten them, he claims, for it is just as effective to confuse them (131).

The Poet is outraged at the Director's argument. In rejecting confusion

16. Goethe, *Werke*, div. 1, vols. 14, 15¹, and 15²; I Abt., Bde. 14, 15¹, 15²; *Faust*, trans. Arndt, ed. Hamlin (English quotations are from this edition and are documented parenthetically in the text by line reference).

and erratic variety, however, he repeats the Director's concern with audience response. Thus he claims unity, harmony, and meaning are the essential means to "kindle every heart" and "conquer every elemental part" (138–51). Unfortunately, the Poet's vision of unity, harmony, and meaning takes him from dramatic action to lyrical meditation of sunsets, flowers, Olympus, the Immortals (151–56). The Merry Person calls him back to the "Now" of stage performance. The Poet may well nourish his lyrical fancy with such visions, for they conjure the enchantment of romance, and romance, in turn, provides the stuff of dramatic spectacle (159–67). Indeed, as the Merry Person insists, any source of speculation will do, so long as it leads the Poet "into the wealth of human living." Here, the Merry Person seems to be working out a reconciliation between the Director and the Poet. In affirming the Poet's lyrical flights of idealism, he turns the results of the Poet's endeavor back to the dramatization of human action and to the "spectacle" and "illusion" of that dramatization (166, 181).

The Poet accepts, at least conditionally, this turn to illusion. To compromise "the thirst for truth" with the "delight in fictions," however, requires the enthusiasm of youth. To meet the expectations of the Merry Person and the Director, the Poet, like Faust later in the play, bargains for youth (192–97). The Merry Person assures him that the recollection of youth will serve him much better than the "reckless whirling dance" of youth itself (204–12). The Director calls for an end to the speeches: it is time for action (214–15). In the concluding lines of the "Prelude, the Director orders that the stage be set.

> You know, upon our German stages
> Each man puts on just what he may;
> So spare me not upon this day
> Machinery and cartonnages.
> The great and little light of heaven employ,
> The stars you may freely squander;
> Cliff-drops and water, fire and thunder,
> Birds, animals, are in supply.
> So in this narrow house of boarded space
> Creation's fullest circle go to pace,
> And walk with leisured speed your spell
> From Heaven through the World to Hell.
> (231–42)

Even though the Poet and Merry Person have reached an agreement of sorts, the Director still has his way. Or, rather, all three, each voicing one aspect of Goethe's own intentions, will continue to assert their conflicting preferences.

The play, thus introduced, pits poetic ideals against the marvels of "machinery and cartonnages." The curtain falls upon the naked stage of the "Prelude in the Theater" and rises upon the grand "Prologue in Heaven" (Fig. 1). In Goethe's sketch, we recognize a mythic grandeur. God, bare-chested in his draped robe, sits upon his cloud-enveloped throne attended by the three Archangels. The light, from the fly-gallery, casts an appropriate gloria around the throne. In the right foreground, also surrounded with clouds, hovers the sphere of the world; in the left foreground, stands Mephisto gesturing toward the world. The scene might just as easily represent Hermes before Zeus. Again, we can observe a triadic structure: God and Mephistopheles appear in place of the Director and the Merry Person, and the Poet is replaced by the opening chorus of Archangels. The Archangels' song of creation (243–71) is followed by the crude jests of Mephisto. Although the source is the *Book of Job*, God's wager with Mephisto is played in a homely rather than a sublime style. Each seems to humor the other. In spite of Mephisto's condescending remarks about "the old gent" (350), Goethe leaves his God just as surely in charge of events as his Director.

Mephisto may think that he is capable of startling man out of his illusions (a role, we must remember, which Goethe recognized in Calderón's Fool), but when Mephisto departs and God has the last word, he tells us that man is too inclined to take things easy; thus God has given him the devil as a companion to make him strive and work. Instead of "falling out of the role," Mephisto reinforces rather than disrupts the harmony of God's World Theater (*Weltbühne*). God, and Goethe, let us know that Mephisto is simply another agent of illusion.

Goethe's opening strategy takes the audience into a dramatic structure of Chinese-boxes, a sequence of alternate realities. Within the "Tragedy," the same strategy persists as the play shifts attention to alternate worlds: the self-searching and metaphysical world of Faust, the demonic world of Mephistopheles, and the bourgeois world of Gretchen. Throughout *Faust*, Part I, the triadic structure enforces the opposition of themes. The love of Faust and Gretchen is presented in seven short scenes (some 600 lines); then, divided by a scene with Faust and Mephistopheles alone in "Forest and Cave," come six more scenes (fewer than 500 lines) in which the love is corrupted by the death of her mother and her brother and Gretchen's guilt and despair. Framing, as well as dividing, the Gretchen episodes are the scenes of Faust's soliloquies and his contest with Mephistopheles ("Night," "Outside the City Gate," "Study," "Forest and Cave," "Dreary Day," "Open Field"—over 2200 lines, the dominant substance of the play). The third sequence of action takes Faust into the demonic world of Mephistopheles. Faust first enters the demonic world, before wooing Gretchen, in "Auerbach's Cellar" and "Witch's Kitchen" (532 lines); he returns to the demonic world, after Gretchen's ruin, in "Walpurgis Night" and "Walpurgis Night's Dream" (564 lines). The demonic scenes, presented in two pairs, frame the scenes of Gretchen's love and ruin. In terms of total length, the scenes in the demonic world of Mephisto balance the scenes in the bourgeois world of Gretchen, and both together (just under 2200 lines) balance the scenes of Faust's mental wrestling. The structure dramatizes the three modes of perception: Faust's, Gretchen's, and Mephisto's.[17]

Even when reading the text, we might well suspect that Goethe intended radically different staging for his episodic realms. Making the most of the pranks (*Streiche*), which Goethe adapted from the chapbook versions of the Faust story, such as Mephisto's in Auerbach's Cellar, performances in England and France freely indulged the magic of mechanical trickery (Figs. 2 and 3). From what we know of the plans for production in 1812, the presentation of scenes from *Faust* in Berlin in 1819, and the first full performance in Weimar in 1829, Goethe called for more modest mechanical effects than the arguments of his Director would seem to indicate. He was especially intrigued by the use of the *laterna magica* in conjuring stage effects. His most elaborate architectural setting was commissioned for the "Cathedral." Perhaps it was his fascination with optics and color theory[18] that prompted him to rely on the trickery of the magic lantern to introduce the supernatural into a contrastingly simple setting.

The appearance of the Earth Spirit in "Night," for example, was to be brought into Faust's study much in the manner of Rembrandt's painting of the Scholar and the Sign of the Microcosm. Except all was to be produced in giant proportions, as Goethe sketched the scene (Fig. 4). At the time of the Berlin performance, he wrote to Count Brühl (2 June 1819):

17. Burwick, *The Haunted Eye: Perception and the Grotesque in Romantic Literature*. This analysis of the triadic structure introduces my explication of the Walpurgisnacht episodes.
18. Goethe, *Werke*, div. 2, vol. 1; *Goethes Farbenlehre*; Goethe, *Theory of Colours*. See also Burwick, *The Damnation of Newton: Goethe's Color Theory and Romantic Perception*.

This representation of the Earth Spirit conforms exactly with my intention. That he looks in through the window is ghostly enough. Rembrandt has used this idea very effectively in an engraved plate. When we, too, intended to take this scene and develop it for production, my conception was also simply to show transparently a colossal head and chest and I thought of adapting it from the well-known bust of Jupiter, for the words "horrible face" refer to the feelings of the observer, who would certainly be frightened by such an apparition, and could therefore be aptly addressed to the figure itself; even here there should appear nothing grimacing or disgusting. How one might, perhaps with flaming hair and beard, to some degree approach the modern idea of the supernatural, on this we had come to no agreement.[19]

Ten years later, when preparations were underway for the full production in Weimar, Goethe had decided that the supernatural scenes could be done in the manner of the popular phantasmagoria. He wrote to W. Zahn requesting him to obtain a magic lantern (12 December 1828):

Prince Radziwill ... had the appearance of the Spirit in the first scene presented in the phantasmagorical manner; that is, in a darkened theater an illuminated head is projected from the rear upon a screen stretched across the background, first as a small image, then gradually increasing in size, so that it seems to be coming closer and closer. This artistic illusion was apparently conjured with a kind of *Laterna Magica*. Could you please find out, as soon as possible, who constructs such an apparatus, how one could obtain it, and what preparations must be made for it?[20]

The conjuration in Faust's study (Fig. 5), a scene written in 1800, was apparently conceived in much the same manner as the Apparition of the

---

19. Goethe, *Werke*, div. 4, vol. 31, 163–64. The undated sketches for *Faust* were collected with Goethe's *Theaterzeichnungen*, presumably executed during his tenure as director of the Weimarer Hoftheater, 1791–1817. Now in the collection of the Nationale Forschungs- und Gendenkstätte, Weimar (NFG/GNM Corp. IVb, 222, 223, 224, 227), they may have been sketched when the scenes were composed or, more probably, in anticipation of performance in 1812, 1819, or 1829. In his *Tag- und Jahresheften*, Goethe records that Wolff had persuaded him to have *Faust* performed in 1812 and he had even begun to prepare stage settings (*Dekorationen und sonstiges Erfordernis*), *Werke*, div. 3, vol. 4.
20. Goethe, *Werke*, div. 4, vol. 45, 80.

Earth Spirit. The demonic poodle has the "flaming hair" which Goethe associated with "the modern idea of the supernatural." Certainly, with the use of the *laterna magica* the "flaming" image could have been enhanced with red or orange tinted glass, and, as was done with the "burning house" in the phantasmagoria of London, Paris, and Berlin,[21] the flames could have been made to flicker with a moiré transparency. The sketch shows the huge transparent head appearing in the framed alcove just beyond Faust's outstretched arm.

Another such trick was to be achieved with the mirror in the Witch's Kitchen (Fig. 6). Sir David Brewster, in a contemporary account of stage illusions wrought with the *laterna magica*, describes the technique of shifting from reflected image to projected image.[22] In Moritz Retzsch's line engraving of this scene (Fig. 7), we see that the witch's kettle occupies center stage, while Faust gazes into the mirror obliquely positioned at the right. In Goethe's sketch, the hearth is to the right and the magic mirror, casting radiant beams, directly faces the audience from center stage, engaging the audience as well as Faust in the vision of the reclining Helena.

It seems likely, too, that the apparition of Gretchen amidst the Walpurgisnacht orgy atop the Brocken was to be achieved as a phantom image cast by the *laterna magica*. Goethe's sketch (Fig. 8) shows Mephisto pointing to the left and tugging Faust by the shoulder to return to the revels, while Faust is turned to the right and stretches out his arms toward the vision of Gretchen that appears in a circle of light against the dark cliffs. Throughout the "Walpurgis Night," Goethe reveals a growing antagonism between what Mephistopheles perceives and what Faust perceives. Mephisto and Faust pause at an abyss to behold the glowing red and gold in the ravine beneath them: Mephisto sees the Mammon-glow of human greed; Faust sees a triumph of golden sparks rising from the black depths to ascend aflame the rocky cliffs. When the phantom of Gretchen appears against the cliffs, Mephisto insists that it is only a magic image, while Faust continues to conjure the memory of Gretchen's physical presence.

Part of the irony in Goethe's dialogue is in Mephisto's revealing declaration that the apparition is but a trick. A more profound dimension of the irony, however, is in Faust's animating the lifeless image. Faust's vision

---

21. *The Magic Lantern; its History and Effects* (London: 1854); see also Rees, *Theatre Lighting in the Age of Gas*.
22. Brewster, *Letters on Natural Magic*, 37–97.

occurs after the satirical dialogue with the Proctophantasmist, who tells the ghosts and demons that they do not really exist. He demands that the poet—and the devil(!)—put a stop to this illusion making. Goethe has it both ways: he introduces a critic of the supernatural, yet renders him a fool in denying the existence of the spirits visibly surrounding him.[23] Goethe thus insists that audience attend to the theatricality of illusion as well as to its dramatic enchantment.

What these sketches reveal is Goethe's own sense of dramatic orientation. Because he utilizes optical effects to enhance the thematic concern with perception, the mechanical aspects of production are not in competition with the aesthetic. Nor do these sketches imply a static setting in which the characters merely enact their roles. The setting (through the moving images of the magic lantern) actually participates in the dramatic action. While he joins the spirit of the age in proclaiming the primacy of the aesthetic experience and the power of the imagination in creating stage illusion, he shares with the Director in the "Prelude" a pragmatic reliance on gimmickry to make the audience "gasp and marvel."

In Hugo we shall observe an extensive concern with dramatic interaction between character and setting. A similar exploitation of setting is evident in *Faust*; it occurs, however, not in dramatic interaction but in a kind of dialogue between Faust and his surroundings. Goethe repeatedly gives to Faust a mode of perception that sees human activity in physical place. In his "Study," Faust struggles against the confinement he feels crushing him. In "Forest" and "Cavern," Faust addresses the sublime power in nature. Significantly, his love for Gretchen commences in his visit to her room. Even in her absence, Faust finds the room bespeaks her presence, her purity, her orderliness and contentment.[24] Although Hugo, too, uses the stage setting to reveal the opposition of purity and perversion in his version of the seduction of innocence, *Le Roi s'amuse*, he leaves the theatricality invisibly contained within the drama. Goethe enforces aesthetic distance by parodying the lovers through Mephisto's antics and by framing and dividing the sequence of scenes dramatizing the wooing and the ruin of Gretchen. He thus transforms the tragedy into a ritual of love and lost innocence.

His stage design for *Romeo and Juliet*, act 5 (Fig. 9), emphasizes the

---

23. Brown, 125. She describes "Walpurgis Night," *Faust I*, and "Charming Landscape," *Faust II*, as, respectively, the "Illusion of Reality" and the "Reality of Illusion."
24. Brown, 99, discusses the significance of Gretchen's absence in this scene.

confinement of the tomb with the vaulting arches that block the proscenium and frame the action within interior recesses. Further, the darkness of the stage, lighted by torches mounted on the pillars and by the indirect light streaming down the stairs, also adds the very sort of somber cave-like quality that, as we shall see, is repeated by Hugo in such plays as *Hernani* and *Les Burgraves*. Where Hugo would insist on making the witches in *Macbeth* demonic and grotesque,[25] however, Goethe would rely on a "classical" staging, presenting the Witches in the manner of a Greek chorus. In his sketch (Fig. 10), we see that Goethe has designed a choric stage at the base of a giant gnarled oak. The foregrounded figure to the left is a detail to indicate the veiled costumes. The details to the right indicate a graveyard setting.

Departing from the more rigorously mimetic stage of the eighteenth century, Goethe's productions in Weimar were designed to alert the audience to the workings of theatrical illusion. Seeing the witches from *Macbeth* arrayed as a Greek chorus ought to have made an audience aware of theatricality. In writing about audience response, however, Goethe seems to uphold Enlightenment aesthetics. He stresses emotional power and denies the intrusion of fantasy: "The spectator must by rights be kept in a state of constant sensory exertion; he may not collect himself mentally, he must follow passionately; his fantasy is utterly silenced, no demands may be made upon it." This pronouncement, from "Ueber epische und dramatische Dichtung," does not argue that illusion must become delusion, or that the reason is somehow extinguished by the excitement of the senses and passion. For Goethe, such a response would mean that the fantasy had taken over.[26] In those moments when a character succumbs to fantasy, expressing inward thoughts or dreams, the audience is supposed to witness a psychological truth. The spectator is not to take this occasion to entertain his or her own private fancy.

Shakespeare's appeal to the fantasy, Goethe asserted in "Shakespeare und kein Ende," was always untheatrical.[27] When he says that the spectator

---

25. Hugo, *Préface de Cromwell*, in *Oeuvres dramatiques et critiques complètes*, 139–53; "Certes, les euménides grecques sont bien moins horribles, et par conséquent bien moins vraies, que les sorcières de *Macbeth*" (142). Hugo's stage designs, sketched in the margins of his plays, are in the manuscript collection at the Bibliothèque Nationale and the Maison de Victor Hugo.

26. Goethe, "Über epische und dramatische Dichtung," in *Werke*, div. 1, vol. 41^2, 223–24; Flemming, *Goethe und das Theater seiner Zeit* 45–47; Carlson, *Goethe and the Weimar Theatre*, 250–58.

27. Goethe, "Shakespeare und kein Ende," in *Werke*, div. 1, vol. 41, 52–71.

should not be able to "collect himself mentally," Goethe does not mean that the audience should remain ignorant of the intellectual problems. In his "Weimarisches Hoftheater," he specifically declares the challenge of the drama to make an audience struggle with intellectual issues.[28] Although the senses are fully involved, the reason is free to observe the illusory nature of the experience.[29] Dramatic illusion works through sympathetic identification with a character. The actor must make us enter into his very being, and the senses should hold our attention to this inward-directed revelation. Neither the dream at the end of *Egmont* nor Gretchen's hallucination in the last scene of *Faust* should stimulate the audience's indulgence in fantasy.

As is evident in his review of Calderón, even in 1822 Goethe continued to emphasize emotional response in dramatic illusion. Nevertheless, with the Romantics he also affirmed illusion as the aesthetic engagement of the creative imagination. His careful discrimination of modes of perception in his *Color Theory* led him to distinguish illusion from delusion in terms that he defined as meticulously as Coleridge. With Coleridge, too, he would affirm that illusion is attained by an act of will. And with both Schlegel and Coleridge, he would insist that the perceiver is conscious of the illusory nature of his perception. The art of illusion may well involve a reflexive or ironic attention to the process of illusion making. In exercising that irony in *Faust*, Goethe not only relied on the words and actions of the characters to remind the audience of the illusion, he emphasized the very theatricality of stage production to enhance as well as to expose illusion.

For Hugo, the paradoxical nature of stage illusion implicated and, depending on the playwright's skill, replicated the essential antagonism confronting all social, political, and religious ideals in the real world. His "history plays" pretend no fidelity to actual historical events. He uses history as a psychological moment to explore possible motives and actions. Hugo is especially concerned with dramatizing the opposition of the practical and the imaginary, and his stage settings provide for the contest between real and irreal.

---

28. Goethe, "Weimarisches Hoftheater," in *Werke*, div. 1, vol. 40, 79.
29. Bennett, *Modern Drama and German Classicism*, 117–88. In summarizing Bennett's argument, I agree with his interpretation of Goethe's "Ueber epische und dramatische Dichtung" and share his frustration that Goethe does not seem to say what he means. Bennett provides, however, a different resolution to the disparity: "I therefore take Goethe's argument concerning the sensualness of drama as a discussion of drama's immediate, not ultimate goal, and I cannot see that the argument is logically consistent otherwise."

As we shall see, he is adroit in evoking vivid offstage action as well as exploiting onstage interaction with the physical setting.

The *Préface de Cromwell* (1827) begins with a commentary on the three ages of poetry. Hugo concludes that Christianity brought to the modern age its prominent and defining characteristic—melancholy. Building upon its primitive and classical antecedents, modern literature exhibits the tension of opposites: "Le génie de la mélancholie et de méditation, le démon de l'analyse et de la controverse." At one extreme, Longinus; at the other, St. Augustine. This inherent cultural polarity, evident in all literature, Hugo finds most pronounced in the antagonism informing the modern drama. In spite of the older separation of dramatic constituents into comedy and tragedy which continues to hamper development, "Le christianisme amène la poésie à la vérité."[30] It is time, Hugo argues, to realize "la vérité": in God's creation the comic is not neatly prescinded from the tragic. The beautiful coexists with the ugly, good with evil, light with darkness, soul with body, beast with intellect, grotesque with sublime. In defending the presence of the grotesque in the drama, Hugo appeals to the traditional principle of *mimesis*. Imitating nature, art should also learn to mingle—without confounding—the antagonistic attributes of creation.

A sustained antagonism is what Hugo proposes to bring to the drama. The Greeks had too keen an awareness of nature to expel all comedy from their tragedy. Hugo cites such comic scenes as the exchange between Menelaus and the portress of the palace in *Helen*, act 1; the Phrygian in *Orestes*, act 4. The grotesque, too, has a venerable tradition in the epic: the Tritons, the Satyrs, the Cyclops. He observes an aesthetic range of grotesquerie: "Polyphème est un grotesque terrible; Silène un grotesque bouffon." In classical drama, the mingling of the comic and tragic was rare and incidental, and in the epic the grotesque was "timide, et cherche toujours à se cacher." For the modern era, the grotesque has acquired a far richer array of implications and has become an essential attribute of experience:

> In contemporary thought, . . . the grotesque plays an immense role. It is found everywhere; on the one hand, it creates the abnormal and the horrible; on the other, the comic and the facetious. It attaches to religion a thousand superstitions, to poetry a thousand picturesque fantasies. . . . it is the grotesque which impels the ghastly antics of the witches' sabbath, which gives Satan his horn, his cloven foot, his

---

30. Hugo, *Préface*, 141.

bat's wings. It is the grotesque, always the grotesque, which now casts into the Christian hell the hideous figures which the severe genius and Dante and Milton will evoke, and again peoples it with the ridiculous forms among which Callot, the burlesque Michelangelo, will disport himself. If it passes from the ideal world to the real world, it provides endless parodies of humanity. Creations of its fantasy are the Scaramouches, the Crespins, the Harlequins, grinning silhouettes of man, types, which altogether unknown to grave antiquity, nevertheless emerged from classic Italy. It is the grotesque, finally, which coloring the same drama from the imagination of the South as from the imagination of the North, exhibit Sganarelle capering about Don Juan and Mephistopheles crawling about Faust.[31]

While his concept of the grotesque draws upon examples common to other definitions of the period, it is significant that Hugo recognizes its demonic and terrifying as well as its ludicrous and farcical dimensions. Some eighteenth-century critics had acknowledged only the grotesque-comic and others had reduced the grotesque to an ornamental subservience. What is important, here, is that within his argument for dramatic antagonism Hugo has not set forth the grotesque in simple opposition to the beautiful or sublime; rather, he has recognized that the grotesque itself derives from conflicting aesthetic elements.

Although he acknowledges that an entire book might be devoted to the use of the grotesque in the arts, Hugo does not elaborate on how that use might contribute to dramatic illusion. He does tell us that the grotesque may provoke "powerful effects," and that it offers "the richest source that nature can offer art." His presumption is simply that the physical as well as the

---

31. Ibid. 142. "Dans la pensée des modernes, ... le grotesque a un rôle immense. Il y est partout; d'une part, il crée le difforme et l'horrible; de l'autre, le comique et le bouffon. Il attache autour de la religion mille superstitions originales, autour de la poésie mille imaginations pittoresques.... c'est lui qui fait tourner dans l'ombre la ronde effrayante du sabbat, lui encore qui donne à Satan les cornes, les pieds de bouc, les ailes de chauve-souris. C'est lui, toujours lui, qui tantôt jette dans l'enfer chrétien ces hideuses figures qu'evoquera l'âpre genie de Dante et Milton, tantôt le peuple de ces formes ridicules au milieu desquelles se jouera Callot, le Michel Ange burlesque. Si du monde idéal il passe au monde réel, il y déroule d'intarissables parodies de l'humanité. Ce sont de créations de sa fantaisie que ses Scaramouches, ces Crespins, ces Arlequins, grimaçantes silhouettes de l'homme, types tout à fait inconnus à la grave antiquité, et sortis pourtant de la classique Italie. C'est lui enfin qui, colorant tour à tour le même drame de l'imagination du Midi et de l'imagination du Nord, fait gambader Sganarelle autour de don Juan et ramper Méphistophélès autour de Faust."

intellectual aspects of human conscious will be stimulated. The aesthetic response involves more than a needed contrast and complement to the sublime: "It seems, on the other hand, that the grotesque is a halting place, a term of comparison, a point of departure, whence one rises toward the beautiful with a fresher, more excited perception."[32] The grotesque challenges and regenerates perception. Furthermore, the grotesque possesses a manifold fecundity: "Le beau n'a qu'un type; le laid en a mille." Classical drama sought tension in a noble character struggling with a "tragic flaw." Christianity brought forth a conception of human character divided into body and soul. The dualism of grotesque body versus sublime soul determined the course of modern drama:

> On the day when Christianity said to man: "Thou art double, thou art composed of two beings: one perishable, the other immortal; one carnal, the other ethereal; one enslaved by appetites, wants, passions, the other elevated on the wings of enthusiasm and reverie; in short, the one always bending down to earth, its mother, the other always darting up to heaven, its fatherland"—on that day the drama was created.[33]

The gargoyles and demons that lurk and leer from the rooftops and spires of the cathedral as well as the hells and purgatories carved in relief over its great arched entrances are the obvious marks of the grotesque in Christian art. But the grotesque also pervades the secular world, from the *châteaux* to the palace. In the drama, the result was a fresh perception of nature and the representation of the real: "The real results from the wholly natural combination of two types, the sublime and the grotesque, which meet in the drama, as they meet in life and in creation."

This principle of contraries prevails over the neoclassical rule mongering and leads Hugo to dismiss the "three unities" and to affirm the validity of mixed genres (the comic in tragedy; the tragic in comedy). Unless vice and

---

32. Ibid., 142. "Il semble, au contraire, que le grotesque soit un temps d'arrêt, un terme de comparaison, un point de départ d'où l'on s'élève vers le beau avec une perception plus fraîche et plus excitée."

33. Ibid., 144. "Du jour où le christianisme a dit à l'homme: 'Tu es double, tu es composé de deux êtres, l'un périssable, l'autre immortel, l'un charnel, l'autre éthéré, l'un enchaîné par les appétits, les besoins et les passions, l'autre emporté sur les ailes de l'enthousiasme et de la rêverie, celui-ci enfin toujours courbé vers la terre, sa mère, celui-là sans cesse élancé vers le ciel, sa patrie'; de ce jour le drama a été créé."

absurdity are seen as copresent with heroism and virtue, there can be no hope of representing the real, the true human condition, upon the stage. The best playwrights have known this and have not conformed to the pseudo-Aristotelian rules. Shakespeare reveals the principle of contraries by introducing the dialogue between the Nurse and Juliet, Romeo and the apothecary, Macbeth and the witches, Hamlet and the gravediggers, Lear and his Fool. The old doctrine of probability in the purist conception of tragedy or comedy resulted in the most improbable plots. Hugo argues that the drama succeeds in representing the real, not by building upon "probability" of events, but by portraying the body-soul dualism.

Unity of action, then, is redefined in terms of *ensemble*. Unity of place, in the constrained conception of neoclassical critics, has limited all action in tragedy to the palace court with the villains conspiring in the porch, peristyle, or antechamber. Comedy is set in the salon with the chicanery relegated to the street. Since violence, vice, and the passions of the grotesque beast were not tolerated onstage, the playwright was forced to report all of the excitement as occurring offstage.

> As a result, everything that is too characteristic, too intimate, too local, to happen in the antechamber or on the street corner—that is to say, the whole drama—takes place in the wings. We see on stage only the turnings in the action; the dealings are elsewhere. Instead of scenes, we have narrative; instead of tableaux, descriptions. From grave personages, placed, like the old chorus, between the drama and us, we hear what is happening in the temple, in the palace, in the public square, until we are tempted repeatedly to call out to them: "Truly! then take us there! It must be very entertaining to behold such a fine sight!"[34]

Hugo, as we shall see, resorts frequently to the devices of offstage action in his own plays. What he objects to, here, is not so much the extension of the

---

34. Ibid. 145. "Il résulte de là que tout ce qui est trop charactéristique, trop intime, trop local, pour se passer dans l'antichambre ou dans le carrefour, c'est-à-dire tout le drame, se passe dans la coulisse. Nous ne voyons en quelque sorte sur le théâtre que les coudes de l'action; ses mains sont ailleurs. Au lieu de scenes, nous avons des récits; au lieu de tableaux, des descriptions. De graves personnages placés, comme le choeur antique, entre le drama et nous, viennent nous raconter ce qui se fait dans le temple, dans le palais, dans la place publique, de façon que souventes fois nous sommes tentés de leur crier: 'Vraiment! mais conduisez-nous donc là-bas! On s'y doit bien amuser, cela doit être beau à voir!' "

boundaries of the drama to include unseen events offstage, but rather the censorship imposed by those guardians of *la dignité* who will not permit us to see certain kinds of action. Unity of place thus becomes a moral law. Not *unity* of place, but direct involvement in the place of dramatic action is what Hugo wants. And that involvement also requires fidelity to historical setting. Instead of unity of place and unity of time, Hugo calls for "la couleur locale" and "la couleur des temps."

The place on the stage must appear as a witness to the historical event; the audience must see it haunted by the event. With his conviction that setting was crucial to effective illusion, Hugo frequently sketched his own stage designs in the margins of his manuscripts. His characters do not merely play upon a decorated stage, they interact with the setting. To conjure reality the playwright requires exact localization: Rizzio cannot be murdered any place but in Mary Stuart's chamber, nor Henry IV any place but in Rue de la Ferronerie. The same specificity applies to time. It is as absurd, Hugo argues, to confine the unfolding of events to twenty-four hours as it is to limit a conspiracy to a peristyle.

He readily grants the neoclassical objection that radical shifts in place and time may disrupt and baffle a spectator's attempts to comprehend the action. These are precisely the difficulties, Hugo adds, that art must overcome. The spectator, after all, is endowed with a facile perception and comprehension: the playwright need only provide the pertinent clue and the spectator will readily follow the unfolding events. But the events themselves must retain a certain unity: "L'oeil ni l'esprit humain ne sauraient saisir plus d'un ensemble à la fois." *Ensemble* involves coherence, not simplicity, of plot. Indeed, subplots converge as lines of perspective in a single vanishing point on the dramatic horizon. That point is the reality of the human condition: body and soul, grotesque and sublime, tragic and comic. *Ensemble*, then, is the stage law of perspective. It is the only law: "Il ne peut pas plus y avoir trois unités dans le drame que trois horizons dans un tableau."

The playwright, like the artist, has full freedom to follow nature. Hugo posits the principle of liberty and declares the artist free from enslavement to imitation. He must not be chained to models and tradition. The only laws he must follow are the laws of nature. While the playwright derives his plot, his dramatic ensemble, directly from nature, he transforms his raw material into art. Art is not nature. The romantic insistence upon absolute nature becomes ludicrous when it deprives art of the right to be art. Hugo offers the example of a performance of *Le Cid*, in which the critic objects, first, that the hero speaks verse not prose; then, should that fault be corrected, that he speaks French not Spanish; if that trespass, too, is amended, the critic will still object that the actor on the stage has no right to pretend that he is the great hero of Spain. Nor need the critic stop here. The principle of absolute nature cannot tolerate mere paintings of trees, mere cardboard facades where castle walls should be.

Hugo's point is clear: art does not presume to duplicate nature. Through a rapport with nature, it strives to represent ideal as well as material life. It represents essences by bringing together the opposing tendencies of nature. The grotesque and the sublime, the real and the ideal, the natural and the imaginative all contribute to the dramatic illusion. Through the tension of opposites, the spectator recognizes the real. Drama, then, may hold up a mirror to nature, but it is a concentrating mirror that focuses and intensifies the light of its images. The stage is an optical point. Our perception of reality tends to be scattered and diffused, whereas our perception of the drama is concentrated. This paradoxical combination of the poetical and the natural is what engenders dramatic illusion: "It imparts to it that vitality of truth and brilliancy which gives birth to illusion, that prestige of reality which arouses the passion of the spectator."[35]

Imaginary scenes, imbued with the same *couleur* as the actual historical events, actually sharpen rather than blur the historical verisimilitude. This is because the combination of the natural and the poetic reveals the body as well as the soul. The focus is so sharply defined that we see the inner workings as well as the outer actions: "L'extérieur, par leurs discours et leurs actions; l'intérieur, par les *a parte* et les monologues; de croiser, en un mot, dans le même tableau, le drame de la vie et le drame de la conscience." Whereas perception in the real world is baffled by surfaces, perception in the theater penetrates to the very core, revealing both the deeds and the motives.

Perception is so thoroughly directed by historical fidelity to time and place, by the attention to local color, that the spectator notices the difference in atmosphere when the curtain rises; however, upon accepting its conventions, he will not be distracted by the difference again until he leaves the theater, when he will find it necessary to readjust to "la couleur locale" in his

---

35. Ibid. 148. "Lui donne cette vie de vérité et de saillie qui enfante l'illusion, ce prestige de réalité qui passionne de spectateur."

own world outside the theater. Local color is sustained by "une ardente inspiration," and the illusion can only be disrupted by a lapse into the commonplace.

When he takes up the problem of representation in the concluding section of the *Préface*, he returns to the evocation of illusion. He refuses to separate scene and situation. Setting participates in dramatic action. Thus he speaks of the "séduction qu'exerçait sur l'imagination de l'auteur cette vaste scène de l'histoire"—and he adds, "De cette scène il a fait ce drame." The play, he admits, grew too large to be presented on the stage. Still, he insists that he has been faithful to the principles he has set forth. In the *Préface*, Cromwell is described in sublime and grotesque dimensions; in the play, however, Cromwell is set before us as a much more monotonous character, who does not expose the extremes of animal vs. spiritual nature. But the plot itself evokes the opposition of the sublime and the grotesque in the political struggle for worldly power between the rival religious factions. The grotesque is abundantly distributed throughout the play, most notably in the antics of Cromwell's quartet of jesters, the bungling of his son Richard, the prophecies of the necromancer Manesse, and the religious fanaticism of Carr.

As immediately becomes clear in the play, Hugo's sense of historical fidelity clearly has more to do with "la couleur locale" than with fidelity to fact, for *Cromwell* opens with a radical twist of history: The Cavaliers and the Roundheads are gathered together in a tavern conspiring to assassinate the Lord Protector. Cromwell, it is feared, aspires to have himself crowned king—a situation which might fit Napoleon more nearly than Cromwell.[36] The dialogue involves a delightful display of stylistic virtuosity. Hugo has the Cavaliers speak like the court poets of Louis XIV, while his Puritans quote the Bible like Huguenots and reason about Divine Will like eighteenth-century Deists or Mechanists. In act 3 the jesters sing demonic songs, and Lord Rochester (the Rochester of Dryden's day, not of Milton's) engages in a debate with Milton on the nature of poetry. The play also involves a complicated game of disguises. Rochester, the most zealous of the Cavaliers, pretends to be a devout Puritan come to serve Cromwell as personal chaplain. Learning of the plan to drug and kidnap him, Cromwell plays along with his "chaplain," drugs his would-be drugger, and re-disguises him as Cromwell. Cromwell then puts on the uniform of sentinel guarding his own gate and

---

36. Descotes, *L'Obsession de Napoléon dans le Cromwell de Victor Hugo*.

watches as the conspirators carry off the wrong victim.[37] The final grotesquery of act 4 is Rochester's confusion upon awakening: He thinks he has died and gone to Hell. The active use of stage setting, a factor to become more prominent in Hugo's dramaturgy, is effectively used in act 5. Carpenters are on stage building a platform, a platform to be used for a coronation—and an execution. The platform serves throughout act 5 as a major symbol for the rise and fall of rulers. The carpenters' macabre reflections are followed, first, by the Roundheads' threat to behead their leader should he go through with the coronation and, then, by Cromwell's trance-like reverie on royal power. He seems ready to mount the platform, but then comes to his senses and restores political order.

Just as illusion making becomes the subject as well as the object of the drama when Goethe takes us into Mephistopheles' world, so too in *Amy Robsart* (1822, first performed in 1828 at the Odéon) and *Les Jumeaux* (1839) Hugo brings his own illusionists onto the stage to perform their pranks. The comic characters in *Les Jumeaux*, for which Hugo completed only the first two acts, are the mountebank Guillot-Gorju and his accomplice Tagus. Hugo opens with a clever variation of the play-within-a-play. The curtain rises to reveal this comic pair, with a mysterious third man identically costumed to switch roles with Guillot-Gorju, setting up their stage, a mere rag hung from a pole, preparing their show of disguises, palm reading, and elixir hawking. The costumes, Hugo notes, are in the style of Callot's *commedia dell' arte* grotesques.

Much in the manner of Bruegel's painting of the huckster who fascinates his dupe with the shell game while his partner steals the dupe's purse,[38] Tagus the trickster also lets the audience witness a thief's skill in illusion making.

> Tagus: Peasant!—my master is a wizard so great that . . .
> (He points a finger to the air, as if to show him something
> far away in the clouds.)
> Do you see that bird?
> Bourgeois: (turning his head) No.
> Tagus: O well!

---

37. On Hugo's use of masks, disguises, and stage charlatanry, see Barrère, *La Fantasie de Victor Hugo*.
38. Stechow, *Pieter Bruegel, The Elder*, 56–59.

> My master, if he wishes, is going to guide his wings, rectilinear, oblique or parallel, through the sphere.
> (He takes the man's purse and puts it into one of his coat pockets.)
> Bourgeois: I don't see the bird.
> Tagus: Look. There! in the air!
> Bourgeois: (after having looked) No.
> Tagus: It is because you have bad eyes, my friend.[39]

This sort of exposé of cony catching may provoke our laughter to the extent that we feel ourselves in co-conspiracy with Tagus and superior to the simple bourgeois.[40] Still, the awareness that we are at the same time being taken in by the illusion of the stage itself may well unsettle our confidence and give an uncomfortable edge to our laughter. And we know that when Tagus pointed, we too searched the empty air above the stage.

The play-within-a-play and the stranger's acting the role of the mountebank keep the audience aware of the physical presence of the stage. The identical costumes of the stranger and the mountebank also deflect the anticipations aroused by the play's title. Hugo cleverly misleads, yet he also alerts his audience to a plot of intrigue in which things are not what they seem. At the same time, he controls the illusion of a street scene, gradually dimming the lights to suggest nightfall; as the scene darkens, a lamplighter

---

39. Hugo, *Les Jumeaux*, Act I:

> Tagus: Manant!—mon maître est un magicien
> Si grand, que . . .
> (Il dresse le doigt en l'air, comme pour lui désigner un objet éloigné dans les nuages.)
>   Voyez-vous cet oiseau?
> Le Bourgeois: (levant la tête)   Non.
> Tagus: Eh bien!
> Mon maître, s'il lui plaît, va lui diriger l'aile
> Selon la sphère droite, oblique ou parallèle.
> (Il prend la bourse du bourgeois dans une de pôches de son gilet.)
> Le Bourgeois: Je ne vois pas l'oiseau.
> Tagus: Regardez. Là! dans
> l'air!
> Le Bourgeois: (apres avoir regardée) Non.
> Tagus: C'est que vous avez de mauvais yeux, mon cher.

40. Bergson, "Le Rire. Essay sur la signification du comique," in *Oeuvres* 381–485; Chahine, *La Dramaturgie de Victor Hugo (1816–1843)*.

comes onstage and lights a streetlamp. Throughout the first act, Hugo makes theatricality and illusion making a major theme. We watch as Tagus assembles and dismantles the stage, and we hear the mountebank tell the secrets of his trade. All the while, Hugo is gradually unfolding the serious plot: The street charlatans are arrested by soldiers and are soon before the Queen. The stranger disguised as a mountebank reveals his identity as Jean, Comte de Créqui.

Hugo's fascination with light-in-darkness is evident in his design for the second act (Fig. 11). The stagefront gaslights have been dimmed; through the setting window to the rear, a limelight casts its sunlike beam:

> A very dark room, with a gothic vault and large stone plates on the floor, bright red velvet trimmed in gold on the walls, deep chairs with golden arms upholstered in tapestry; the whole aspect is sinister and magnificent. On the left, in a *pan coupé*, a wide bed, the hangings of red damask alternating with tapestry; the canopy supported by columns and a bed of sculpted gold; on the bed, a spread of rich lace. On the right, in the *pan coupé* of the corner opposite, a high fireplace, decorated with a *fleur de lys*. This plaque is so large that the entire rear of the fireplace is covered by it. Also on the right a table covered with a velvet cloth and standing upon a carpet of Gobelin tapestry. Upon the table, a Venetian mirror. Upon the bed, a large ivory Christ on an ebony cross; this Christ isn't a Jansenist one—that is to say, with outstretched arms. In a corner, to the right close to the table, part of the drapery is torn and exposes the bare stone wall, on which can be seen strange carved designs, A large nail has been tossed onto the table. The room receives light only through the long barred window in the rear which can be reached by three high stone steps. The ray of light passing through the window is clearly projected onto the pavement. The opening of the window reveals the enormous thickness of the walls.[41]

---

41. Hugo, *Les Jumeaux*, Act II, stage directions: "Une chambre très sombre à voûte ogive, pavée en larges dalles, tendue en velours écarlate à crépines d'or, meublée de grands fauteuils à bras doré et à dossiers de tapisserie; d'un aspect à la fois sinistre et magnifique. A gauche, dans un pan coupé, un large lit de damas rouge et de tapisserie alternés, à colonnes, à dais et à ched d'or sculpté, revêtu d'un riche couvre-pied de dentelle. A droite, dans un autre pan coupé, une haute cheminée, garnie de sa plaque fleurdelysée. Cette plaque est si grande qu'elle occupe entièrement le fond de la cheminée. A droite également, une table recouverte d'un tapis de velours et posée sur un tapis des Gobelins carré. Sur la table un miroir de Venise. Au-dessus du lit, un grand christ d'ivoire sur

The furnishings are similar to the "somptueuse et sombre" setting in *Ruy Blas*, act 4. When we discuss *Ruy Blas*, we shall point out how such details as the chimney and the Venetian mirror literally "play a role." The place, Hugo has said, should be a witness to the event ("un témoin terrible et inséparable"). The setting must thus reflect emotional atmosphere and personality. The setting to *Les Jumeaux*, act 2, carefully detailed in Hugo's design and description, serves as an apt psychological reflection of the Man in the Mask, as apt as the image in the mirror which he will study when he comes on stage.[42] The chiaroscuro effect of the back-lit stage is to be functionally used by the actor who paces in and out of the shadows and climbs the steps to peer through the barred window. Props—such as the nail on the table— are not incidental decorations: they become instruments of dramatic action. In spite of the stark contrast to the street-show setting in the opening, Hugo maintains thematic parallels: theatrical pretense, disguise, intrigue. Because Hugo has already established the pattern of concealed identity in act 1 ("L'Homme," who becomes Count Jean), the audience listens to the soliloquy of "Le Masque" for clues of the identity to be revealed.

In *Amy Robsart*, Hugo's grotesque villains are the conniving Varney, the evil sorcerer Alasco, and the sorcerer's apprentice Flibbertigibbet. The plot, which Hugo adapted from Scott's *Kenilworth*, involves the victimization of Amy, secretly married to Leicester, who is the favorite of Queen Elizabeth. Varney persuades Leicester to do away with Amy so that he can rise to power under the Queen's preferment. Hugo shows considerable dexterity in manipulating offstage strategies to counter that inept neoclassical use of the offstage that had prompted his frustrated complaint: "Vraiment! mais conduisez-nous donc là-bas! On s'y doit bien amuser, cela doit être beau à voir!" To be sure, Hugo teases his audience with exterior places that cannot be seen, but he uses his offstage space actively, not merely referentially.

In the opening act, Leicester looks out of the window at rear stage and comments on the cloudless sky beyond. Later, Amy throws a dagger out of the open window. The villain Varnery announces that the sorcerer "est

---

ébène, non janséniste, c'est-à-dire les bras étendus.—Dans un coin, à droite, près de la table, une partie de la tenture a été déchirée et laisse voir à nu la muraille, sur laquelle on distingue quelques dessins étranges gravés dans la pierre. Un grand clou est jeté sur la table.—La chambre ne reçoit de jour que par une longue fenêtre grillée qui est au fond et à laquelle on parvient par trois hautes marches de pierre. Le rayon de lumière qui passe par cette fenêtre vient se projeter visiblement sur le pavé. La baie de la fenêtre fait voir l'énorme épaisseur de la muraille."

42. Chancerel, "Victor Hugo, metteur en scène, décorateur et costumier."

enfermé là-haut dans la chambre secrète"; shortly thereafter, Alasco descends the staircase as if there were, in fact, a secret chamber somewhere "upstairs" above the stage. These simple gestures of interaction with the stage setting contribute greatly to enhancing the illusion and extending the boundaries of confined place. The conclusion exhibits a stunning reversal of that moral nicety which advocated all bloodshedding be relegated to offstage. At first, Hugo seems in conformity, for poor Amy is sent by Varney and Alasco, who pretend to help her escape, out to a passageway with a false staircase. As soon as she puts her weight on the first step it will fall open and she will plunge to her death. Amy steps through the door; from offstage the audience hears "un grand bruit, pareil à la chute d'un madrier pesant" (in Scott's *Kenilworth:* "the door of the countess' chamber opened, and in the same moment the trap door gave way. There was a rushing sound—a heavy fall—a faint groan, and all was over"). But then Hugo defies the guardians of "la dignité" of French theater. With the death of his heroine, he left the violence (except for the sound effects) to the imagination. The villains, however, perish painfully on stage. In Scott's novel, the conspirators die later, one poisoned, another jailed, a third starved. Hugo burns them alive in a fiery finale in the style of Pixérécourt's *Marguerite d'Anjou.*[43]

It may seem foolish to make so much of Hugo's ingenious stagecraft in *Amy Robsart,* for in spite of his collaboration with Delacroix, who assisted with costumes and settings, the play failed on opening night. Its grotesque elements were too erratic, its hero too weak, its development too shallow and melodramatic to do justice to Scott's narrative. Nevertheless, Hugo had obviously learned much from his experimentation with stage effects, and he continued to exercise the possibilities of character interaction with setting. In *Marie Tudor* (act 1), a stone breaks a pane of glass in the window and falls near the Queen. In *Lucrèce Borgia* (act 2,) the impulsive Gennaro, enraged over the wickedness of this infamous family, crosses the stage (set as the Grand Square of Ferrare, with the Borgia Palace on the right), leaps onto the stone steps to reach the latticed balcony, and with his dagger hacks at the large stone escutcheon; from the golden-lettered *BORGIA* upon the white

43. Hugo, *Amy Robsart*, in *Oeuvres Dramatiques et Critiques Complètes*, 130–31: "On entend tout à coup un bruit affrueux derrière la porte masquée, elle s'ouvre avec violence, une lueur rouge et tremblante s'en échappe ... La lueur devient de plus en plus ardente. On entend au dehors comme un sifflement de flammes.... L'incendie fait des progrès, les flammes arrivent par la porte masquée, le toit se crèvasse, le mur se lézarde, une pluie de feu commence à tomber du faite de la tour.... Il diparaît par une crévasse du toit qui s'écroule et ensevelit Varney et Alasco."

marble he removes the first letter, leaving the savage pun *ORGIA* to mark their domain.

Hugo's play with sound effects also contributes to his dramatic conjuring. He uses sound to heighten suspense and to enhance the illusion of offstage action. In *Amy Robsart*, Hugo's directions call for the repeated punctuation of events throughout the play by the clang of an iron door being closed offstage; act 5 adds the sound of Amy's plunge to death. In the opening scene of *Les Jumeaux*, Guillot-Gorju points to the back of the square and announces that three knocks will be heard in "ce coin noir." The signal, of course, is later heard. Probably the most stunning instance is the sound of the horn in *Hernani*.

The "battle" at the first performance of *Hernani* at the Comédie français in 1830 is famous as the grand confrontation between the Romanticists and the Neoclassicists. The play must be seen as an ideological statement as well as a Romantic play. Although Don Carlos rises above the kind of follies in which we see him through the first three acts, Hugo has nevertheless portrayed a rather foolish king. In the very opening scene we watch as he hides in a closet, where he stays for a good part of act 1. Worse, in his amorous pursuit he is challenged by a bandit who makes a much more heroic impression than the king. The plot is the rivalry between Don Carlos, Don Ruy Gomez, and Hernani for the love of Dona Sol. The first three acts, respectively entitled "Le roi," "Le bandit," and "Le viellard," ring the changes on the rivalry. The first act is set in her chambers, the second in Saragossa, the third in the grand gallery of the de Silva castle in Aragon. Each act involves concealment and turns upon a confrontation that is resolved only by the appeal to honor.

In act 2, Hugo has the King disguise himself as the bandit in order to meet with Dona Sol, whom he then tries to abduct. Hernani intervenes, but spares Don Carlos's life (Fig. 12). The setting is a conventional street scene; Hugo, however, creates an effective illusion of depth and distance with the street rounding the building on the left, the recessed passage right rear, and Dona Sol's elevated balcony above the patio to the right. The darkened stage is illuminated with unseen "street lamps" in the recesses and light shining through the façade windows. Tricked by the disguised Don Carlos, Dona Sol descends from the balcony to the street where the confrontation occurs. The setting for act 3 is a gallery. Don Ruy Gomez addresses the portraits of his forebears as images of his own identity. With old age upon him, he transforms his responsibility to tradition and the family line into a justification for taking his young and beautiful ward, his niece, as his bride. He calls upon them for judgment of Hernani, who in a subsequent scene, adds a dimension of irony to the proud exhibition of noble lineage, by hiding in a secret chamber behind one of the portraits. The planned wedding is disrupted first by Hernani and then by Don Carlos, who this time succeeds in abducting Dona Sol. Hernani acknowledges that his life is forfeit because of his trespass, and he gives his horn to Don Ruy, pledging to kill himself upon hearing the horn blown. He asks to live only until he has killed the abductor.

Act 4 is set in the torch-lit tomb of Charlemagne. Here Don Carlos, in a manner contrasting to Don Ruy Gomez, calls upon the tradition of the past, the spirit of Charlemagne, to give him wisdom and guidance as he assumes the crown. When he discovers Don Ruy and Hernani hiding in the underground labyrinth, he reveals his new strength and confidence in pardoning the assassins and restoring to Hernani his nobility and estate. The final act, which opens with the marriage celebration of Hernani and Dona Sol, teases the audience with the illusion of a "happy ending," for the marriage, of course, is immediately blighted by the sound of the horn. The appearance of Don Ruy as the harbinger of death in the final scene of *Hernani* (Fig. 13) was the signal for the outbreak of battle at the first performance (Fig. 14).

Although it is merely a hasty sketch (Fig. 15), Hugo's stage design for *Le Roi s'amuse* (1832) reveals how thoroughly and profoundly he could incorporate his principle of opposition into the very setting of the dramatic action. As we have seen, Goethe kept the three worlds of Faust, Mephistopheles, and Gretchen separate and demonstrated their interaction through such visual devices as the demonic apparitions in Faust's study or the vision of Gretchen atop the Blocksberg. Hugo, however, divides his stage into two opposing worlds. As his sketch reveals, the right half of the stage front opens into a tree lined street that turns and runs along the full back stage, which is lined with houses. Hugo has sketched in the rooftops of many houses and several doors opening onto the street. Thrusting high above the rooftops is the tower (yes, it is phallic) of the King's castle. Below, stage left, is the enclosed garden and chateau of Triboulet and his daughter Blanche. While the walls seem to protect the privacy of the garden, one door in the upper right corner opens onto the public street. Through this door comes Triboulet, having met with the mercenary cutthroat Saltabadil; through this door comes the King, eager to claim the virginity of Triboulet's daughter.

Because *Le Roi s'amuse* is well known through Piavi's adaptation for Verdi's *Rigoletto*, it may help our understanding of Hugo's stagecraft to stress the two crucial differences between the play and the opera. First, in the opera, the Duke turns into a decent fellow who seems actually to fall in love with the innocent girl whom he has seduced; in the play, the King remains an ever-lusting womaniser who quickly forgets his last conquest in pursuit of the next. Second, in the opera, Rigoletto is only indirectly guilty of his daughter's death; in the play, Tribolet himself, albeit not knowing her identity, kills her. Although Piavi made other changes (he omits, for example, Hugo's poet, Clément Marot), these two significantly alter the dramatic tensions which Hugo had developed with his divided stage.

In terms of Hugo's body-soul dualism, only Blanche is sublime; all the other characters are grotesques. But as Hugo observed: "Le beau n'a qu'un type; le laid en a mille." The manifold forms of the ugly are set forth in pairs with a studied sense of contrast and opposition. The King ought to possess the virtues of royal dignity and authority, but he is haughty and cruel, perverting his power to demean his courtiers, exploit his subjects, and gratify his sexual whims. If the King had a conscience, it would no doubt look and speak very much like Triboulet, deformed in mind and body. His sole power in court is his quick and cunning wit, and he uses it to make jests of the courtiers whose wives and daughters have been seduced by the King. Triboulet has one redeeming virtue, his devoted and doting love for his daughter. Just as Triboulet is set in counterpart to his King, so too he stands in contrast to Saltabadil, who is a skillful opportunist at court, but more murderous and greedy than any of the sordid crowd in the street surrounding the garden of innocent Blanche. Triboulet's weapon is "une langue acérée," Saltabadil's "une lame pointue." Finally there is the seductive Maguelonne, sister of Saltabadil, as much of a mercenary opportunist as her brother, but whose trade is in arousing desires rather than in cutting throats. And she, of course, stands in contrast to the pure and innocent Blanche. All of Hugo's carefully schemed duality and opposition is brought into conflict at the walls that divide his stage in act 2.

While his two contrasting worlds appeared only in alternate scenes, or remained hidden, or offstage in *Amy Robsart* and *Hernani*, Hugo brings them both onto the stage at the same time in *Le Roi s'amuse*. The Edenic garden is penetrated by the snake, for mere garden walls cannot protect virtue from vice. Revenge and lust both enter through the garden door, and the masses soon storm the sanctuary. As act 2 draws to a close, Triboulet lends his hand to what he presumes is another affair with a lady at court. He thus unwittingly sanctions the seduction of his daughter. The first act displays Triboulet as the perverted wit, whose taunting brings down the wrathful curse of the humiliated courtier Saint-Vallier. By the end of the second act, Saint-Vallier's curse begins to be fulfilled. Triboulet's wit gives way to rage, and he utters his own passionate curse of revenge. Acts 1 and 3 take place in the court and the King's chambers. In Acts 4 and 5, Hugo provides another variation on the divided set. Here the stage has a river and Saltabadil's hideaway with two rooms. The divided stage no longer represents the fragile protection of virtue against vice, but rather the complications of revenge, duplicity, and deceit. Just as the action goes on simultaneously on both sides of the garden wall in act 2, in act 4 we watch what is going on outside as well as inside the hovel, and upstairs as well as downstairs. The characters in one room are being exposed or betrayed by those in the other room: we witness the King's passion for coldhearted sexual gratification, Saltabadil's for coldblooded murder, Triboulet's for revenge, Maguellone's for opportunistic coquetry, and, still in sublime contrast to them all, Blanche's for saintly goodness in her martyr's death. Here, again, *Le Roi s'amuse* avoids the sentimentality of the opera version: the King remains an unmitigated scoundrel and the Father must recognize his own part in the viciousness that destroyed virtue.

Hugo's stage design for *Ruy Blas* (1838), act 1, represents Le Salon de Danaé in the Royal Palace of Madrid (Fig. 16). Hugo describes the setting:

> To the left, a large window with a golden frame and small panes. On both sides, in a *pan coupé*, a low door leading to some interior apartment. At the rear, a huge dividing partition, made of glass, opens onto a long gallery. This gallery, which crosses the entire theater, is hidden by immense curtains which hang from top to bottom of the glass partition. A table, an armchair, and writing materials.[44]

By the end of this first act, Hugo will have fully exploited every dimension of his stage design, with a grand opening up of space when the long gallery is

---

44. Hugo, *Ruy Blas*, Act I, stage directions: "A gauche, une grande fenêtre à châssis doré et à petits carreaux. Des deux côtés, sur un pan coupé, une porte basse donnant dans quelque appartement intérieur. Au fond, une grande cloison vitrée à châssis dorés s'ouvrant par une large porte également vitrée sur une longue galerie. Cette galerie, qui traverse tout le théâtre, est masquée par d'immenses rideaux qui tombent du haut en bas de la cloison vitrée. Un table, un fauteuil, et ce qu'il faut pour écrire."

exposed to view and the audience beholds the arrival of the Queen. As the curtain rises, Don Salluste enters through the small door on the left, followed by Gudiel and Ruy Blas, who carry parcels for Don Salluste's departure. With the very opening lines, Hugo begins to make use of this sumptuous and complex setting. Don Salluste commands his servant, Ruy Blas, to close the door and open the window. In telling contrast to the opening scene of *Amy Robsart*, where first Leicester and then Amy are much occupied with exploring the offstage world beyond the windows, Don Salluste discovers nothing of interest outside the palace: "Ils dorment encor tous ici—le jour va naître." He then launches his long introspective account of his fall from power because he has refused to obey the Queen's order for him to marry the chambermaid whom he has seduced. He seeks revenge against the Queen.

Don Salluste's opening command not only engages Ruy Blas in direct interaction with the setting, it also establishes the master-servant relationship. The master will command his servant to sit at the table and write a love letter, signing it Don César, as well as a personal statement of his service as a lackey, signing it Ruy Blas. The master will then order him to discard his livery and put on the clothes of a nobleman. To each count and marquis who then arrive in the salon, Ruy Blas is introduced as Don Salluste's cousin, Don César. Finally, when the Queen's entourage passes through the long gallery, the master gives a closing command: Charm that woman and be her lover.

While Don Salluste's revenge plot—to gain power over the Queen by revealing that her lover is a mere servant (neatly reversing his own disgrace over an affair with a chambermaid)—is perfectly transparent to the audience, Ruy Blas realizes the consequences of his assumed role only when he sees the Queen threatened. Act 2 begins in the Queen's chambers. Here again, the windows and doors give us no access to an outside world. As with the many doors in the opening scene, this setting is also thematically revealing precisely because the windows and doors offer no escape. Every room in *Ruy Blas* is a prison cell, and even the Queen is a prisoner in her sumptuous chambers. In act 3, we see Ruy Blas wielding power in court as the favorite of the Queen (another point to compare with *Amy Robsart*); when alone with Don Salluste, however, we see poor Ruy Blas once again opening and closing windows.

Even while the tensions are mounting, the audience is amused by the caprices of the real Don César, a more carefully wrought grotesque character than we find in any of the other plays. Upon his surprise visit to his cousin in act 1, Hugo emphasizes the contrast between his rough manners and tattered costume and the elegant grandeur of the palace. Ruy Blas recognizes him as an old friend, and, not knowing that he is a renegade nobleman who has squandered his fortune, greets him as a brother and a man of the people. To this friend, Ruy Blas confesses his hopeless love for the Queen, a confession which Don Salluste then puts to use. In act 4, Don César arrives at Don Salluste's house and almost succeeds in destroying the villainous plot. The scene provides a sustained example of Hugo's technique of building illusion out of a character's interaction with setting. The would-be hero enters by climbing out of the fireplace (he has slid down the chimney). He puts on the fine clothes that are set out, admires his reflection in the mirror, eats the meal that he finds on the table, and commands an entire solo scene, talking to himself and to the furnishings of the room. This scene ironically replicates the scene of Ruy Blas's putting on courtly dress in act 1. The renegade ruffian of the streets now wears the garb of his true identity. Not only Ruy Blas is costumed as Don César, so too is Don César. The comedy of errors begins when a page enters, addresses him, to his surprise, as Don César. In rapid succession he is offered quantities of gold and silver by attending lackeys, which he greedily accepts; then a duenna tells him that "Une dame / Reçoit un rendez-vous de l'ami son âme" and asks him to sign a billet doux, which he gladly signs; next he is challenged by Don Guritan, whom he kills in a duel. When Don Salluste arrives, Don César gloats at having disrupted his cousin's plan to expose a rendezvous between a commoner and the Queen. He calls the Alcade and the guards to take away the banished Don Salluste. The villain, however, is not so easily foiled. He tells the Alcade that his accuser is an impostor and a thief, not the real Don César at all. The clothing that he wears is embroidered, of course, with Don Salluste's name. And no witness will recognize him as the Don César whom they have seen at the palace.

Act 4 is a clever reversal of disguise, but its only purpose is to exhibit the grotesque comedy of Don César. The dramatic resolution has only been delayed. The events of act 5 are swift. Don Salluste has the Queen in his trap. As he savors his revenge in revealing the true identity of her lover and announcing that she is disgraced and banished from the throne, he is confronted by Ruy Blas (Fig. 17), who challenges him with vehement understatement: "Je crois que vous venez d'insulter votre reine!" He assumes his right to duel as a gentleman, not as a mock-nobleman. Precisely because of

Ruy Blas's insistence upon the decorum of the duel, it is fought according to neoclassical rules—offstage. Don Salluste is killed. In the final scene, asking the Queen's pardon for having deceived her, Ruy Blas drinks poison.

Hugo was much taken with the bleak panorama of ruined castles he saw on his trip along the Rhine with his mistress, Juliette Drouet. His principle of enhancing the real with the imaginary to attain aesthetic truth is evident in the union of the historical with the mythic past in his sketch of "Le Burg à la Croise" (Fig. 18), which depicts Hugo's vision of a former unity between the Church and the feudal barons; a turreted wall joins castle and cathedral. In *Les Burgraves* (1843) Hugo constructs his own imaginative account of the dissipation of an heroic age following the reign of Kaiser Frederick Barbarossa. The play opens upon a scene in the ancient gallery of the Castle Heppenheff (Fig. 19). We have already observed in *Hernani* an example of Hugo's use of the portrait gallery as a stage device to develop interaction between character and setting. But the first glimpse into this gallery gives the audience an unsettling foreboding: the frescoes high along the walls may reveal scenes of valor and victory, but below all the portraits have been turned to face the wall. Hugo's stage directions reveal that a second level is built into the colonnade under the roman arches at the rear of the stage. The gallery is built around the tower on the right. The door to the tower leads into the dungeon. Along the left wall, under the mural, is a grand door and a small window through which a beam of light illuminates the shadowy stage. The vacant throne facing the audience from the proscenium is an apt symbol of the fall from empire. The gallery, Hugo adds, should appear "délabré et inhabité."

As the curtain rises, a ceremonial procession is seen: "La partie du château qu'on aperçoit par les archivoltes du promenoir au fond du théâtre semble éclairée et illuminée à l'intérieur, quoiqu'il fasse encore grand jour. On entend venir de ce côté du burg un bruit de trompettes et de clairons, et par moments des chansons chantées à pleine voix au cliquetis des verres." Men in chains follow at the rear of the procession. This remarkable assembly continues to be heard offstage, as an aged crone, dressed in tatters and chains, steps to the center of the stage. Guanhumara's opening vow of revenge against the princess expresses an epic conflict that has endured through three generations and which is dramatically contained in this three-act play. Once a ravishing Corsican beauty, she is now the personification of an abiding hate ("cette esclave est la haine!") resulting from the jealous conflict in which Job attempted to murder both her and his ward, who was in fact his younger brother. The enmity then fostered years of war as the brother, Frederick Barbarossa, becomes emperor, and Job rallies the burgraves to rebellion.

In the first act, Guanhumara offers a potion to save the life of Otbert's beloved Regina, for which Otbert must pledge to murder Fosco. Unknown to Otbert, Fosco is Job, and Job is his father. The act closes with the return of Frederick, who has been wandering as a beggar doing penance for having desecrated the tomb of Charlemagne. The plotted patricide in the present reenacts the attempted fratricide of the past. In both cases the identity of the victim is unknown, and both crimes take place in the dungeon vault, "humide et hideux," the setting of the final act. Here, Job and Frederick and Guanhumara are reconciled, and the latter act to prevent Otbert from killing Job. Otbert is then revealed to be Yorghi, the long-lost son and heir to the empire. The complexity of concealed and revealed identities (Guanhumara was once the Corsican maiden Ginevra; Job has taken the name Fosco; Frederick is the beggar Donato; Otbert is the long-lost Yorghi) functions as more than a mere artifice of plot. Each of the two names has its own epoch in this ancient conflict; the names, that is, designate periods of time during which a character had assumed one or the other identity.

The nature of *Les Burgraves*, as critics have pointed out, is epic rather than dramatic.[45] It failed on its first performance in 1843, yet it is a far different sort of failure than *Amy Robsart*. In the late play, no less than in the early one, he has persisted in experimenting with ways to extend the boundaries of the stage. The early play failed not because of the experimentation but because of shallow characterization and inept development of plot. The late play may succeed as literary accomplishment, but fails on the stage precisely because the experimentation has exceeded the possibilities of theater performance. The epic sweep is too vast. Hugo said in his *Préface de les Burgraves* that he saw in this story the mythic conflict of the Titans and Olympians, of Cain and Abel. His dramatic characters are intended to be mythic giants, and the great conflicts of the past are supposed to be contained within the present action.

The problem remains that the events of the mythic past, which are more interesting than those of the degenerate present, are narrated rather than acted. Bound, then, to extensive narrative dialogue, Hugo has reasserted dramatic tension by ironically undermining the narrators. As one character

---

45. Affron, 62–82; Houston, *Victor Hugo*, 64–66.

tells a fragmentary tale of past rivalries and battles, other characters scoff and deny the credibility of the story. The slave Hermann assumes the role of cynical disbeliever in the legend of Frederick and Job, while Guanhumara prowls the stage as living testimony of its truth. Illusion resides in the awful past that is made to haunt the present.

In *Faust*, Goethe radically departed from the neoclassical form he adhered to in *Clavigo* and *Iphigenie auf Tauris*. In taking his material from a folk tradition fraught with magic and occult lore, he sought to recreate on the stage, not a reality shackled by the norms of verisimilitude and probability, nor even a world overwhelmed by superstition and the supernatural, but a world experienced by ambitious, passionate, and self-divided man (Faust: "Two souls dwell, alas, within by breast"). Hugo, similarly, dramatized the sublime and the grotesque of man's body-soul dualism. His prime concern in all his plays was to free the stage of the mimetic constraints, to infuse the real with the imaginative, to turn false "unity" into the tension and opposition of human experience, and to enhance stage illusion through dynamic interaction and intimacy between character and place, between the stage and the physical world.

7

Illusion and Metadrama: Coleridge and Tieck

While the lack of significant drama in England during the Romantic period is usually attributed to the public clamor for melodrama and spectacle, the fact remains that all of the major poets—Blake, Wordsworth, Coleridge, Byron, Shelley, Keats—attempted, at least experimentally, to write plays. Several of Byron's plays were later staged by Macready, who made *Werner* a regular part of his repertory. Shelley's *The Cenci*, which attracted attention in *fin de siècle* theater and in Artaud's Theater of Cruelty, has also been revived in three major twentieth-century productions.[1] Only Coleridge, however, was successfully staged in his own day. The 1813 performance of *Remorse*, in spite of the weak performance of Rae in Ordonio, brought welcome applause and financial reward to the poet.[2] The irony that his audience probably enjoyed it for all the wrong reasons could not have diminished his delight in the lucrative run of twenty performances. He would, to be sure, have been fully aware of ironic disparity between his dramatic theme and the popular response, for in his public

---

1. Cave, "Romantic Drama in Performance."
2. To Sara Coleridge, January 1813, *Collected Letters of Samuel Taylor Coleridge* III, 430–31.

lectures he had already denounced the superficial fascination with sensational effects and the failure to attend to the subtler appeals of the imagination.[3]

The turning point in the plot is provided by a spectacular scene in the third act. Accompanied by eerie music and incantational song, a sorcerer conjures before an altar in a darkened alcove—already a stock scene in 1719 when Abbé Du Bos gave examples of stage spectacles and the artifices of illusion.[4] Coleridge adds a new and stunning surprise: the smoldering incense suddenly blazes with a bright phosphorous flash illuminating above the altar the painting of an assassination. This is certainly the sort of trickery that many in the audience had paid their money to see. Coleridge, however, has constructed the scene as an ironic reversal of the villain's stratagem to overwhelm his victim with delusion. The intended victim grows disgusted with the mystical mockery and walks out before this *coup de théâtre* occurs. What is more, the hero whispers to her on her way out that she is right to reject such mawkish displays. Not delusion (the surrender of reason to emotional sensations) but illusion ("the willing suspension of disbelief") is the proper engagement of the imagination thematically endorsed and dramatized in *Remorse*.

It is this metadramatic exploitation and repudiation of stage trickery that Coleridge shares with Tieck. In the last chapter, we observed how both Goethe and Hugo sought to elaborate and refine the interaction between character and stage setting. Coleridge and Tieck, as we shall see in the present chapter, ironically undermine their own stunning stage effects. In Coleridge's *Remorse*, the phosphorescent explosion upon the wizard's altar is deliberately exposed as hoax yet has its dramatic effect when its intended purpose "backfires" upon the villain. In Tieck's *Der gestiefelte Kater*, the fictive audience cannot comprehend the metadramatic play with illusion but are utterly dazzled by the elaborate setting "borrowed" from *The Magic Flute*. While it is certainly not irrelevant that both Tieck and Coleridge studied the attributes of illusion in Shakespeare's drama, these two plays have very little in common beyond their peculiar irony in ridiculing the stage apparatus. They both respond, however, to the prevailing rivalry between the aesthetics and mechanics of illusion. Picking up on that rivalry, described above in Goethe's *Triumph of Sensibility* and the "Prelude in the

---

3. Coleridge, *Lectures 1808–1819: On Literature*, in *The Collected Works of Samuel Taylor Coleridge* I, 563; *Letters* IV, 720.

4. Du Bos, "Que le plaisir que nous avons au Théâtre n'est point produit par l'illusion" (section 43), *Réflexions critiques sur la poésie et sur la peinture*, 451–57.

Theater" to his *Faust*, the present chapter will review Arnim's reply to Brentano's denunciation of stage decorations and will conclude with a few words on the conflicting sources of illusion as thematic and dramatic issues in Kleist, Byron, and Shelley.

Charles Lamb's prologue for Coleridge's *Remorse* closes with a contrast between Shakespeare's barren stage and the decorated stage of "a more liberal age." While Coleridge has the benefit of the "painted scene," Lamb still prizes the setting "seen only by the intellectual eye." For Coleridge's play, too, the illusion provided by the mind's eye is clearly intended to dominate. Indeed, the power of illusion secured by volitional control of the imagination is a major concern of Coleridge's tragedy, for this is the power that sustains Teresa's love and the power that mediates Ordonio's repentance. At odds with illusion, of course, is delusion. Those who lack volitional control over their own fancy fail to comprehend the rational clarity of perception of those who do. The crucial difference is established in the opening scenes and the contest between the two continues to provide dramatic tension throughout the play.

Only twice in the play does Coleridge deliberately exploit the "painted scene." For most scenes he offers only brief indications for setting. The altar scene, of course, requires elaborate attention. The cave scene (act 4) also involves detailed interaction with the setting, for he develops suspense and anticipation through character response to physical place—moonlight breaking through a crevice, the deep abyss, dark recesses. Irony is derived from confusions of what is seen, imagined, and not seen. In the next scene, however, all he needs is the image of a dungeon gate—it does not matter whether the stage props show us a Gothic or a Saracenic Castle. The opening scene is supposed to represent the coast of Granada. How that scene is viewed has virtually nothing to do with the props. It is all in the mind of the beholder.

As Alvar steps onto his native shore after six years' absence, how he "sees" depends upon rational discrimination and volitional control of the emotions. In order to behold with "filial awe" the "land of my fathers," he must will to "forget my anguish and their crimes" (2–9). In this opening scene, Alvar declares to Zulimez his plan to sway his brother to remorse, rather than to seek revenge (19). Alvar himself at this moment, however, lacks full control over his thoughts. His abiding vision of Teresa's love has been undermined by his brother's lie. Coleridge shows him wavering between doubt and faith, his image of Teresa's innocence

(54–59)[5] disrupted by the tale of her "perfidy" (38). Donning his disguise as Moor, Alvar declares that the report of his death will sustain the illusion:

> And what the mind believes impossible,
> The bodily sense is slow to recognize.
> (108–9)

Teresa's actions, in scene 2, refute this formula. The false report of Alvar's death is what her "mind believes impossible," yet her "bodily sense" is very much alert. As Alvar has stated it, the mind has succumbed to a false report; relying on her own instincts, Teresa rejects what is false. Himself the victim of deception, Valdez consequently must consider Teresa "the victim of a useless constancy" (17). The situation distinguishes between illusion, willfully conjured, and delusion, which overwhelms the reason. Teresa thus embodies the problem of imaginatively informed vs. pathologically perverted perception. She begins by describing her capacity "To shape sweet visions, and live o'er again / All past hours of delight" (24–25); but her illusions are not merely memories, for she is also able to invent new meetings with Alvar, "to frame adventures / Most terrible and strange, and hear him tell them" (28–29). Coleridge's note on Valdez's response to this latter state of imagination is inserted here.

> Stage direction (MS note to 1st edition): "Here Valdez bends back, with a smile of *wonder* at the witness of the Fancy, which Teresa noting, she checks her enthusiasm, and in a persuasive half-pleading tone and action exemplifies her meaning in the little Tale included in the Parenthesis."[6]

Teresa then offers, as an example contrasting to her visions, a tale of actual delusion; "a crazy Moorish maid / Who drest her in her buried lover's

---

5. Coleridge, "To William Wordsworth," in *Complete Poetical Works* I, 403–5. Coleridge borrowed these lines (54–55), which refer to the blighted hope of the French Revolution "summoned homeward" to strengthen "man's absolute self." In the play, Teresa has taken the place of Hope as "The Angel of Vision." Coleridge acknowledged the self-plagiarism in his manuscript note: "May not a man, without breach of the 8th Commandment, take out of his left pocket and put into his right?"

6. Coleridge's manuscript note was revised and printed in the second and third editions (1829). Stage direction: "Here Valdez bends back, and smiles at her wildness, which Teresa noticing, checks her enthusiasm, and in a soothing half-playful tone and manner, apologizes for her fancy, by the little tale in parenthesis."

clothes," (30–31) and played upon the lute "the selfsame tune / He used to play, and listened to the shadow / Herself had made" (33–35).[7] When she goes on to tell of her own experience, Teresa emphasizes the full consciousness and control she exercises over her thoughts. To marry Ordonio, and then to confront Alvar upon his return, provokes a thought of horrid shame: "Oh what a thought!" Valdez, who has no comprehension of Teresa's capacity to reason with visual images, declares her "thought" irrational and meaningless. "A thought? even so! mere thought! an empty thought!" (50). Once again, illusion is condemned as delusion.

In the next scene, Monviedro, the Inquisitor who is zealously devoted to persecuting the Moors, arrives with Alhadra. She has identified Ordonio as witness to her husband's Christian faith. At the mention of Isidore's name, Ordonio is startled and mentally unsettled. Monviedro, whose business as interrogator makes him alert to signs of guilt, observes Ordonio's response: "What, is he ill, my Lord? how strange he looks!" (143) "The drops did start and stand upon his forehead!" (151). Aware that Isidore could testify against him if he were taken prisoner and tortured, Ordonio hatches a plot to do away with the unwanted witness to his guilt. Alhadra's survival instincts also make her, no less than Monviedro, an alert reader of character. She observes Ordonio's inward turmoil and declines his "hospitality."

Left alone with Teresa, Alhadra begins to seethe in her angry lust for revenge. The dramatic "action" exists only in the dialogical opposition between Alhadra's wishful "vision" of herself pushing Monviedro off a cliff, and Teresa's gentle plea for compassion even to one's enemies. Alhadra tells the tale of her imprisonment. When Teresa, experiencing the horror of the tale, responds: "O Heaven! it is too horrible to hear," Alhadra contrasts the imaginative experience of the listener with the real experience of the teller: "What was it then to suffer?" We here see for the second time, Coleridge turning to a narrative mode, yet sustaining a dramatic relationship between storyteller and listener.

The storytelling device is used a third time in Teresa's interview with Alvar (disguised as a "Moresco chieftain"). When he mentions his "frightful dream," Teresa defines dream as memory (past), but also acknowledges dream as prophecy (future). Alvar, seeking to test her, equates dream experience with the guilty conscience: "The Past lives o'er again / In its effects,

---

7. Cf. "Constancy to an Ideal Object" and "Phantom and Fact," in Coleridge, *Complete Poetical Works*.

and to the guilty spirit / The ever-frowning Present is its image" (274–76). As he tells his dream of being betrayed by his friend and his beloved, she again enters into the telling and seems "lost in thought." She explains that "From morn to night, I am myself a dreamer, / And slight things bring on me the idle mood" (292–93). Alvar concludes his "dream" with an account of his prayer for "remorse." Here, Alhadra cannot understand that he has not dreamt of revenge. Teresa, however, perceives the dream as similar to her own: "My soul is full of visions all as wild" (321). She senses in his presence some hauntingly familiar, yet unrecognized, image. She confesses that her own dreaming now "tricks" her perception:

> Your mien is noble, and, I own, perplexed me
> With obscure memory of something past,
> Which still escaped my efforts, or presented
> Tricks of fancy pampered with long wishing.
> (325–28)

Act 2 opens in "Wild mountainous country, near Isidore's house." The storytelling is used again, but here it is in the context of conspiracy, and Ordonio must assure himself that the scene is "secured from listeners" and safe from an audience of listening spies. This denial of audience puts the audience in the theater in a paradoxical position, for the spectators in the audience are asked to play at nonexistence. Ordonio wants Isidore to disguise himself and act a role, giving Teresa "proof" (the miniature portrait) that Alvar is dead. Ordonio describes the necessary posturing to "play the sorcerer":

> Why, you can utter with a solemn gesture
> Oracular sentences of deep no-meaning,
> Wear a quaint garment, make mysterious antics.
> (30–32)

As opposed to a "willing suspension of disbelief," this dramatic ploy is supposed to bring firm belief. Ordonio has mistaken Teresa's reveries as a superstitious indulgence of occult "nonsense":

> Yet still a tale of spirits works upon her.
> She is a lone enthusiast, sensitive,
> Shivers, and cannot keep the tears in her eye:
> And such do love the marvelous too well

> Not to believe it. We will wind up her fancy
> With a strange music, that she knows not of—
> With fume of frankincense, and mummery,
> Then leave, as one sure token of his death,
> That portrait, which from off the dead man's neck
> I bade thee take, the trophy of thy conquest.
> (37–46)

In his plot to use the playacting to delude Teresa, Ordonio endorses a theory of theatrical illusion that is counter to Coleridge's. Ordonio goes on to reveal how he learned the secret of the miniature portrait. As an eavesdropping "audience," he spied upon the lovers in their farewell tryst. Isidore now learns, for the first time, that the man whom Ordonio had ordered him to kill was Ordonio's own brother. When Isidore refuses to take part in the plot, Ordonio dismisses the qualms of conscience as the illusion of virtue: "A gust of the soul! i'faith it overset me. O 'twas all folly!—all! idle as laughter!" (134–35). Isidore tells of the wizard who came to the ruins to pick strange herbs by moonlight and, when accosted by agents of the Inquisitor ("whose spies / Lurk everywhere"), told them to tell Ordonio that he had the power to "bring the dead to life again" (163). As Ordonio departs to seek the wizard, he suddenly halts and points offstage: "Who lurks there! Have we been overheard?" An audience has listened after all. Isidore assures him, however, that the audience is only a poor witless "idiot boy."

Alhadra and Alvar meet in Isidore's cottage (II.ii). Suspicious of Alvar's disguise, she calls upon him to serve as leader "If what thou seem'st thou art." Borrowing from the Bible the image of "through a glass darkly" and from Shakespeare the conceit on anamorphic art,[8] Coleridge has Alvar answer that for the present, "Time . . . still unrolls / The volume of concealment," but in the future all will be revealed:

> As in the optician's glassy cylinder,
> The indistinguishable blots and colours
> Of the dim past collect and shape themselves,
> Upstarting in their own completed image
> To scare or to reward.
> (11–15)

---

8. 1 Corinthians 13:12; *Richard II*, II.ii. 18–20: "Like perspectives, which rightly gazed upon / Show nothing but confusion, ey'd awry / Distinguish form."

The visual imagery continues, as Zulimez tells the story of Alvar as an artist. From the text of the play, Coleridge deleted twenty-eight lines on Alvar's painting of the assassination, but he preserved the passage in a note to the second and subsequent editions. The five lines substituted in the text merely confirm the power of the artist to conjure illusion: "You can call up past deeds, and make them live / On the blank canvas" (43–44). The deleted lines tell of Alvar's schooling under "that divine old man, / . . . the famous Titian!" Here, Titian is the mighty conjurer, who "changed the blank canvas to a magic mirror, / That made the absent present; and to shadows / Gave light, depth, substance, bloom, yea, thought and motion." Alvar is the diligent pupil who learns to bring to canvas the awful images of his assassins: "So vivid were the forms within his brain, / His very eyes, when shut, made pictures of them."[9]

After Alhadra's departure, Ordonio enters the hut and challenges the wizard to fulfill his boast "to bring the dead to life again." Ordonio sees the Moorish wizard as a clever charlatan, and he convinces him to play the conjuror's part that Isidore had refused. Again, Ordonio describes the theatrics for deluding Teresa. Alvar now has the miniature portrait, which he had surrendered to his assassin; he knows, as well, Teresa's devoted constancy. Act 2 closes with Alvar's self-recriminations for having doubted Teresa's abiding love, and he pledges to use his painting to arouse Ordonio's feelings, to "wake the hell within him, / And rouse a fiery whirlwind in his conscience" (177–78).

For the conjuring scene at the beginning of act 3, the stage directions specify "A Hall of Armory, with an Altar at the back of the Stage. Soft Music from an instrument of Glass or Steel."[10] Ordonio has even arranged for a concealed choir to sing to the eerie whine of the glass or steel harmonica. Because Teresa has described herself as a dreamer, Ordonio has presumed that she is easily deluded by the marvelous. Her first reaction, however, when she enters this setting prepared for the sorcerer's conjuration is to declare that she disapproves of such "mockery." Surprised by her response, Ordonio asks her if she does not believe in "preternatural influ-

---

9. Coleridge declares that he preserves these lines not for their relevance to the drama, but because they contain "a slight, yet not unfaithful profile of one, who still lives"—Sir George Beaumont.

10. Coleridge refers to those instruments played by rubbing with resinous cloth or leather. The glass harmonica invented by Benjamin Franklin (1762) was played by rubbing with wet fingers glass bowls that were made to spin by a gear mechanism driven by a pedal.

ence" or in the presence of spirits. Once again, Teresa states the difference between illusion and delusion:

> Say rather that I have imagined it
> A possible thing: and it has sooth'd my soul
> As other fancies have; but ne'er seduced me
> To traffic with the black and frenzied hope
> That the dead hear the voice of witch or wizard.
>
> (III.i.23–27)

In explaining his task as "wizard," Alvar says that he proposes to "uncover all concealed guilt." He calls upon innumerable dead, who work their "dread illusion" upon the desert sands, and then upon the "Soul of Alvar," whom he bids to "pass visible before our mortal sense." The song, heard from "Behind the Scenes" accompanied by the same eerie music, is a blending of the occult and the sacred liturgy—the "Miserere Domine." While Valdez and even Ordonio fall under the spell of the sham sorcery, Teresa refuses to take part in "these lawless mysteries, / This dark provoking of the hidden Powers" (117–18). As she leaves, Alvar praises her faith and wisdom. Only the guilty need to behold his revelation. The smoldering incense suddenly blazes up with an intense flash, revealing the painting of the assassination concealed in the darkness above the altar. Ordonio cries out "Duped! duped! duped!"—thinking that Isidore has revealed to the wizard the dark secret of the murder. At this moment, the Inquisitor enters and takes the sorcerer prisoner.

Alone in the chapel (III.ii), Teresa contrasts the serenity with the troubled forebodings of the preceding scene at the sorcerer's altar. Here she feels herself in a "cloudless" trance. Her unburdened reverie is disturbed by Valdez, who has interpreted the picture as certain proof of Alvar's horrible murder. Teresa, by calling attention to the rays of light that take on the stained coloring of the chapel windows, suggests that fancy, too, may take on other hues. Valdez turns her reply into an accusation of her self-delusion:

> My child, we must not give religious faith
> To every voice which makes the heart a listener
> To its own wish.
>
> (III.ii.34–36)

Yet he is willing, she answers, to give credence to "impious sorcery" and none to her own prayers. Coleridge's dialogue addresses the possibility of relying on faith to discern truth amidst falsehood.[11] Valdez, no less than Teresa, claims to have perceived the truth. When he describes to her the picture of the fallen Alvar clutching "some relique / More dear than was his life," she "sees" what he had not—the "relique" is her own portrait.

At this point Ordonio enters. Valdez continues describing the painting and the sorcerer's words, and again Ordonio cries out that he has been "Dup'd! dup'd! dup'd!" by the traitor Isidore. Dialogue lapses here into dual monologues. Both Valdez and Ordonio voice their private thoughts, not listening to each other but merely grasping phrases. Valdez declares that he only attended the sham sorcery supposing it to be an "innocent stratagem" arranged by Ordonio "to remove the doubts / Of wild Teresa—by fancies quelling fancies." Ordonio transforms the phrase into "fancies opposed by fancies," taking it as the rationale for his murderous deceptions. Life itself becomes a delusion, and murder is no more than giving "a morsel to the hungry worms / Somewhat too early." As Ordonio's declaration of the "dream" of life grows more fantastic, Valdez steps back in alarm, fearing that "excess of feeling / . . . hath unhinged his brain" (III.ii.105–6). Teresa, however, approaches and "places herself directly before Ordonio." She has heard the guilt in his mad ravings about leaving the corpse to rot in the sun. Teresa has been accused of so cherishing delusion that she cannot discern reality, but it is Ordonio who is caught up in delusion and struggles ineptly to regain his perception of the real world. He looks blankly upon the woman before him: "Teresa? or the phantom of Teresa?" (115). Teresa answers that she is only the phantom; the real Teresa has perished with Alvar. She demands to know where his body has been buried. He describes a "rocky grave" where "the fir-grove sighs" (127). Rather than recognizing his son's guilt, Valdez declares that he only names what was revealed in the "magic imagery" of the sorcerer's painting. Ordonio's delusion was provoked by the "supernatural shews" and his "hopeless love" for Teresa has driven him to "give reality / To the creatures of his fancy" (142–43). This, of course, is precisely the same diagnosis Valdez has earlier used to explain Teresa's behavior.

Lured to the cave by a letter from Ordonio, Isidore waits in darkness (IV.i). Indeed, it is the very darkness of this "painted scene" that Coleridge

---

11. Coleridge, *The Notebooks of Samuel Taylor Coleridge* III, §3592 (August–September 1809).

exploits. It is a scene for "seeing things." Isidore begins to describe a dream, when he sees something moving in the shadows. As he searches into the darkness, Ordonio enters from another recess. Isidore explains that he "saw something moving." Ordonio steps forward with his torch to investigate and declares that it was only a weed nodding and dripping in an underground pool (IV.i.18–20).[12] Again Coleridge relies on storytelling to heighten anticipation. The murder is rehearsed three times before it takes place. Isidore tells it twice; then, reversing the actor-audience relationship, Ordonio tells his version.

First we see Isidore reenacting the adventure that had just occurred while he awaited Ordonio's arrival. The floor of the cavern has a deep gaping hole. By "filling the void," the "shadowy moonshine" has played a trick on his eyes. The moonlight "so counterfeited substance, / That my foot hung aslant adown the edge." He would have plunged to his death, had he not been saved by an icy hand that pulled him back from the abyss. Ordonio smiles at what he considers a superstitious tale. The optical illusion and the mysterious rescue, Isidore declares, strangely repeat his dream of the previous night, and he narrates the dream in which he saw himself about to fall down the very same chasm and was saved by Alhadra who wakened him from his troubled sleep. Ordonio next tells his tale, a tale of a mind troubled by "phantom thoughts," holding "dalliance" with shadows, until "this human hand / . . . gave a substance and reality / To that wild fancy." Isidore rightly guesses that Ordonio is revealing his own guilt-ridden and treacherous thoughts. By the time Ordonio turns his obscure threat into a direct accusation, Isidore is prepared for the assault. They fight. Isidore is overcome and hurled down the gaping chasm.

The next scene takes us into the castle dungeon. Still unaware of the Moorish wizard's true identity, Teresa has come to the dungeon to rescue him. As has already been well established, Valdez's role in this play has been to inform Teresa of her delusions. In act 3, he also became the observer of Ordonio's delusions. He now tells Teresa that the "wizard haunts thee" (IV.ii.22), insinuating that his masculine bearing has worked its "wonder" on her feminine frailty. He has repeatedly complained that she has cruelly abused Ordonio's love for her. In previous scenes, he has accused her of deluded constancy to Alvar; he now suggests that she is fickle and too easily attracted to a stranger. Teresa replies by verbally conjuring a painting of

---

12. Cf. "This Lime Tree Bower my Prison," in Coleridge, *Complete Poetical Works*, 17–20.

Alvar. Her act is set in direct comparison to the scene of sorcery: "O that I had indeed the sorcerer's power.—/ I would call up before thine eyes the image / Of my betrothed Alvar, of thy first-born" (49–51). She presents to his "mind's eye" her ideal hero, "kingly," "tender," "genial," "spiritual," "the joy, the triumph of our kind." Then she tells him to take this portrait and "place beside him / Ordonio's dark perturbed countenance." How, she demands of Valdez, could he bid her to turn from Alvar and "To take in exchange that brooding man, who never / Lifts up his eye from the earth, unless to scowl" (73–74). This confrontation is interrupted by a peasant with a letter from Zulimez promising to "reveal a secret."

The final scene of act 4 is set in "Mountains by moonlight." Alhadra has summoned the Moorish warriors. Here is still another episode of storytelling. Alhadra tells of seeking her husband and hearing his dying groan from the abyss in the dark cave. Counting on the impassioned response of her audience, she ends her tale of Isidore's murder by calling on the Morescoes to avenge his death.

At the beginning of act 5, Teresa enters the dungeon cell to free the prisoner, whom she still believes is a Moorish chieftain. Alvar returns the portrait to Teresa, revealing his identity. Their reunion is interrupted by the sound of the prison gate. Teresa conceals herself in the shadows. Ordonio arrives, bringing poisoned wine. Alvar refuses to drink and dashes the goblet to the ground. While Ordonio spits threats and curses, Alvar begs him to cleanse his conscience, to surrender his guilt to contrition and remorse. Ordonio angrily rejects the plea: ". . . remorse! remorse! / Where got'st thou that fool's word? Curse on remorse!" (169–70). Ordonio thinks the Moorish wizard means to taunt him with Alvar's name:

> Ha! it chokes thee in the throat,
> Even thee; and yet I pray thee to speak it out.
> Still Alvar! —Alvar! —howl it in my ear!
> Heap it like coals of fire upon my heart,
> And shoot it hissing through my brain!
> (177–81)

As in Marlowe's *Dr. Faustus*, the guilty sinner believes a fiery damnation inevitable and is unable to seek salvation through contrition and confession of guilt. The gradual revelation of Alvar's identity parallels the preceding scene with Teresa. While Teresa cherished a phantom image of love,

Ordonio has been persecuted by an image of guilt. The shift from image to reality prompted her ready embrace. Ordonio, however, rages with fear and anger:

> Spirit of the dead!
> Methinks I know thee! ha! my brain turns wild
> At its own dreams! —off —off, fantastic shadow!
> (190–92)

Teresa intervenes, and together with Alvar, they work upon Ordonio's conscience. Coleridge draws upon the language of confession and penitence: "Call back thy soul, Ordonio." "Heal. O heal him, Heaven." Just as Ordonio confesses his sins and admits his guilt, Alhadra bursts in with her armed Morescoes. Teresa begs them spare Ordonio, "He doth repent! See, see, I kneel to thee! / O let him live!" These Christian gestures mean nothing to Alhadra. She has come for blood. She plunges her sword into Ordonio. Accepting death as a blessing, Ordonio dies with the word: "Atonement!" (255). Valdez arrives with armed servants and Zulimez, too late to save his younger son, but now aware of his elder son's return. He gives his blessing to Teresa and Alvar, and Alvar closes the final act with his affirmation of the truth of conscience and the restorative power of remorse.

When the curtain rises in Tom Stoppard's *The Real Inspector Hound* (1968), "the audience appear to be confronted by their own reflection in a huge mirror." The stage, decorated as the drawing room in an English manor, seems to be situated between rows of seats facing each other on opposite sides. Before the action begins on stage, one theater critic in the front row is joined by a second; a dialogue commences about a third critic and about the play, "a whodunnit," which we are told has already begun.[13] Beginning a play with members of the audience discussing the play to be played is the same peculiar metadramatic gambit which Ludwig Tieck employed in *Puss-in-Boots* (*Der gestiefelte Kater*, 1797).[14] Stoppard's play contains a spoof of Agatha Christie's *The Mousetrap;* Tieck parodies scenes from *The Magic Flute*. The ironic tensions of an Aristophanic *parabasis* or a Shakespearean play-within-a-play are complicated by Tieck and Stoppard,

---

13. Stoppard, *The Real Inspector Hound* (1968); see Cahn, *Beyond Absurdity: The Plays of Tom Stoppard*, and Londré, *Tom Stoppard*.

14. Tieck, *Der gestiefelte Kater* (1797), ed. Kreuzer (1984). Subsequent quotations are from this edition; translations are my own.

for the fictive spectators do not simply provide an alternate frame of reality, another level of dramatic illusion; instead of remaining discretely separated as spectators and commentators, they become entangled in the other action on stage. Like Moon and Birdboot in Stoppard's play, Bötticher, Leutner, Wiesener, Fischer, Müller, and Schlosser satirically parody the pretensions of critics and the prejudices of theatergoers. While they may seem to be mere commentators, we soon realize that they are central characters in the dramatic action.

In his review, August Wilhelm Schlegel observed that *Puss-in-Boots* is "a play about a play."[15] Schlegel's formula helps distinguish Tieck's strategy from a "play within a play," but it scarcely prepares us for the constant implications of what is "not in the play." What belongs in the play, supposedly, is a dramatization of Perrault's *Le chat botté*. In terms of eighteenth-century tenets of dramatic illusion, the very choice of fable would render the illusion impossible.[16] The audience expects the realism of bourgeois characters in a domestic setting, not the antics of a talking cat. Moreover, the interaction on stage of actors, audience, playwright, critics deliberately confuses the boundaries of "play" and "not play." The denial of illusion becomes the most bewildering aspect of illusion.

When the curtain is raised "too soon" in act 3, for example, the playwright is revealed in a desperate attempt to arrange last-minute stage effects with the theater technician. The uproar in the audience, which "disrupted" the performance of act 2, has convinced the playwright that he must add the trickery of stage machinery to save his play. The technician considers his role in manipulating the machinery an impromptu ad-libbing. We seem to be catching the playwright in the act of conspiring with the technician to appropriate the "water and fire" display from *The Magic Flute*. The intrusion of the playwright and technician is further complicated by the intrusion of

15. Schlegel, review of Tieck's *Ritterblaubart* and *Der gestiefelte Kater*, in *Jenaische Allgemeine Litteraturzeitung*, rpt. in *Kritische Schriften* (1828), I, 311–18. See also Kokott, "Das Theater auf dem Theater im Drama der Neuzeit. Eine Untersuchung über die Darstellung der theatralischen Aufführung durch das Theater auf dem Theater in ausgewählten Dramen von Shakespeare, Tieck, Pirandello, Genet, Ionesco und Beckett."

16. Perrault, *Contes de ma mère l'oye* (1697). Lessing, *Abhandlungen über die Fabel* (1759), in *Werke*, ed. Göpfert, et al., V, 402–4, grants that a fable may engender aesthetic illusion but argues its inappropriateness to the stage; on Gozzi's fiabesque drama and its influence on Tieck, see Rusack, *Gozzi in Germany*; Feldmann, *Die Fiabe Carlo Gozzis. Die Entstehung einer Gattung und ihre Transposition in das System der deutschen Romantik*; Marelli, "Ludwig Tiecks frühe Märchenspiele und gozzische Manier."

the audience. The fictive audience grapples with the very paradox set before the actual audience: the presumptions of destroying illusion (the curtain has risen prematurely) and of substituting mechanical for aesthetic illusion (the audience has grown impatient with the play, so the playwright seeks to distract them with dazzling stage machinery) are themselves illusory. The metadramatic illusion cannot "expose" the dramatic illusion, it can only pretend to.

"What are these people doing in Gottlieb's house?" asks one of the audience. "Who raised the curtain?" asks the stage technician. After the embarrassed playwright runs from the stage, the audience tries to make sense of the intrusion:

> Wiesener: Was this a part of the play?
> Neighbor: Of course—it motivates the changes which are to follow.

At this juncture the King is heard, offstage, refusing to make his entrance and be laughed at. Since the setting is the peasant's hovel, the King ought not to make an appearance here anyway, but the clown, Jackpudding, volunteers to step forward and save the performance. Under the strictures of the Enlightenment, Jackpudding had been banished from the stage.[17] His reappearance in Tieck's play deliberately challenges neoclassical taste—a fact immediately noted by the fictive audience:

> Müller: What is Jackpudding doing in the peasant's house?
> Schlosser: He probably wants to hold an insipid monologue.[18]

The word "insipid" (*abgeschmackt*) is pivotal in the ensuing dialogue with the audience, for they begin by denouncing his "bad taste" yet are led all too easily to approve his "taste." In chapter 2 we noted that in his earlier essay, "Shakespeare's Use of the Marvelous" (1793), Tieck had declared that an

---

17. Gottsched, *Versuch einer Critischen Dichtkunst vor die Deutschen.*
18. Tieck, *Der gestiefelte Kater,* 42–43:

> Wiesener: Gehört denn das zum Stück?
> Nachbar: Natürlich, —das motiviert ja die nachherigen Verwandlungen.
>
> . . . .
>
> Muller: Wie kömmt den der Hanswurst nun in die Bauernstube?
> Schlosser: Er wird gewiß einen abgeschmackten Monolog halten wollen.

"insipid" lapse would destroy illusion, yet he went on to describe how the "burlesque and insipid" could enlarge the comic dimensions of dramatic illusion."[19] Tieck was apparently guilty of logical inconsistency in his essay, but in creating a similar turnabout in his play, he is deliberately challenging audience expectations. In the process of converting "bad taste" to proper "taste," Jackpudding informs the audience that his own immediate presence, as well as the scene which they have just witnessed and the conclusion to the previous act, do not belong in the play:

> Jackpudding: The curtain was raised too soon. It was a private discussion, which would not have occurred on stage were the space in the wings not so terribly narrow. If you experienced an illusion, then it truly is much the worse. Please be so good as to eradicate the illusion from yourselves, for only now, understand that I mean after I am gone, will the act actually begin. Between you and me, all of the preceding did not belong to the matter. But you shall be repaid. In stark contrast, there will now be presented much that is quite relevant to the matter. I talked to the playwright, and he promised me there would.[20]

Tieck inculcates the illusion that there is no illusion. Claiming to have stepped out of his role in order to speak directly as actor to the audience, Jackpudding tells us that, if we mistakenly experienced illusion, we should uproot it from our minds. We should ignore the false illusion; the true illusion is to follow. At this juncture, the "insipid" clown persuades the audience that it is the playwright who is insipid. The playwright steps forth to denounce the intrusion of Jackpudding and to insist that he had only allowed his appearance, not to oppose critical principles but to prepare for a degree of fantasy. Jackpudding assures the audience that the playwright is lying and reminds them that this scene, too, does not belong in the play.

---

19. Tieck, "Shakespeares Behandlung des Wunderbaren," *Kritische Schriften* I, 50, 56.
20. Tieck, *Der gestiefelte Kater*, 43–44: "Der Vorhang war zu früh aufgezogen. Es war eine Privatunterredung, die gar nicht auf dem Theater vorgefallen wäre, wenn es zwischen den Kulissen nicht so abscheulich eng gewesen wäre. Sind Sie also illudiert gewesen, so ist es wahrlich um so schlimmer, sein Sie dann nur so gütig, diese Täuschung aus sich wieder auszurotten, denn von jetzt an, verstehn Sie mich, nachdem ich weggegangen bin, nimmt der Akt erst eigentlich seinen Anfang. Unter uns, alles Vorhergehende gehört gar nicht zur Sache. —Aber Sie sollen entschädigt werden, es wird im Gegenteil bald manches kommen, was sehr zur Sache gehört, ich habe den Dichter selber gesprochen und er hat's mir zugeschworen."

When the "real" play then recommences, however, Tieck does not relinquish the metadramatic counterillusion. Actor and character are confounded in Gottlieb's dialogue with his cat:

> Hinze: Upon my word, I will make your fortune.
> Gottlieb: Then it must be soon, very soon, for it is growing late. It is already half past seven, and the comedy will be over at eight.
> Hinze: What in the devil are you saying?
> Gottlieb: Oh, I was lost in thought, —Look! I wanted to say, How beautiful is the sunrise. —The damned prompter mumbles, and when I try to say something extemporaneously, it always comes out wrong.
> Hinze (whispering): Pull yourself together, otherwise the whole play will break into a thousand pieces.[21]

Evening and morning become simultaneous events as Gottlieb appeals to both offstage and onstage time. Even in warning Gottlieb against his errant (but only apparent) ad-libbing, Hinze steps out of his role as cat to speak as a player. Tieck's *dramatis personae* extend beyond the usual limits of stage to include other provinces of theater: the audience and the critics, the characters and the players, the stage crew including prompter and technician, and the playwright himself. These groups do not remain discrete. Beginning with the playwright's response to the uproar in the audience in the Prologue, the boundaries become more and more entangled.

In act 1, the audience intrudes to judge the play. By act 3, the confusions of illusion and reality have become so thoroughly complicated that, when the Fool and the Wiseman of the King's court are called upon to judge the play, Tieck can entertain a multiple paradox: whether the judges are also

---

21. Ibid., 45.
> Hinze: Auf mein Wort, ich will Dich glücklich machen.
> Gottlieb: Bald, sehr bald muß es kommen, sonst ist es zu spät, es ist schon halb acht und um acht is die Komödie aus.
> Hinze: Was zum Teufel ist denn das?
> Gottlieb: Ah, ich war in Gedanken. —Sieh! wollt' ich sagen, wie schön die Sonne aufgegangen ist. —Der verdammte Souffleur spricht so undeutlich, und wenn mann dann manchmal extemporieren will, geht's immer schief.
> Hinze (leise): Nehmen Sie sich doch zusammen, das ganze Stück bricht sonst in tausend Stücke.

players in the play, whether there is an audience in the play, indeed, whether there is a play at all. The prize, a splendid hat decorated with gold and jewels, is displayed atop a high standard, but the debate seems irreconcilable. The Wiseman says the play is good, the Fool argues that it is bad:

> Leander: I maintain that there is wit in the play.
> Jackpudding: I maintain that there is none.
> Leander: You are a fool. How can you judge whether there is wit?
> Jackpudding: And you are a scholar. What do you know about wit?
> Leander: Many characters are well developed.
> Jackpudding: Not a one.
> Leander: It must be admitted, even if I drop all other points, that the public is well drawn in the play.
> Jackpudding: The public never has any character.
> Leander: This insolence almost amazes me.
> Jackpudding: (to the public) Isn't he a foolish person? We now have an intimate understanding and we sympathize in matters of taste. He opposes my opinion and wants to maintain that at least the public in *Puss-in-Boots* is well drawn.
> Fischer: The public? There is no public in the play.[22]

Jackpudding wins the prize by cunning. He persuades the cat to doff his boots, climb the pole, and fetch the hat. In complying, Hinze steps out of his role as hunter, not as actor but as cat. Only afterward does Hinze learn that

---

22. Ibid., 48–49.
> Leander: Ich behaupte, es ist Witz darin.
> Hanswurst: Ich behaupte, es ist keiner darin.
> Leander: Du bist ein Narr, wie willst Du über Witz urteilen.
> Hanswurst: Und Du bist ein Gelehrter, was willst Du von Witz verstehn!
> Leander: Manche Charaktere sind gut durchgeführt.
> Hanswurst: Kein einziger.
> Leander: So ist, wenn ich auch alles übrige fallen lasse, das Publikum gut darin gezeichnet.
> Hanswurst: Ein Publikum hat nie einen Charakter.
> Leander: Über diese Frechheit möcht' ich fast erstaunen.
> Hanswurst (*gegen das Parterre*): Ist es nicht ein närrischer Mensch? Wir stehn nun beide auf Du und Du, und sympathisieren in Ansehung des Geschmacks und er will gegen meine Meinung behaupten, das Publikum im gestiefelten Kater sei wenigstens gut gezeichnet.
> Fischer: Das Publikum? Es kömmt ja kein Publikum in dem Stücke vor.

by helping Jackpudding to his victory, he has opposed the play in which he has the title role. For his part, Jackpudding confesses that he debated only in jest for he had never heard of the play.

In executing his repeated turnabouts of illusion and reality, Tieck not only gives new dimension to dramatic illusion, he also provides a critique of established notions about illusion and aesthetic experience. Beginning with the intrusions of the audience in the Prologue, Tieck assaults preconceptions about the nature of dramatic illusion. A conventional prologue, declaring the poet's rationale for the play and his willingness to accept the judgment of the audience, would typically involve an actor speaking directly to the audience, presumably in his own person. Tieck opens instead with members of the audience who raise such a tumult that the playwright must come forward to beg their indulgence. The fictive audience, of course, has already judged. Although they now reject and now applaud, their fickle response is not unpredictable. They always approve theatrical display and trite sentimentality; they have no patience for metadramatic provocations—which are, of course, the very substance of Tieck's play about a play.

Reacting to the title, the spectators in the prologue survey the anticipated possibilities. If *Puss-in-Boots* is a children's tale, a *Kindermärchen* as the subtitle declares, why is it being presented to an adult audience? Perhaps it is a fiabesque opera, in the manner of *The Magic Flute*, but what is an opera without music?[23] Perhaps it is a "family tableau," the kind of domestic play advocated by Diderot and popularized on the German stage by Iffland and Kotzebue.[24] Perhaps the pretense of the children's tale is only a satirical ploy, a coded discourse for revolutionary polemics. Any of these possibilities would follow established genre and satisfy audience expectations. Tieck represents the spectators as thoroughly conditioned by Enlightenment aesthetics and unprepared for the metadramatic strategies in which he has engaged them. Because witches, ghosts, and supernatural phantoms were deemed inappropriate in an enlightened age, the audience is quick to denounce fairy-tale elements. When it is reported that the poet is busy backstage helping an actor into a cat costume, the audience confronts a dramatic

23. Tieck discusses the fantastic in Mozart's *Der Zauberflöte* in his introductory essay to *Das Ungeheuer und der verzauberte Wald* (1800), in *Schriften*, 28 vols. (Berlin: G. Reimer, 1828–1854), XI, xlviii–lvi; see also *Ludwig Tieck. Dichter uber ihre Dichtungen*, ed. Schweikert, I, 180–87.

24. Diderot, *Le Fils naturel* (1757) and *La Pére de Famille* (1758), in *Oeuvres complètes* VII, 23–84 and 187–298; Iffland, *Verbrechen aus Ehrfurcht* (1784) and *Der Spieler* (1796), in *Dramatische Werke*; Kotzebue, *Menschenhaß unf Reue* (1789), in *Sämtliche Werke* III, 1–80.

situation at odds with accepted genre. Their protest against the violation of good taste brings forth the poet. His request, "Allow me a hearing for a minute before you damn me," may exercise the usual rhetorical ploy of a prologue, but Tieck has reversed the situation. The public, here, have become the actors and the playwright is reduced to mere spectator. He does not manipulate the dramatic event; he is manipulated by it. The cathartic response expected from the audience is suffered instead by the playwright. He is overwhelmed not by the production but by the debate over the production: "Never before has anything frightened me to such a degree; I am pale and trembling."

The two stages of aesthetic response—the resistance and acquiescence described in the essay on "Shakespeare's Use of the Marvelous"—are reasserted, but also redefined, in the comic confusion of the fictive audience in *Puss-in-Boots*. During the first stage, the audience must be carefully seduced into accepting the illusory conditions. If dramatic *mimesis* is adequately coherent, awareness of the deception is gradually lulled so that incongruities no longer disrupt the experience. This "non-disruption of illusion" may be the effect of the suasive power of the play, but it is also the cause of increased imaginative participation. When disruption is avoided, tolerance is secured and the illusory experience is reinforced. During the second stage, the audience puts aside its suspicions and willingly accepts the seduction.[25] In *Puss-in-Boots*, the befuddled interruptions of the audience reveal compelling and compulsive attributes of illusion that have nothing to do with a "willing suspension of disbelief." Knowing that it is illusion, even rejecting the incongruities, does not enable the audience to escape the illusory trap. In showing his fictive audience ensnared in confusion, Tieck challenges his real audience with the paradoxicality of illusion.

In the first act, when the cat speaks, his master is surprised, but the audience, just beginning to adjust to a "family tableau," is completely unsettled:

> The Critics (*in the audience*): —The cat speaks? —What does this mean?
> Fischer: It is impossible for me to enter into a reasonable illusion.
> Müller: Before letting myself have such an illusion, I would rather never see another play for the rest of my life.

---

25. Tieck, "Shakespeares Behandlung des Wunderbaren," in *Kritische Schriften* I, 42–50; see discussion of this essay in chapter 2 above.

That illusion is supposed to be grounded in an emotional response, yet constructed through rationally persuasive *mimesis*, is the paradox of eighteenth-century theory. The requirement of a "reasonable illusion" (*vernünftige Illusion*) has been disrupted. Hinze's account of his talking, however, is unquestioningly accepted by Gottlieb: the two pledge camaraderie and promptly turn the discussion to Gottlieb's welfare. Tieck's spectators object to the apparent irrationality; nevertheless, they find themselves caught up in the dramatic situation:

> Fischer: Friends, what has happened to our hope for a family tableau?
> Leutner: This is almost too insane.
> Schlosser: It's as if I were dreaming.[26]

The cobbler, who measures Hinze for his boots, has no difficulty in recognizing the cat as a cat—but also as a customer: "Would you be so kind, sir, as to pull in your claws, or nails. I have already scratched myself." While the process of initiation and acceptance poses no problem for Gottlieb or the cobbler, the fictive audience are wary of the illusion. Later in act 2, members of the audience are still struggling with the cat's identity:

> Fischer: What upsets me is that not a single person in the play wonders about the cat; the King and all the rest respond as if it were a usual occurrence.
> Schlosser: All this fantastic stuff makes my head spin.[27]

---

26. Tieck, *Der gestiefelte Kater*, 11, 12:

> Die Kunstrichter (*im Parterre*). —Der Kater spricht? —Was ist denn das?
> Fischer: Unmöglich kann ich da in eine vernünftige Illusion hineinkommen.
> Müller: Eh' ich mich so täuschen lasse, will ich lieber zeitlebens noch kein Stück wieder sehn.
>
> . . . .
>
> Fischer: Freunde, wo ist unsre Hoffnung zu einem Familiengemälde geblieben?
> Leutner: Es ist doch fast zu toll.
> Schlosser: Ich bin wie im Traum.

27. Ibid., 34:

> Fischer: Was mich nur ärgert, ist daß sich kein Mensch im Stück über den Kater wundert; der König und alle tun, als müßte es so sein.
> Schlosser: Mir geht der ganze Kopf von dem wunderlichen Zeug herum.

The actor playing the cat is deliberately confounded with the cat playing the hunter. Shaking hands with Hinze, Jackpudding releases his firm grip when sharp claws scratch him. When Hinze steps out of his role as hunter, as in the debate between the Fool and the Wiseman, he climbs like a cat. During the rebellious protest of the audience at the end of act 2, Tieck's stage note explains that amidst the stamping and whistling of the spectators, "all the actors forget their roles." Yet in forgetting his role as hunter, Hinze has clambered up a pillar. Once the poet has helped the actor into his cat costume, the actor becomes the cat.

In acting his role as hunter, Hinze must gird himself to his task—a comic dilemma in which Tieck parodies the tragic hero's struggle between his nobler and baser instincts.

> Now, fortune be with me! —When I recollect that this stubborn goddess of fortune seldom favors cleverly conceived plans, that she much prefers to demolish the understanding of mortals, then I am inclined to lose all courage. Yet be still my heart, a king's realm is worth the effort, even if it means working and sweating a bit for it.

Tieck complicates the dilemma; "working and sweating" are at odds with regal pretensions, and hunting fowl, even to win a king's favor, trespasses against the popular cult of sensibility as well as against Hinze's feline instincts.

> It is my sad fate that I can never hear a bird singing without a compulsion to eat it: Nature! Nature! why dost thou ever thus disrupt my most tender feelings, why hast thou made me so? —I am almost tempted to remove my boots and stealthily climb yon tree.

The song of the nightingale gives rise to conflicting emotions, and the same music has the virtue—not of soothing the savage beast—but of rising above the rude noises from the audience.

> The nightingale has a good nature. She does not allow even this militant music to disrupt her song—she must taste delicious. I forget my hunt in these sweet dreams.[28]

28. Ibid., 27–28:

The parodistic dimensions are not merely heaped together, they interpenetrate. The hunter pauses in his hunt to indulge "sweet dreams" on the nightingale's song. But Hinze's thoughts on how they sing are inseparable from thoughts on how they taste. In this mockery of "Sensibility," Hinze has trespassed decorum and the audience registers protest. Hinze, however, turns the situation around by transferring the breach of decorum to the perpetrators of "militant music."

At this point a pair of wooing lovers cross the field, provoking further conflict—the lovers disturb the hunter and *vice versa*. The fictive audience, of course, shout loud bravos for the lovers, although they are left to ponder whether the scene has any relevance for the play as a whole. Hinze's following speech, while it continues to play upon his manifold identity as cat, hunter, and actor, nevertheless manages to thrill the audience as a bravura piece on duty vs. impulse. They applaud wildly and call for an encore *da capo*. Twice Tieck shows us Hinze as hunter in the field. In both scenes Hinze delivers "grand" speeches, and in both Hinze's call to duty is contrasted with an interlude of young lovers. When we see them the second time, their gushing exchange of love vows has given way to disenchantment and recriminations. The audience may claim to want realism, but they delight in sentimental effusion. The lovers' spat is uncomfortably real, and the audience wants no part of it.

In satirizing the public, Tieck aims several salvos at the self-proclaimed arbiter of taste. The critic Böttiger is scarcely disguised in the character of Bötticher. Tieck objects to Böttiger's celebration of the actor Iffland not because attributes of his acting have been overlooked, rather because his

> Nun, Glück stehe mir bei! —Wenn ich freilich bedenke, daß diese eigensinnige Glücksgöttin so selten die klug angelegten Pläne begünstigt, daß sie immer darauf ausgeht, den Verstand der Sterblichen zu Schanden zu machen, so möchte ich allen Mut verlieren. Doch, sei ruhig mein Herz, ein Königreich ist schon der Mühe wert, etwas dafür zu arbeiten und zu schwitzen.
>
> . . . .
>
> Es ist fatal, daß ich nichts kann singen hören, ohne Lust zu kriegen, es zu fressen: Natur! Natur! warum störst Du mich dadurch immer in meinen allerzartesten Empfindungen, daß Du mich so eingerichtet hast? —Fast krieg' ich Lust, mir die Stiefeln auszuziehen und sacht den Baum dort hinanzuklettern.
>
> . . . .
>
> Die Nachtigall hat eine gute Natur, das sie sich durch diese kriegerische Musik nicht einmal unterbrechen läßt, —delikat muß sie schmecken; ich vergesse meine ganze Jagd über diese süßen Träume.

talents have been overstated. Worse, admiration for the player replaces attention to the play. Böttiger's pedantry and preoccupation with voice and gesture are parodied in Bötticher's critique of the cat. Following act 1, Bötticher discourses on the cat costume as a Greek mask, pointing out how the "mask" is not that of a black cat, but of a white cat with a few black spots—a distinction, of course, which the actor has captured perfectly in mime.[29] After the fiasco at the end of act 2, while other members of the audience praise the ballet (borrowed from *The Magic Flute*) that has "saved" the play, Bötticher recounts the actor's stunning performance as a cat: the gesture upon removing a rabbit from his sack, the grimace of fear when an eagle lands on his head, and, above all, the transformation from cat into hunter with no other props or costume than a pair of boots—an illusion that allows us to see the cat as well as the hunter. Such slight suggestions, Bötticher exclaims, are always most dramatic. When Bötticher goes into raptures over "the infinite refinement with which the cat always holds his cane," his neighbors denounce him as "more boring than the play" and throw him out of the theater.[30]

Schlosser, who in the prologue had speculated that the play may be a "revolutionary piece," finds his suspicions confirmed in the final act with Hinze's overthrow of the tyrant Popanz. But Schlosser's perception is no less constrained and superficial than Bötticher's. Tieck's satire implicates the illusory nature of all political authority. He had already "exposed" the illusion of authority in the tavern scene of act 1: After escaping military conscription by crossing the border, a deserter banters with the soldiers who have pursued him while they enjoy a beer. The law, here, is a game; the deserter has "won." Still it is a vicious and dangerous game, as Tieck demonstrates when he takes us into the court of Popanz, whose power is deception and terror. We see him first as a rhinoceros, administering "justice" to a poor peasant who must sell his land to pay the sentence against him. The peasant ignores his rhinoceros shape and responds only to his cruel law. The civil servant, who comes to bribe, fears not the law but is

---

29. Böttiger, *Entwicklung des Ifflandschen Spiels in vierzehn Darstellungen auf dem Weimarer Hoftheater im Aprilmonath 1796.*

30. Tieck, *Der gestiefelte Kater*, 24–25, 40, 46. Because this Iffland-like actor can express the nuance of the cat's "einige schwarze Flecke," Tieck may be suggesting that his player has borrowed certain touches from two other members of the Berlin National Theater: Ferdinand and Louise Fleck. In the 1812 version, Bötticher is not thrown out, but merely gagged like Papageno; in the last scene, the gag explodes from his mouth and he breaks forth with even more exaggerated praise of "das einzige Talent dieses unvergleichlichen Mannes" (*Schriften* V, 269–71, 279–80).

frightened by Popanz in his human shape. Before relinquishing his gold, he persuades Popanz to assume a less intimidating form. Popanz becomes a mouse—a political transformation aptly anticipating the scene which Tieck has adapted from Perrault's version of tale. Hinze then replays the sly game with the magician's transforming art, leaping on the tyrant become mouse and shouting a revolutionary cry: "Freedom and Equality!—the law is devoured—now the Third Estate has arrived and Gottlieb rules." In the fictive audience, Schlosser reacts as a political conservative outraged by this voice of political radicalism.[31] The real audience, however, is left with the absurdity of the puss-in-boots as revolutionary hero. The *Tiers état* is only another reign of fantasy and folly.

The attempt to provide illusion through technological gimmickry, rather than to conjure illusion through the imaginative participation of the audience, may have satisfied the popular fascination with elaborate settings, but it inevitably subordinated the players and the play. Flamboyant stage decorations are suitable for the opera, Tieck later wrote, but they offer a poor substitute for true dramatic illusion. In direct proportion to the success of these sensational effects, the audience is distracted and prevented from experiencing "a noble intellectual pleasure."[32] The fictive audience of *Puss-in-Boots* is easily seduced into mindless delight by spectacular stage designs and stunning theatrical effects. Tieck gives his critique an ironic twist by having the audience in the final scene applaud not the play but a stage setting borrowed from another production.

In the interlude following act 1, one of the spectators calls the playwright "a great man" for having imitated *The Magic Flute*. Act 2 concludes with a parody of the spell Papageno casts over Monostatos and the slaves with his Glockenspiel. After the "false" opening of act 3, exposing the conspiracy to "put all the machinery into play" should the audience again grow unruly, the scene proper begins in Gottlieb's hut. No sooner has Hinze declared that he is ready to "go through fire" for his master, than the audience is ready to be treated to "the decorations from the Magic Flute with the water and fire." This absurd expectation is fulfilled. When Hinze's revolutionary proclamation ("the law is devoured—now the Third Estate has arrived") provokes another uproar in the audience, once more the pacifier appears with the Glockenspiel, this time

---

31. Tieck, *Der gestiefelte Kater*, 6, 23, 56, 58. In the 1812 version, Schlosser has changed his politics; he applauds the revolutionary speech and calls for a repeat performance of the play "um all die großen Winke, die tiefe Andeutungen zu fassen" (*Schriften* V, 269).

32. Tieck, Preface to *Dramaturgische Blätter* (1825), in *Kritische Schriften* III, xviii.

singing Sarastro's "In these hallowed halls" ("In diesen heil'gen Hallen"), while the "fire-and-water" scene is revealed on stage. One spectator takes malicious pleasure in anticipating the cat going through the trial, but Hinze pushes Gottlieb into Tamino's role. Although he cannot comprehend why the setting has changed, Hinze tells his master that "since it has gone this far anyway, you must go through the fire here and then through the water there." When the curtain falls on this final scene, the audience calls out for an encore—not for the players, but for the setting. The curtain goes up again to reveal the "fire-and-water" decorations and Jackpudding steps forward to accept the curtain call in behalf of the scenery.[33]

While the play with illusion in *Puss-in-Boots* may be rightly cited as example of Romantic irony, it is a mistake to think that Tieck has departed from Schlegel's definition of Romantic irony as "a permanent *parabasis*."[34] In order to consider *Puss-in-Boots* as progenitor of anti-Illusionist theater,[35] it would be necessary to claim that once illusion is ironically countered, it is effectively exposed and dispelled. The *parabasis* would, then, have but a momentary effect, whereupon illusion would be permanently vanquished. Instead, we find illusion disrupted, but only to provoke more complex illusions. The confusion of the fictive spectators more aptly expresses Tieck's purpose:

> Fischer: Tell me, please, how this can happen—the play itself—it comes again as a play in the play.
> Schlosser: It won't take many such circumstances to drive me crazy. As I said at the outset, this is the aesthetic pleasure which one is supposed to have here.
> Leutner: No tragedy has ever affected me as much as this farce.[36]

---

33. Tieck, *Der gestiefelte Kater*, 24, 39, 46, 58, 59, 61; Tieck refers to Johann Jakob Engel's production of *Die Zauberflöte* at the Berlin National Theater in 1794.
34. Furst, *Fictions of Romantic Irony*, 24–30; Gillespie, "Young Tieck and the Romantic Breakthrough"; Szondi, "Friedrich Schlegel und die romantische Ironie. Mit einer Beilage über Tiecks Komödien"; Heimrich, "Der Begriff der Parekbase in der Ironie-Terminologie Friedrich Schlegels"; Strohschneider-Kohrs, *Die romantische Ironie in Theorie und Gestaltung*, 128–46; Immerwahr, *The Esthetic Intent of Tieck's Fantastic Comedy;* Lussky, *Tieck's Romantic Irony*.
35. Ernst Nef, "Das Aus-der-Rolle-Fallen als Mittel der Illusionszerstörung bei Tieck und Brecht"; Günzel, *König der Romantik. Das Leben des Dichters Ludwig Tieck*, 15.
36. Tieck, *Der gestiefelte Kater*, 30:

> Fischer: Sagt mir nur, was das ist, —das Stück selbst, —das kommt wieder als Stück im Stücke vor—

Rather than destroying illusion, the "intrusions" and the "asides" add new dimensions to the aesthetic awareness. The very self-conscious questioning of illusion provides Tieck with his provocational technique in combining satire and fantasy.

At the outset of his literary career, Clemens Brentano looked to the theater as his destined province. From 1800 to 1803, he sketched plans for over a dozen plays and brought several to publication: *Gustav Wasa* (1800), *Ponce de Leon* (1801; published 1804), and *Die lustigen Musikanten* (The Merry Musicians, 1802; published 1803).[37] The satirical thrust of these early efforts reveals that Brentano, like Tieck, opposed the popular productions of Iffland and Kotzebue. When Kotzebue ridiculed Friedrich and August Wilhelm Schlegel in *Der hyperborische Esel* (The Hyperborean Jackass, 1799), Brentano came to the defense of the young romantics with a farce in the manner of *Puss-in-Boots*. Brentano's *Gustav Wasa* was meant as a counterattack on Kotzebue, who had written a historical play of the same title.[38] The polemic may have been addressed against Kotzebue, but Brentano was so adept in mimicking the style of *Puss-in-Boots* that Tieck thought himself the target of a devastating parody.[39] In spite of his appropriation of Tieck's "play about a play" strategy, Brentano develops none of the metadramatic possibilities. When a drunken actor is interviewed in the tavern, or when the fictive audience studies the playbill in the theater, there is no turnabout confusion of what is not "in" the play. He is so completely preoccupied with the intertextual confrontations of parody and the witty polemics of satire that he pays no attention to the self-reflexive implications of his dramatic situations. Because he is not concerned with elaborating or extending the ironic awareness of illusion, it would be a mistake to expect that Brentano's *Gustav Wasa* would

---

        Schlosser: Ich bin ohne viele Umstände verrückt, —sagt' ich's doch gleich, das ist der Kunstgenuß, den man hier haben soll.
        Leutner: So hat mich noch kein Trauerspiel angegriffen, wie diese Posse.

37. Brentano, *Werke;* also presently available are seventeen of the projected thirty-six volumes in the new historical-critical edition, *Sämtliche Werke und Briefe;* for an overview of the dramatic works in the manuscript collection (Freies Deutsches Hochstift), see Pfeiffer-Belli, *Clemens Brentano. Ein romantisches Dichterleben.*

38. Kotzebue, *Der hyperboreische Esel oder Die heutige Bildung; Gustava Wasa.*

39. Caroline Schelling to Friedrich Schleiermacher, 16 June 1800, *Caroline und Dorothea Schlegel in Briefen,* 327: Brentano "hat eine Farce geschrieben, 'Gustav Wasa', worin er glaubt der Tieck des Tiecks zu seyn; es ist aber herzlich dumm und toll, und klingt doch wie Tieck ungefähr, so daß sich dieser tüchtig darüber erboßt, und darum hat er ihn auch so derb mitgenommen im *Journal*"; Tieck, "Der neue Hercules am Scheideweg," in *Poetisches Journal* (Jena 1800), 81ff; reprinted as "Der Autor, ein Fastnachtsschwank," in *Schriften* XIII, 267ff.

deliberately provoke, as did Tieck's *Puss-in-Boots*, the metadramatic complications of illusory relationships between playwright and players, players and characters, characters and audience.

Although *Gustav Wasa* caused a stir in the romantic circle of Jena,[40] it impressed no one as a play for the stage. *The Merry Musicians*, a "Singspiel," is the only one of Brentano's plays to gain success on the stage. The original music was composed by Peter Ritter, who directed the performances in Mannheim in 1804 and 1805. E. T. A. Hoffmann provided his own musical setting and produced the comic opera at the Warsaw German Theater in April 1805. In his appraisal of *The Merry Musicians*, Hoffmann repeats Hamlet's remark to the players: " 'The play . . . pleased not the million; 'twas caviare to the general.' " Hoffmann liked it—not in spite of but because of its fantastic excesses. Again following the example of Tieck's fiabesque drama, Brentano had appropriated the *commedia dell' arte* masques. "But! —Holy Gozzi," exclaimed Hoffmann, "what misbegotten creatures have been produced out of the attractive characters of that jovial mischievousness."[41]

Ponce de Leon was Brentano's contribution for the prize competition announced in Goethe's *Propyläen*. After reviewing the thirteen plays submitted, Schiller said that "not one of them can be used; most are beneath criticism." And Goethe, when Brentano pressed him for a response, answered that "a public review was omitted because none of the submitted works seemed suitable for performance in the theater."[42] Brentano had the play published in 1804, but he had to wait another ten years for an occasion to have it staged. The revised version, *Valeria oder Vaterlist* (Valeria, or Paternal Cunning, 1813), was performed in Vienna (18 February 1814). It flopped. Not his play but the production, according to Brentano, should be blamed for the failure; in his critical reviews for the *Dramaturgischen*

40. Arnim, *Achim von Arnim und Clemens Brentano*, 20–21; Brentano, *Clemens Brentano. Dichter über ihre Dichtungen*, 88–93; Thalmann, "Clemens Brentano, *Gustav Wasa*," in *Provokation und Demonstration in der Komödie der Romantik*.

41. Hoffmann to Theodor Hippel, 26 September 1805, *E. T. A. Hoffmann, Briefwechsel* I, 193–94: "Der Text mißfiel—es war Kaviar für das Volk wie Hamlet sagt . . . Vorzüglich nahm man daran einen Aerger, daß sich die komischen Masken der Italiäner darinn herumdrehen, Truffaldin, Tartaglia und Pantalone. Aber! —Heiliger Gozzi, was für Mißgeburten wurden hier auch aus den anziehenden Gestalten des jovialen Muthwillens!" See also Allroggen, *E. T. A. Hoffmanns Kompositionen. Ein chronologisch-thematisches Verzeichnis seiner musikalischen Werke mit einer Einführung*, 26–27, 43–61.

42. Brentano, *Clemens Brentano. Dichter über ihre Dichtung*, 97–101; Schiller to Körner, October 1801, Goethe to Brentano, 16 October 1802, in Brentano, *Werke* IV, 911–12.

Beobachter (25 February and 11 March 1814), he vented his anger at the misdirected attention to stage design rather than to the acting.

In subsequent reviews, Brentano continued to take the theater to task for undermining dramatic illusion.[43] As Achim von Arnim observed, Brentano adhered to an outmoded theory of illusion which had long since been recognized as nonsense. Illusion should be opposed to delusion, not to reality. Only children or fools, Arnim objected, would mistake a theater performance for reality. Yet Brentano persisted in upholding that "most stupid response."[44] Perhaps it was because Brentano held such a naive notion of dramatic illusion that he never plays with illusion in his own drama. We noted above that even in mimicking Tieck, Brentano ignored the situations which seemed to call for metadramatic reversals. The same observation may be made of *Ponce de Leon;* since half the characters put on disguises and play roles to fool the other half, Brentano would seem to have abundant occasion to exploit presumptions about appearances. But there is no irony of revealed and concealed identities. If a character should step in and out of a role, Brentano keeps the "trespass" contained within the plot. He neither thematizes the problem of perception, nor allows the character to reflect on the duplicity or theatricality of role playing.

With the secret return of Don Sarmiento, who plans to observe as an unknown stranger the behavior of his son and daughters, Brentano opens his play with an intrigue of deception and disguise. We see Valeria dressing Ponce in his Venetian mask in the first scene of act 1, and by the final scene at the masked ball, all the characters have entered into the world of *commedia dell' arte* (Porporino as Harlequin, Valeria as Columbine, Valerio as Pantaloon). Through the third, fourth, and fifth acts, the audience is treated to more complicated disguises, as Valerio plays the housemaster at Sarmiento's estate and Porporino, Sarmiento's yet unidentified bastard son, plays tailor,

---

43. Brentano, "Über das moderne Theaterwesen im größten Teile von Europa, vielleicht überall. Bei Gelegenheit des *Achilles* von Paer." *Berlinische Nachrichten*, no. 137 (16 November 1815); "Über die auf der modernen Europäischen Schaubühne zur Hauptsache gewordenen Nebensachen, Kostüm und Schauspiel Kunst," *Berlinische Nachrichten*, nos. 141, 143 (25, 30 November 1815); in *Werke* II, 1127–34.

44. Arnim to Savigny, 17 December 1815, *Arnims Briefe an Savigny, 1803–1831*, 132–34: "Kinder und Narren lassen sich von den Kunstwerken wohl einen Augenblick täuschen, auch wohl Thiere in der Geschichte des Protogenes zu weilen die Auflösung dieser Täuschung ist aber die dümmste Empfindung, die ein Mensch haben kann, von einer Täuschung, das für wirklich zu halten, was sich im Abbilde darstellt, kann sowenig im Dichter wie im Schauspieler und in der Dekorazion bestreiten."

and portrait painter, and soldier, and doctor. When Valeria arrives disguised as the Moorish maiden, Flametta, she fools her father so thoroughly that he cannot recognize her even when she acquiesces to his request and "pretends" to be his daughter, and she fools her former lover not only by concealing her true identity, but also by tricking him in the dark to mistake her for his new love.[45] Brentano, however, uses none of these situations to initiate the audience, overtly or covertly, into the pretenses of illusion. He certainly gives the audience opportunity to enjoy Valeria's dual identity, but he never suspends one illusion to impose another.

When Brentano read the tales of Hoffmann in 1816, he described the self-reflexive strategy. Making it clear that he did not approve of the "irony of falling out of the work," he declares it "outmoded" and goes on to confess "a certain aversion to all literature which reflects itself." Brentano likens this mode of narrative to "pissing in the snow," or "blasting into the air in order to see the winter breath, the tobacco smoke, and even yourself crystallized on the icy window of life."[46] Admittedly, this response to Hoffmann comes late in Brentano's career, but his attitude toward self-reflexive irony and multiple levels of illusion is not at odds with his own earlier literary practice.

Although Brentano's *Godwi* (1801) has been cited as a novel of romantic irony, Ingrid Strohschneider-Kohrs argues that Brentano is incapable of romantic irony precisely because he never escapes the bondage of his own subjectivity in order to observe illusion critically. In the tradition of Cervantes, Sterne, and Jean Paul, he may seem to play continually with illusion, or, imitating Tieck, to suspend willfully the very illusion which his narrative engenders.[47] Yet whenever the fictive narrator "abandons" his narrative in a

---

45. Arntzen, "Das Speil der Maskierten"; Maurer-Adam, "Deklamatorisches Theater. Dramaturgie und Inszenierung von Clemens Brentanos Lustspiel *Ponce de Leon*."

46. Brentano to E. T. A. Hoffmann, January 1816, *Hoffmann, Briefwechsel* II, 82–83: "Welch glücklicher Erdmann sind Sie, mit solcher Lust in den Schnee zu pissen, in die Luft zu knallen, den Winterhauch zu betrachten und selbst den Tabacksrauch, und sich selbst an ein Eisfenster des Lebens an zu gestirnen. Was Sie geschrieben, hat mich mannichfaltig gefreut, aber daß Sie es gethan eben so sehr verwundert, denn stellen Sie sich vor ich möchte die Lichter ausputzen meinen Schatten nicht zu sehen, die Spiegel verhängen, das Spiegelbild nicht zu erblicken, und dieser Schatten, dieses Spiegelbild von mir in Ihrem Buch hat mich darum oft geängstet, weswegen ich nicht begreifen kann, daß Sie das Ihre selbst drinn sehen und zeigen mochten. Seit längerer Zeit habe ich ein gewisses Grauen vor aller Poesie, die sich selbst spiegelt ... die Ironie des aus dem Stückfallens allein schien sich mir überlebt, ich halte es für frühere Arbeit." See also Brentano's letter to Arnim, 3 February 1816, *Achim von Arnim und Clemens Brentano*, 343–45.

47. Kerr, *Godwi. Ein Kapitel deutscher Romantik*, 64–67, 77, 79; Friedemann, "Die romantische Ironie"; Friedemann, *Die Rolle des Erzählers in der Epik*, 88.

moment of disillusionment or self-critical scorn, there is no objective stance, no Aristophanic *parabasis*, no alternate perspective in which the author reveals the illusory process and exposes the limits of authorship. Instead, as Strohschneider-Kohrs points out, the expressions of disillusion continue the subjectivity and sentimentality. The narrator may shift from rapture to self-ridicule, but he still indulges the introspective, expressive, and confessional modes. In turning narrative attention to the fictive narrator in the act of narrating, Brentano achieves no liberated objectivity.[48]

We need not be surprised, then, that in his critical essays Brentano speaks of a purity of illusion that has been defiled by intrusions of theatrical display. Exaggerated attention to stage designs, he argues, has subordinated playwright and player. To emphasize stage effects over the dramatic art is a perversion not just of aesthetic sensibility, but of intellect and morality. Dramatic illusion, as defined by Brentano, is conjured exclusively through the art of the playwright and actor:

> How ridiculous and blundering is the imputation concerning decorations, that they should promote illusion, for they are precisely that part of a performance which, by their very nature, cannot provide illusion. A four-cornered room with three walls, a terrible prison with more open space than walls, a deserted wilderness from which one peers into a crowded gathering, . . . besides the characters who always turn to the open side, and monologues which, since they seldom occur in real life, by no means fulfill the presupposed causal necessity of gross illusion. Nothing should provide illusion on the stage but *the poet* and *the actor*, both alone are capable, and by entrusting them so little with illusion as now happens, one has brought forth a theater, brought forth so incurably, such as our modern one is. The whole modern deposition of decorations makes all illusion utterly impossible. Only from one point in the theater is the perspective accurate; from all other points must the scenery, the better it is, appear the worse, collapsing into the most unnatural and untrue;

---

48. Strohschneider-Kohrs, *Die romantische Ironie in Theorie und Gestaltung*, 337–41. Furst, *Fictions of Romantic Irony*, 123, observes a similar bondage in Jean Paul's irony, in which a "pervasive and invasive self-consciousness" blurs the distinction "between illusion and truth": "Such extreme awareness of self leads not only to a heightened creative consciousness, but also to a menacing self-doubt; for the ego perceived in the mirror may after all be nothing more than an illusion in an illusory universe."

indeed a truly illusory *trompe l'oeil* in the current deposition must cause the spectator, who experiences the illusion, the greatest discomfort, disturbance, and confusion, if the non-illusion of the actor and poet are not strong enough to help him out of the dream.[49]

Brentano wants dramatic illusion to reside completely in the mimetic principle. In witnessing "the imitation of human action" as accomplished by playwright and player, the spectator has all the illusion that is necessary to the drama.[50] Arnim objected strongly to the narrow constraints Brentano wished to impose not only on the theatrical production but on actor and poet as well.

In his correspondence with Savigny, who had accused him of reacting too harshly to Brentano, Arnim explained his objections and attempted to reaffirm the play with illusion as an important part of illusion. Tieck had made the point that illusion in Shakespeare was wrought without decorations.[51] When Brentano repeats the argument, he omits Tieck's account of the historical conditions. In presuming to write on the theater, Arnim says, "a critic should be aware of its history and ought to have thought at least as much about its theory as other people." Brentano's essay sins in its neglect

---

49. Brentano, *Werke* II, 1134: "Wie lächerlich und stolpernd ist die Zumutung an die Dekoration, sie solle die Täuschung erheben, da sie grade der Teil der Darstellung ist, der, seiner Natur nach, nicht täuschen kann. Eine viereckte Stube von drei Wänden, ein schrecklicher Kerker, der mehr offnen Raum als Mauer hat, eine wilde Einöde, aus welcher man in die größte Gesellschaft blickt, ... dabei immer die Wendung der Handelnden gegen die offne Seite, und die an sich plumpe Täuschung keineswegs voraussetzende Notwendigkeit des Monologs, der selten im wahren Leben vorkommt. Nichts soll täuschen auf der Bühne, als *der Dichter* und *der Schauspieler*, beide allein sind es im Stand, und ihnen die Täuschung so wenig anmutend, als es jetzt geschieht, hat man ein Theater erzogen, so inkurabel erzogen, als das moderne es ist. Die ganze moderne Disposition der Dekorationen macht alle Täuschung rein unmöglich, nur aus einem Punkte des Theaters ist die Perspektiv richtig, aus allen andern Punkten, muß das Gemälde, um so besser es ist, um so mehr sich so höchsten Unnatur und Unwahrheit zusammenstürzen und schieben; ja ein wirklich täuschendes Gemälde bei der jetzigen Disposition muß den Zuschauer, des es täuscht, wenn er nicht auf jenem einzigen Punkt sitzt, aufs höchste beunruhigen, ängstgen und verwirren, wenn ihm das Nichttäuschen der Schauspieler und Dichter nicht stark genug aus dem Traum hälfe."

50. Neureuter, *Das Spiegelmotiv bei Clemens Brentano. Studie zum romantischen Ich-Bewußtsein*, documents in Brentano's works an extensive and deliberate concern with mimetic reflection. He also acknowledges that ironic multiplicity of illusion ("das übermütige Spiel mit den verschiedenen Wirklichkeitsebenen, das oft zitierten amüsanten Paradigmata des 'Aus-dem-Stücke-Fallens,'" 165) interests Brentano less than artistic illusion as a reflection of human action or an image of more exalted being, 106–8, 162–68, 183–86.

51. Tieck, *Poetisches Journal* (Jena, 1800), no. 1, 18–20; no. 2, 459–72; Tieck, *Kritische Schriften* I, 148–70.

of both history and theory. As Arnim points out, Brentano's objections to theater decorations might just as well be levied against painting. The frame around a landscape painting is no less effective in separating the viewer from the scene and reminding him of the illusion than the proscenium arch and the prompter's box in the middle of the stage. Brentano fails to appreciate the capacity of the audience "to enjoy through the fantasy" ("mit der Phantasie geniessen"). Since all aesthetic experience derives from the capacity to complement what the artist offers, a spectator should have no difficulty in adjusting his view from an oblique perspective.[52] Arnim knows, of course, what has irritated Brentano: "The entire essay would not annoy at all if it were in a biography of Clemens as a document to the performance of his *Ponce;* the individual, conscious of his efforts and his good intentions and the obstacles which he encountered there, explains openly what happened to him at the Viennese Theater. Generalized, all is false."[53]

The notion that art was supposed to be perceived as a reality, in Arnim's judgment, rendered the old theory of illusion untenable nonsense. What might provide for a tenable theory of illusion Arnim had pondered in his "Theoretical Investigation" ("Theoretische Untersuchung," October 1812). He approaches this investigation through the creative process. To what extent does the author indulge illusion in his effort to create a work?

> My theory of poetic discovery, . . . how the fantasy is only then true, when in creating illusion it experiences illusion itself; how the under-

---

52. Arnim to Savigny, 17 December 1815, *Arnims Briefe an Savigny, 1803–1831*, 132–34. Brentano drew the argument on stage decoration from Schinkel: "Den Antheil Schinkels an den Bemerkungen über Dekorazion kenne ich, der weiß von dem Unnützen der Dekorazion eigentlich nichts, so weit theoretisiert er nie, sondern arbeitet nur sehr ehrlich daran, einiges was ihm von Dekorazionsmalerei unzweckmässig scheint und was Burnat inbesondre durch sein Ungeschick fehlt zu verbessern. Seine Vorschläge haben einiges Gute, er hat sie mir einmal ganz ausführlich gezeigt, aber auch manches, was der Natur vieler Theaterstücke durchaus unangemessen ist, sie sind aus dem Standpunkte der Mahlerey lobenswerth, obgleich auch gute Dekorazionen derohne gedacht werden können." In his editorial commentary, Härtl notes that Schinkel was to have designed the stage decorations for Arnim's *Festspiel beim Feste des allgemeinen Friedens* in 1814; at this time, Schinkel sent to Iffland his memorandum ("Reformvorschläge zu Theaterbau und Dekorationswesen") —these ideas were further developed in Schinkel's "Entwürfe" of 1815; see Harken, "Die Bühnenbilder K. F. Schinkels, 1798–1834," 77–99.

53. Arnim to Savigny, 17 December 1815, *Arnims Briefe an Savigny, 1803–1831*, 132–34: "Die ganze Aufsatz in einer Biographie von Clemens bey Gelegenheit der Aufführung seines Ponce würde durchaus nicht kränken, der Einzelne, seiner Mühe sich bewußt und seines guten Willens und der Hindernisse, die ihm dort entgegenstanden, erklärt frey, was ihm am Wiener Theater entgegenstand, verallgemeinert ist alles falsch."

standing only then feels certainty, when through seeking the truth it verifies itself; thus, for example, applied to drawing, beauty, which is truth, is first present to the fantasy when that which is perceived in my head and which I want to represent, through which I want to engage people in illusion, has possessed me so thoroughly that ultimately I can no longer distinguish it from the thing perceived, and I even lose altogether the thing perceived, or can only bring it forth through the created image. Where the truth of fantasy encounters the truth of understanding, there resides the highest human feeling—we call it religion.[54]

The certainty that Arnim affirms here in the creative act was also endorsed by other romantic thinkers. Keat's concluded his "Ode on a Grecian Urn" (1820) by insisting on the equation: " 'Beauty is truth, truth beauty', — that's all / Ye know on earth, and all ye need to know." Coleridge's essay "On Certainty" (1809), as we may recall from chapter 5, also denounced the notion that a work of art should produce "actual Delusion" or that we should mistake "the picture for reality." Coleridge had no difficulty in linking "faith" with "certainty" because both derived from an "Instinctive Pursuit of a sufficient ground." Through its imaginative grasp of that otherwise unattainable ground, art provides a "sense of Power" and with it the conviction "that there *is* a certain ground." Just as Arnim turned to Klopstock's *Messiah* to demonstrate a union of the "truth of fantasy" and

54. Arnim, "Theoretische Untersuchung" (October 1812), in *Achim von Arnim und Jacob und Wilhelm Grimm*, 242–43; "Meine Theorie poetischer Erfindung, ... wie die Phantasie nur dann wahr sei, wenn sie täuschend sich selbst täuscht, wie der Verstand nur dann Ueberzeugung fühlt, wenn er von der Wahrheit, die er sucht, selbst wahr gemacht wird: so z.B. auf Zeichnung angewendet, so ist da erst eine Schönheit, und das ist Wahrheit, der Phantasie vorhanden, wenn das Angeschaute im Kopfe, das ich darstellen möchte, womit ich die Leute täuschen möchte, mich selbst so ergreift, daß ich es zuletzt nicht mehr von dem Angeschauten unterscheiden kann, ja sogar dieses Angeschaute gänzlich verliere, oder erst wieder durch das erschaffene Bild hervorbringen kann. Wo sich Wahrheit der Phantasie und Wahrheit des Verstandes begegnet, da ist das höchste menschliche Gefühl, wir nennen das Religion. ... Sehr oft halten wir mit Unrecht ein religiöses Gedicht für schöner als jedes andre, zu Klopstocks Zeit den Messias: mehr ist es uns aber in jedem Falle als das schönste andre, ohne daß wir darum ein blos phantastisches herabsetzen wollen; denn der Mensch, der sich immerdar nur in der Berührung von Phantasie und Verstand aufhalten wollte, ohne jene beiden Kräfte selbst zu achten und erkennen zu wollen, würde bald in einer vollkommen Nichtigkeit versinken, vorüber religiöse Gemüther gewisser Zeiten (Süßianer, Zinzindorfianer ...) so häufig bis zur Gottlosigkeit klagen. Die Tugend liegt nur in der Vereinigung des religösen innern Menschen mit der äußeren Welt, bloße Verstandes-, bloße Phantasietugend ist leer."

"truth of understanding," Coleridge found his example in the combination of biblical and fictive matter in Milton's *Paradise Lost*.[55]

Although Arnim wants fantasy and understanding to touch, he does not expect the one to overwhelm the other. To be sure, the fantasy "in creating illusion . . . experiences illusion itself," but it is a self-conscious and rationally alert illusion. Arnim's "Theoretical Investigation" was written as a part of his ongoing debate with the Brothers Grimm concerning *Kunstpoesie* as opposed to *Naturpoesie*—a false distinction as Arnim saw it. Jacob Grimm had disparaged *Des Knaben Wunderhorn* (vol. 1 1805; vols. 2 and 3 1808), the collaborative effort of Arnim and Brentano, for falsifying the folk tradition.[56] Arnim replied that the folk tales gathered by the Brothers Grimm were no more authentic, for they were composites, thoroughly revised by the editors. Worse, the very presumption of publishing a definitive record of the folk tradition was a lethal blow to that tradition: "Fixed folk tales will ultimately be the death of the whole world of folk tales." Many romantic poets, including Arnim and Brentano, were involved in perpetuating the folk tradition.

Telling and retelling requires a vital participation in the world of *Märchen*. Arnim emphasizes illusion as the fundamental attribute of storytelling. The telling requires participation, experiencing illusion while creating illusion. Through the telling "the inventive talent" is aroused in both teller and auditor, aroused and thus also perpetuated. The telling of folk tales provides a way of initiating children into the creative process. Gifted with a natural instinct for this "highest truth of fantasy" and "essence of all poetic invention," the child is readily caught up in creating and experiencing illusion. Because telling and retelling tales are such natural occurrences, Arnim argues against Jacob Grimm's terminology: "All distinction between *Kunstpoesie* and *Naturpoesie* becomes a mere joke." The distinction is possible only because we can prescind one telling from another, but that act itself results from the "power of making and experiencing illusion" and can never be isolated as a fixed moment in history because the retelling continues.[57]

---

55. Coleridge, *The Notebooks of Samuel Taylor Coleridge* III, §3592 (August–September 1809).
56. Jacob Grimm to Arnim, 9 July 1811, *Achim von Arnim und Jacob und Wilhelm Grimm*, 131.
57. Arnim to Jacob Grimm, 22 October 1812, *Achim von Arnim und Jacob und Wilhelm Grimm*, 223–24: "Fixierte Märchen würden endlich der Tod der gesammten Märchenwelt sein. Das hat aber auch nichts auf sich; das Kind erzählt schon anders, als es im selben Augenblicke von der Mutter gehört, ich habe oft herzlich darüber lachen müssen, da entstehen Wunder, man weiß nicht wie. Die Hauptsache ist, daß das erfindende Talent immerfort geweckt werde; denn nur darin geht den Kindern eine freudige Selbstbeschäftigung auf. . . . so täuschend und doch getäuscht und darum in der höchsten Wahrheit der Phantasie ist der Märchensinn der Kinder—und bis zum

The drama, as Arnim explains it, grows out of the dynamic interaction of storytelling. It relies on the same commitment to illusion but brings it out of the small social gathering into a large public arena. The actor, of course, does not merely tell a story with animated gesture, he enters into the story and becomes one of its characters. Because the theater is a public institution, the history of the theater is a social and political history. In his "Erzählungen von Schauspielen" (Tales of the Drama, 1803), Arnim had observed the political repercussions in Parisian theater under Napoleon.[58] Because dramatic illusion is an affect of the concerns and needs of the audience, the critic should consider social conditions when attempting to understand the changes in theatrical performance. Thus Arnim faulted Brentano for failing to consider historical conditions when he denounced the mechanics of illusion.

The elaborate attention to the mechanics of illusion was nourished by a popular fascination with advances in technology—the optical trickery that Goethe brought onto the stage, and the lighting effects that intrigued Hugo. On the other hand, the romantic exaltation of the imagination also gave new impetus to the aesthetics of illusion and to the attributes of consciousness and perception. The problematic perception of self and other, for example, directs the action in Kleist's *Amphitryon* (1807). To seduce Alkmene, Jupiter must disguise himself as her husband Amphitryon. For Plautus this had provided appropriate matter for sexual ribaldry and comedy of errors. For Molière the seduction plot served as a humorous apology for the monarch's presumption of nuptial rights. But for Kleist the problem is truly one of perception and illusion. Alkmene sees in her "transformed" husband only the idealization she has always perceived. Jupiter cannot seduce her in his own person, for she is absolutely devoted to Amphitryon.[59] Conflicting sources of illusion also provide thematic and dramatic motifs in Byron's *Manfred* (1817), where his "vigil" of self becomes a mandate for all other characters whom he directs to "Look upon me," "Watch me, or watch me in my watchings." As Stuart Curran has shown, Shelley conceived his *Charles*

Höchsten das Wesen aller poetischen Erfindung, und durchaus aller Unterschied zwischen Kunst- und Naturpoesie ein bloßer Spaß, der selbst wieder aus dieser täuschend getäuschten Kraft hervorgegangen ist, und für die Phantasie eine Wahrheit haben kann, die in der Geschichte sich nirgends bekundet."

58. Arnim, *Achim von Arnim und Clemens Brentano*, 67–68; Arnim, "Erzählungen von Schauspielen."

59. Hoffmeister, *Täuschung und Wirklichkeit bei Heinrich von Kleist*.

The First (1821) as an elaborate metadramatic effort "to present a drama that looked continually into itself as into a mirror even as it represented itself to readers or auditors as a spectacle to contemplate and through which to contemplate themselves." Shelley adapted the self-reflexive techniques of Calderón to dramatize the psychological dilemma of illusion, "the sense that everywhere you look in the world you are victimized by your own illusions as well as the illusions of others."[60]

As Arnim's critique of Brentano makes clear, the old conception of illusion could no longer be used to justify the practices of writing, staging, or acting a play. The new conception implicated a conscious awareness of illusory technique. But even here we have observed considerable differences in bringing theory into practice. Goethe and Hugo both sought to integrate the illusory devices of the stage into the dialogue and action. Coleridge and Tieck also give explicit attention to stage devices. But their technique is to repudiate rather than to integrate their props. When Tieck "borrows" the elaborate settings of *The Magic Flute*, his stage joke is that the machinery of illusion breaks down. Coleridge's most effective stage props and settings cannot be seen. Neither of the two paintings, the props which command much attention on the stage, can be seen by the audience. The miniature of Teresa can only be intimately viewed by the characters. And Alvar's painting of his own "assassination," unless it were a canvas as large as John Martin's *Deluge*, could not possibly be seen beyond the first row of Drury Lane when it is revealed on the darkened stage by a flash of gunpowder. The cave scene, too, is designed primarily to allow the characters to interact with their own dark thoughts. But for Coleridge and Tieck, no less than for Goethe and Hugo, the drama is made to confront the very conventions of illusion making.

Illusion, then, becomes for the Romantics more than a fascination with aesthetic experience or with the possibilities of stagecraft. The phenomena of illusion offer insight into the ambiguities of knowledge and the frail and fallible access we have to self, others, and the world. Schlegel and Coleridge taught their generation a new way of looking at the drama, of watching their own watching. As we have seen in the dramatic works of Goethe, Hugo, Coleridge, and Tieck, the Romantics endeavored to transform the deliberations of philosophy and critical theory into the very substance and subject matter of dramatic representation.

60. Curran, "Shelleyan Drama."

Bibliography

Primary Sources

[anon.] "Rezension: Theorie der schönen Künste und Wissenschaften, von Riedel." In *Neue Bibliothek der schönen Wissenschaften und der freyen Künste* 7, no. 1. Leipzig: Dyckische Buchhandlung, 1768, 38–75.
[anon.] "Rezension: Trauerspiele von C. F. Weiße." In *Allgemeine deutsche Bibliothek* (1782). 136–37.
d'Alembert, Jean le Rond. "Genève" (1757). In *Encyclopédie, ou Dictionnaire raisonné des sciences, des arts et des métiers*. 3d ed. 36 vols. Geneva: Pellet, 1777–99. VII, 578.
Arnim, Achim von. *Arnims Briefe an Savigny, 1803–1831*. Ed. Heinz Härtl. Weimar: Hermann Böhlaus Nachfolger, 1982.
———. *Achim von Arnim und Clemens Brentano*. Ed. Reinhold Steig. Stuttgart and Berlin: J. G. Cotta, 1894. Reprint. Bern: Herbert Lang, 1970.
———. *Achim von Arnim und Jacob und Wilhelm Grimm*. Ed. Reinhold Steig. Stuttgart and Berlin: J. G. Cotta, 1904. Reprint. Bern: Herbert Lang, 1970.
———. "Erzählungen von Schauspielen." In *Europa* II (1803), 140–92. Facsimile reprint of Friedrich Schlegel's *Europa*. Ed. Ernst Behler. Stuttgart: Cotta, 1963.
Batteux, Charles. *Les Beux Arts réduits à un même principe*. Paris, 1746. Reprint. Geneva: Slatkine, 1969.
Baumgarten, Alexander Gottlieb. *Aesthetica*. 2 vols. Frankfurt: I. C. Klayb, 1750–58.
Beaumarchais, Pierre Augustin Caron de. *Oeuvres complètes*. Paris: Merlin, 1767.
Berkeley, George. *Works*. 4 vols. Ed. Alexander Fraser. Oxford: Clarendon Press, 1871.

Bodmer, Johann Jacob. *Brief-Wechsel von der Natur des poetischen Geschmackes.* Zurich: C. Orell, 1736. Reprint. Stuttgart: Metzler, 1966.
———. *Critische Abhandlung von dem Wunderbaren in der Poesie.* Zurich: C. Orell, 1740. Reprint. Stuttgart: Metzler, 1966.
———. *Critische Briefe.* Zurich: Heidegger und Comp., 1746. Reprint. Hildesheim: Georg Olms, 1969.
———, and Johann Jacob Breitinger. *Von dem Einfluß und Gebrauche der Einbildungs-Krafft zur Ausbesserung des Geschmackes.* Frankfurt/Leipzig, 1727.
Böttiger, Karl August. *Entwicklung des Ifflandschen Spiels in vierzehn Darstellungen auf dem Weimarer Hoftheater im Aprilmonath 1796.* Leipzig: G. J. Göschen, 1796.
Brecht, Bertolt. *Gesammelte Werke.* 20 vols. Ed. Elisabeth Hauptmann. Frankfurt: Suhrkamp, 1967.
Breitinger, Johann Jacob. *Critische Dichtkunst.* 2 parts. Zurich: C. Orell, 1740.
Brentano, Clemens. *Clemens Brentano. Dichter über ihre Dichtungen.* Ed. Werner Vortriede and Gabriele Bartenschlager. Munich: Heimeran, 1970.
———. *Sämtliche Werke und Briefe.* Ed. Ludwig Behrens, Wolfgang Frühwald, and Hartwig Schultz. Frankfurt: Freies Deutsches Hochstift, 1975– .
———. *Werke.* 4 vols. Vol. 1, ed. Wolfgang Frühwald, Bernhard Gajek, and Friedhelm Kemp. Vols. 2–4, ed. F. Kemp. Munich: Carl Hanser, 1963–68; 2d ed. 1978.
Brewster, Sir David. *Letters on Natural Magic, Addressed to Sir Walter Scott.* London: John Murray, 1832.
Brooke [Broke], Arthur. *The Tragicall History of Romeus and Juliet* (1562). Ed. P. A. Daniel. New Shakespeare Society Publications. Series III: Originals and analogues. London: Trubner, 1875.
Burke, Edmund. *A Philosophical Enquiry into the Origin of our Ideas of the Sublime and the Beautiful. The Second Edition, With an introductory Discourse concerning Taste.* London: Dodsley, 1759.
———. *A Philosophical Enquiry into the Origin of our Ideas of the Sublime and Beautiful* (1756; rev. 1757). In *The Speeches and Writings of Edmund Burke.* 12 vols. Boston: Little, Brown, 1901. I, 138–55.
Calderón de la Barca, Pedro. *La Hija del Aire.* In *Obras completas (Dramas).* Ed. L. Astrana Marin. Madrid: M. Aguilar, 1933.
Calepio, Pietro di. *Paragon della Poesia tragica d'Italia con quella di Francia.* Zurich: M. Rordorf, 1732.
Cazotte, Jacques. *Le Diable amoureux.* Naples [i.e. Paris: Legay], 1772.
Chladenius, Johann Martin. *Einleitung zur richtigen Auslegung vernünfftiger Reden und Schrifften.* Leipzig: Carl Hermann Hemmerde, 1742. Reprint. Düsseldorf: Stern-Verlag Janssen, 1969.
Clairon, Claire-Joseph. *Mémoires d'Hippolyte Clairon, et réflexions sur l'art dramatique.* Paris: F. Buisson, an VII de la République [1799].
Coleridge, Samuel Taylor. *Biographia Literaria.* 2 vols. Ed. James Engell and Walter Jackson Bate. In *The Collected Works of Samuel Taylor Coleridge* 7. London: Routledge & Kegan Paul; Princeton: Bollingen, 1983.
———. *Coleridge's Shakespearean Criticism.* 2 vols. Ed. Thomas Middleton Raysor. London: Constable, 1930. Rev. ed. London: Dent, 1960.
———. *Collected Letters of Samuel Taylor Coleridge.* 6 vols. Ed. Earl Leslie Griggs. Oxford: Clarendon Press, 1956–71.
———. *Complete Poetical Works.* 2 vols. Ed. Ernest Hartley Coleridge. Oxford: Clarendon Press, 1912.
———. *Essays on His Times.* 3 vols. Ed. David Erdman. In *The Collected Works of Samuel Taylor Coleridge* 3. London: Routledge & Kegan Paul; Princeton: Bollingen, 1978.

———. *Lectures 1808–1819: On Literature.* 2 vols. Ed. Reginald A. Foakes. In *The Collected Works of Samuel Taylor Coleridge* 5. London: Routledge & Kegan Paul; Princeton: Bollingen, 1986.
———. *Literary Remains.* 4 vols. Ed. H. N. Coleridge. London: Pickering, 1836–39.
———. *The Notebooks of Samuel Taylor Coleridge.* Vols. 1–4 Text, vols. 1–4 Notes. Ed. Kathleen Coburn. Bollingen Series 50. Vols. 1 and 2, New York: Bollingen Foundation/Pantheon Books, 1957–61. Vols. 3 and 4, Princeton: Bollingen Foundation/Princeton University Press, 1973–90.
———. *Table Talk.* Ed. T. Ashe. London: George Bell and Sons, 1888.
———, and William Wordsworth. Marginalia in Richard Payne Knight, *Analytical Inquiry into the Principles of Taste.* 3d ed. London, 1806. Huntington Rare Book 1157.
Collier, Jeremy. *A Short View of the Immorality and Profaneness of the English Stage, Together With the Sense of Antiquity upon this Argument.* London: Printed for S. Keble, R. Sarc, & H. Hindmarsh, 1698.
Cooper, Anthony Ashley, third earl of Shaftesbury. *Characteristics of Men, Manners, Opinions, and Times.* 3 vols. 1711. Rev. ed. London: J. Darby, 1714. 3d ed. J. Darby, 1723.
Corneille, Pierre. *Oeuvres.* 7 vols. Ed. M. Ch. Marty-Laveaux. Paris: Les Grands Ecrivains de France, 1862.
———. *IIIe Discours* (1660). In *Théâtre complet.* Paris: Pléiade, 1950. II, 6–82.
———. *Writings on the Theatre.* Ed. H. T. Barnwell. Oxford: Blackwell, 1965.
Cramer, Johann Andreas. *Von dem Wesen der biblischen Poesie. Poetische Übersetzungen der Psalmen.* Leipzig, 1735. 2d ed., rev. (4 vols. in 2). Leipzig: Breitkopf und Sohn, 1763–64.
Darwin, Erasmus. "The Loves of the Plants." Part 2 of *The Botanic Garden.* Litchfield, 1789. London: J. Johnson, 1789. 2d ed. 1790.
De Quincey, Thomas. *The Collected Writings of Thomas De Quincey.* 14 vols. Ed. David Masson, London: Black, 1896–97.
———. *Selected Essays on Rhetoric.* Ed. Frederick Burwick. Carbondale: Southern Illinois University Press, 1969.
Descartes, René. *Discours de la méthode.* Leyden: I. Maire, 1637.
———. *Meditationes de prima philosophia.* Paris: Apud Michaelem Sol, 1641.
Diderot, Denis. *Mémoires, correspondance et ouvrages inédits de Diderot.* 4 vols. Paris: Paulin, 1830–31.
———. *Oeuvres complètes.* 20 vols. Ed. J. Assézat and M. Tourneaux. Paris: Garnier, 1875–77.
———. *Oeuvres esthétiques.* Ed. P. Vernière. Paris: Garnier, 1959.
———. *The Paradox of Acting.* Trans. Walter Herries Pollock (1883), and William Archer, *Masks or Faces? A Study in the Psychology of Acting* (1888), with an introductory essay by Lee Strasberg. Ed. Eric Bentley. New York: Hill & Wang, 1957.
———. *Paradoxe sur le comédien, avec recueilles et présentées sur l'art du comédien.* Ed. Marc Blanquet. Paris: Librairie Théâtrale, 1958.
———. *Salon de 1765.* Ed. Else Marie Bukdahl and Annette Lorenceau. Paris: Hermann, 1984.
———. *Salons.* 4 vols. Ed. Jean Seznec and Jean Adhémar. Oxford: Clarendon Press, 1957–67.
Du Bos, Jean Baptist. *Réflexions critiques sur la poésie et sur la peinture.* 1st ed. Paris, 1719. 7th ed. 3 vols. Paris: Pissot, 1770. Reprint. Geneva: Slatkine, 1967.
Engel, Johann Jacob. *Über Handlung, Gespräch und Erzählung.* Leipzig: Dyckische Buchhandlung, 1774. Reprint. Ed. Ernst Theodor Voss. Stuttgart: Metzler, 1964.

Garrick, David. *Private Correspondence.* 2 vols. Ed. James Boaden. London: H. Colburn & R. Bentley, 1831–32.
Garve, Christian. "Laokoön-Rezension." In *Allgemeine deutsche Bibliothek* 9 (1769), 328–58.
Gerstenberg, Heinrich Wilhelm. *Briefe über Merkwürdigkeiten der Literatur* (1766–67). Letter 20. In *Sturm und Drang. Dichtungen und theoretische Texte.* 2 vols. Ed. Heinz Nicolai. Darmstadt: Wissenschaftliche Buchgesellschaft, 1971. I, 112–20.
Gleim, Johann Wilhelm Ludwig. *Briefwechsel zwischen Gleim und Ramler.* 2 vols. Ed. Carl C. Schüddekopf. Bibliothek des Litterarischer Vereins in Stuttgart. Tübingen, 1906–7.
Goethe, Johann Wolfgang von. *Farbenlehre.* Ed. Rupprecht Matthaei. Ravensburg: Otto Maier, 1971.
———. *Faust.* Trans. Walter Arndt, ed. Cyrus Hamlin. New York: W. W. Norton, 1976.
———. *Italienische Reise.* Ed. Herbert von Einem. Munich: C. H. Beck, 1978.
———. *Theory of Colours.* Trans. and annotated by Sir Charles Lock Eastlake. London: John Murray, 1840. Reprint (with an introduction by Deane B. Judd). Cambridge, Mass.: MIT Press, 1970.
———. *Werke.* 143 vols. By order of the Grand Duchess Sophie von Sachsen. Weimar: Hermann Böhlau, 1887–1919.
———. *Wilhelm Meisters Lehrjahre.* Berlin: Johann Friedrich Unger, 1795.
Gottsched, Johann Christoph. *Versuch einer Critischen Dichtkunst vor die Deutschen.* 1730; 2d ed. 1737; 4th ed. 1751. Reprint. Darmstadt: Wissenschaftliche Buchgesellschaft, 1962.
Gozzi, Carlo. *Fiabe Teatrali.* Ed. Paolo Bosisio. Rome: Bulzoni, 1984.
Handke, Peter. *Publikumsbeschimpfung.* In *Prosa Gedichte Theaterstücke Hörspiele Aufsätze.* Frankfurt, 1969.
Hazlitt, William. *Collected Works.* 14 vols. Ed. A. R. Waller and Arnold Glover. London: Dent, 1902–4.
———. *Hazlitt on Theatre.* Ed. William Archer and Robert Lowe. London: Walter Scott, Ltd., 1895. Reprint. New York: Hill & Wang, 1956.
Hédelin, François, Abbe d'Aubignac. *Pratique du théâtre.* Paris: chez Antoine de Sommaville, 1657.
Hegel, G.W.F. *Werke.* 21 vols. Ed. Eva Moldenhauer and Karl Markus Michel. Frankfurt: Suhrkamp, 1970.
Herder, Johann Gottfried. *Sprachphilosophische Schriften.* Ed. Erich Heintel. Hamburg: Meiner, 1960.
———. *Werke.* 33 vols. Ed. Bernard Suphan. Berlin: Wiedmann, 1877–1913. Reprint. Hildesheim: Georg Olms, 1967.
Hill, Aaron. *The Actor.* 2d ed. London: R. Griffiths, 1755.
Hoffmann, E.T.A. *E.T.A. Hoffmann, Briefwechsel.* 3 vols. Ed. Hans von Müller and Friedrich Schnapp. Munich: Winkler, 1967–69.
Home, Henry, Lord Kames, *Elements of Criticism.* 2 vols. 6th ed. Edinburgh: J. Bell and W. Creech, 1785.
Houdar de La Motte, Antoine. *Les Paradoxes littéraires de La Motte.* Ed. B. Julien. Paris: Librairie Hachette, 1859.
Hugo, Victor. *Oeuvres dramatiques et critiques complètes.* Ed. Francis Bouvet. Paris: Jean-Jacques Pauvert, 1963.
Hutcheson, Francis. *An Essay on the Nature and Conduct of the Passions and Affections with Illustrations on the Moral Sense.* London: Sold by J. Osborn & T. Longman, 1728.
———. *Inquiry into the Origin of our Ideas of Beauty and Virtue.* 1725.

———. *Sittenlehre der Vernunft*. Trans. Gotthold Ephraim Lessing. Leipzig: Wendler, 1756.
———. *A System of Moral Philosophy*. 2 vols. London: Sold by A. Millar, 1755.
Iffland, August Wilhelm. *Dramatische Werke*. 20 vols. Leipzig: G. J. Göschen, 1798–1802.
Johnson, Samuel. *A Dictionary of the English Language*. London, 1755.
———. *The Works of Samuel Johnson*. 16 vols. Cambridge: Harvard Cooperative Society, 1912.
Kant, Immanuel. *Werke*. 6 vols. Ed. Wilhelm Weischedel. Darmstadt: Wissenschaftliche Buchgesellschaft, 1966.
Keats, John. *Letters, 1814–1821*. 2 vols. Ed. Hyder Edward Rollins. Cambridge: Harvard University Press, 1958.
———. *Poems*. Ed. Jack Stillinger. Cambridge: Belknap Press, 1978.
Knight, Richard Payne. *An Account of the Remains of the Worship of Priapus . . . to which is added, A Discourse on the Worship of Priapus and its connections with the Mystic Theology of the Ancients*. London: T. Spilsbury, 1786.
———. *Analytical Inquiry into the Principles of Taste*. 3d ed. London: T. Payne, 1806.
Kotzebue, August von. *Gustava Wasa*. In *Neue Schauspiele* 7. Leipzig: Paul Gotthelf Kummer, 1801.
———. *Der hyperboreische Esel oder Die heutige Bildung* (1799). In *Lustspiele*. Leipzig: Paul Gotthelf Kummer, 1800.
———. *Sämtliche Werke*. 10 vols. Leipzig: Eduard Kummer, 1867.
Lamb, Charles. *Charles Lamb on Shakespeare*. Ed. Joan Coldwell. Gerrards Cross: Colin Smythe, 1978.
———. *Works*. 12 vols. Ed. Alfred Ainger. Boston: Merrymount Press, 1888.
La Mesnardière, Hippolyte-Jules de. *La Poétique*. Paris: chez Antoine de Sommaville, 1640.
Leibniz, Gottfried Wilhelm. *Kleine Schriften zur Metaphysik*. Ed. H. H. Holz. Darmstadt: Wissenschaftliche Buchgesellschaft, 1965.
Lessing, Gotthold Ephraim. *Werke*. 8 vols. Ed. Herbert G. Göpfert, et al. Munich: Carl Hanser, 1970–79.
———. *Werke*. 25 vols. Ed. J. Petersen and W. von Olshausen. Berlin, Leipzig, Vienna, Stuttgart: Deutsches Verlagshaus Bong & Co., 1925–29.
———, Moses Mendelssohn, and Friedrich Nicolai. *Briefwechsel über das Trauerspiel*. Ed. Jochen Schulte-Sasse. Munich: Winkler, 1972.
Lewes, George Henry. Review: A. W. Schlegel, *Essais littéraires et historiques*. In *Foreign Quarterly Review* 32 (1843), 87–99.
———. "Shakespear's Critics: English and Foreign." In *Edinburgh Review* 90 (1849), 21–41.
Locke, John. *An Essay on Human Understanding* (1690). Ed. A. S. Pringle-Pattison. Oxford: Clarendon Press, 1924.
The Magic Lantern; its History and Effects; together with an Explanation of the Method of producing Dissolving Views, the Chromotope, Phantasmagoria, etc. London: A. N. Myers, 1854.
Marivaux, Pierre Carlet de Chamblain de. *Théâtre complet*. Ed. Marcel Arnand. Paris: Bibliothèque de la Pléiade, 1955.
Marmontel, Jean François. "Illusion." *Encyclopédie, ou Dictionnaire raisonné des sciences, des arts et des métiers*. 3d ed. 36 vols. Geneva: Pellet, 1777–79. VIII.
———. *Poétique François*. 2 vols. Paris: Lesclapart, 1763.
Meier, Georg Friedrich. *Abbildung eines Kunstrichters*. Halle: Carl Hermann Hemmerde, 1745.

———. *Anfangsgründe aller schönen Künste und Wissenschaften.* 3 vols. Halle: Carl Hermann Hemmerde, 1748–50; 2d ed. 1754.
———. *Versuch einer allgemeinen Auslegungskunst.* Halle: Carl Hermann Hemmerde, 1757. Reprint. Düsseldorff: Stern-Verlag Janssen, 1965.
Mendelssohn, Moses. *Gesammelte Schriften.* 7 vols. Ed. G. B. Mendelssohn. Leipzig: Brockhaus, 1843–45.
———. *Gesammelte Schriften.* Ed. Ismer Elbogen, Julius Guttmann, Eugene Mittwoch. Berlin: Friedrich Fromann, 1929–32. Reprint. Stuttgart: Friedrich Fromann, 1972.
Mercier, Louis Sébastien. *Du Théâtre, ou nouvel essai sur l'art dramatique.* Amsterdam: E. van Harrevelt, 1773.
Nicolai, Friedrich. "Abhandlung vom Trauerspiel." In *Bibliothek* 1, no. 1. (Leipzig: J. G. Dyck, 1757). 17–68.
Perrault, Charles. *Contes de ma mère l'oye* (1697). Paris: R. Hilsum, 1937.
Pirandello, Luigi. *Sei personaggi in cerca d'autore.* Firenze: R. Bemporad, 1921. Reprinted in *Maschere Nude* 3. Milan: Mondadori, 1948–49.
Plato. *The Collected Dialogues.* Ed. Edith Hamilton and Huntington Cairns. Princeton: Princeton University Press, 1961.
Pope, Alexander. *Peri Bathous, or the Art of sinking in Poetry,* in *Works.* 12 vols. London: Aaron Hill, George and Thomas Tonson, John Linnot and James Bathurst, 1764. Vol. 7, 111–95.
Porto, Luigi da. *Istoria novellamente ritrovata di due nobili amanti.* Venice: Benedetto de Bendoni [ca. 1530].
Richter, Jean Paul. *Werke.* 10 vols. Ed. Norbert Miller and Wilhelm Schmidt-Biggemann. Munich: Carl Winter, 1960–85.
Riedel, Friedrich Just. *Theorie der schönen Künste und Wissenschaften. Ein Auszug aus den Werken verschiedenen Schriftsteller.* Jena: Cuna, 1767.
Robinson, Henry Crabb. *The Correspondence of Henry Crabb Robinson with the Wordsworth Circle.* Ed. Edith J. Morley. Oxford, 1927.
———. *Henry Crabb Robinson on Books and their Writers.* 3 vols. Ed. Edith Morley. London: Dent, 1938.
Rousseau, Jean-Jacques. *Oeuvres.* 18 vols. Paris: Deterville, 1817.
Schelling, Caroline Michaelis. *Caroline. Briefe aus der Frühromantik.* 2 vols. Ed. Erich Schmidt. 1913. Reprint. Bern: Herbert Lang, 1970.
———. *Caroline und Dorothea Schlegel in Briefen.* Ed. Ernst Wieneke. Weimar: G. Kiepenheuer, 1914.
Schelling, Friedrich W. J. *Sämtliche Werke.* 14 vols. Stuttgart: Cotta, 1856–61.
———. "Über das Verhältnis der bildenden Künste zu der Natur" (1807). In *Werke.* Ed. Manfred Schröter. Munich: C.H. Beck und R. Oldenbourg, 1959. 3d vol. (supplementary), 388–429.
Schiller, Friedrich. *Briefe.* Ed. Gerhard Fricke. Munich: Carl Hanser, 1955.
———. *Sämtliche Werke.* 5 vols. Ed. Gerhard Fricke, Herbert G. Göpfert, Herbert Stubenrauch. Munich: Carl Hanser, 1962.
Schink, Johann Friedrich. *Dramaturgische Fragmente.* 4 vols., continuous pagination. Graz: Widmannstättische Schriften, 1781–82.
Schlegel, August Wilhelm. *August Wilhelm Schlegels Briefwechsel mit seinen Heidelberger Verlegern.* Ed. Erich Jenisch. Heidelberg: Carl Winter, 1922.
———. *A Course of Lectures on Dramatic Art and Literature.* Trans. John Black. 2 vols. London: Baldwin, Craddock, and Joy, 1815. Rev. ed. A.J.W. Morrison. London: G. Bell & Sons, 1889.
———. *Kritische Schriften.* 2 vols. Berlin: Georg Reimer, 1828.

---. *Kritische Schriften und Briefe.* 7 vols. Ed. Edgar Lohner. Stuttgart: Kohlhammer, 1962-74.
---. *Sämtliche Werke.* 12 vols. Ed. Eduard Böcking. Leipzig, 1846-47. Reprint. 16 vols., Hildesheim: Georg Olms, 1971-72.
---. *Vorlesungen über dramatische Kunst und Literatur.* 2 vols. in 3. Heidelberg: Mohr und Zimmer, 1809-11; 2d ed. 1817.
---. *Vorlesungen über dramatische Kunst und Literatur.* 2 vols. Ed. Giovanni Vittorio Amoretti. Bonn: Kurt Schröder, 1923.
---. "Ueber Litteratur, Kunst und Geist des Zeitalters." In *Europa* 2, no. 1 (1803), 3-95; Reprint. Ed. Ernst Behler. Stuttgart: Cotta, 1963.
Schlegel, Friedrich. *Friedrich Schlegels Briefe an seinen Bruder August Wilhelm.* Ed. Oskar F. Walzel. Berlin: Speyer und Peters, 1890.
---. *Kritische Ausgabe.* Ed. Ernst Behler, Hans Eichner, Jean-Jacques Anstett. Munich, Paderborn, Vienna: Schöningh, 1967- .
Schmid, Christian Heinrich. "Über das bürgerliche Trauerspiel" (1768). In *Literarische Chronik.* Ed. J. G. Heinzmann. III (1788), 212.
Schubert, Gotthelf Heinrich. *Ansichten von der Nachtseite der Naturwissenschaft.* Dresden: Arnold, 1808.
Shakespeare, William. *Complete Works.* Ed. Hardin Craig. Chicago: Scott, Foresman, 1959.
---. *Dramatische Werke.* 9 vols. Trans. August Wilhelm Schlegel. Berlin: Unger, 1797-1810; 2d ed. 1825-33.
Stendhal (= Henri Beyle). *Oeuvres complètes.* 25 vols. Ed. Georges Eudes. Paris: Pierre Larrive, 1946-56.
---. *Racine et Shakespeare.* Paris: Bossange, 1823. Reprinted in *Oeuvres complètes* 13. Paris: Le Divan, 1927-37.
Stoppard, Tom. *The Real Inspector Hound.* New York: Grove Press, 1968.
Styles, John. *An Essay on the Character, Immoral, and Antichristian Tendency of the Stage.* Newport, Isle of Wight: Medina Press; London: Williams and Smith, 1806.
Sulzer, Johann Georg. "Täuschung" (1774). In *Allgemeine Theorie der schönen Künste.* 4 vols. Leipzig: Weidmann, 1794. IV, 514-16.
Tieck, Ludwig. *Der gestiefelte Kater* (1797). Ed. Helmut Kreuzer. Stuttgart: Reclam, 1984.
---. *Kritische Schriften.* 4 vols. Leipzig: F. A. Brockhaus, 1848-52; Reprint. Berlin: de Gruyter, 1974.
---. *Ludwig Tieck. Dichter über ihre Dichtung.* 3 vols. Ed. Uwe Schweikert. Munich: Heimeran, 1971.
---. Introduction to *Das Ungeheuer und der verzauberte Wald* (1800). In *Schriften.* 28 vols. Berlin: G. Reimer, 1828-54. XI, xlviii-lvi.
Valdastri, Idelfonso. "Dissertazione sopra il quesito quali vantaggi, e svantaggi abbiano rimpetto alla Tragedia, e alla Commedia, quelle, che diconsi Tragedie Cittadinesche, e quali sieno le peculiari leggi costitutive di questo genere, oltre le comuni agli altri, cavandole dalla specifica, ed intima indole loro, per dimostrare qual grado di perfezione possa ottenersi, presentata dal Signor Abate Idelfonso Valdastri Modenese al Concorso dell' anno MDCCXC e coronata dalla Reale Accademia di Scienze e Belle Lettere di Mantova." Mantova, 1792.
"Valdastri Preisschrift." *Neue Bibliothek der schönen Wissenschaften und der freyen Künste* 52, no. 1. Leipzig: Dyckische Buchhandlung, 1794. 103.
Voltaire, François-Marie Arouet de. *Le Brutus, avec un discours sur la tragédie.* Paris: Josse, 1731.
---. *Oeuvres complètes.* 92 vols. [duodecimo Kehl], de l'Imprimerie de la société littéraire typographique, 1785.

Weiße, Christian Felix. Preface to *Das Fanatismus, oder Jean Calas. Ein Historisches Schauspiel in fünf Aufzügen, Samt einer kurzen Geschichte von seinem Tode.* Frankfurt und Leipzig: Dykische Buchhandlung, 1780.

———. *Selbstbiographie.* Ed. Christian Ernst Weiße and Samuel Gottlob Frisch. Leipzig: Georg Voß, 1806.

Wolff, Christian. *Psychologia empirica.* Frankfurt: Renger, 1732.

———. *Theologia naturalis.* Frankfurt: Renger, 1736–37.

Wordsworth, William, and Dorothy Wordsworth. *The Letters of William and Dorothy Wordsworth* II. *The Middle Years,* Part 1, 1806–11. Ed. Ernest de Selincourt, rev. Mary Moorman. Oxford: Clarendon Press, 1969.

Wordsworth, William, and Samuel Taylor Coleridge. *Lyrical Ballads.* Ed. R. L. Brett and A. R. Jones. London: Methuen, 1963.

Secondary Sources

Abrams, Meyer Howard. *A Glossary of Literary Terms.* 5th ed. New York: Holt, Rinehart and Winston, 1988.

Adams, Joseph Quincey. *A Life of William Shakespeare.* Boston: Houghton Mifflin, 1923.

Adorno, Theodor. *Ästhetische Theorie.* Frankfurt: Suhrkamp, 1973.

———. *Negative Dialektik.* 3d ed. Frankfurt: Suhrkamp, 1970.

———. *Zur Metacritik der Erkenntnistheorie: Studien über Husserl und die phenomenologische Antinomien* (1956). Frankfurt: Suhrkamp, 1970.

Affron, Charles. *A Stage for Poets. Studies in the Theatre of Hugo and Musset.* Princeton: Princeton University Press, 1971.

Allroggen, Gerhard. *E.T.A. Hoffmanns Kompositionen. Ein chronologisch-thematisches Verzeichnis seiner musikalischen Werke mit einer Einführung.* Regensburg: Gustav Bosse, 1970.

Anthony, Sister Rose, S.C. *The Jeremy Collier Stage Controversy, 1698–1726.* New York, 1937. Reprint. New York: Benjamin Blom, 1966.

Arntzen, H. "Das Spiel der Maskierten." In *Die ernste Komödie.* Munich: Nymphenburger Verlagshandlung, 1968. 156–68.

Badawi, Mohamed Moustafa. *Coleridge: Critic of Shakespeare.* Cambridge: Cambridge University Press, 1973.

Barish, Jonas. *The Antitheatrical Prejudice.* Berkeley and Los Angeles: University of California Press, 1981.

Barrère, Jean-Bertrand. *La Fantasie de Victor Hugo.* 3 vols. Paris: J. Corti, 1949–60.

———. "Le Lustre et la rampe. Petite note sur la conception de la scéne selon Victor Hugo." In *La Revue d'histoire du théâtre* 1, no. 4 (1948–49), 282–86.

Bate, Jonathan. *Shakespeare and the English Romantic Imagination.* Oxford: Clarendon Press, 1986.

Bate, Walter Jackson. *Negative Capability: The Intuitive Approach in Keats.* Cambridge: Harvard University Press, 1939.

———. "The Sympathetic Imagination in Eighteenth-Century English Criticism." In *Journal of English Literary History* 12 (1945), 144–64.

Belavel, Yvon. *L'Esthétique sans Paradoxe de Diderot.* Paris: Gallimard, 1950.

Bennett, Benjamin. *Modern Drama and German Classicism.* Ithaca and London: Cornell University Press, 1979.

Bergson, Henri. "Laughter" (*Le Rire*). Trans. Fred Rothwell. In *Comedy.* Ed. Wylie Sypher. Garden City: Doubleday, 1956. 61–190.

———. *Oeuvres*. Paris: Presses Universitaires de France, 1959. 2d ed. 1963.
———. *Le Rire. Essai sur la signification du comique*. Paris: F. Alcan, 1900.
Bodensiek, K. H. "Von der romantischen Illusion." In *Geistige Welt* 2 (1947), 82–84.
Bremner, Geoffrey. *Order and Change. The Pattern of Diderot's Thought*. Cambridge: Cambridge University Press, 1983.
Brinker, Menachim. "Aesthetic Illusion." In *Journal of Aesthetics and Art Criticism* 36 (1977–78), 191–96.
Brown, Jane. *Goethe's Faust. The German Tragedy*. Ithaca: Cornell University Press, 1986.
Brown, Joseph Epen. *The Critical Opinions of Samuel Johnson*. New York: Russel & Russel, 1961.
Burwick, Frederick. "Coleridge, Schlegel, and Animal Magnetism." In *English and German Romanticism: Cross-Currents and Controversies*. Ed. James Pipkin. Heidelberg: Carl Winter, 1985.
———. *The Damnation of Newton: Goethe's Color Theory and Romantic Perception*. Berlin and New York: de Gruyter, 1986.
———. *The Haunted Eye: Perception and the Grotesque in English and German Romanticism*. Heidelberg: Carl Winter, 1987.
———. "Romantic Drama: From Optics to Illusion." In *Literature and Science. Theory and Practice*. Ed. Stuart Peterfreund. Boston: Northeastern University Press, 1990. 167–208.
Cahn, Victor L. *Beyond Absurdity: The Plays of Tom Stoppard*. Rutherford: Farleigh Dickinson, 1979.
Carlson, Marvin. *Goethe and the Weimar Theatre*. Ithaca: Cornell University Press, 1978.
Carr, Leslie. "Diderot and the Paradox of the Spectator." Diss., University of Connecticut, 1980.
———. "Painting and the Paradox of the Spectator in Diderot's Art." In *Studies on Voltaire and the Eighteenth Century* 193 (1980), 1690–98.
Cave, Richard Allen. "Romantic Drama in Performance." In *The Romantic Theatre*. Gerrards Cross: Colin Smythe, 1986. 79–104.
Chahine, Samia. *La Dramaturgie de Victor Hugo (1816–1843)*. Paris: A. G. Nizet, 1971.
Chancerel, Léon. "Victor Hugo, metteur en scène, décorateur et costumier." In *La Revue d'histoir du théâtre* 4, no. 3 (1952), 232.
Chouillet, J. "La formation des idées esthétiques de Diderot." Diss., Université de Lille, 1973.
Curran, Stuart. "Shelleyan Drama." In *The Romantic Theatre*. Ed. Richard Allen Cave. Gerrards Cross: Colin Smythe, 1986. 68–71.
Daemmrich, Horst. "Illusion, Möglichkeit und Grenzen eines Begriffs." In *Lessing Yearbook* 1 (1969), 88–98.
Derbolav, Josef. *Der Dialog "Kratylos" im Rahmen der platonischen Sprach- und Erkenntnisphilosophie*. Saarbrücken: West-Ost-Verlag, 1953.
———. "Das Problem des Metasprachlichen in Platons 'Kratylos.'" In *Lebendiger Realismus. Festschrift für Johannes Thyssen*. Ed. Klaus Hartmann with Hans Wagner. Bonn: Bouvier, 1962.
Derrida, Jacques. *La voix et le phénoméne*. Paris: Editions du Seuil, 1967.
Descotes, Maurice. *L'Obsession de Napoléon dans le Cromwell de Victor Hugo*. Paris: Lettres modernes, 1967.
Deuchler, Florens. "Diderots Traktat über das Schöne." In *Jahrbuch für Ästhetik und allgemeine Kunstwissenschaft* 3 (1955/57), 197–224.
Dieckman, Herbert. *Cinq Leçons sur Diderot*. Paris: Société de publications romanes et françaises, 1959.

———. Review: "Yvon Belavel, *L'Esthétique sans paradoxe de Diderot.*" In *Romanic Review* 42 (1951), 63–65.
Fayolle, Roger. "Criticism and Theory." In *The French Romantics.* 2 vols. Ed. D. G. Charlton. Cambridge: Cambridge University Press, 1984. II, 248–73.
Feldmann, Helmut. *Die Fiabe Carlo Gozzis. Die Entstehung einer Gattung und ihre Transposition in das System der deutschen Romantik.* Cologne: Böhlau, 1971.
Flemming, Willi. *Goethe und das Theater seiner Zeit.* Stuttgart; W. Kohlhammer, 1968.
Foakes, Reginald A. "Form to his Conceit: Shakespeare and the uses of Stage Illusion." In *Proceedings of the British Academy, London* 66 (1980), 103–19.
———. "Repairing the Damaged Archangel." In *Essays in Criticism* 24 (1974), 423–27.
Foucault, Michael. *Les mots et les choses.* Paris: Gallimard, 1966.
Frenzel, Herbert. *Geschichte des Theaters. Daten und Dokumente.* Munich: DTV, 1979.
Fried, Michel. *Absorption and Theatricality. Painting and Beholder in the Age of Diderot.* Berkeley: University of California Press, 1980.
Friedeman, Käte. *Die Rolle des Erzählers in der Epik.* Leipzig: H. Haessel, 1910.
———. "Die romantische Ironie." In *Zeitschrift für Ästhetik und allgemeine Kunstwissenschaft* 13 (1919), 270–82.
Fruman, Norman. *Coleridge: The Damaged Archangel.* New York: George Braziller, 1971.
Furst, Lilian R. *Fictions of Romantic Irony.* Cambridge: Harvard University Press, 1984.
Gadamer, Hans-Georg. *Wahrheit und Methode.* Tübingen: Mohr, 1960. 3d rev. ed., 1972.
Gebhardt, Peter. *Schlegels Shakespeare-Übersetzungen. Untersuchungen zu seinem Übersetzungsverfahren am Beispiel des Hamlet.* Göttingen: Vandenhoeck und Ruprecht, 1970.
Gerth, Klaus. *Studien zu Gerstenbergs Poetik.* Göttingen: Vandenhoeck und Ruprecht, 1960.
Gillespie, Gerald. "Young Tieck and the Romantic Breakthrough." In *Theater Three* 4 (Spring 1988), 31–44.
Gombrich, Ernst H. *Art and Illusion. A Study in the Psychology of Pictorial Representation.* Princeton: Princeton University Press, 1960. Rev. 1961.
Gray, Terence. "The Festival Theatre in Cambridge." In *Theatre Arts Monthly* 10 (September 1926), 585–86.
———. "This Age in the Theatre." In *Bookman* 32 (October 1932), 11.
Greiner, Walter. "Deutsche Einflüsse auf die Dichtungstheorie von Samuel Taylor Coleridge: Eine neue untersuchung über den Einfluß von Tetens, Kant und Schelling auf Coleridge." Diss. Universität Tübingen 1957.
Griggs, Earl Leslie. "The Willing Suspension of Disbelief." In *Elizabethan Studies and Other Essays in Honor of George F. Reynolds.* Boulder: University of Colorado Press, 1945. 272–85.
Günzel, Klaus. *König der Romantik. Das Leben des Dichters Ludwig Tieck.* Tübingen: Wunderlich, 1981.
Guthke, Karl S. "Das bürgerliche Drama des 18. und frühen 19. Jahrhunderts." In *Handbuch des deutschen Dramas.* Ed. Walter Hinck. Düsseldorf: Bagel, 1980.
Hamilton, James R. " 'Illusion' and the Distrust of Theatre." In *Journal of Aesthetics and Art Criticism* 41, no. 1 (Fall 1982), 39–50.
Hardy, Swana. *Goethe, Calderon, und die romantische Theorie des Dramas.* Heidelberg: Carl Winter, 1965.
Harken, Ulrike. "Die Bühnenbilder K. F. Schinkels, 1798–1834." Diss., Universität Kiel, 1974.
Haßelbeck, Otto. *Illusion und Fiktion. Lessings Beitrag zur poetologischen Diskussion über das Verhältnis von Kunst und Wirklichkeit.* Munich: Wilhelm Fink, 1979.

Heidsieck, Arnold. "Der Disput zwischen Lessing und Mendelssohn über das Trauerspiel." In *Lessing Yearbook* 11 (1979), 7–34.

———. "Lessing as Aesthetic Thinker. An Essay on the Systematic Structure of Lessing's Aesthetics." In *Lessing Yearbook* 15 (1983), 177–211.

Heimrich, Bernhard. "Der Begriff der Parekbase in der Ironie-Terminologie Friedrich Schlegels." In *Fiktion und Fiktionsironie in Theorie und Dichtung der deutschen Romantik.* Tübingen: Max Niemeyer, 1968. 59–65.

Helmholtz-Phelan, Anna Augusta. *The Indebtedness of Samuel Taylor Coleridge to August Wilhelm Schlegel.* Madison: University of Wisconsin Press, 1907. Reprint. New York: Haskell House, 1971.

Hobson, Marian. *The Object of Art. The Theory of Illusion in Eighteenth-Century France.* Cambridge: Cambridge University Press, 1982.

———. "Le 'Paradoxe sur le comédien' est un paradoxe." In *Poétique* 15 (1973), 320–39.

Hoffmeister, Elmar. *Täuschung und Wirklichkeit bei Heinrich von Kleist.* Bonn: Bouvier, 1968.

Hogsett, Charlotte. "Jean Baptiste Du Bos on Art as Illusion." In *Studies on Voltaire and the Eighteenth Century* 73 (1970), 161.

Houston, John Porter. *Victor Hugo.* New York: Twayne, 1974.

Huhn, Thomas. "Adorno's Aesthetics of Illusion." In *Journal of Aesthetics and Art Criticism* 44, no. 2 (Winter 1985), 181–89.

Husserl, Edmund. *Ideen zu einer reinen Phänomenologie und phänomenologische Philosophie.* 1913. 2d ed. 1922. Reprint. Tübingen: Max Niemeyer, 1980.

———. *Phantasie, Bildbewußtsein, Erinnerung.* Ed. Eduard Marbach. The Hague: Martinus Nijhoof, 1980.

Immerwahr, Ray. *The Esthetic Intent of Tieck's Fantastic Comedy.* Seattle: University of Washington Press, 1953.

Iser, Wolfgang. "Akte des Fingierens. Oder: Was ist das Fiktive im fiktionalen Text?" In *Funktionen des Fiktiven. Poetik und Hermeneutik* 10. Munich: Fink, 1983. 121–52.

Issacharoff, Michael. "How Play Scripts Refer: Some Preliminary Considerations." In *On Referring in Literature.* Ed. Anna Whiteside and Michael Issacharoff. Bloomington and Indianapolis: Indiana University Press, 1987.

Jackson, J. R. de J. "Coleridge on Dramatic Illusion and Spectacle in the Performance of Shakespeare's Plays." In *Modern Philology* 62 (1964–65), 13–21.

Jakobson, Roman, and Morris Halle. *Fundamentals of Language.* Janua linguarum, no. 1. Mouton: 's Gravenhage, 1956.

Jauß, Hans Robert. "Anmerkungen zum idealen Gespräch." *Das Gespräch. Poetik und Hermeneutik* 11. Munich: Fink, 1984. 467–72.

———. "Der dialogische und der dialektische *Neveu de Rameau* oder: Wie Diderot Sokrates und Hegel Diderot rezipierte." In *Das Gespräch. Poetik und Hermeneutik* 11. Munich: Fink, 1984. 393–419.

———. "Diderots Paradox über das Schauspiel (Entretiens sur le Fils naturel)." In *Germanisch-Romanische Monatsschrift* 24 (1961), 380–413.

———. "Der literarische Prozeß des Modernismus von Rousseau bis Adorno." In *Epochenschwelle und Epochenbewußtsein. Poetik und Hermeneutik* 12. Munich: Fink, 1987. 243–68.

———. "Nachahmungsprinzip und Wirklichkeitsbegriff in der Theorie des Romans von Diderot bis Stendhal." In *Nachahmung und Illusion. Poetik und Hermeneutik* 1. Munich: Fink, 1964. 157–78.

Jordan, John. *Thomas De Quincey, Literary Critic.* Berkeley: University of California Press, 1952.

Kerr, Alfred. *Godwi. Ein Kapitel deutscher Romantik.* Berlin: G. Bondi, 1898.

Kluckhohn, Paul. *Das Ideengut der deutschen Romantik.* Tübingen: Max Niemeyer, 1953.
Knabe, Peter-Eckhard. "Illusion," In *Schlüsselbegriffe des kunsttheoretischen Denkens in Frankreich von der Spätklassik bis zum Ende der Aufklärung.* Düsseldorf: L. Schwann, 1972. 299–304.
Köhler, Wolfgang. *Gestalt Psychology: An Introduction to New Concepts in Modern Psychology.* New York: Liveright, 1947.
———. *The Selected Papers of Wolfgang Köhler.* Ed. Mary Henle. New York: Liveright, 1971.
Kokott, Jörg Henning. "Das Theater auf dem Theater im Drama der Neuzeit. Eine Untersuchung über die Darstellung der theatralischen Aufführung durch das Theater auf dem Theater in ausgewählten Dramen von Shakespeare, Tieck, Pirandello, Genet, Ionesco und Beckett." Diss., Universität Köln, 1968.
Koopmann, Helmut. *Drama der Aufklärung. Kommentar zu einer Epoche.* Munich: Winkler, 1979.
Köpke, Rudolf. *Ludwig Tieck. Erinnerungen aus dem Leben des Dichters nach dessen mündlichen und schriftlichen Mitteilungen.* 2 vols. Leipzig, 1855. Reprint. Darmstadt: Wissenschaftliche Buchgesellschaft, 1970.
Krieger, Murray. "Mediation, Language, and Vision in the Reading of Literature." In *Interpretation: Theory and Practice.* Ed. Charles S. Singleton. Baltimore: Johns Hopkins University Press, 1969.
———. *Poetic Presence and Illusion.* Baltimore: Johns Hopkins University Press, 1979.
———. *Words about Words about Words. Theory, Criticism, and the Literary Text.* Baltimore: Johns Hopkins University Press, 1988.
Lambert, Pauline. *Réalité et ironie. Les jeux de l'illusion dans le théâtre de Marivaux.* Fribourg/Suisse: éd. univ., 1973.
Lancaster, H. C. *French Tragedy in the Time of Louis XV and Voltaire, 1715–1774.* Baltimore: Johns Hopkins University Press, 1950.
Lobsien, Eckard. *Theorie literarischer Illusionsbildung.* Stuttgart: Metzler, 1975.
Londré, Felicia Hardison. *Tom Stoppard.* New York: Ungar, 1981.
Lussky, Alfred. *Tieck's Romantic Irony.* Chapel Hill: University of North Carolina Press, 1932.
Marelli, Adriani. "Ludwig Tiecks frühe Märchenspiele und gozzische Manier." Diss., Universität Köln, 1968.
Martin, R. L. *The Paradox of the Liar.* New Haven: Yale University Press, 1970.
Maurer-Adam, R. "Deklamatorisches Theater. Dramaturgie und Inszenierung von Clemens Brentanos Lustspiel *Ponce de Leon*." In *Aurora* 40 (1980), 71–99.
McFarland, Thomas. *Coleridge and the Pantheist Tradition.* Oxford: Clarendon Press, 1969.
———. "Coleridge's Plagiarisms Once More: A Review Essay." In *Yale Review* 63 (1974), 252–86.
———. *Originality and Imagination.* Baltimore: Johns Hopkins University Press, 1985.
———. *Romanticism and the Forms of Ruin. Wordsworth, Coleridge, and Modalities of Fragmentation.* Princeton: Princeton University Press, 1981.
———. *Shapes of Culture.* Iowa City: University of Iowa Press, 1987.
McKenna, Wayne. *Charles Lamb and the Theatre.* New York: Harper & Row, 1978.
McLeish, Kenneth. *The Theatre of Aristophanes.* New York: Taplinger, 1980.
Merleau-Ponty, Maurice. *L'oiel et l'esprit.* Paris: Gallimard, 1964.
———. *Phénoménologie de la perception.* Paris: Gallimard, 1945.
Michelson, Peter. "Die Erregung des Mitleids durch die Tragödie." In *Deutsche Vierteljahresschrift* 40 (1960), 557ff.
Morrill, Dorothy I. "Coleridge's Theory of Dramatic Illusion." In *Modern Language Notes* 42 (November 1927), 436–44.

Mortier, Roland. *Diderot en Allemagne 1750–1850*. Paris: Presses Universitaires de France, 1954.
——. *Diderot in Deutschland, 1750–1850*. Trans. Hans G. Schürmann. Stuttgart: Metzler, 1972.
Nef, Ernst. "Das Aus-der-Rolle-Fallen als Mittel der Illusionszerstörung bei Tieck und Brecht." In *Zeitschrift für deutsche Philologie* 83 (1964), Heft 2, 191–215.
Neureuter, Hans Peter. *Das Spiegelmotiv bei Clemens Brentano. Studie zum romantischen Ich-Bewußtsein*. Frankfurt: Athenäum, 1972.
Nivelle, Armand. *Kunst- und Dichtungstheorien zwischen Aufklärung und Klassik*. Berlin: de Gruyter, 1960.
Orsini, Gian. "Coleridge and Schlegel Reconsidered." In *Comparative Literature* 16 (1964), 97–118.
——. *Coleridge and the German Idealists*. Carbondale: Southern Illinois University Press, 1969.
Pfeiffer-Belli, Wolfgang. *Clemens Brentano. Ein romantisches Dichterleben*. Freiburg im Breisgau: Herder, 1947.
Pikulik, Lothar. *"Bürgerliches Trauerspiel" und Empfindsamkeit*. Cologne, Graz: Böhlau, 1966.
Pillau, Helmut. *Die fortgedachte Dissonanz. Hegels Tragödientheorie und Schillers Tragödie*. Munich: Wilhelm Fink, 1981.
Poundstone, William. *Labyrinths of Reason. Paradox, Puzzles, and the Frailty of Knowledge*. New York: Doubleday, 1988.
Prudhoe, John. *The Theatre of Goethe and Schiller*. Totowa, NJ: Rowman and Littlefield, 1973.
Rath, Norbert. "Dialektik des Scheins—Materialien zum Scheinbegriff Adornos." In *Ästhetischer Schein*. Ed. Willi Oelmüller. Paderborn, Munich, Vienna, Zurich: Schöningh, 1982. 51–61.
Rees, Terence. *Theatre Lighting in the Age of Gas*. London: Society for Theatre Research, 1978.
Reis, Timothy J. *Toward Dramatic Illusion: Theatrical Technique and Meaning from Hardy to Horace*. New Haven: Yale University Press, 1971.
Robertson, J. G. *Lessing's Dramatic Theory*. Cambridge: Cambridge University Press, 1929. 2d ed. 1965.
Rudowski, Victor Anthony. *Lessing's Aesthetica in nuce*. Chapel Hill: University of North Carolina Press, 1971.
Rusack, Hedwig Hoffmann. *Gozzi in Germany*. New York: Columbia University Press, 1930.
Sartre, Jean-Paul. *L'Imaginaire: Psychologie phénoménologique de l'imagination*. Paris: Gallimard, 1940.
Sauer, Thomas G. *A. W. Schlegel's Shakespearean Criticism in England, 1814–1846*. Bonn: Bouvier, 1981.
Schenkel, Martin. *Lessings Poetik des Mitleids*. Bonn: Bouvier, 1984.
Schipperges, Heinrich. *Welt des Auges. Zur Theorie des Sehens und Kunst des Schauens*. Basel: Herder Freiburg, 1978.
Schmidt, Jochen. *Die Geschichte des Genie-Gedankens in der deutschen Literatur, Philosophie und Politik 1750–1945*. 2 vols. Darmstadt: Wissenschaftliche Buchgesellschaft, 1985.
Schmitt, Albert R. "Christian Felix Weißes *Jean Calas*—Dokumentarisches Theater im 18. Jahrhundert." In *Aufnahme—Weitergabe: Literarische Impulse um Lessing und Goethe*. Ed. John A. McCarthy and Albert A. Kipa. Hamburg: Buske, 1982. 2–30.

Schneider, Elisabeth. *Coleridge, Opium, and Kubla Khan*. Chicago: University of Chicago Press, 1953.
Schneider, Ferdinand Josef. *Theodor Gottlieb von Hippel in den Jahren von 1781 und die erste Epoche seiner literarischen Tätigkeit*. Prag: Taussig & Taussig, 1911.
Schulz, Gerhard A. *Literaturkritik als Form der ästhetischen Erfahrung*. Eine Untersuchung am Beispiel der literatur-kritischen Versuch von Samuel Taylor Coleridge und August Wilhelm Schlegel über das Shakespeare-Drama *Romeo und Julia*. Frankfurt: Peter Lang, 1984.
Shearer, Edna Aston, and Julian Ira Lindsay. "Wordsworth and Coleridge Marginalia in a Copy of Richard Payne Knight's *Analytical Inquiry into the Principles of Taste*." In *Huntington Library Quarterly* 1, no. 1 (October 1937), 63–99.
Sherman, Carol. *Diderot and the Art of the Dialogue*. Geneva: Librairie Droz, 1976.
Stechow, Wolfgang. *Pieter Bruegel, The Elder*. New York: Abrams, 1969.
Strohschneider-Kohrs, Ingrid. *Die romantische Ironie in Theorie und Gestaltung*. Tübingen: Niemeyer, 1960. 2d ed. 1977.
Strube, Werner. "Ästhetische Illusion. Ein kritischer Beitrag zur Geschichte der Wirkungsästhetik des 18. Jahrhunderts." Diss., Universität Bochum, 1971.
Szondi, Peter. "Friedrich Schlegel und die romantische Ironie. Mit einer Beilage über Tiecks Komödien." In *Satz und Gegensatz*. Frankfurt: Suhrkamp, 1964. 5–24.
Thalmann, Marianne. "Clemens Brentano, *Gustav Wasa*." In *Provokation und Demonstration in der Komödie der Romantik*. Berlin: E. Schmidt, 1974. 71–77.
Thorslev, Peter. "The Romantic Mind Is Its Own Place." In *Comparative Literature* 15, no. 3 (Summer 1963), 250–68.
Todorov, Tzvetan. *The Fantastic* (= *Introduction à la littérature fantastique;* Paris: Editions du Seuil, 1970). Trans. Richard Howard. Cleveland, Ohio: Case Western, 1973.
Villiers, André. "A propos du *Paradoxe* de Diderot." In *Revue d'Histoire du Théâtre* 4 (1952), 379–81.
―――. "Illusion dramatique et dramaturgie classique." *XVIIe Siècle* 73 (1966), 4–21.
Walton, Kendall L. "Appreciating Fiction: Suspending Disbelief or Pretending Belief?" *Dispositio* 5, no. 13–14 (1980), 1–18.
―――. "Fearing Fictions." *Journal of Philosophy* 75, no. 1 (January 1978), 5–27.
―――. "How Remote are Fictional Worlds from the Real World?" In *Journal of Aesthetics and Art Criticism* 37, no. 1 (Fall 1978), 11–23.
―――. *Mimesis as Make-Believe. On the Foundations of the Representational Arts*. Cambridge: Harvard University Press, 1990.
―――. "Points of View in Narrative and Depictive Representation." In *Nous* 10, no. 1 (March 1976), 49–61.
Wasserman, Earl R. "The Sympathetic Imagination in Eighteenth-Century Theories of Acting." In *Journal of English and Germanic Philology* 46 (1947), 264–72.
Wellek, René. "Coleridge." In *A History of Modern Criticism*. New Haven: Yale University Press, 1955. II, 151–87.
Wenzel, Heinz. *Das Problem des Scheins in der Ästhetik: Schillers Ästhetische Briefe*. Cologne, 1958.
Wierlacher, Alois. *Das Bürgerliche Drama. Seine theoretische Begründung im 18. Jahrhundert*. Munich: Wilhelm Fink, 1968.
Wilson, Arthur M. *Diderot*. New York: Oxford University Press, 1972.

Index

acting, 17, 130–33, 206, 302
  changing fashions, 72, 149, 207, 231, 302
  gesture, delivery, movement, 4, 55, 58, 60, 95–96, 100, 103, 203
  studied control vs. feeling the part, 44–47, 60–62, 73–74
  vs. staging, 231, 267–69, 281, 297, 302
Addison, Joseph, 88
admiration, 84, 87, 89
Adorno, Theodor, 6, 9–11, 13
Aeschylus, 129, 156, 184
Aesop, 94
aesthetic complementation, 100, 104, 106, 108, 112, 156, 187–88, 299
aesthetic distance, 2, 41, 79, 111, 120
aesthetic experience, 2, 7, 19, 116
  as community response, 138–43
  as passive submission, 20, 26, 99–100, 103, 186, 187, 193, 200, 209, 222
  as rational or emotional, 8–9, 71, 81–82, 84–93, 96, 113, 116, 117, 153, 161, 184, 186, 205–7, 234–36, 244–45, 248, 287
  as sensual, 17, 22, 56, 59–60, 82, 86, 87, 106–7, 109, 111–12, 114, 120, 128, 142, 147, 200, 244–45
aesthetic immediacy, 2, 7, 36, 41
aesthetic judgment, 6, 7, 60, 61, 90–91, 93, 109, 227
affect, 10, 29, 94, 203
Alembert, Jean Le Rond d', 25, 29
Alfieri, Vittorio, 150
allegory, 65, 175
alterity, 120, 163, 179
anachronism, 95, 102

anamorphic art, 273
anticipation, 51, 72, 73, 98, 99, 139, 168, 180, 217, 254, 269, 277
anti-illusion, 5, 6, 9, 11, 61, 123–24, 232
appearance, 6, 15, 27, 119, 124–25, 168, 234
Archer, William, 45
Ariosto, 227
Aristophanes
  Acharnians, 147–48
  parabasis, 4, 11, 148–49, 279, 292, 297
Aristotle, 86, 87, 101, 119, 136, 154–55, 217, 224, 237, 249
Arnim, Achim von, 269, 295, 298–303
art and nature; artifice and reality, 175–77, 203–4, 234–36, 251, 283
Artaud, Antonin, 5, 267
as-if, 11, 12
associationism, 193, 200, 207, 222
audience response, 43, 237–38, 244
  co-conspiracy, 4, 75, 113, 149, 254
  fictive audience on stage, 165–66, 279–92
  "secretly" addressed by players, 75–79, 149, 152, 158, 162
Augustine, St., 246

Badawi, M. M, 192, 193
ballet, 235–36
Bannister, John, 76–77, 79
Barish, Jonas, 5
Barnum, Phineas T., 50
Bate, Walter Jackson, 160
Batteux, Charles, 26
Baumgarten, Alexander Gottlieb, 81, 116
Beaumarchais, Pierre-Augustin Caron, 41

320 Index

beautiful, 7, 14, 55–57, 105, 115, 117, 125, 199, 208, 234, 246–48
Beckett, Samuel, 5, 9
Bennett, Benjamin, 99
Bensley, Robert, 77, 79
Berkeley, George, 38, 217
Beaumont, Sir George, 199
Bible, 217, 252
　I Corinthians, 273
　Genesis, 215
　Job, 239
bienséance, 53, 55
Black, John, 153 n. 37, 177, 193, 195 n. 16
Bodmer, Johann Jacob, 46, 64, 82, 116, 118, 212
Böttiger, Karl August, 289–90
Boileau, Nicolas, 153
Bonaparte, Napoléon, 34, 252, 302
Brecht, Bertolt, 5, 9
　Verfremdungseffekt, 6
Brentano, Clemens, 269, 293–99, 301–3
　Godwi, 296
　Gustava Wasa, 293–94
　Die lustige Musikanten, 293–94
　Ponce de Leon, 293–95, 299
　Valeria oder Vaterlist, 294–96
Breitinger, Johann Jacob, 107, 116
Brewster, Sir David, 242
Brown, J. E., 29
Bruegel, Pieter, 253
Brühl, Karl Friedrich Moritz Paul, Count, 240–41
Burke, Edmund, 38, 200–201
Byron, Lord (George Gordon), 267, 269
　Manfred, 182, 302
　Werner, 267

Calderón de la Barca, Pedro, 152, 170, 235–36, 239, 245, 303
Calepio, Pietro de, 46
Callot, Jacques, 247, 253
catharsis, 22, 84–86, 145–46
causality, 48–51, 56, 68, 93, 98, 105, 128, 154, 156, 160, 174, 180, 184–85, 217, 222
Cazotte, Jacques, 70
certainty, 216–17, 221
Cervantes, Miguel de, 221, 227, 296
character
　action (*proairesis* and *praxis*), 154–55, 237–38
　comic *naiveté*, 158
　meditation and observation, 211, 218, 220, 223–24, 227
　motives, 131–32, 145, 164, 171, 183, 187

revealed or concealed, 135, 164, 175, 295
stock, 157, 171
tragic flaw (*hamartia*), 145, 248
Chardin, Jean-Baptiste-Siméon, 58
chiaroscuro, 233, 256, 269
chorus, 144–45, 148, 239, 244, 249
Christie, Agatha, 279
Cicero, 117
Clairon, Claire-Joseph, 44, 73
Coleridge, Samuel Taylor, 16, 17, 26, 33, 37, 47, 75, 99, 106, 189, 245
　Biographia Literaria, 192, 193, 215, 222–26
　Lectures, 4, 41, 46, 72, 77, 177, 191–99, 203–29, 231, 303
　"On Certainty," 216, 221, 300–301
　Remorse, 5, 17, 218, 267–79
　plagiarism, 125–26, 127–28, 154, 191–96, 214, 219
　"poetic faith" ("temporary Faith," "Half-Faith"), 196, 206, 209, 214–16, 221, 223–26, 300
　"primary imagination," 83
　"reconciliation of opposites," 74, 225–26
　"willing suspension of disbelief," 12, 37, 38, 48, 63, 87, 96, 128, 188, 194, 196–97, 210, 212, 215, 221–224, 226, 229, 268, 272, 286
Collier, Jeremy, 19, 20–21, 22, 82
Collier, John Payne, 191, 214
comic relief, 179
commedia dell'arte, 151, 157, 247, 253, 294–95
Condorcet, Antoine Nicolas de, 21
Congreve, William, 77, 79
Copeau, Jacques, 44
Corneille, Pierre, 23, 41, 100, 153, 157, 194, 251
costume, 53, 58, 253, 257, 290
coup de théâtre, 54, 168, 268, 303
Cramer, Johann Andreas, 116
credibility, 30, 49, 76
Cromwell, Oliver, 252
cultural tradition, 129, 133, 140
Cumberland, Richard, 225
Curran, Stuart, 302–3

Dante, 227, 247
Darwin, Erasmus, 2, 14, 32, 35, 37, 120, 197
deception, 5, 17, 20, 35, 38, 66, 67, 91, 93, 115, 116, 121, 153, 162, 166, 168, 182, 184, 189, 201, 205, 209, 228, 261, 270, 276, 290, 295
dédoublement, 62, 75

Delacroix, Eugène, 257
De Quincey, Thomas, 43, 127
Derrida, Jacques, 9, 11–12, 13, 14
Descartes, René, 82, 216
dialogue, 134–36, 139–40, 150, 161–63, 166, 180, 201, 206, 208, 252, 276, 281
Diderot, Denis, 2, 4, 17, 32–33, 36–37, 41–60, 82, 99–101, 119, 137, 197, 219, 233, 285
  "Beau," 46, 55–56
  Les Bijoux indiscrets, 42, 57–58, 100
  Discours sur la poésie dramatique, 42, 47, 51, 53, 75
  Entretiens sur le Fils naturel, 42, 45, 53–55, 58, 234
  Paradox sur le comédien, 42, 44–52, 58, 60, 73–74, 128
  Salon de 1767, 42, 45, 46,
difference, 13, 46, 212–14, 228–29
disbelief (*prosaische Unglaube*), 188, 219, 221
disguise (*Verkleidung*), 4, 17, 77, 128, 164–66, 168, 170, 172–73, 177, 179, 185–87, 189, 253, 256, 258, 262–63, 270, 272–73, 275, 295–96
disinterestedness, 7, 15–16, 120, 125
dissiumulation (*Verstellung*), 164–66, 168, 170, 173, 177, 179, 180, 181, 183, 185–87, 295–96
domestic drama, 47, 52–55, 58, 72, 81, 118–19, 213, 233, 280
Dryden, John, 252
Du Bos, Jean-Baptiste, 3, 26, 55–56, 59–60, 82, 85, 93, 94, 113, 120, 212, 268
Dusmenil, M., 73
Dussane, Beatrix, 44

eidetic intuition, 11
Emery, John, 76
Engel, Johann Jacob, 134
enthusiasm, 116
Epicurus, 217
Euripedes, 129, 147–48, 156, 246
externality ("Outness"), 217

fable, 94–95, 97, 171, 280
fancy, 28, 172
fantasy, 11, 63–70, 117, 124, 134, 150, 152, 160, 163, 168, 172, 244–45, 275, 279, 287, 291, 293, 299–301
Farquhar, George, 79
Favart, Charles Simon, 97
feigned actions. *See* dissimulation
fiabesque drama, 63, 71, 151, 285, 294

Foakes, Reginald, 29 n. 27, 188, 192–94, 218
folk tale, 69, 72, 151, 168, 176, 301
"fourth wall," 51–52, 74–75, 297
Foucault, Michel, 12
freedom, 15, 104–6, 121, 123–24, 146, 160
Fruman, Norman, 192, 193
Furst, Lilian, 43 n. 7, 292 n. 34

Gadamer, Hans Georg, 9, 15–16, 121
Galvani, Luigi, 121
Garrick, David, 41, 44, 46, 73
genius, 116–17, 196, 227, 247
Gerstenberg, Heinrich Wilhelm, 116–17
gestalt shift, 13
Godwin, William, 21
Goethe, Johann Wolfgang von, 4, 17, 232–45, 268, 294, 302–3
  Clavigo, 266
  Dichtung und Wahrheit, 233
  Egmont, 65, 245
  Farbenlehre, 240, 245
  Faust, 232, 235–43, 245, 247, 253, 259, 266, 268–69
  Iphigenia auf Tauris, 266
  Italienische Reise, 39
  "Shakespeare und kein Ende," 244–45
  Der Triumph der Empfindsamkeit, 234, 268
  "Über epische und dramatische Dichtung," 244
  Über Kunst und Altertum, 235–36, 239
  "Über Wahrheit und Wahrscheinlichkeit der Kunstwerke," 233
  "Weimarisches Hoftheater," 245
  Wilhelm Meister, 130–32, 183
Goldoni, Carlo, 53, 150–51
Gombrich, Ernst H., 9, 16, 188
Gottsched, Johann Christoph, 64, 151, 281 n. 17
Gozzi, Carlo, 5, 71, 150–52, 280 n. 16, 294
Gray, Terence, 5
Greuze, Jean-Baptiste, 55
Griggs, Earl Leslie, 194
Grimm, Jacob, 301
Grimm, Wilhelm, 301
grotesque, 33, 69, 71, 174, 184, 244, 246–53, 257, 260, 262–63, 266
Guizot, François, 35

hallucination, 197–99, 209, 224, 245
Hamann, Johann Georg, 42
Handke, Peter, 5
Hanswurst, 151, 237, 281–92
Haßelbeck, Otto, 101

Hazlitt, William, 115
heautonomy, 125
Hédelin, François, abbé d'Aubignac, 41
Hegel, G. W. F., 6, 7–9, 11, 17, 116
Helmholtz-Phelan, Anna, 191–92
Herder, Johann Gottfried, 13, 37, 120–22, 125, 127, 197
hermeneutics, 107, 132
Hippel, Theodor Gottlieb von, 118
historical fidelity, 101–2, 118, 245, 250–52
historical sources, 49, 143, 186–87, 264
history, compared to fiction, 202, 215, 225, 301
history of ideas, 1–2
Hobson, Marian, 3
Hoffmann, E. T. A., 294
Homer, 20
Horace, 59, 224
Hugo, Victor, 4, 17, 233, 243–66, 268, 302–3
  Amy Robsart, 253, 256–58, 260, 262, 265
  Les Burgraves, 232, 244, 264–66
  Cromwell, 252–53
  Hernani, 244, 258–60, 264
  Les Jumeaux, 253–56, 258
  Marie Tudor, 257
  Lucrèce Borgia, 257–58
  "Préface de *les Burgraves*," 265
  "Préface de *Cromwell*," 33, 219, 246–52
  Le Roi s'amuse, 243, 259–61
  Ruy Blas, 256, 261–64
Hume, David, 223
Husserl, Edmund, 9, 11–12, 13, 14, 15
Hutcheson, Francis, 31, 56, 83, 84, 94

ideal, 9, 46, 55, 124, 147, 237–38, 302
idem in alio, 13, 14, 15, 212, 228
identity, 120, 160–61, 171
Iffland, August Wilhelm, 285, 289
illusion
  alternating belief and disbelief, 2, 35, 120, 196–97, 202, 206, 210
  alternating rational and emotional response, 96, 109–10, 113, 205
  awareness of, 6, 12, 16, 17, 30, 33, 38, 47–48, 60, 76, 92, 94, 101, 109, 111–14, 116, 119, 138, 143, 158, 160, 178, 184–85, 188–89, 193, 201–2, 205–7, 210, 212, 235–36, 245, 269, 286, 301–3
  bipolar or bimodal, 3
  compared to dream, 2, 31–32, 35, 37, 62, 63–64, 66–67, 120–23, 124, 153–54, 194–95, 197, 210, 221, 223, 287, 298
  conditional, 66, 137, 144, 183, 187, 286
  counterfeit or false, 28, 100, 105, 156, 216, 282
  disruption of (*Illusionszerstörung*), 4–5, 11, 17, 27, 36, 52, 60, 62–64, 66–68, 70–72, 85, 92, 96, 98–100, 103, 105, 111, 119, 124, 136, 149–50, 152, 156, 158, 162–63, 206–7, 210, 235–36, 252, 280–82, 286, 292–93
  distinguished from delusion, 7, 16, 26, 38, 41, 181, 185, 193, 195, 197, 216, 225, 245, 268–70, 273, 274, 300
  dual perception, 113–15, 164, 166, 175–76, 178, 193, 203–5, 245
  ensemble of effects, 143, 161, 250
  fits of forgetfulness or delusion, 201, 205–7, 288
  identification, 3, 119, 121–22, 160, 162
  ideological influence, 5–6, 11, 134, 141, 162, 290, 302
  interrupted induction, 109, 112–14
  intuitive, 61, 92
  involuntary, 2, 14, 32–33, 37, 38, 48, 64, 66, 119, 154, 195, 197
  no conscious awareness of means, 109, 115, 299
  optical, 4, 12, 13, 16, 38, 128, 144, 277
  perfect or complete, 20, 26–27, 31–34, 36, 37, 46, 74, 100, 119, 144, 200, 219, 223, 233–34, 297
  pretending belief (make-believe), 37–38, 301
  psychological process of, 220, 224, 299–301
  reason overwhelmed by emotion, 2, 26, 44, 48, 64, 72, 86–92, 94, 99, 103, 109–10, 112–13, 128, 161, 184, 188, 193, 201, 268, 287, 301
  revealed, 175, 243, 282–83, 292
  resistance and acquiescence, 66, 143, 286
  sensual involvement, 7, 9, 82, 86–87, 109, 111, 112, 114, 142, 144, 147
  simulataneous observing and forgetting, 138, 143, 187, 201, 206
  spontaneity, 12, 77, 88, 136, 149, 160, 183, 189, 201, 206, 232, 283
  symmetry of, 168–69
  thematization of, 4, 17, 72, 126, 128, 174, 181, 189, 192, 196, 210, 220, 268, 302
  vicarious response, 3
  visual and verbal, 14, 97, 103–5, 110, 217
  voluntary, volitional control, 12, 14, 30, 32–33, 48, 63–64, 66, 121–22, 128, 153–54, 188, 193–98, 206, 209–10, 221–22, 227–29, 245, 269–70

images, 116, 117, 122
  counterfeit (*eidolon, phantasma*), 20, 27, 39, 93
  "humanizing," 208
  ideal (*eikon*), 20, 27, 30, 39
  mental existence of, 12
  negative reality, 228
  visual, 107, 110, 217–18, 241–42, 271, 274
  vivid power, 220–22
imagination, 4, 15, 17, 38, 75, 104, 106, 115–17, 120, 123, 126, 129, 130, 132, 146, 156–57, 159–61, 164, 171, 172, 178, 186, 188, 192, 203–4, 206, 208, 212–15, 226–27, 268, 302
  constitutive and reproductive, 106–7
  dangers of, 27–29, 220
  impotency of, 188, 219
  intuitive, 83, 133, 215, 217, 224
  volitional control, 210–11, 222–23
imitation, 10, 20, 44, 46, 58, 83, 86, 87, 89, 91–94, 100–101, 103, 109–11, 113, 116, 117, 123–24, 150, 159, 177, 200, 210, 212–13, 216, 234, 237, 246, 298
  distinguished from copy, 72, 209, 211–12, 214, 223, 225–29
  "mirror of life," 28, 79, 118–19, 251, 274
immediacy. *See* aesthetic immediacy
immorality, 19–26, 113, 141, 157
improbability, 123, 156, 171, 224, 227–29
inspiration, 116–17, 154, 252
interest, 51, 155–56, 207
intersubjectivity, 17
irrational, 31, 71–72, 82, 183–85, 224, 270–71, 277, 187
irony, 5, 13, 15, 17, 61, 69, 147, 150, 152, 161–65, 170–71, 179, 186, 189, 236, 259, 263, 267, 291, 293, 295
  dramatic, 136, 153, 164
  romantic, 11, 62–63, 153, 279–94, 296–97
  self-reflexive, 27, 158, 232, 242–43, 245, 268, 296
Iser, Wolfgang, 12

Jackpudding. *See* Hanswurst
Jackson, J. R. de J., 194
Jakobson, Roman, 13
Jauß, Hans Robert, 43 n. 7, 58, 135 n. 19
Johnson, Samuel, 21, 27–31, 156, 163, 167, 196, 224
Jordan, Dorothy, 77

Kames, Henry Home, Lord, 31–32, 120, 197
Kant, Immanuel, 6–7, 9, 11, 15, 16, 17, 65 n. 44, 106, 116, 120, 121, 125, 146–47, 177, 188
Keats, John, 115, 160, 211 n. 42, 267, 300
Kemble, John Philip, 206
Kenrick, William, 29 n. 27
Kleist, Heinrich von, 269
  Amphitryon, 302
Klopstock, Friedrich Gottlieb, 225, 300
Kotzebue, August von, 285
  Gustava Wasa, 293
  Der hyperborische Esel, 293
Knight, Richard Payne, 192–93, 199–208, 215, 219, 222, 224, 227
Krieger, Murray, 13–14, 15, 16, 17

Lamb, Charles, 42, 74–79, 199, 269
Lamb, Mary, 199
La Mesnardière, Hippolyte Jules Pilet de, 41
La Motte, Houdar de, 155
language
  games, 137, 168
  metrical, 134, 136, 251
  persuasive power, 92
  visual referentiality, 217
Leibniz, Gottfried Wilhelm, 82, 84, 90, 94, 112, 114, 116
Lessing, Gotthold Ephraim, 2, 60, 115–16, 125, 127, 128, 137, 161, 197
  Briefe, die neueste Literatur betreffend, 88, 94, 136
  Briefwechsel über das Trauerspiel, 83–94, 102, 105, 109, 111, 112
  Hamburgische Dramaturgie, 4, 57, 95–103, 119, 134
  Laokoon, 38, 103–9, 110, 129 n. 5
Lillo, George, 52
local color, 250–52
Locke, John, 56–57, 209
Longinus, 59, 117, 246
Louis XVIII, 34

Macready, William, 267
Maffei, Francesco Scipione, 98
magic, 151, 157, 172–75, 214–15, 240–42, 285, 291
magic lantern (*laterna magica*), 232, 240–43
Malebranche, Nicolas, 217
manipulation, 51, 150, 179, 181, 183, 286
mannerism, 150, 157–58, 188, 236
Marivaux, Pierre Carlet de Chamblain de, 5, 157–59
Marlowe, Christopher
  Doctor Faustus, 175, 278

Marmontel, Jean-François, 2, 33, 68, 97
Martin, John, 303
marvelous, 49, 65, 67–72, 175–76, 272, 274
masque, 167, 236, 294
McFarland, Thomas, 192, 223, 227
mechanic form, 127, 129, 133, 155, 159, 192, 214
mediation, 13, 14, 16, 44, 57, 59, 72, 82, 86, 89, 93, 94, 97, 103, 124, 159, 177, 181, 194, 197
Meier, Georg Friedrich, 82, 107
Mendelssohn, Moses, 2, 15, 42, 60, 61, 62, 64, 73, 83–94, 109–16, 120, 128, 197
meontic (in contrast to mimetic), 227
Mercier, Louis-Sébastien, 2
Merleau-Ponty, Maurice, 12
mesmerism, 121
metadrama, 5, 6, 17, 27, 61, 71, 119, 229, 234–35, 268, 279–303
metaphor, 13–14, 17, 107, 182
Metastasio, Pietro Trapassi, 150
metonymy, 13–14
Michelangelo, 247
Milton, John, 221, 227, 247, 252
  Paradise Lost, 182, 215, 221, 225–26, 301
mime, 140, 231
mimesis. *See* imitation
mimetic drama, 17, 23, 64, 236, 244
moderation, 68
Molière, Jean-Baptiste Poquelin, 24, 52, 153, 157–58, 194, 302
Molino, Tirso de
  Don Juan, 226, 247
Morgan, Mary (Brent), 218
Mozart, Wolfgang Amadeus
  Die Zauberflöte, 268, 279, 285, 290–92, 303
multistability, 13
music, 143, 150, 268, 274–75, 294

Necker cube, 12, 13, 16
negative capability, 160, 211 n. 42
new historicism, 1
Newton, Sir Isaac, 209
Nicolai, Christoph Friedrich, 2, 83–94, 112, 113, 120, 197
novelty and familiarity, 225

opera, 150, 213, 223, 236, 260–61, 285, 291
organic form, 127, 129, 133, 159, 192, 214
Orsini, Gian, 192

painting and poetry compared, 103–4, 107–8
Palmer, John, 79

paradox, 6, 42, 43, 63, 69, 70, 101, 123, 125, 158, 182, 251, 272, 281, 286
  of acting, 44–52, 60–62, 73–74, 137
  of knowledge and *naiveté*, 161
  of pleasure in pain, 111, 115, 145–46, 161
  of representation, 6, 15, 16, 17, 20, 39, 44, 47, 58, 219, 283–84
parody, 147–48, 163, 165, 279–80, 289, 291, 293
participation, imaginative involvement, 38, 47, 62, 118, 121, 128, 136, 142–43, 146–49, 152, 180–81, 184, 187, 196, 210, 228, 234–35, 245, 286, 291
passions, aroused or excited, 86–87, 91, 94, 109, 128, 142, 161
perception, 6, 38, 55, 57, 83, 90, 95, 103, 122, 132–33, 146, 160, 175, 181, 182, 184, 189, 220, 240, 243, 272, 275, 295, 302
Perrault, Charles, 280, 291
phantasmagoria, 232, 241
phenomenology, 12, 112
Piave, Francesco Maria, 260
Pirandello, Luigi, 5, 61
Pixérécourt, René Charles Guilbert de, 257
plastic and picturesque, 127, 129, 156, 159, 214
Plato, 19–20, 21, 25, 26, 27, 30, 46, 55, 141, 154
Plautus, 302
play, in artistic expression or experience, 14, 15, 38, 79, 104, 114, 121, 124–25, 140, 149, 227, 296, 298
play within a play, 5, 164–66, 174, 183, 186, 236, 253–54, 279
play about a play, 166–67, 280, 292–93
Plautus, 165
poetic justice, 145
politics, 9, 16, 17, 138, 141, 162, 290, 302
Pope, Alexander
  Peri Bathous, or the Art of Sinking in Poetry, 217
presence, 12, 13–14, 117, 161, 208
probability, 27, 50, 53, 67, 137–38, 156, 164, 175, 210, 224, 227–29, 249
propaganda, 162
proscenium arch, 157, 244, 299
psychomachia, 175, 181

Quintilian, 59

Racine, Jean, 23, 33–36, 57, 153, 155, 157, 194
Radziwill, Prince, 241

Ramler, Karl Wilhelm, 115
Raysor, T. M., 188, 193–94
real and ideal, 143, 212, 220, 226–27, 245, 251
  beau réel (Diderot), 46, 56, 57
  higher reality (Goethe), 233–34
  modèle ideal (Diderot), 46–47, 49, 58, 234
realism, 79, 94, 118–19
religion and drama, 21
Rembrandt Hermensz van Rijn, 240–41
representative, 224, 226
Retzsch, Moritz, 242
Richardson, Samuel, 115
Richter, Jean Paul, 129 n. 5, 296
Ritter, Peter, 294
Riedel, Friedrich Just, 117
Robinson, Henry Crabb, 191, 199, 218
role playing, 4, 74, 128, 164–65, 170, 178, 187, 262–63, 277, 295–96
  deliberate revelation of, 77–78, 152, 158, 165, 282–85
  stepping out of role, 4–5, 75, 149, 232, 239, 280, 282–85, 296–97
romanticism, 34, 129, 159
Rousseau, Jean-Jacques, 2, 16, 17, 21, 22–26, 197

Sartre, Jean-Paul, 12
Savigny, Friedrich Carl von, 298
Schelling, Friedrich, 106, 177 n. 63, 209 n. 37
Schiller, Friedrich, 14–15, 17, 123–25, 294
Schink, Johann Friedrich, 2, 26–27, 31, 119
Schlegel, August Wilhelm, 4, 17, 61–62, 99, 127–89, 245, 293
  "Etwas über Shakespeare," 130–34
  "Über den dramatischen Dialog," 134–38
  "Über literatur, Kunst und Geist des Zeitalters," 138–39
  Vorlesungen, 4, 62, 125–26, 127, 129, 139–88, 191–97, 209–11, 213–14, 218, 220, 228 n. 75, 229, 303
Schlegel, Caroline, 127
Schlegel, Friedrich, 4, 62–63, 106, 127, 129 n. 5, 159, 292, 293
Schmid, Christian Heinrich, 118
Schröder, Friedrich Ludwig, 73
Scott, Sir Walter, 256–57
self-delusion, 162, 167, 171–73, 185, 220, 275
self-referential, self-reflexive, 11, 12, 14, 98–99, 103, 119, 147–48, 164, 166, 189, 229, 236, 293, 303
semiotics, 107, 109–10, 112
Seneca, 153

sensation, 117, 122, 213, 268
sensibility, 45, 48, 81, 91, 123, 160, 209, 234, 288–89
sensory certainty (sinnliche Gewißheit), 8
sensory intuition, 59, 109–10, 113–14
sentimental tragedy, 81
Shaftesbury, Anthony Ashley Cooper, 3rd Earl of, 31, 56, 83, 94
Shakespeare, William, 30, 33–35, 62, 64, 66, 99, 120, 125, 127–34, 146, 150, 152, 157, 159–87, 189, 194, 227, 231, 236, 244, 268–69, 298
  his intentionality (Absichtlichkeit), 164, 177, 192–93, 196, 208–10, 229
  his judgment, 192–93, 196, 208–12, 214, 218–20, 227–29
  All's Well That Ends Well, 137, 167–70, 178
  Antony and Cleopatra, 30, 156, 186
  As You Like It, 172, 204
  The Comedy of Errors, 164–65
  Coriolanus, 206
  Cymbeline, 175, 177–78, 180–81
  Hamlet, 64, 71, 97, 130–32, 137, 163, 166, 167, 181–85, 198, 202, 203, 215, 249, 294
  Henry IV, 186–87, 215
  Henry V, 213, 219, 229
  Julius Caesar, 136–37
  King Lear, 163, 184–86, 202, 203, 215
  Love's Labour's Lost, 166–67, 171–72
  Macbeth, 34, 35, 64, 71, 160, 163, 175, 184–85, 203, 219–20, 244, 249
  Measure for Measure, 169–71, 207
  The Merchant of Venice, 171, 229
  A Midsummer-Night's Dream, 64, 70, 71, 173–74
  Much Ado About Nothing, 168–69, 178
  Othello, 3, 33, 36, 180–81, 185, 206
  Richard II, 273
  Romeo and Juliet, 179–80, 243–44, 249
  The Taming of the Shrew, 165–66, 236
  The Tempest, 61, 64, 65, 67–70, 71, 160, 163, 173–75, 181, 192, 214–15, 217, 221
  Twelfth Night, 77, 172–73
  The Two Gentlemen of Verona, 164–65
  Venus and Adonis, 208
  The Winter's Tale, 175, 178, 180
Shelley, Percy Bysshe, 267, 269
  Charles the First, 302–3
Sheridan, Richard Brinsley, 77
signs, 11, 12, 13, 20, 57, 106, 109, 114
  arbitrary and natural, 107–8, 112–13
  verbal and visual, 110

Smith, Adam, 105
Socrates, 20
Sophocles, 105, 129, 143, 146
    Antigone, 154–55
spatiality, 104–5, 107–8, 110, 120–21
spectacle, 231, 238, 267–68
Spenser, Edmund, 227
stage manager, as character role, 170–71, 173, 183
staging
    character interaction with props, 4, 148, 232, 234, 246, 250, 252–66, 268–69, 272, 280, 303
    concealing reference to, 98–99, 103
    divided stage, 259–61
    lighting, 233, 239, 254–56, 258–59, 264, 269, 275, 302
    machinery and decor, 53, 58, 92, 143, 144, 157, 187, 203–4, 206–9, 213, 231–33, 236, 239–43, 250, 254–60, 268–69, 274, 291–92, 295, 297–99, 302–3
    off-stage action, 232, 246, 249–50, 256–57, 260, 262, 265
    sound effects, 258–59
    visual effects, 4, 17, 143, 231–33, 239–43, 257, 268, 303
Stanislavski, Konstantin, 45
Stendhal (= Henri Beyle), 2, 14, 33–36, 37, 219
Sterne, Laurence, 296
stimulus-response mechanism, 105
Stoppard, Tom, 5, 61
    The Real Inspector Hound, 279–80
Strohschneider-Kohrs, Ingrid, 296–97
Stuart, Daniel, 221
Styles, John, 19, 21–22
subjectivism, 9, 15, 16, 32, 111, 159, 296–97
subject-object dialectics, 10, 55, 217, 220
sublime, 7, 38, 88, 146, 199, 200, 247–48, 250–52, 260, 266
subplot, 169, 173, 175, 186, 250
Sulzer, Johann Georg, 37, 122–23, 197
supernatural, 64–65, 68–72, 86, 95, 96–97, 98, 103, 173, 175, 182, 184, 214–15, 223–25, 233, 240–43, 266, 274–76, 285
surprise, 51, 64, 68, 70, 71, 99
symbols, 11, 91, 107, 144, 218, 223, 226, 253
sympathy, 2, 4, 31, 56, 83–86, 89–91, 93–95, 97, 99, 102–3, 105–6, 108–9, 112, 128, 130, 133, 162, 188, 201–2, 205, 209, 222, 236, 245
synecdoche, 13

tableau, 54–55, 249, 286
Talma, François-Joseph, 36
temporality, 104–5, 107–8, 110, 120–21
Terence, 158
Tieck, Ludwig, 42, 61–75, 268, 296, 298, 303
    Bemerkungen, 62, 73–74
    Der gestiefelte Kater, 5, 17, 61, 63, 150, 268, 279–94
    Prinz Zerbino, 150
    Shakespeare's Behandlung des Wunderbaren, 62–72, 281–82, 286
    Die verkehrte Welt, 150
Titian, 274
Todorov, Tzvetan, 70
Tolkien, John Ronald Reuel, 12
Tomalin, J., 212
tragic and comic combined, 160, 163–64, 246–50
transform (*Verwandlung*), 173–74
trompe l'oeil, 144, 298

unity
    of effect, 180
    of interest, 155–56
    of time, place, action, 30, 34–36, 85, 120, 153–57, 160, 186, 194–95, 212, 248–50
    of understanding, 157

Valdastri, Idelfonso, 119–20, 121
Verdi, Giuseppe, 260
Vergil, 104
verisimilitude (*vraisemblance*), 49, 53, 55, 72, 163–64, 251
Vernet, Claude Joseph, 58
Voltaire, François Marie Arouet, 24, 41, 97, 157
voyeurism, 149

Walton, Kendall, 37, 222 n. 68
Weiße, Christian Felix, 2, 118–19
Wellek, René, 192, 193
Wellington, Sir Arthur Wellesley, Duke of, 34
Wilson, Robert, 5
Wolff, Christian, 82, 84, 90, 94, 112, 114, 116
Wordsworth, William, 74, 192, 199, 207–8, 217, 223–27, 267
Wycherley, William, 79

Zahn, W., 241